NEW PERSPECTIVES ON

The Internet

9th Edition

INTRODUCTORY

The Internet

9th Edition

INTRODUCTORY

Gary P. Schneider
Jessica Evans

COURSE TECHNOLOGY
CENGAGE Learning

Australia • Brazil • Japan • Korea • Mexico • Singapore • Spain • United Kingdom • United States

COURSE TECHNOLOGY
CENGAGE Learning®

New Perspectives on the Internet, 9th Edition, Introductory

Vice President, Careers and Computing: David Garza

Executive Editor: Marie L. Lee

Associate Acquisitions Editor: Amanda Lyons

Senior Product Manager: Kathy Finnegan

Product Manager: Leigh Hefferon

Associate Product Manager: Julia Leroux-Lindsey

Director of Marketing: Elisa G. Roberts

Associate Marketing Manager: Adrienne Fung

Marketing Coordinator: Michael Saver

Developmental Editor: Kim T. Crowley

Senior Content Project Manager:
    Jennifer Goguen McGrail

Composition: GEX Publishing Services

Art Director: Marissa Falco

Text Designer: Althea Chen

Cover Designer: Roycroft Design

Cover Art: Image Copyright Lukáš Hejtman, 2012;
    used under license from Shutterstock.com

Copyeditor: Suzanne Huizenga

Proofreader: Camille Kiolbasa

Indexer: Rich Carlson

For product information and technology assistance, contact us at
Cengage Learning Customer & Sales Support, 1-800-354-9706
For permission to use material from this text or product, submit all
requests online at **www.cengage.com/permissions**
Further permissions questions can be emailed to
permissionrequest@cengage.com

Some of the product names and company names used in this book have been used for identification purposes only and may be trademarks or registered trademarks of their respective manufacturers and sellers.

Microsoft and the Office logo are either registered trademarks or trademarks of Microsoft Corporation in the United States and/or other countries. Course Technology, Cengage Learning is an independent entity from the Microsoft Corporation, and not affiliated with Microsoft in any manner.

Disclaimer: Any fictional data related to persons or companies or URLs used throughout this book is intended for instructional purposes only. At the time this book was printed, any such data was fictional and not belonging to any real persons or companies.

Library of Congress Control Number: 2012932418

ISBN-13: 978-1-111-52912-3

ISBN-10: 1-111-52912-4

Course Technology
20 Channel Center Street
Boston, MA 02210
USA

Cengage Learning is a leading provider of customized learning solutions with office locations around the globe, including Singapore, the United Kingdom, Australia, Mexico, Brazil, and Japan. Locate your local office at:
international.cengage.com/global

Cengage Learning products are represented in Canada by Nelson Education, Ltd.

To learn more about Course Technology, visit **www.cengage.com/course technology**

To learn more about Cengage Learning, visit **www.cengage.com**

Purchase any of our products at your local college store or at our preferred online store **www.cengagebrain.com**

Printed in the United States of America
1 2 3 4 5 6 7 8 9 16 15 14 13 12

Preface

The New Perspectives Series' critical-thinking, problem-solving approach is the ideal way to prepare students to transcend point-and-click skills and take advantage of all that the Internet has to offer.

In developing the New Perspectives Series, our goal was to create books that give students the software concepts and practical skills they need to succeed beyond the classroom. We've updated our proven case-based pedagogy with more practical content to make learning skills more meaningful to students.

With the New Perspectives Series, students understand *why* they are learning *what* they are learning, and are fully prepared to apply their skills to real-life situations.

About This Book

"This text engages students by providing workplace scenarios designed to help them personally connect with the concepts and applications presented. The new visual overviews greatly enhance each tutorial as they provide a snapshot to the lessons."

—Paulette Comet
The Community College
of Baltimore County

This book provides thorough coverage of using the Internet and its technologies, and includes the following:

- Hands-on steps for searching the Web and evaluating the available resources to determine their validity, credentials, timeliness, and accuracy
- Hands-on steps for using Microsoft Internet Explorer, Mozilla Firefox, and Google Chrome, and for creating and using a Windows Live Hotmail email account
- In-depth and expanded coverage of social networks, wireless technology and networks, security countermeasures for various types of threats, and protecting individual privacy and avoiding identity theft

New for this edition!

- Each session begins with a Visual Overview, a new two-page spread that includes colorful, enlarged graphics with numerous callouts and key term definitions, giving students a comprehensive preview of the topics covered in each session, as well as a handy study guide.
- New ProSkills boxes provide guidance for how to use the Web in real-world, professional situations.
- Comprehensive ProSkills exercise at the end of Tutorial 5 integrates the skills students learn in the tutorials with one or more of the following soft skills: decision making, problem solving, teamwork, verbal communication, and written communication. This comprehensive exercise provides an opportunity for students to complete more challenging, thought-provoking assignments that reinforce the critical thinking skills taught in the tutorials.

System Requirements

This book assumes that Microsoft Internet Explorer 9 (or higher), Mozilla Firefox 5 (or higher), or Google Chrome, and Windows 7 are installed. (Students using Internet Explorer 8 (or lower) or Firefox 4 (or lower) and Windows Vista or XP can still complete the steps in this book, but they might encounter some differences.) Note that the figures and steps in this edition were written using Windows 7; therefore, Windows Vista/XP users might notice minor differences in the figures and steps. This book assumes that students have a complete installation of the Web browser and its components, an Internet connection, and are able to create an email account. Because the Web browser or email account students use might be different from those used in the figures in this book, students' screens might differ slightly; this difference does not present any problems for students completing the tutorials.

"The clear step-by-step instructions, real-world data files, and helpful figures make New Perspectives texts excellent for courses taught in the classroom, the hybrid/blended format, or entirely online."

—Sylvia Amito'elau
Coastline Community
College

VISUAL OVERVIEW

PROSKILLS

INSIGHT

TIP

REVIEW

APPLY

REFERENCE

GLOSSARY/INDEX

The New Perspectives Approach

Context
Each tutorial begins with a problem presented in a "real-world" case that is meaningful to students. The case sets the scene to help students understand what they will do in the tutorial.

Hands-on Approach
Each tutorial is divided into manageable sessions that combine reading and hands-on, step-by-step work. Colorful screenshots help guide students through the steps. Trouble? tips anticipate common mistakes or problems to help students stay on track and continue with the tutorial.

Visual Overviews
New for this edition! Each session begins with a Visual Overview, a new two-page spread that includes colorful, enlarged screenshots with numerous callouts and key term definitions, giving students a comprehensive preview of the topics covered in the session, as well as a handy study guide.

ProSkills Boxes and Exercises
New for this edition! ProSkills boxes provide guidance for how to use the software in real-world, professional situations, and related ProSkills exercises integrate the technology skills students learn with one or more of the following soft skills: decision making, problem solving, teamwork, verbal communication, and written communication.

InSight Boxes
InSight boxes offer expert advice and best practices to help students achieve a deeper understanding of the concepts behind the software features and skills.

Margin Tips
Margin Tips provide helpful hints and shortcuts for more efficient use of the software. The Tips appear in the margin at key points throughout each tutorial, giving students extra information when and where they need it.

Assessment
Retention is a key component to learning. At the end of each session, a series of Quick Check questions helps students test their understanding of the material before moving on. Engaging end-of-tutorial Review Assignments and Case Problems have always been a hallmark feature of the New Perspectives Series. Colorful bars and brief descriptions accompany the exercises, making it easy to understand both the goal and level of challenge a particular assignment holds.

Reference
Within each tutorial, Reference boxes appear before a set of steps to provide a succinct summary and preview of how to perform a task. In addition, each book includes a combination Glossary/Index to promote easy reference of material.

Our Complete System of Instruction

Coverage To Meet Your Needs

Whether you're looking for just a small amount of coverage or enough to fill a semester-long class, we can provide you with a textbook that meets your needs.

- Brief books typically cover the essential skills in just 2 to 4 tutorials.
- Introductory books build and expand on those skills and contain an average of 5 to 8 tutorials.
- Comprehensive books are great for a full-semester class, and contain 9 to 12+ tutorials.

So if the book you're holding does not provide the right amount of coverage for you, there's probably another offering available. Go to our Web site or contact your Course Technology sales representative to find out what else we offer.

CourseCasts – Learning on the Go. Always available…always relevant.

Want to keep up with the latest technology trends relevant to you? Visit our site to find a library of podcasts, CourseCasts, featuring a "CourseCast of the Week," and download them to your mp3 player at http://coursecasts.course.com.

Our fast-paced world is driven by technology. You know because you're an active participant—always on the go, always keeping up with technological trends, and always learning new ways to embrace technology to power your life.

Ken Baldauf, host of CourseCasts, is a faculty member of the Florida State University Computer Science Department where he is responsible for teaching technology classes to thousands of FSU students each year. Ken is an expert in the latest technology trends; he gathers and sorts through the most pertinent news and information for CourseCasts so your students can spend their time enjoying technology, rather than trying to figure it out. Open or close your lecture with a discussion based on the latest CourseCast.

Visit us at http://coursecasts.course.com to learn on the go!

Instructor Resources

We offer more than just a book. We have all the tools you need to enhance your lectures, check students' work, and generate exams in a new, easier-to-use and completely revised package. This book's Instructor's Manual, ExamView testbank, PowerPoint presentations, data files, solution files, figure files, and a sample syllabus are all available on a single CD-ROM or for downloading at http://www.cengage.com/coursetechnology.

SAM: Skills Assessment Manager

SAM is designed to help bring students from the classroom to the real world. It allows students to train and test on important computer skills in an active, hands-on environment.

SAM's easy-to-use system includes powerful interactive exams, training, and projects on the most commonly used Microsoft Office applications. SAM simulates the Office application environment, allowing students to demonstrate their knowledge and think through the skills by performing real-world tasks, such as bolding text or setting up slide transitions. Add in live-in-the-application projects, and students are on their way to truly learning and applying skills to business-centric documents.

Designed to be used with the New Perspectives Series, SAM includes handy page references, so students can print helpful study guides that match the New Perspectives textbooks used in class. For instructors, SAM also includes robust scheduling and reporting features.

Content for Online Learning

Course Technology has partnered with the leading distance learning solution providers and class-management platforms today. To access this material, visit www.cengage.com/webtutor and search for your title. Instructor resources include the following: additional case projects, sample syllabi, PowerPoint presentations, and more. For students to access this material, they must have purchased a WebTutor PIN-code specific to this title and your campus platform. The resources for students might include (based on instructor preferences): topic reviews, review questions, practice tests, and more. For additional information, please contact your sales representative.

Acknowledgments

Creating a textbook is a collaborative effort in which authors and publisher work as a team to provide the highest quality book possible. We appreciate the many contributions of our Course Technology team, including Marie Lee, Executive Editor; Amanda Lyons, Associate Acquisitions Editor; Kathy Finnegan, Senior Product Manager; Leigh Hefferon, Product Manager; Julia Leroux-Lindsey, Associate Product Manager; and Jennifer Goguen McGrail, Senior Content Project Manager. We also would like to thank Christian Kunciw and his outstanding team of Quality Assurance testers for their many contributions in error-checking and fine-tuning this book's content throughout its development, and Marisa Taylor, Senior Project Manager at GEX Publishing Services, for guiding this book through the production process. Words cannot express our gratitude for the outstanding work of our Development Editor, Kim Crowley. Throughout this book's development, Kim has provided limitless and much appreciated encouragement and support, and her many excellent suggestions have significantly improved this book. Finally, we offer our heartfelt thanks to Robin Romer, for her substantial contributions to this edition of the book; to Katherine Pinard, who has contributed to this book in the past and also authored the book's adaptation for other markets; and to Janice Jutras, for her exceptional skill and diligent efforts to secure permissions for this text.
–Gary P. Schneider
–Jessica Evans

Dedication

To the memory of my brother, Bruce. – G.P.S.
To Hannah and Richard. – J.E.

www.cengage.com/ct/newperspectives

BRIEF CONTENTS

INTERNET   Level I Tutorials

TABLE OF CONTENTS

Browser Basics

Using Web Browser Software

INTERNET

Case | *Danville Animal Shelter*

The Danville Animal Shelter is an organization devoted to helping improve the welfare of animals, particularly unwanted pets, in the local Danville area. Trinity Andrews, the director of the shelter, is always looking for ways to improve the services it offers to the community.

The shelter is a charitable organization that is supported mainly by contributions from the local community. Trinity budgets the limited funds that the shelter receives to do the most good for the animals. One of the most important functions of the shelter is to let people in the community know about the pets available for adoption. Advertising in the local newspaper or on television stations is very expensive. Another problem is that the pets available for adoption change from day to day and, by the time a news story or ad runs, the pet that is featured often has been adopted. Although newspaper and television advertising and promotion can be a good way for the shelter to get its general message out to the community, these outlets are not the best way to let people know about specific pets that are available for adoption.

You have volunteered at the shelter for several years, and Trinity heard that you were learning to use the Internet. Trinity wants you to help identify ways to use the Internet to let the community know about the shelter and, in particular, about specific pets that are available for adoption. To do this, you need to learn more about using a Web browser.

Note: If you are using Microsoft Internet Explorer as your Web browser, you should complete Session 1.1. If you are using Mozilla Firefox as your Web browser, then skip Session 1.1 and complete Session 1.2.

STARTING DATA FILES

SESSION 1.1 VISUAL OVERVIEW

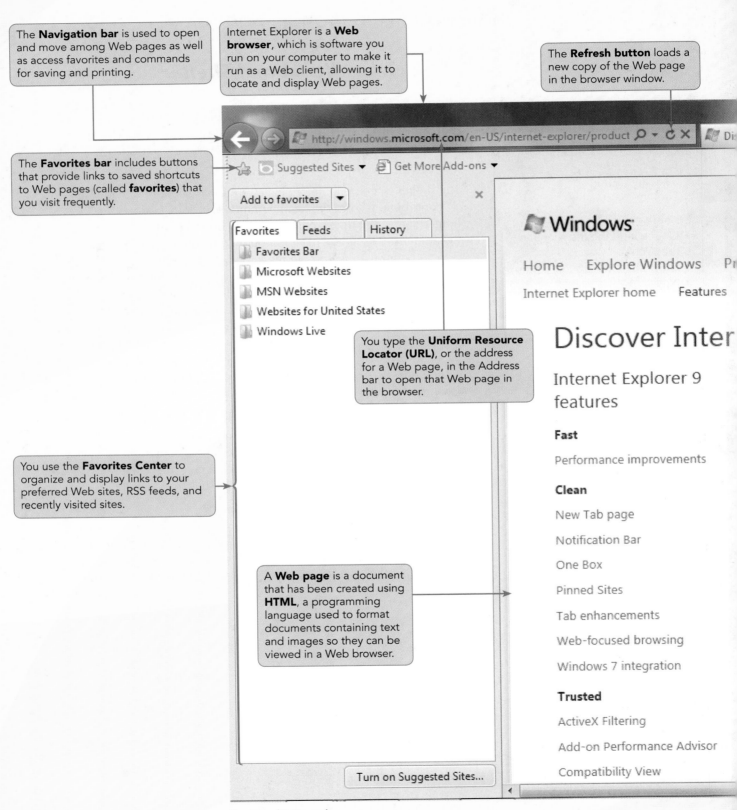

The **Navigation bar** is used to open and move among Web pages as well as access favorites and commands for saving and printing.

Internet Explorer is a **Web browser**, which is software you run on your computer to make it run as a Web client, allowing it to locate and display Web pages.

The **Refresh button** loads a new copy of the Web page in the browser window.

The **Favorites bar** includes buttons that provide links to saved shortcuts to Web pages (called **favorites**) that you visit frequently.

You type the **Uniform Resource Locator (URL)**, or the address for a Web page, in the Address bar to open that Web page in the browser.

You use the **Favorites Center** to organize and display links to your preferred Web sites, RSS feeds, and recently visited sites.

A **Web page** is a document that has been created using **HTML**, a programming language used to format documents containing text and images so they can be viewed in a Web browser.

http://windows.microsoft.com/en-US/internet-explorer/product

Suggested Sites ▾   Get More Add-ons ▾

Add to favorites ▾

Favorites   Feeds   History

Favorites Bar
Microsoft Websites
MSN Websites
Websites for United States
Windows Live

Turn on Suggested Sites...

Windows

Home   Explore Windows   Pr

Internet Explorer home   Features

Discover Inter

Internet Explorer 9 features

Fast

Performance improvements

Clean

New Tab page

Notification Bar

One Box

Pinned Sites

Tab enhancements

Web-focused browsing

Windows 7 integration

Trusted

ActiveX Filtering

Add-on Performance Advisor

Compatibility View

Courtesy of © Microsoft

MICROSOFT INTERNET EXPLORER

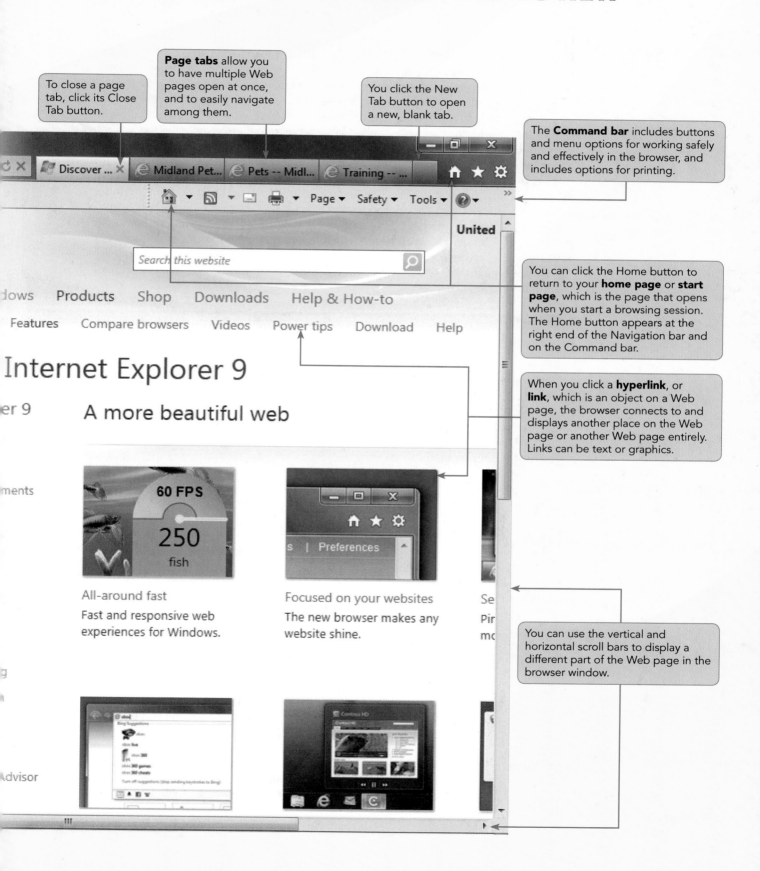

To close a page tab, click its Close Tab button.

Page tabs allow you to have multiple Web pages open at once, and to easily navigate among them.

You click the New Tab button to open a new, blank tab.

The **Command bar** includes buttons and menu options for working safely and effectively in the browser, and includes options for printing.

You can click the Home button to return to your **home page** or **start page**, which is the page that opens when you start a browsing session. The Home button appears at the right end of the Navigation bar and on the Command bar.

When you click a **hyperlink**, or **link**, which is an object on a Web page, the browser connects to and displays another place on the Web page or another Web page entirely. Links can be text or graphics.

You can use the vertical and horizontal scroll bars to display a different part of the Web page in the browser window.

The Internet and the Web

Computers can be connected to each other in a configuration called a **network**. When networks are connected to each other, the system is called an **interconnected network** or **internet** (with a lowercase "i"). The **Internet** (with an uppercase "i") is a specific interconnected network that connects computers all over the world using a common set of interconnection standards. Although it began as a computer science project sponsored by the U.S. military, the Internet today allows people and businesses all over the world to communicate with each other in a variety of ways.

The part of the Internet known as the **World Wide Web** (or the **Web**) is a collection of files that reside on computers, called **Web servers**, that are connected to each other through the Internet. Most files on computers, including computers that are connected to the Internet, are private; that is, only the computer's users can access those files. The owners of the computer files that make up the Web have made the files publicly available by placing them on the Web servers. Thus, anyone who has a computer connected to the Internet can obtain access to the files.

When you use an Internet connection to become part of the Web, your computer becomes a **Web client**. A **Web browser** is software that allows your computer to connect to, locate, retrieve, and display Web content. You can read Appendix A to learn more about the history of the Internet and the Web, how they work, and the technologies behind their operation.

Choosing a Browser

There are a variety of Web browsers available. Some of the most common are Microsoft Internet Explorer, Mozilla Firefox, Google Chrome, Apple Safari, and Opera. You can download and install these browsers for free, enabling you to choose the one you want. All Web browsers have similar features, but some are more robust and others are more streamlined. To help evaluate and decide which Web browser you want to use, you can read reviews, explore the product pages, take tours or demos of the browsers, and download and try them.

Hypertext Markup Language and Hyperlinks

The public files on Web servers are ordinary text files, much like the files created and used by word-processing software. To enable Web browser software to read these files, the text must be formatted according to a generally accepted standard. The standard used on the Web is **Hypertext Markup Language (HTML)**. HTML uses codes, or **tags**, that tell the Web browser software how to display the text contained in the text file. For example, a Web browser reading the following line of text

```
<B>A Review of the Book <I>Wind Instruments</I></B>
```

recognizes the <B> and </B> tags as instructions to display the entire line of text in bold and the <I> and </I> tags as instructions to display the text enclosed by those tags in italic. Different Web clients that connect to this Web server might display the tagged text differently. For example, one Web browser might display text enclosed by bold tags in a blue color instead of displaying the text in bold. A text file that contains HTML tags is called an **HTML document**.

HTML provides a variety of text formatting tags that can be used to indicate headings, paragraphs, bulleted lists, numbered lists, and other text enhancements in an HTML document. (You will learn more about HTML tags in Tutorial 8.) The real power of HTML, however, lies in its anchor tag. The **HTML anchor tag** enables Web designers to link

HTML documents to each other. Anchor tags in HTML documents create **hypertext links**, which are instructions that point to other HTML documents or to another section of the same document. Hypertext links also are called **hyperlinks** or **links**. The linked HTML documents can be on the same computer or on different computers. These computers can be anywhere in the world if they are connected to the Internet. When a Web browser displays an HTML document, it is often referred to as a **Web page**.

Starting Microsoft Internet Explorer

Microsoft Internet Explorer is the Microsoft Web browser; it is installed with all recent versions of the Windows operating system software. In this session, you will use the Internet Explorer Web browser to do your work for the Danville Animal Shelter. This introduction assumes that you have Internet Explorer installed on your computer.

To start Internet Explorer:

1. Click the **Internet Explorer** button on the taskbar. The Internet Explorer browser window opens.

   Trouble? If the Internet Explorer button does not appear on the taskbar, click the Start button on the taskbar, point to All Programs, and then click Internet Explorer. If you cannot find Internet Explorer on the All Programs menu, ask your instructor or technical support person for help. The program might be installed in a different location on the computer you are using.

2. If the program window does not fill the screen entirely, click the **Maximize** button on the title bar. Your screen should look similar to the Session 1.1 Visual Overview.

   Trouble? Your computer will open to the home page for your installation of Internet Explorer, or no page at all.

   Trouble? The Session 1.1 Visual Overview shows the Internet Explorer program window with the Command bar, Favorites bar, and Favorites Center displayed. Some or all of these may be hidden on your screen. You will learn how to customize the program window later in this session. In addition, other programs can add icons and toolbars to the Internet Explorer program window. So if you are using a computer that has been used by other people or your own computer on which other software has been installed, you might see icons and toolbars that are not shown in the Session 1.1 Visual Overview.

   Trouble? The Session 1.1 Visual Overview shows the Favorites Center open on the left side of the browser window. Your Favorites Center might not be open on your screen. This is not a problem; you will open the Favorites Center later in this session.

The very first time Internet Explorer starts, only the Navigation bar is displayed in the program window. The Navigation bar contains the Address bar for opening Web pages; the Back and Forward buttons for navigating among previously visited pages; the tabs for open Web pages; and the Home, Tools, and View favorites, feeds, and history buttons to access the most common Command bar functions. This streamlined version provides more screen space for viewing Web pages.

You can, however, display additional toolbars, including the Command bar and the Favorites bar, which are shown the Session 1.1 Visual Overview. You can also customize the toolbars by deleting icons and adding new icons. Internet Explorer allows you to change the toolbar settings because some people like to have many commands available on the screen, while others prefer to have more space available for displaying the Web page. Also, other software programs installed on your computer can place icons on the Internet Explorer toolbars so that you can use these programs from within Internet Explorer. As a result, your Internet Explorer browser window might have different toolbars displayed or the toolbars might contain icons not shown in the Visual Overview.

Customizing the Internet Explorer Window

In Internet Explorer, you can display or hide the menu bar and toolbars as needed. The menu bar and toolbars are hidden by default. When they are hidden, more of the Web page is displayed in the browser window. To display the menu bar or a toolbar, right-click a blank area of the Navigation bar, and then click the corresponding option on the shortcut menu. If the Command bar is displayed, you can click the Tools button on the Command bar, point to Toolbars, and then select or deselect the corresponding option to display or hide the menu bar or a toolbar.

At any point, you can switch to **Full screen mode**, which temporarily hides the program window—the title bar, the Navigation bar, the menu bar, and any toolbars as well as the Windows taskbar—leaving only the Web page visible on your screen. You can select the Full screen option by clicking Tools on the Command bar, and then clicking Full screen. When the window is in Full screen mode, you can display the hidden toolbars by pointing to the top of the screen. When you move the pointer away from the toolbars, they will become hidden again. To exit Full screen mode, point to the top of the screen until the toolbars appear, click the Tools button on the Command bar, and then click Full screen to remove the check mark and deselect this option.

REFERENCE

Hiding and Restoring Toolbars in Internet Explorer

- To switch to Full screen mode, click the Tools button on the Command bar, and then click Full screen (or click the Tools button on the Navigation bar, point to File, and then click Full screen, or press the F11 key).
- To temporarily restore the toolbars in Full screen mode, point to the top of the screen until the toolbars appear.
- To exit Full screen mode, point to the top of the screen to display the toolbars, click the Tools button on the Command bar, and then click Full screen (or click the Tools button on the Navigation bar, point to File, and then click Full screen, or press the F11 key).
- To display or hide individual toolbars, right-click a blank area of the Navigation bar, and then click a toolbar name on the shortcut menu. If the toolbar name is already checked, the toolbar will be hidden when you click the name. If the toolbar name is not checked, the toolbar will be displayed when you click the name.

Next, you will customize the Internet Explorer window by displaying and hiding the toolbars. In these tutorials, you will use the Command bar and Favorites bar, so you will leave them displayed.

To display and hide toolbars in Internet Explorer:

1. Right-click a blank area of the Navigation bar. A shortcut menu opens, listing the available toolbars. A check mark appears to the left of each toolbar that is displayed.

2. Click **Menu bar** on the shortcut menu to select this option and place a check mark next to it. The menu bar appears below the Navigation bar.

   Trouble? If the menu bar disappears, it was already displayed. Continue with Step 4.

3. Right-click a blank area of the Navigation bar, and then click **Menu bar** on the shortcut menu to uncheck this option and hide the menu bar. This on-off, or toggle, function works for all of the toolbars on the shortcut menu.

4. If the Favorites bar is not displayed, right-click a blank area of the Navigation bar, and then click **Favorites bar**. The Favorites bar appears below the Navigation bar.

5. If the Command bar is not displayed, right-click a blank area of the Navigation bar, and then click **Command bar**. The Command bar appears to the right of the Favorites bar. You can temporarily hide these toolbars.

6. Click the **Tools** button on the Command bar, and then click **Full screen**. The Web page fills the entire screen.

   Trouble? If the toolbars do not immediately roll up out of view, move the pointer away from the top of the screen.

7. Point to the top of the screen. The toolbars scroll back down into view.

8. Click the **Tools** button on the Navigation bar, point to **File**, and then click **Full screen** to deselect this option and redisplay the toolbars.

> **TIP**
>
> Another way to switch Full screen mode on and off is to press the F11 key.

Now that you are familiar with the tools in the browser window, you are ready to navigate to a Web site.

Navigating Web Pages

To identify a particular Web page's exact location on the Internet, Web browsers rely on an address called a Uniform Resource Locator (URL). The URL is the address of a specific Web page. Every Web page has a unique URL. A URL is a four-part addressing scheme that tells the Web browser:

- The protocol to use when transporting the file
- The domain name of the computer on which the file resides
- The path for the folder or directory on the computer in which the file resides
- The name of the file

So in the URL *http://www.nytimes.com/pages/sports/index.htm*, the *http://* is the transfer protocol, which is the set of rules that computers use to move files from one computer to another. The two most common protocols used to transfer files on the Internet are Hypertext Transfer Protocol (HTTP) and File Transfer Protocol (FTP). The second part of the URL, the domain name, is *www.nytimes.com* and this references the location of the computer on which the Web page resides; *www* indicates the computer is connected to the Web, *nytimes* is the name of the Web site, and *.com* identifies the Web site as being a commercial organization. The */pages/sports* portion of the URL provides the path for the folder in which the Web page file is located, and the last portion of the URL, *index.htm*, is the filename.

Entering a URL in the Address Bar

You can use the Address bar, which is located on the Navigation bar, to enter a specific URL and go directly to that Web page. For example, you can enter the complete URL for a Web site, such as http://www.cnn.com, to load that Web page in the browser. As you begin to type, a list opens, displaying pages you have previously visited that begin with the letters you are typing; you can select a URL and press the Enter key to return to that Web page. Also, Internet Explorer will try to complete partial URLs that you type in the

Address bar. For example, if you type cnn.com, Internet Explorer will convert it to http://www.cnn.com and load the Web page at that URL.

If you don't see the URL you want in the Address bar list, you can enter a partial URL or a search word; Internet Explorer will open the search engine selected for your browser. A **search engine** performs a search based on the text you type in a search box—in this case, the Address bar—and displays the search results. You can click any link in the search results to go to that Web page. You will learn more about search engines in Tutorial 3.

INSIGHT

Understanding Home Pages

The term "home page" is used at least three different ways on the Web, and it is sometimes difficult to tell which meaning people intend when they use the term. The first definition of home page indicates the main page that all of the other pages on a particular Web site are organized around and link back to. This home page is the first page that opens when you visit that Web site. The second definition of "home page" is the first page that opens when you start your Web browser. This type of home page might be an HTML document on your own computer. Some people create such home pages and include hyperlinks to Web sites that they frequently visit. If you are using a computer on your school's or employer's network, its Web browser might be configured to open the main page for the school or firm. The third definition of "home page" is the Web page that a particular Web browser loads the first time you use it. This page usually is stored at the Web site of the firm or other organization that created the Web browser software. Home pages that meet the second or third definitions are sometimes called start pages.

Trinity wants you to start your research by examining the Midland Pet Adoption Agency's Web site. She has provided the URL for the site's home page.

To load the Midland Pet Adoption Agency's home page:

1. Click in the **Address bar** to select the URL, and then type **www.midlandpet.com**. This is the URL for the Midland Pet Adoption Agency Web site.

   Trouble? The Address bar might display a list of suggested URLs as you type; ignore these suggestions and continue typing.

2. Press the **Enter** key. The home page of the Midland Pet Adoption Agency Web site loads, as shown in Figure 1-1.

Figure 1-1	Midland Pet Adoption Agency Web page

Courtesy of © Microsoft; © Cengage Learning

Written Communication: The Importance of Organization in a Web Site

Web sites are written communications media just as printed brochures and newsletters are. When visiting a Web site, you can learn a great deal about how to create a Web site for your organization, just as you can learn to design brochures by reading brochures produced by other organizations. The writing that appears on a Web site's pages must be organized to reflect the organization's communication goals for the site. For example, the Midland Pet Adoption Agency's main page includes links to information that it believes Web site visitors will be seeking, such as:

- Pets available for adoption (including their names and pictures)
- Training programs offered
- The agency's emergency clinic
- Directions to the agency and contact information

The Midland Pet Adoption Agency's Web site is organized so that each of these information sets appears on its own Web page. The links are organized on the home page in order of importance, from left to right. For example, the first link next to the Home page link is the Pets link, which opens a page of information about pets available for adoption. This is the agency's primary mission and is the most important set of information it wants to convey to site visitors.

Another important point in organizing the Web site is that the navigation tools (in this case, the links) should appear in the same place and in the same form on every page. This consistent structure reinforces the site visitors' knowledge that the site is well organized and tells them that they are still on the same Web site. For example, the Home page link appears in the upper-left corner of all the site's pages, providing the visitors a consistent means to return to the site's main page. The use of common color combinations and consistent headers and graphics (for example, the use of the same two graphics at the top of each page, along with the reminder to "Take me home today!") reinforces the primary message of the Web site, which is to encourage visitors to stop by and adopt a pet, and conveys a sense of urgency regarding doing so.

Good written communications are clearly organized around a theme that conveys the message while guiding readers to the most important information in a direct way. You can accomplish this in a Web site by understanding what your site's visitors will be looking for, and structuring your site to organize that information and make it easy to find.

Clicking Links

Most Web pages include links to other Web pages. A link might open a Web page that is related to the original Web page, such as the Pets link on the Midland Pet Adoption Agency home page, which opens a page listing pets available for adoption. A link could also be a link to a company, such as the Course Technology link at the bottom of the home page. Other times, a link could open a Web page with related information or an advertised product or service. The easiest way to move from one Web page to another is to click a link on the open Web page. You'll use links to open the Training Programs and Pets Web pages.

To use links to navigate the Midland Pet Adoption Agency Web site:

1. On the Midland Pet Adoption Agency home page, point to the **Training Programs** link, as shown in Figure 1-2. The pointer changes to the shape of a hand with a pointing index finger, and a ScreenTip listing the URL to which the link points appears near the bottom of the browser window.

Figure 1-2	Using a hyperlink

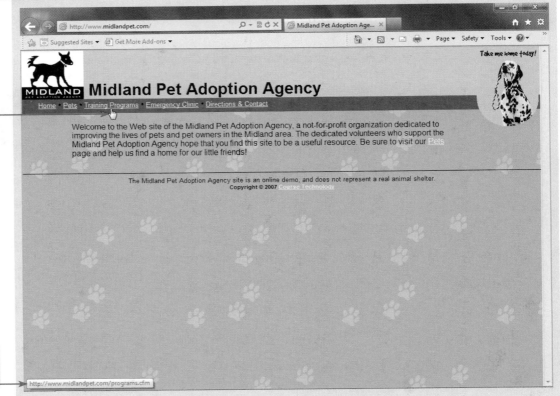

pointer shape changes when positioned over a hyperlink

ScreenTip shows the URL to which the hyperlink points

Courtesy of © Microsoft; © Cengage Learning

2. Click the **Training Programs** link. The Training Programs Web page opens in the browser window.

3. On the Training Programs Web page, click the **Pets** link. The Pets page opens in the browser window.

4. On the Pets Web page, click the **Meet Maxie** link. The Web page with information about the cat named Maxie opens in the browser window.

Moving Among Visited Web Pages

The Back and Forward buttons on the Navigation bar let you navigate among the pages you have just visited. When you first start Internet Explorer, these buttons are grayed out. After you visit more than one Web page in a browsing session, the Back button changes to blue, indicating that it is active and available. Clicking the Back button returns the browser to the previous Web page you visited. You can continue clicking the Back button until you reach the first page you viewed when you started Internet Explorer. Once you click the Back button, the Forward button changes to blue, and you can click the Forward button to return to later pages you have visited.

As you move among the pages you visited, you might want to reload, or refresh, a Web page you return to. The Refresh button on the Navigation bar loads a new copy of the Web page that currently appears in the browser window. Internet Explorer stores a copy of every Web page it displays on your computer's hard drive in a Temporary Internet Files folder in the Windows folder. Storing this information increases the speed at which Internet Explorer can display pages as you move back and forth through the Web pages you have visited because the browser can load the pages from a local disk drive instead of reloading them from the remote Web server. When you click the Refresh button, Internet Explorer contacts the Web server to see if the Web page has changed since it was stored in the Temporary Internet Files folder. If it has changed, Internet Explorer gets the new page from the Web server; otherwise, it loads the copy stored on your computer.

You'll use the Back, Forward, and Refresh buttons to navigate among the Web pages you visited on the Midland Pet Adoption Agency Web site.

To navigate among visited pages on the Midland Pet Adoption Agency Web site:

1. Point to the **Back** button on the Navigation bar. A ScreenTip appears, listing the page that will be displayed if you click the button, as shown in Figure 1-3. In this case, the Pets page will be displayed.

| Figure 1-3 | Using the Back button |

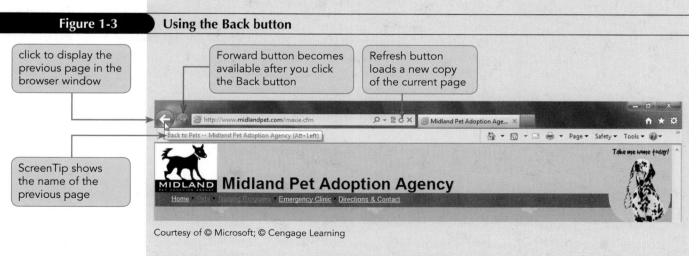

Courtesy of © Microsoft; © Cengage Learning

2. Click the **Back** button to return to the Pets page.

3. Click the **Back** button to return to the Training Programs page.

4. Point to the **Forward** button on the Navigation bar. A ScreenTip appears, listing the page that will be displayed if you click the button. In this case, the Pets page will be displayed.

5. Click the **Forward** button to return to the Pets page.

6. Click the **Refresh** button in the Address bar to load a new copy of the Pets page. Because the content on the page hasn't been updated, you won't see any differences on the refreshed page.

Returning to Internet Explorer's Home Page

When you click the Home button on the Navigation bar or the Command bar, the browser displays the home (or start) page for your installation of Internet Explorer. You can select one or more pages to display as the default home page. If you select multiple pages, each page opens in a separate tab when you click the Home button. You can set the page or pages you want to use as the default home page in the Internet Options dialog box, which you open from the Tools button on the Command bar. You can also open a Web page and then set it as your home page or as one of your home page tabs in the Add or Change Home Page dialog box, which you open from the Home button arrow on the Command bar.

REFERENCE

Changing the Default Home Page in Internet Explorer

- Click the Tools button on the Navigation bar or Command bar, and then click Internet options to open the Internet Options dialog box.
- To use the current page, use Internet Explorer's default page, or use a blank page as the home page, click the corresponding button in the Home page section on the General tab.
- To specify a home page, type the URL of that Web page in the Home page box. To open multiple home pages on separate tabs, type the URL for each home page on separate lines in the Home page box.
- Click the OK button.

or

- Open the Web page you want to use as your home page.
- Click the Home button arrow on the Command bar, and then click Add or change home page to open the Add or Change Home Page dialog box.
- Click the Use this webpage as your only home page option button or the Add this webpage to your home page tabs option button.
- Click the Yes button.

You will use the Home button to return to your browser's home page, and then you will view the home page settings.

To view the settings for your browser's home page:

1. Click the **Home** button on the Navigation bar. The home page for your browser appears in the browser window. This is the same page that opened when you started your browser at the beginning of this session.

2. Click the **Tools** button on the Navigation bar, and then click **Internet options**. The Internet Options dialog box opens, displaying the General tab, which provides options for specifying your home page, or a series of home page tabs. See Figure 1-4.

TIP

Many organizations set the home page defaults on all of their computers and then lock those settings.

Figure 1-4	**Internet Options dialog box**

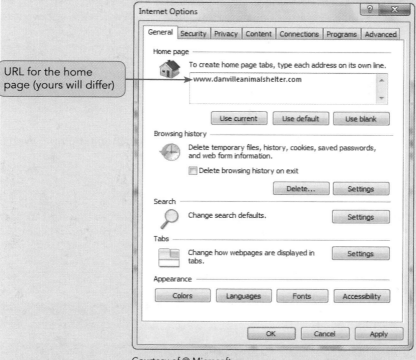

URL for the home page (yours will differ)

Courtesy of © Microsoft

To use the currently loaded Web page as your home page, you would click the Use current button. To use the default home page that was installed with your copy of Internet Explorer, you would click the Use default button. If you do not want a page to open when you start your browser, you would click the Use blank button. If you want to specify a home page other than the current, default, or blank page, you would type the URL for that page in the Home page box.

3. Click the **Cancel** button to close the dialog box without making any changes.

Using the Page Tabs

So far, all the Web pages you have visited have been displayed on the same tab. You can open additional page tabs on the tab row next to the Address bar and load different Web pages on each tab instead of opening additional Web pages in separate browser windows. This tabbed browsing technique is especially useful when you need to open many pages or move frequently back and forth among multiple Web pages.

There are several methods for opening a Web page in a new tab. You can click the New Tab button on the tab row, and then open a Web page as usual. You can right-click a link on a Web page, and then click the Open in new tab command on the shortcut menu. Or, you can press the Ctrl key as you click a link. To close a tab, you click the Close Tab button on that page tab. If you have only one tab open, closing that tab also exits Internet Explorer. Conversely, if you try to exit Internet Explorer when you have more than one tab open, a dialog box opens, asking whether you want to close the current tab or all open tabs.

REFERENCE

Opening Web Pages in Tabs

- Click the New Tab button on the tab row.
- In the Address bar, enter the URL for the Web page you want to open in the new tab.

or

- Right-click a link on the displayed Web page, and then click Open in new tab on the shortcut menu.

or

- Press the Ctrl key as you click a link on the displayed Web page.

You'll use page tabs to open and navigate among multiple Web pages.

To use page tabs in Internet Explorer:

1. On the tab row, click the **New Tab** button. A second tab appears in the browser window and the New Tab page opens, displaying a list of sites you've visited recently and frequently. See Figure 1-5.

Figure 1-5 New tab open

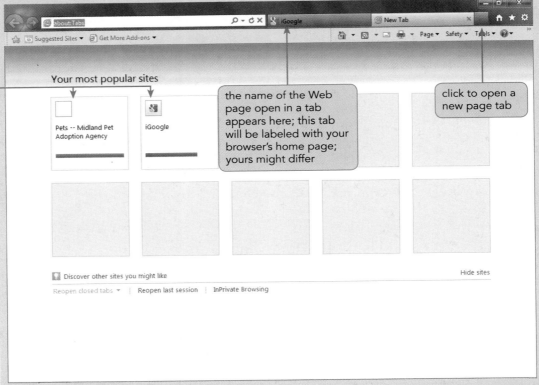

links to recently visited sites appear in these boxes; yours will differ

the name of the Web page open in a tab appears here; this tab will be labeled with your browser's home page; yours might differ

click to open a new page tab

Courtesy of © Microsoft

2. Type **www.midlandpet.com/pets.cfm** in the Address bar, and then press the **Enter** key. The Pets page opens and is labeled on the page tab.

3. On the Pets page, right-click the **Home** link, and then click **Open in new tab** on the shortcut menu. A third tab appears on the tab row labeled "Midland Pet Adoption Agency." To display this page in the browser window, you need to click the new tab.

4. Click the **Midland Pet Adoption Agency** tab on the tab row on the Navigation bar. The home page is displayed in the browser window.

TIP

To see the entire title and URL of a Web page in a ScreenTip, point to its page tab.

5. Press and hold the **Ctrl** key, click the **Training Programs link**, and then release the Ctrl key. The Training -- Midland Pet Adoption Agency page opens in a new tab.

6. Click the **Training -- Midland Pet Adoption Agency** tab. The tab for the training programs is displayed, as shown in Figure 1-6. Notice that the page tabs become smaller as you open additional tabs, and the text identifying the Web pages displayed on the tab becomes truncated.

| **Figure 1-6** | **Internet Explorer with four tabs open** |

Courtesy of © Microsoft; © Cengage Learning

7. Point to the **Pets -- Midland Pet Adoption Agency** tab, and then click the **Close Tab** button that appears. The tab closes.

8. On the Training -- Midland Pet Adoption Agency tab, click the **Close Tab** button. The tab closes and the home page for the Midland Pet Adoption Agency site reappears in the browser window.

9. Click the **Close Tab** button on the tab for your browser's home page. The Midland Pet Adoption Agency home page is the only open tab in the browser window.

You like the format of the Midland Pet Adoption Agency's home page, so you want to make sure that you can go back to that page later if you need to review its contents. You can write down the URL so you can refer to it later, but Internet Explorer makes it easier to return to a previously visited Web page using the Favorites Center.

Using the Favorites Center

The Favorites Center lets you store and organize a list of Web pages that you have visited so you can return to them easily. The View favorites, feeds, and history button located next to the Home button at the right end of the Navigation bar opens the Favorites Center. The Favorites Center has three tabs: Favorites, Feeds, and History. The Favorites tab allows you to create a **favorite**, which is a stored shortcut containing the URL of a Web page. You create, organize, and access your stored favorites on the Favorites tab. The Feeds tab is used to store and organize **RSS feeds**, which provide content published by a Web site that is updated often. The History tab records your browsing activity by organizing and storing the URLs of the Web sites you have visited by date, site, most visited, order visited today, or search history.

Creating and Organizing Favorites

As you use the Web to find information, you can create favorites so you can easily return to sites of interest. You might very quickly find yourself creating so many favorites that it is difficult to find a specific favorite. When you start accumulating favorites, it is helpful to keep them organized so that you can quickly locate the site you need. On the Favorites tab, you can add, delete, and organize favorites into folders that best suit your needs and working style. You can also add favorites that you want to access very frequently to the Favorites bar, which is a toolbar that appears below the Address bar on which you create buttons to access favorites. Keep in mind that the favorites and folders you create are available only on the computer on which you are working.

REFERENCE

Creating a Favorite

- Open the Web page you want to save as a favorite.
- Click the View favorites, feed, and history button on the Navigation bar to open the Favorites Center, and then click the Add to favorites button to open the Add a Favorite dialog box (or right-click a blank area of the Web page, and then click Add to favorites on the shortcut menu).
- If necessary, type a title for the Web page in the Name box.
- If necessary, click the Create in arrow and click a folder in which to store the favorite.
- To create a new folder in which to store the favorite, click the New folder button to open the Create a Folder dialog box. Type the name of the new folder in the Folder Name box, and then click the Create button to close the Create a Folder dialog box.
- Click the Add button in the Add a Favorite dialog box.

or

- Open the Web page you want to save as a favorite.
- Click the View favorites, feed, and history button on the Navigation bar to open the Favorites Center, click the Add to favorites button arrow, and then click Add to Favorites bar (or click the Add to Favorites bar button on the Favorites bar).

You will save the URL for the Midland Pet Adoption Agency Web page as a favorite, and create a Pet Adoption Agencies folder in which to store this favorite.

To create a favorite and a folder to store a link to the agency's home page:

1. With the Midland Pet Adoption Agency home page open, click the **View favorites, feeds, and history** button on the Navigation bar to open the Favorites Center.

2. If necessary, click the **Favorites** tab to display a list of Favorites on your computer. See Figure 1-7.

| Figure 1-7 | **Favorites Center** |

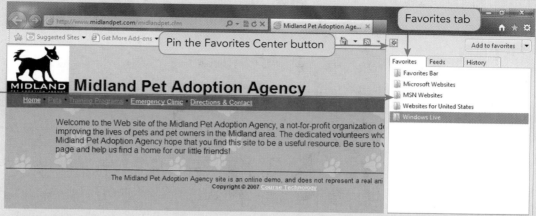

click a folder icon to open the folder and display the favorites stored in it; your list of folders and favorites might differ

Courtesy of © Microsoft; © Cengage Learning

The Favorites Center opens on the right side of the browser window, overlapping the Web page displayed. When you are working in the Favorites Center, you might prefer to dock it on the left side of the browser window using the Pin the Favorites Center button in the upper-left corner of the Favorites Center so that it doesn't obstruct the Web pages you are viewing.

 3. Click the **Pin the Favorites Center** button in the upper-left corner of the Favorites Center. The Favorites Center remains open, and appears along the left side of the browser window; the Midland Pet Adoption Agency home page is fully visible as well.

 4. In the Favorites Center, click the **Add to favorites** button. The Add a Favorite dialog box opens.

 5. If the text selected in the Name box is not "Midland Pet Adoption Agency" (without the quotation marks), type **Midland Pet Adoption Agency**. You want to store the Midland Pet Adoption Agency favorite in a new folder.

 6. Click the **New folder** button. The Create a Folder dialog box opens. The Create in box indicates the new folder will be stored as a subfolder within the Favorites folder.

 7. Type **Pet Adoption Agencies** in the Folder Name box, and then click the **Create** button. The Create a Folder dialog box closes, the Pet Adoption Agencies folder is added to the Favorites tab, and you return to the Add a Favorite dialog box.

 8. Click the **Add** button to create the favorite and close the dialog box. The favorite is saved in the Pet Adoption Agencies folder on the Favorites tab. You can test the favorite by opening it from the Favorites Center.

 9. On the Midland Pet Adoption Agency home page, click the **Emergency Clinic** link to open that page in your browser.

 10. In the Favorites Center, click the **Pet Adoption Agencies** folder to open it, as shown in Figure 1-8.

Figure 1-8	Favorites Center with new folder and favorite

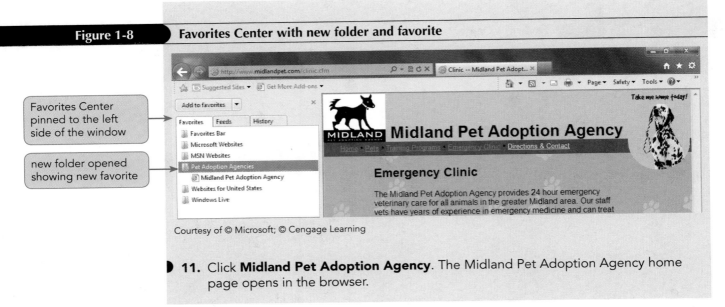

Favorites Center pinned to the left side of the window

new folder opened showing new favorite

Courtesy of © Microsoft; © Cengage Learning

▶ **11.** Click **Midland Pet Adoption Agency**. The Midland Pet Adoption Agency home page opens in the browser.

In the previous set of steps, you created a favorite and a folder in which to store it. You can also create folders and move existing favorites into these folders on the Favorites tab of the Favorites Center. You can reorganize the favorites and folders stored in the Favorites Center at any point, such as by creating new folders and rearranging favorites and folders within folders.

You saved the Midland Pet Adoption Agency's URL as a favorite, which you stored in a new folder named Pet Adoption Agencies in the Favorites Center. Because Trinity might want you to collect information about adoption agencies in different states as you conduct your research, you will organize the information about adoption agencies by state. The Midland Pet Adoption Agency is located in Minnesota, so you will put information about the Midland Pet Adoption Agency in a separate folder named MN (the two-letter abbreviation for Minnesota) within the Pet Adoption Agencies folder. As you collect information about other agencies, you will add folders for the states in which they are located, too.

To move the Midland Pet Adoption Agency favorite into a new folder:

▶ **1.** In the Favorites Center, right-click the **Pet Adoption Agencies** folder, and then click **Create new folder** on the shortcut menu. A new folder appears in the Favorites Center, with the default folder name "New folder" selected.

▶ **2.** Type **MN** as the folder name, and then press the **Enter** key to rename the folder. Now that you have created a folder, you can move your favorite for the Midland Pet Adoption Agency Web page into the new folder.

▶ **3.** If necessary, click the **Pet Adoption Agencies** folder to open it, and then click and drag the **Midland Pet Adoption Agency** favorite to the new MN folder, as shown in Figure 1-9.

Figure 1-9   **Favorite being moved to a new folder**

ScreenTip indicates where the selected favorite will be moved

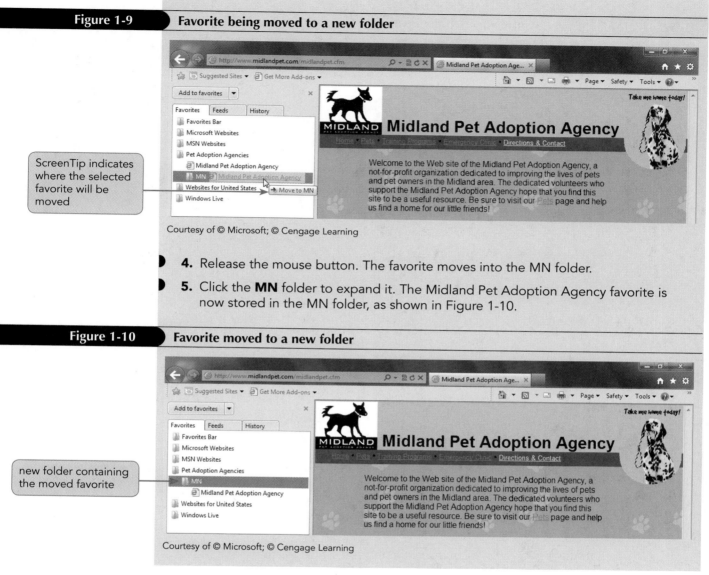

Courtesy of © Microsoft; © Cengage Learning

4. Release the mouse button. The favorite moves into the MN folder.

5. Click the **MN** folder to expand it. The Midland Pet Adoption Agency favorite is now stored in the MN folder, as shown in Figure 1-10.

Figure 1-10   **Favorite moved to a new folder**

new folder containing the moved favorite

Courtesy of © Microsoft; © Cengage Learning

You realize that you will need to go to the Midland Pet Adoption Agency home page frequently. Although it's easily available from the Favorites Center, it would be even faster to access that page from the Favorites bar.

You'll add the Midland Pet Adoption Agency's URL as a link on the Favorites bar.

To add the Midland Pet Adoption Agency home page to the Favorites bar:

1. Click the **Add to Favorites** bar button on the Favorites bar. A button appears on the Favorites bar labeled with the Web page's title, as shown in Figure 1-11.

   Trouble? If the Favorites bar doesn't appear on your screen, right-click the blank area to the right of the page tabs, and then click Favorites bar on the shortcut menu.

Figure 1-11 **Favorite added to the Favorites bar**

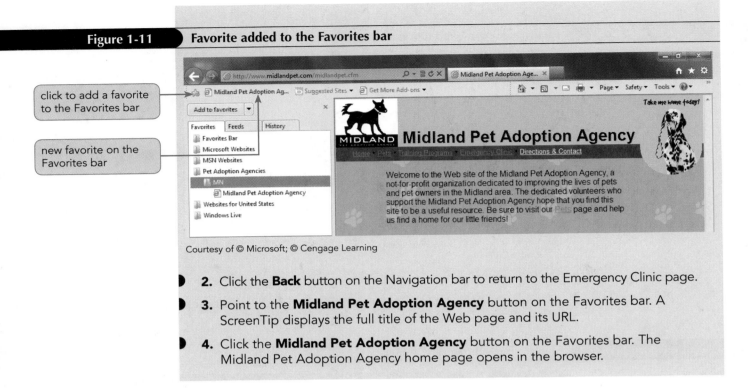

click to add a favorite to the Favorites bar

new favorite on the Favorites bar

Courtesy of © Microsoft; © Cengage Learning

2. Click the **Back** button on the Navigation bar to return to the Emergency Clinic page.

3. Point to the **Midland Pet Adoption Agency** button on the Favorites bar. A ScreenTip displays the full title of the Web page and its URL.

4. Click the **Midland Pet Adoption Agency** button on the Favorites bar. The Midland Pet Adoption Agency home page opens in the browser.

Deleting Favorites and Folders from the Favorites Center

Creating favorites is a great way to keep track of sites you know you want to visit on a regular basis. However, sometimes you no longer want to visit a site, such as when you saved favorites related to a specific project. Other times, the URL for a site has changed or the site no longer exists. In all these instances, you'll want to delete the favorites and the folders in which they are stored. You can delete a specific favorite, or you can delete a folder in the Favorites Center. When you delete a folder, the folder and all of its contents are moved to the Recycle Bin.

To delete the folders and favorites you created:

1. In the Favorites Center, right-click the **Midland Pet Adoption Agency** favorite in the MN folder, and then click **Delete** on the shortcut menu. The favorite is deleted.

2. In the Favorites Center, right-click the **Pet Adoption Agencies** folder, and then click **Delete** on the shortcut menu. The Delete Folder dialog box opens so you can confirm that you want to move the folder to the Recycle Bin.

3. Click the **Yes** button. The folder and all of its contents are deleted from the Favorites Center.

4. Click the **Close the Favorites Center** button on the Favorite Center's title bar to close the Favorites Center.

5. On the Favorites bar, right-click the **Midland Pet Adoption Agency** link, and then click **Delete** on the shortcut menu. The favorite is deleted from the Favorites bar.

Navigating Web Pages Using the History List

Creating favorites is a great way to keep track of sites you know you want to visit on a regular basis. Another way to return to a site that you have visited recently is with the history list. The history list, which you open by clicking the History tab in the Favorites Center, is useful when you know you visited a site recently, but you did not create a favorite and you cannot recall the URL of the site. From the History tab, you can view a list of the sites that were visited on that computer during the last three weeks. You can display the history of visited sites organized by date, by site, by sites most visited, or by the order visited on a single day. You can also use the History tab to search for a specific site. To return to a specific Web page, just click its link in the history list.

Not every site that you visit as you research pet adoption sites for Danville Animal Shelter will warrant being saved as a favorite. The history list will be helpful if you want to show Trinity the breadth of sites you visited during your research. You will view the history list next.

To view the history list for this session:

TIP

If you are using a computer in a computer lab or a public computer, the history list will include sites visited by anyone who has used the computer, not just you.

1. Click the **View favorites, feeds, and history** button on the Navigation bar, and then click the **History** tab in the Favorites Center. The pages that you have visited are grouped by date of visit, so the last icon in the list is labeled "Today" and includes Web sites you visited today. The other icons are labeled with the names of days of the week (Monday, Tuesday, and so on) if Internet Explorer has been used regularly. If not, the icons will be labeled with week names (Last Week, Two Weeks Ago, and so on).

2. Click the **Today** icon to open a list of folders for the Web sites you visited today. Clicking a folder opens a list of the links to each page on that site that you visited today in the order in which you visited them.

TIP

You can see the full URL of any item in the history list by pointing to that item.

3. Click the **midlandpet (www.midlandpet.com)** folder. See Figure 1-12. Each page you visited on the Midland Pet Adoption Agency site is stored in this folder in the order you visited it. Notice the home page for the site appears in the list more than once because you navigated back to that page from the other pages on the site. To return to a particular page, click that page's entry in the list.

Figure 1-12 | **History tab in the Favorites Center**

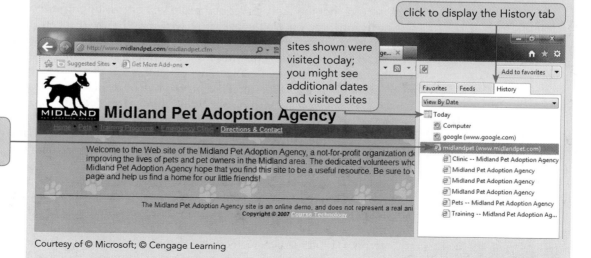

click to display the History tab

sites shown were visited today; you might see additional dates and visited sites

click a folder to display the list of pages visited on that Web site

Courtesy of © Microsoft; © Cengage Learning

> **4.** Click the **Training -- Midland Pet Adoption Agency** link to navigate to that page. The Favorites Center closes and the Training Programs page for the Midland Pet Adoption Agency appears in the browser window.

INSIGHT

Erasing Your Browsing History

In some situations, such as when you are finishing a work session in a school computer lab or on any public computer, you might want to remove the list of Web sites that you visited from the history list of the computer on which you had been working. Erasing your browsing history helps protect your personal information and guard your privacy when working on a shared computer. You can delete your browsing history in Internet Explorer by clicking the Tools button on the Navigation bar or Command bar, and then clicking Internet options to open the Internet Options dialog box. In the Browsing history section of the General tab, click the Delete button to open the Delete Browsing History dialog box. Click the History check box to select it (unless it is already selected). If any other check boxes are selected, click each of them to clear the selections. After ensuring that only the History box is checked, click the Delete button to erase the entire browsing history stored on the computer.

Managing Cookies

All Web browser users should know about the use of cookies. A **cookie** is a small text file that a Web server saves on the hard drive of the computer that is running the Web browser software. A cookie is used to store information about your visit to a specific Web site, such as your login name and password, which pages you viewed, and your shopping cart information if you purchased something from the Web site. By storing this information on your computer, the Web server can retrieve the information when you return to that site, enabling it to perform functions such as automatic login, which makes it easier to sign in to Web pages you have visited before. However, the user often is unaware that cookie files are being written to the computer's hard drive.

When the site you are visiting places a cookie on your computer, it is called a **first-party cookie**. However, many cookies are written by companies that sell advertising on Web pages. The advertising elements of the Web page are delivered by the advertisers' Web servers, not the Web server of the site you are visiting. These cookies record which ads have appeared on Web pages you have viewed. Advertisers use these cookies to determine which ads they will deliver the next time you open a Web page. This can be beneficial because it prevents sites from showing you the same ads over and over again. On the other hand, many people believe that this sort of user tracking is an offensive invasion of privacy. Cookies that are placed by companies other than the company whose Web site you are visiting are called **third-party cookies**.

Most Web browsers, including Internet Explorer, allow you to block cookies from your computer or to specify general categories of cookies (such as first-party or third-party) to block. In Internet Explorer, you can specify privacy settings that control the writing of cookie files to your computer's hard drive. You can specify which types of cookies to block or you can block particular types of cookies from specific sites. These options are available on the Privacy tab in the Internet Options dialog box. You will learn more about the different types of cookies, how they work, and how best to deal with them in Tutorial 6.

Internet Explorer stores each cookie in a separate file. You can delete the cookies from your computer at any time or whenever you exit Internet Explorer. To delete all of the cookies stored on your computer, click the Tools button on the Navigation bar or the

Command bar and then click Internet options to open the Internet Options dialog box. On the General tab, click the Delete button in the Browsing history section to open the Delete Browsing History dialog box. In this dialog box, you click the Cookies check box to select it (unless it is already selected). Clear any other check boxes for items you do not want to delete, and then click the Delete button.

Because some cookies benefit users, you might not want to delete all of the cookies on your computer. For example, if you regularly visit a site that requires you to log in, the Web server can store your login information in a cookie on your computer so you do not have to type your user name each time you visit the site. You should always consider carefully whether the advantages of cookies outweigh the disadvantages for you before you delete all of your Internet Explorer cookies.

Trinity wants you to check the privacy settings related to cookies in Internet Explorer on your computer.

To view privacy settings for cookies in Internet Explorer:

1. Click the **Tools** button on the Navigation bar, and then click **Internet options**. The Internet Options dialog box opens.

2. Click the **Privacy** tab. See Figure 1-13.

| Figure 1-13 | Privacy tab in the Internet Options dialog box |

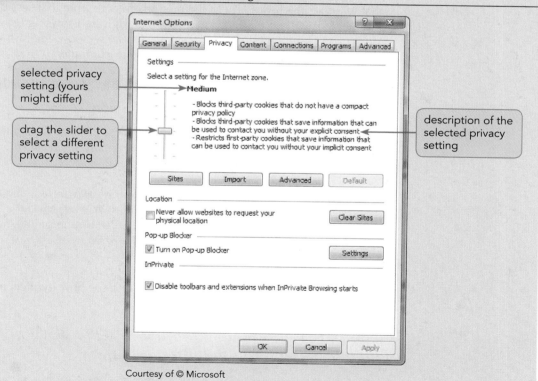

Courtesy of © Microsoft

3. Click and drag the slider control in the Settings section to examine the various settings available that control placement of first-party and third-party cookies on your computer.

4. Click the **Cancel button** to close the Internet Options dialog box without saving any changes to the privacy settings.

Private Web Browsing

As you have learned, Internet Explorer stores a considerable amount of information about your Web browsing activity. It stores a list of all the Web pages you have viewed in the history list, and it stores cookies that can contain information about your logins and passwords. It even stores information about which ads have been displayed on the Web pages you have viewed.

Internet Explorer also stores copies of all or part of the Web pages you visit on whatever computer you are using. If you do not wish to have this information stored, you can use Internet Explorer in InPrivate Browsing mode. In **InPrivate Browsing mode**, Internet Explorer does not store your browsing history, cookies, or copies of the Web pages you visit. In other words, there is no record in Internet Explorer of what sites you visited and what you looked at. When you are using a computer other than your own (such as a friend's computer or a computer at work, school, or another public location), InPrivate Browsing mode can help protect your privacy and security.

To start InPrivate Browsing, you can click the New Tab button to open a new tab, and then click the InPrivate Browsing link. You can also start an InPrivate Browsing session by clicking the Safety button on the Command bar or by clicking the Tools button on the Navigation bar, pointing to Safety, and then clicking InPrivate Browsing, which then opens a new browser window with the "InPrivate is turned on" page displayed in the browser window, the InPrivate label on the page tab, and the InPrivate indicator to the left of the Address bar.

As you visit Web pages in the InPrivate Browsing browser window or in any tabs in that window, the history list of the session, cookies from that session, and temporary Internet files will be tracked only while the InPrivate Browsing browser window is open. When you close the InPrivate Browsing browser window, the history list, cookies, and temporary Internet files are removed from your computer.

REFERENCE

Opening an InPrivate Browsing Session

- Click the New Tab button to open a new tab and then click the InPrivate Browsing link (or click the Tools button on the Navigation bar, point to Safety, and then click InPrivate Browsing; or click the Safety button on the Command bar, and then click InPrivate Browsing).
- Enter a URL in the Address bar to navigate to a Web site, and navigate to other Web pages by clicking links or open pages in other tabs as usual.
- To turn off InPrivate Browsing, click the Close button on the Internet Explorer title bar to close the browser window and all open tabs.

You will try an InPrivate Browsing session to see how it differs from the Web browsing you have done earlier in this session.

To start an InPrivate Browsing session:

1. Click the **Safety** button on the Command bar, and then click **InPrivate Browsing**. A new browser window opens, displaying a Web page with the message "InPrivate is turned on." The Address bar has the blue InPrivate indicator next to it, and the text "about:InPrivate" appears selected in the Address bar. See Figure 1-14.

| Figure 1-14 | InPrivate Browsing mode |

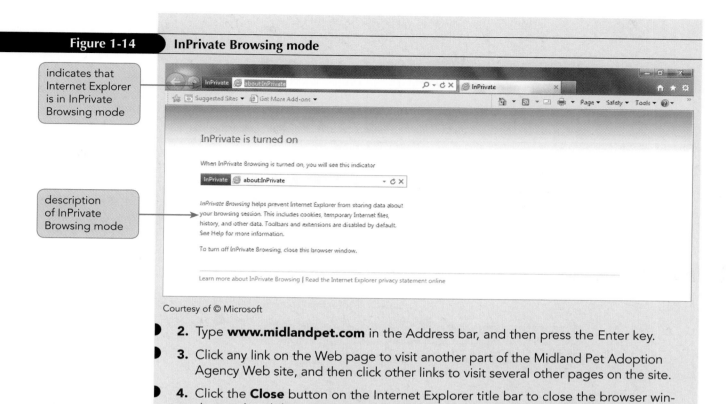

Courtesy of © Microsoft

> **2.** Type **www.midlandpet.com** in the Address bar, and then press the Enter key.

> **3.** Click any link on the Web page to visit another part of the Midland Pet Adoption Agency Web site, and then click other links to visit several other pages on the site.

> **4.** Click the **Close** button on the Internet Explorer title bar to close the browser window and end the InPrivate Browsing session. You return to the browser window displaying the Midland Pet Adoption Agency Training page.

If you examine the browser's history listing, you will see that it includes no record of the Web pages you just visited. Although the browser does not record the pages you have visited (or other information, such as cookies), the network server that connects the computer to the Internet might have software that does. Therefore, it is best not to rely on InPrivate Browsing mode to keep private the Web pages you visit while using a computer at work or another public location.

Getting Help in Internet Explorer

Internet Explorer has an online Help system that includes information about how to use the browser and how it is different from previous versions of the browser. It also provides tips for exploring the Internet.

REFERENCE

Using Internet Explorer Help

- Click the Help button on the Command bar, and then click Internet Explorer Help (or press the F1 key) to open the Windows Help and Support window.
- Click the Browse Help button on the toolbar in the Windows Help and Support window.
- Click a link to access information on a specific Help topic or type a search term or query in the Search Help box, and then click the Search Help button.
- Click the Close button on the Windows Help and Support window.

Trinity wants you to learn more about InPrivate Browsing. You will use Internet Explorer Help to find more information about this feature.

To use Internet Explorer Help:

1. Click the **Help** button on the Command bar, and then click **Internet Explorer Help**. The Windows Help and Support window opens.

2. Click the **Browse Help** button on the toolbar to open the Contents page. You can explore any of the items in the Help system by clicking the topics links on this page. You can also type search terms or queries into the Search Help box.

3. Type **inprivate browsing** in the Search Help box and then click the **Search Help** button. The Windows Help and Support window displays a list of results for the search term, as shown in Figure 1-15.

| Figure 1-15 | Windows Help and Support window |

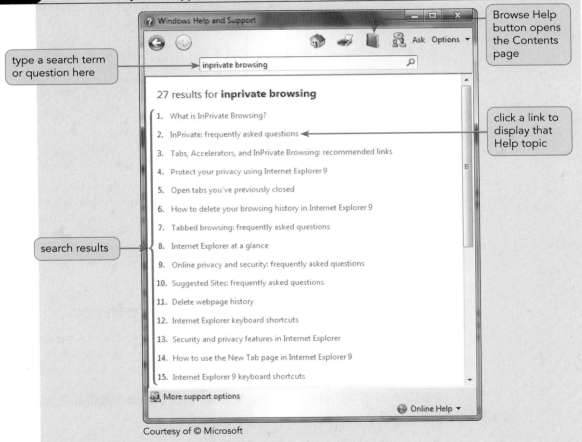

Courtesy of © Microsoft

4. Click the **InPrivate: frequently asked questions** link to open a page of frequently asked questions about InPrivate Browsing.

5. Click the **What is InPrivate Browsing?** link, and read the paragraph that appears under the link.

6. When you are finished, click the **Close** button on the Windows Help and Support window title bar.

Saving Web Page Content

At times you will want to refer to the information that you have found on a Web page without having to return to the site. In Internet Explorer, you can save entire Web pages, particular graphics, or selected portions of Web page text.

Saving an Entire Web Page

When you save the entire Web page, you use the Save Webpage dialog box, which is similar to the Save As dialog box in other programs. To open the Save Webpage dialog box, click the Tools button on the Navigation bar, point to File, and then click Save as. You can also click the Page button on the Command bar, and then click Save as to open the Save Webpage dialog box.

Internet Explorer by default saves the complete Web page, including the graphic page elements along with the Web page's text and the HTML markup codes. You can select a different format from the Save as type list in the Save Webpage dialog box. The Webpage, HTML only format saves the Web page's text along with the HTML markup codes. The Text File format saves the Web page's text without the HTML markup codes. The Web Archive, single file format saves the Web page in a proprietary archive format (the .mht format) that can be read by Internet Explorer Web browsers, but not necessarily other Web browsers. Avoiding the Internet Explorer proprietary format will ensure that anyone using another Web browser can read the page you saved.

You will save the Midland Pet Adoption Agency home page to show to Trinity. This Web site will provide Trinity an example of a well-designed site with appropriate text and graphics.

To save the Midland Pet Adoption Agency home page:

1. Return to the Midland Pet Adoption Agency home page.

2. Click the **Page** button on the Command bar, and then click **Save as**. The Save Webpage dialog box opens.

3. Navigate to and select the **Tutorial.01\Tutorial** folder included with your Data Files. This is the location where you will save the Web page.

   Trouble? If you don't have the starting Data Files, you need to get them before you can proceed. Your instructor will either give you the Data Files or ask you to obtain them from a specified location (such as a network drive). In either case, make a backup copy of the Data Files before you start so that you will have the original files available in case you need to start over. If you have any questions about the Data Files, see your instructor or technical support person for assistance.

4. Type **Midland Pet Home Page IE** in the File name box.

5. Click the **Save as type** arrow, and then click **Webpage, complete (*.htm, *html)** to select this format if it is not already selected.

6. Click the **Save** button. The Save Webpage dialog box closes. The Web page for the Midland Pet Adoption Agency's home page is saved in the location you specified.

Saving an Image from a Web Page

Most Web pages include graphics or pictures to provide interest, illustrate a point, or present information. You can save a graphic or picture instead of the entire Web page.

REFERENCE

Saving an Image from a Web Page

- Right-click the image on the Web page that you want to save, and then click Save picture as on the shortcut menu to open the Save Picture dialog box.
- Navigate to the location in which you want to save the image, and change the default filename, if necessary.
- Click the Save button.

The Directions & Contact Web page also includes a street map that shows the location of the Midland Pet Adoption Agency. You will save this map to show Trinity as well.

To save the street map image:

1. Click the **Directions & Contact** link to open the Web page that contains the address and phone number for the Midland Pet Adoption Agency.

2. On the Directions & Contact page, scroll the page as needed to display the map.

3. Right-click the **map**, and then click **Save picture as** on the shortcut menu to open the Save Picture dialog box.

4. Navigate to and select the **Tutorial.01\Tutorial** folder included with your Data Files. This is the location where you will save the map graphic.

5. Type **Midland Pet Map IE** as the filename, and then click the **Save** button to save the graphic.

INSIGHT

Understanding Copyright for Web Page Content

A **copyright** is the legal right of the author or other owner of an original work to control the reproduction, distribution, and sale of that work. A copyright comes into existence as soon as the work is placed into a tangible form, such as a printed copy, an electronic file, or a Web page. Copyright laws can place significant restrictions on the way that you can use information or images that you copy from another entity's Web site. Because of the way a Web browser works, it copies the HTML code as well as the graphics and media files to your computer before it can display them in the browser. Just because copies of these files are stored temporarily on your computer does not mean that you have the right to use them in any way other than having your computer display them in the browser window.

The United States and most other countries have copyright laws that govern the use of photocopies, audio or video recordings, and other reproductions of authors' original work. The copyright exists even if the work does not contain a copyright notice. If you do not know whether material that you find on the Web is copyrighted, the safest course of action is to assume that it is.

U.S. copyright law has a **fair use** provision that allows a limited amount of copyrighted information to be used for purposes such as news reporting, research, and scholarship. The source of the material used should always be cited. Commercial use of copyrighted material is much more restricted. You should obtain permission from the copyright holder before using anything you copy from a Web page. The copyright holder can require you to pay a fee for permission to use the material from the Web page. The steps in this tutorial are designed so that your use of copyrighted Web pages and elements of those pages falls within the fair use provisions of U.S. copyright law.

Copying Text from a Web Page

You can also copy and paste portions of a Web page to a file or email. This can be helpful when you want to save specific information from a Web page, such as a schedule of events, directions to a location, or information about a place.

Trinity plans to visit the Midland Pet Adoption Agency while she is traveling in Minnesota next week. She wants to contact Midland's director and schedule a meeting. You can copy and paste the agency's address and telephone number from its Web site into a document or an email for Trinity.

To copy and paste text from the Midland Pet Adoption Agency Web site:

1. On the Directions & Contact page, select the address and telephone number for Midland Pet Adoption Agency at the top of the page.

2. Right-click the selected text, and then click **Copy** on the shortcut menu to copy the selected text to the Clipboard, which is a temporary storage area in Windows.

3. Click the **Start** button on the taskbar, point to **All Programs**, click the **Accessories** folder, and then click **WordPad** to start the program and open a new document.

4. On the Home tab on the WordPad Ribbon, click the **Paste** button to paste the text into the WordPad document, as shown in Figure 1-16.

| Figure 1-16 | **WordPad document with pasted text** |

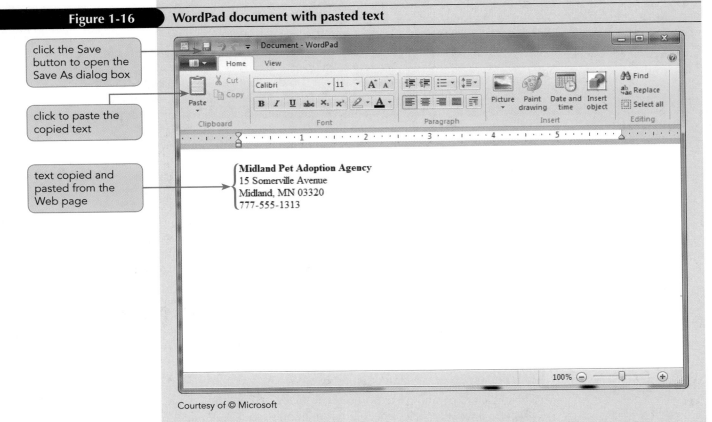

click the Save button to open the Save As dialog box

click to paste the copied text

text copied and pasted from the Web page

Midland Pet Adoption Agency
15 Somerville Avenue
Midland, MN 03320
777-555-1313

Courtesy of © Microsoft

5. Click the **Save** button on the WordPad Quick Access Toolbar to open the Save As dialog box.

6. Navigate to and select the **Tutorial.01\Tutorial** folder included with your Data Files. This is the location where you will save the WordPad document.

7. Click the **Save as type** button, and then click **Rich Text Format (RTF)** if necessary.

8. Type **Midland Pet Contact Info IE** in the File name box, and then click the **Save** button. The address and phone number of the agency are now saved in a text file for future reference.

9. Click the **Close** button on the WordPad title bar to close it.

Printing a Web Page

TIP

If you encounter a page that is difficult to print, be sure to look on the Web page for a link to a version of the page that is designed to be printed.

Sometimes you will want to print a Web page. This might occur when you want to keep a printed page for reference, save a record or receipt of an online purchase, or have a coupon to use at a local store or restaurant. As with other programs, you can send the displayed page directly to the printer by clicking the Print button on the Command bar, or you can select options in the Print dialog box by clicking the Print button arrow on the Command bar and then clicking Print. The Print dialog box includes options for selecting a printer, setting a page range, and specifying the number of copies to print.

You can also use the Page Setup dialog box to change aspects of a Web page printout, including the page size and orientation, margins, and headers and footers that print at the top and bottom of the page, respectively. The default header prints the Web page title in the left section, nothing in the center section, and the page number and the total number of pages in the right section. The default footer prints the URL in the left section, nothing in the center section, and the date in the right section. To open the Page Setup dialog box, click the Print button arrow on the Command bar, and then click Page setup.

Before printing a Web page, you should preview what the printout will look like to ensure that it will print in the best way possible. For example, you want to ensure that extra or unnecessary pages won't print, that the printed page is legible, and that what will print is what you wanted to print. This extra step helps you to save resources, including paper and printer ink. To open the Print Preview window, click the Print button arrow on the Command bar, and then click Print preview. The Print Preview window shows how the current Web page will look on the printed page. It also provides access to common printing options. From the toolbar, you can open the Print dialog box, change the page orientation, open the Page Setup dialog box, toggle headers and footers on or off, change the number of pages in the preview, and adjust the print size. Changing the print size enables you to shrink the Web page to fit better on the page or enlarge the Web page on the printout so it's more legible.

REFERENCE

Printing the Current Web Page

- Click the Print button on the Command bar to print the current Web page with the default print settings.
or
- Click the Print button arrow on the Command bar, and then click Print to open the Print dialog box.
- On the General tab, select the printer you want to use, specify the page range you want to print, and set the number of copies to print.
- Click the Print button.

You will preview a copy of the Midland Pet Adoption Agency home page, and then print it.

To preview and print the Midland Pet Adoption Agency home page:

1. Return to the Midland Pet Adoption Agency home page.

2. Click the **Print button arrow** on the Command bar, and then click **Print preview**. The Print Preview window opens. See Figure 1-17.

Figure 1-17   **Print Preview window**

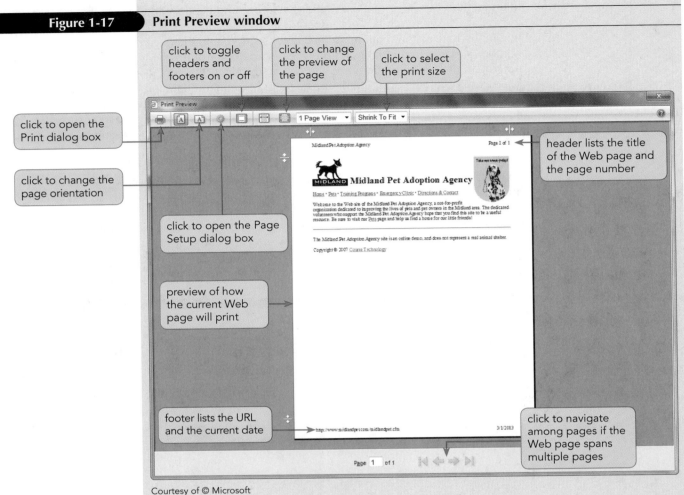

Courtesy of © Microsoft

The preview looks fine, so you will print the page.

3. Click the **Close** button on the title bar to close the Print Preview window.

4. Click the **Print button arrow** on the Command bar, and then click **Print** to open the Print dialog box.

5. Make sure that the printer selected in the Select Printer box is the printer you want to use; if not, click the icon of the printer you want to use to change the selection.

6. If necessary, click the **Pages** option button in the Page Range section of the Print dialog box, and then type **1** in the text box to specify that you only want to print the first page. (If the text box already contains a "1" you do not need to change it.)

7. Make sure that the Number of copies box displays **1**.

8. Click the **Print** button to print the Web page and close the Print dialog box.

9. Click the **Close** button on the Internet Explorer title bar to close the Web browser.

You have copies of the Midland Pet Adoption Agency home page and map that will show Trinity how to get to the agency during her trip to Minnesota. Trinity will be able to use her Web browser or other software to open the files and print them.

In this session, you worked with Internet Explorer as you browsed the Midland Pet Adoption Agency Web site. You navigated among pages, worked with favorites, reviewed the history list, saved and copied Web pages, and printed a Web page from the site.

REVIEW

Session 1.1 Quick Check

1. Briefly explain the difference between a network and the Internet.
2. What is a hypertext link?
3. What is a URL?
4. What is a favorite?
5. If you have recently visited a Web site, but cannot recall the URL and didn't save it as a favorite, what feature can you use to return to that site?
6. Briefly explain what a cookie is.
7. What is InPrivate Browsing mode?
8. Can you use an image you save from someone else's Web site on your Web site? Explain your answer.
9. Why should you preview what the printout will look like before printing a Web page?

Note: If your instructor assigned Session 1.2, continue reading. Otherwise, complete the Review Assignments and Case Problems at the end of this tutorial.

SESSION 1.2 VISUAL OVERVIEW

The **Firefox button** opens a menu with options for all the main functions and features in the browser.

Firefox is a **Web browser**, which is software you run on your computer to make it run as a Web client, allowing it to locate and display Web pages.

Page tabs allow you to have multiple Web pages open at once, and to easily navigate among them.

The **Navigation toolbar** is used to open and move among Web pages and search for Web pages.

You type the **Uniform Resource Locator (URL)**, or the address for a Web page, in the Location bar to open that Web page in the browser.

A **Web page** is a document that has been created using **HTML**, a programming language used to format documents containing text and images so they can be viewed in a Web browser.

You use the **Library** to organize and display links to your preferred Web sites and view the History list of recently visited sites.

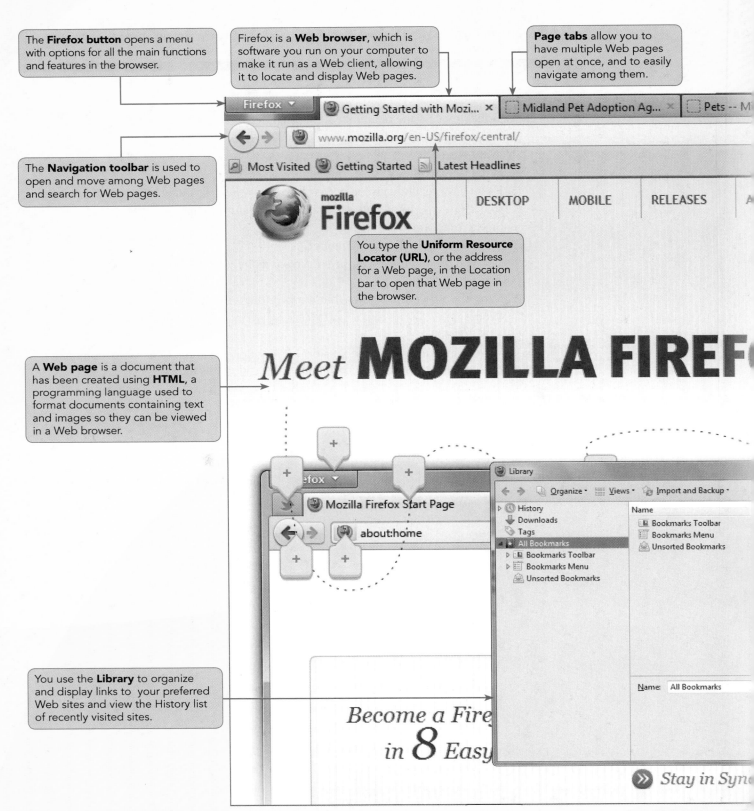

Courtesy of The Mozilla Foundation

MOZILLA FIREFOX

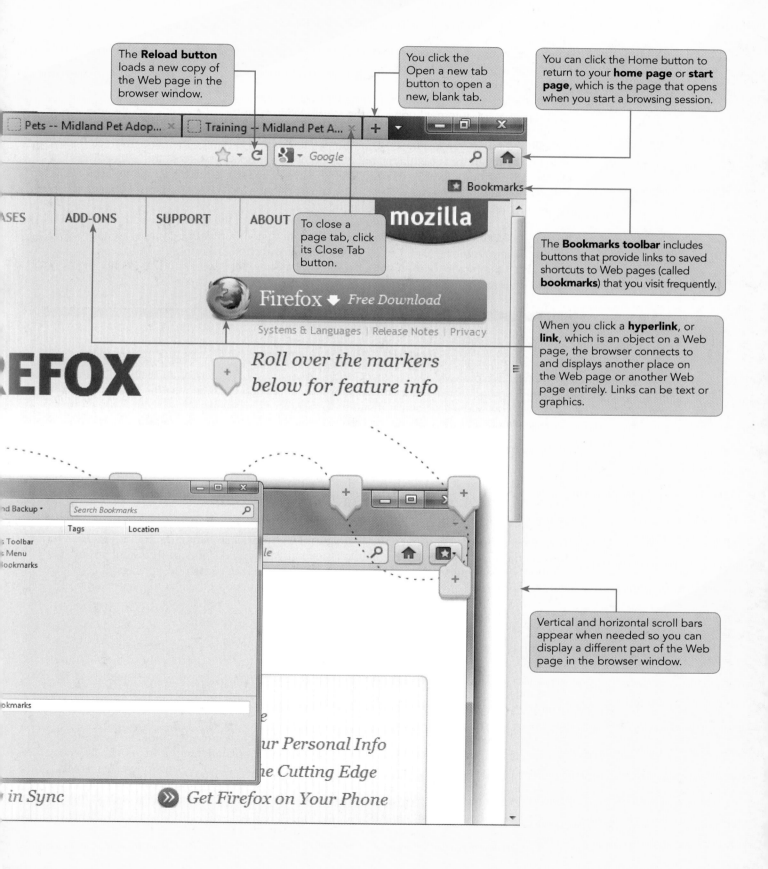

The **Reload button** loads a new copy of the Web page in the browser window.

You click the Open a new tab button to open a new, blank tab.

You can click the Home button to return to your **home page** or **start page**, which is the page that opens when you start a browsing session.

To close a page tab, click its Close Tab button.

The **Bookmarks toolbar** includes buttons that provide links to saved shortcuts to Web pages (called **bookmarks**) that you visit frequently.

When you click a **hyperlink**, or **link**, which is an object on a Web page, the browser connects to and displays another place on the Web page or another Web page entirely. Links can be text or graphics.

Vertical and horizontal scroll bars appear when needed so you can display a different part of the Web page in the browser window.

Roll over the markers below for feature info

The Internet and the Web

Computers can be connected to each other in a configuration called a **network**. When networks are connected to each other, the system is called an **interconnected network** or **internet** (with a lowercase "i"). The **Internet** (with an uppercase "i") is a specific interconnected network that connects computers all over the world using a common set of interconnection standards. Although it began as a computer science project sponsored by the U.S. military, the Internet today allows people and businesses all over the world to communicate with each other in a variety of ways.

The part of the Internet known as the **World Wide Web** (or the **Web**) is a collection of files that reside on computers, called **Web servers**, that are connected to each other through the Internet. Most files on computers, including computers that are connected to the Internet, are private; that is, only the computer's users can access those files. The owners of the computer files that make up the Web have made the files publicly available by placing them on the Web servers. Thus, anyone who has a computer connected to the Internet can obtain access to the files.

When you use an Internet connection to become part of the Web, your computer becomes a **Web client**. A **Web browser** is software that allows your computer to connect to, locate, retrieve, and display Web content. You can read Appendix A to learn more about the history of the Internet and the Web, how they work, and the technologies behind their operation.

INSIGHT

Choosing a Browser

There are a variety of Web browsers available. Some of the most common are Microsoft Internet Explorer, Mozilla Firefox, Google Chrome, Apple Safari, and Opera. You can download and install these browsers for free, enabling you to choose the one you want. All Web browsers have similar features, but some are more robust and others are more streamlined. To help evaluate and decide which Web browser you want to use, you can read reviews, explore the product pages, take tours or demos of the browsers, and download and try them.

Hypertext Markup Language and Hyperlinks

The public files on Web servers are ordinary text files, much like the files created and used by word-processing software. To enable Web browser software to read these files, the text must be formatted according to a generally accepted standard. The standard used on the Web is **Hypertext Markup Language (HTML)**. HTML uses codes, or **tags**, that tell the Web browser software how to display the text contained in the text file. For example, a Web browser reading the following line of text

```
<B>A Review of the Book <I>Wind Instruments</I></B>
```

recognizes the <B> and </B> tags as instructions to display the entire line of text in bold and the <I> and </I> tags as instructions to display the text enclosed by those tags in italics. Different Web clients that connect to this Web server might display the tagged text differently. For example, one Web browser might display text enclosed by bold tags in a blue color instead of displaying the text in bold. A text file that contains HTML tags is called an **HTML document**.

HTML provides a variety of text formatting tags that can be used to indicate headings, paragraphs, bulleted lists, numbered lists, and other text enhancements in an HTML document. (You will learn more about HTML tags in Tutorial 8.) The real power of HTML, however, lies in its anchor tag. The **HTML anchor tag** enables Web designers to link HTML documents to each other. Anchor tags in HTML documents create **hypertext links**, which are instructions that point to other HTML documents or to another section of the same document. Hypertext links also are called **hyperlinks** or **links**. The linked HTML documents can be on the same computer or on different computers. These computers can be anywhere in the world if they are connected to the Internet. When a Web browser displays an HTML document, it is often referred to as a **Web page**.

Starting Mozilla Firefox

Mozilla Firefox is a Web browser currently maintained by the Mozilla Foundation. If you want to use Firefox as your Web browser, you usually need to download and install the software. In this session, you will use the Firefox Web browser to do your work for the Danville Animal Shelter. This introduction assumes that you have Firefox installed on your computer.

To start Firefox:

1. Click the **Start** button on the taskbar, point to **All Programs**, and then click **Mozilla Firefox**. After a moment, Firefox opens.

   Trouble? If you cannot find Mozilla Firefox on the All Programs menu, check to see if a Mozilla or Firefox shortcut icon appears on the desktop, and then double-click it. If you do not see the shortcut icon, ask your instructor or technical support person for help. The program might be installed in a different location on the computer you are using.

2. If the program window does not fill the screen entirely, click the **Maximize** button on the title bar. Your screen should look similar to the Session 1.2 Visual Overview.

   Trouble? The Session 1.2 Visual Overview shows the Mozilla Firefox Start page, which is the page that Firefox opens the first time the program is started after being installed on a computer. Your computer will almost certainly be configured to open to a different Web page, or no page at all.

   Trouble? The Session 1.2 Visual Overview shows the Mozilla Firefox program window with the Navigation toolbar and Bookmarks toolbar displayed with the new tabs opened on top. Some of these may be hidden on your screen. You will learn how to customize the program window later in this session. In addition, other programs can add icons and toolbars to the Firefox program window. So if you are using a computer that has been used by other people, or your own computer on which other software has been installed, you might see icons and toolbars that are not shown in the figure.

   Trouble? If the Bookmarks toolbar shown in the Session 1.2 Visual Overview is not displayed on your screen, click the Firefox button, point to Options, and then click Bookmarks Toolbar to check this option and display the toolbar.

   Trouble? If you don't see a page tab in the browser window as shown in the Session 1.2 Visual Overview, then your browser is set to hide page tabs when only one Web site is open. Click the Firefox button, point to Options, and then click Options to open the Options dialog box. Click the Tabs icon in the Options dialog box, and then click the Always show the tab bar check box to select it. Click the OK button to close the dialog box.

The very first time Firefox starts, only the Firefox button and the Navigation toolbar are displayed in the program window. The Firefox button provides access to all of the features and functions available in Firefox. The Navigation toolbar contains the Location bar for opening Web pages, the Go back one page and Go forward one page buttons for navigating among previously visited pages, the Search bar for finding specific Web pages, and the Home and Bookmarks buttons to go to your start page or favorite sites. This streamlined version provides more screen space for viewing Web pages.

You can, however, display additional toolbars, including the Bookmarks toolbar, which is shown in the Session 1.2 Visual Overview. You can also customize the toolbars by deleting icons and adding new icons. Firefox allows you to change the toolbar settings because some people like to have many commands available on the screen, while others prefer to have more space available for displaying the Web page. Also, other software programs installed on your computer can place icons on the Firefox toolbars so that you can use these programs from within Firefox. As a result, your Firefox browser window might have different toolbars displayed or the toolbars might contain icons not shown in the Visual Overview.

Customizing the Firefox Window

In Firefox, you can display or hide the menu bar and toolbars as needed. When the menu bar and toolbars are hidden, more of the Web page is displayed in the browser window. The menu bar and most toolbars are hidden by default. To display the menu bar or a toolbar, right-click a blank area of the Navigation toolbar, and then click the corresponding option on the shortcut menu. You can also display or hide the menu bar or a toolbar by clicking the Firefox button, pointing to Options, and then clicking the corresponding option to display or hide the menu bar or a toolbar.

At any point, you can switch to **Full Screen mode**, which temporarily hides the program window—the Firefox button, the Navigation toolbar, and any other toolbars as well as the Windows taskbar—leaving only the Web page visible on your screen. You can switch to Full Screen mode by clicking the Firefox button and selecting Full Screen on the menu. When the window is in Full Screen mode, you can display the hidden toolbars by pointing to the top of the screen. When you move the pointer away from the toolbars, they will become hidden again. To exit Full Screen mode, point to the top of the screen until the toolbars appear, right-click a blank area above the Navigation toolbar, and then click Exit Full Screen Mode on the shortcut menu.

REFERENCE

Hiding and Restoring Toolbars in Firefox

- To switch to Full Screen mode, click the Firefox button, and then click Full Screen (or press the F11 key).
- To temporarily restore the toolbars in Full Screen mode, point to the top of the screen until the toolbars appear.
- To exit Full Screen mode, point to the top of the screen to display the toolbars, right-click a blank area above the Navigation toolbar, and then click Exit Full Screen Mode on the shortcut menu (or press the F11 key).
- To display or hide individual toolbars, click the Firefox button, point to Options, and then click a toolbar name on the menu (or right-click a blank area of the Navigation toolbar, and then click a toolbar name on the shortcut menu). If the toolbar name is already checked, the toolbar will be hidden when you click the name. If the toolbar name is not checked, the toolbar will be displayed when you click the name.

Next, you will customize the Firefox window by displaying and hiding the toolbars. In these tutorials, you will use the Navigation toolbar and the Bookmarks toolbar, so you will leave them displayed.

To display and hide toolbars in Firefox:

1. Click the **Firefox** button, and then point to **Options**. A menu opens, listing the available toolbars. A check mark appears to the left of each toolbar that is displayed.

2. Click **Navigation Toolbar** on the menu to remove the check mark and deselect this option. The Navigation toolbar is hidden.

   Trouble? If the Navigation toolbar appears, it was already hidden. Continue with Step 4.

3. Click the **Firefox** button, point to **Options**, and then click **Navigation Toolbar** to display the toolbar. This on-off, or toggle, function works for all of the toolbars.

4. Click the **Firefox** button, point to **Options**, and then click **Menu Bar** on the menu to display the menu bar.

   Trouble? If the menu bar disappears, it was already displayed. Continue with Step 6.

5. Right-click a blank area of the Navigation toolbar, and then click **Menu Bar** on the shortcut menu to hide the menu bar.

6. If the Bookmarks toolbar is not displayed, click the **Firefox** button, point to **Options**, and then click **Bookmarks Toolbar**. The Bookmarks toolbar appears below the Navigation toolbar. You can temporarily hide the Firefox button and the toolbars.

7. Click the **Firefox** button, and then click **Full Screen**. The Web page fills the entire screen.

   Trouble? If the toolbars do not immediately roll up out of view, move the pointer away from the top of the screen.

8. Point to the top of the screen. The toolbars scroll back down into view.

   Trouble? If the toolbars don't scroll back into view, this feature is not working on your computer. Press the F11 key to exit Full Screen mode and skip Step 9.

9. Right-click a blank area on the Navigation toolbar, and then click **Exit Full Screen Mode** to redisplay the toolbars.

TIP

Another way to switch Full Screen mode on and off is to press the F11 key.

Now that you are familiar with the tools in the browser window, you are ready to navigate to a Web site.

Navigating Web Pages

To identify a particular Web page's exact location on the Internet, Web browsers rely on an address called a Uniform Resource Locator (URL). The URL is the address of a specific Web page. Every Web page has a unique URL. A URL is a four-part addressing scheme that tells the Web browser:

- The protocol to use when transporting the file
- The domain name of the computer on which the file resides
- The path for the folder or directory on the computer in which the file resides
- The name of the file

So in the URL *http:www.nytimes.com/pages/sports/index.htm,* the *http://* is the transfer protocol, which is the set of rules that computers use to move files from one computer to another. The two most common protocols used to transfer files on the Internet are Hypertext Transfer Protocol (HTTP) and File Transfer Protocol (FTP). The second part of the URL, the domain name, is *www.nytimes.com* and this references the location of the computer on which the Web page resides; *www* indicates the computer is connected to the Web, *nytimes* is the name of the Web site, and *.com* identifies the Web site as being a commercial organization. The */pages/sports* portion of the

URL provides the path for the folder in which the Web page file is located, and the last portion of the URL, *index.htm*, is the filename.

Entering a URL in the Location Bar

You can use the Location bar, which is located on the Navigation toolbar, to enter a specific URL and go directly to that Web page. For example, you can enter the complete URL for a Web site, such as http://www.cnn.com, to load that Web page. As you begin to type, a list opens, displaying pages you have previously visited that begin with the letters you are typing; you can select a URL and press the Enter key to return to that Web page. Also, Firefox will try to complete partial URLs that you type in the Location bar. For example, if you type cnn.com, Firefox will convert it to www.cnn.com and load the Web page at that URL.

If you don't see the URL you want in the Location bar list, you can use the Search bar on the Navigation toolbar to find a specific Web site. You enter a partial URL or a search word in the Search bar, and Firefox contacts the search engine selected for your browser. A **search engine** performs a search based on the text you type in a search box—in this case, the Location bar—and displays the search results. You can click any link in the search results to go to that Web page. You will learn more about search engines in Tutorial 3.

INSIGHT

Understanding Home Pages

The term "home page" is used at least three different ways on the Web, and it is sometimes difficult to tell which meaning people intend when they use the term. The first definition of home page indicates the main page that all of the other pages on a particular Web site are organized around and link back to. This home page is the first page that opens when you visit that Web site. The second definition of "home page" is the first page that opens when you start your Web browser. This type of home page might be an HTML document on your own computer. Some people create such home pages and include hyperlinks to Web sites that they frequently visit. If you are using a computer on your school's or employer's network, its Web browser might be configured to open the main page for the school or firm. The third definition of "home page" is the Web page that a particular Web browser loads the first time you use it. This page usually is stored at the Web site of the firm or other organization that created the Web browser software. Home pages that meet the second or third definitions are sometimes called start pages.

Trinity wants you to start your research by examining the Midland Pet Adoption Agency's Web site. She has provided the URL for the home page.

To load the Midland Pet Adoption Agency's home page:

1. Click in the **Location bar** to select the current URL, and then type **www.midlandpet.com**. This is the URL for the Midland Pet Adoption Agency Web site.

   Trouble? The Location bar might display a list of suggested URLs as you type; ignore these suggestions and continue typing.

2. Press the **Enter** key. The home page of the Midland Pet Adoption Agency Web site loads, as shown in Figure 1-18.

Figure 1-18	Midland Pet Adoption Agency Web page

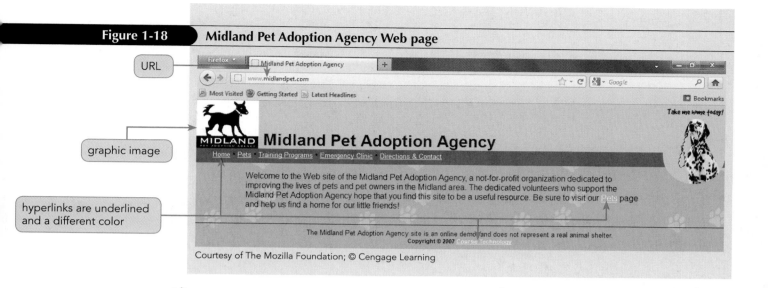

Courtesy of The Mozilla Foundation; © Cengage Learning

Written Communication: The Importance of Organization in a Web Site

Web sites are written communications media just as printed brochures and newsletters are. When visiting a Web site, you can learn a great deal about how to create a Web site for your organization, just as you can learn to design brochures by reading brochures produced by other organizations. The writing that appears on a Web site's pages must be organized to reflect the organization's communication goals for the site. For example, the Midland Pet Adoption Agency's main page includes links to information that it believes Web site visitors will be seeking, such as:

- Pets available for adoption (including their name and pictures)
- Training programs offered
- The agency's emergency clinic
- Directions to the agency and contact information

The Midland Pet Adoption Agency's Web site is organized so that each of these information sets appears on its own Web page. The links are organized on the home page in order of importance, from left to right. For example, the first link next to the Home page link is the Pets link, which opens a page of information about pets available for adoption. This is the agency's primary mission and is the most important set of information it wants to convey to site visitors.

Another important point in organizing the Web site is that the navigation tools (in this case, the links) should appear in the same place and in the same form on every page. This consistent structure reinforces the site visitors' knowledge that the site is well organized and tells them that they are still on the same Web site. For example, the Home page link appears in the upper-left corner of all the site's pages, providing the visitors a consistent means to return to the site's main page. The use of common color combinations and consistent headers and graphics (for example, the use of the same two graphics at the top of each page, along with the reminder to "Take me home today!") reinforces the primary message of the Web site, which is to encourage visitors to stop by and adopt a pet, and conveys a sense of urgency regarding doing so.

Good written communications are clearly organized around a theme that conveys the message while guiding readers to the most important information in a direct way. You can accomplish this in a Web site by understanding what your site's visitors will be looking for and structuring your site to organize that information and make it easy to find.

Clicking Links

Most Web pages include links to other Web pages. A link might open a Web page that is related to the original Web page, such as the Pets link on the home page, which opens a page listing pets available from the Midland Pet Adoption Agency. A link could also be a link to a company, such as the Course Technology link at the bottom of the home page. Other times, a link could open a Web page with related information or an advertised product or service. The easiest way to move from one Web page to another is to click a link in the open Web page. You'll use links to open the Training Programs and Pets Web pages.

To use links to navigate the Midland Pet Adoption Agency Web site:

1. On the Midland Pet Adoption Agency home page, point to the **Training Programs** link, as shown in Figure 1-19. The pointer changes to the shape of a hand with a pointing index finger, and a ScreenTip listing the URL to which the link points appears in the lower-left corner of the browser window.

Figure 1-19	Using a hyperlink

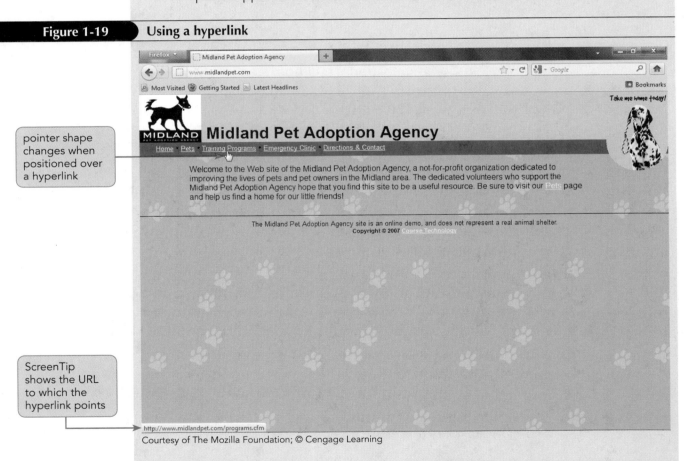

pointer shape changes when positioned over a hyperlink

ScreenTip shows the URL to which the hyperlink points

Courtesy of The Mozilla Foundation; © Cengage Learning

2. Click the **Training Programs** link. The Training Programs Web page opens in the browser window.

3. On the Training Programs Web page, click the **Pets** link. The Pets page opens in the browser window.

4. On the Pets Web page, click the **Meet Maxie** link. The Web page with information about the cat named Maxie opens in the browser window.

Moving Among Visited Web Pages

The Go back one page and Go forward one page buttons on the Navigation bar let you navigate among the pages you have just visited. After you visit more than one Web page, the arrow in the Go back one page button changes to black, indicating that the button is active and available. Clicking the Go back one page button returns the browser to the previous Web page you visited. You can continue clicking the Go back one page button until you reach the first page you viewed when you started Firefox. Once you click the Go back one page button, the arrow in the Go forward one page button changes to black, and you can click the Go forward one page button to return to later pages you have visited. You can also right-click either button to display a list of the Web pages you have visited during the session and click a specific name to return to that page.

As you move among the pages you visited, you might want to reload, or refresh, a Web page you return to. The Reload current page button on the Navigation toolbar loads a new copy of the Web page that currently appears in the browser window. Firefox stores a copy of every Web page it displays on your computer's hard drive in a Temporary Internet Files folder in the Windows folder. Storing this information increases the speed at which Firefox can display pages as you move back and forth through the Web pages you have visited because the browser can load the pages from a local disk drive instead of reloading them from the remote Web server. When you click the Reload current page button, Firefox contacts the Web server to see if the Web page has changed since it was stored in the Temporary Internet Files folder. If it has changed, Firefox gets the new page from the Web server; otherwise, it loads the copy stored on your computer.

You'll use the Go back one page, Go forward one page, and Reload current page buttons to navigate among the Web pages you visited on the Midland Pet Adoption Agency Web site.

To navigate among visited pages on the Midland Pet Adoption Agency Web site:

1. Right-click the **Go back one page** button on the Navigation toolbar. A shortcut menu listing the pages you visited so far appears, as shown in Figure 1-20. The current page is in bold type. Clicking the button displays the previous page—in this case, the Pets page. Or you can click any page name on the shortcut menu to return directly to that page.

Figure 1-20	Navigating among pages

click to return to a more recently viewed page

click to load a new copy of the current page

click to display the previous page in the browser; right-click to open a list of recently viewed pages; click a name to return to that page

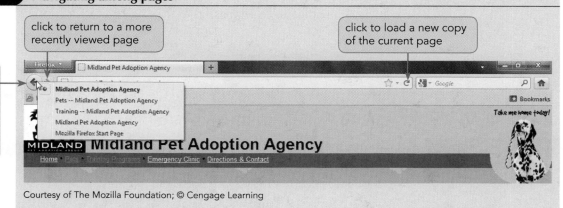

Courtesy of The Mozilla Foundation; © Cengage Learning

2. Click **Training -- Midland Pet Adoption Agency** to return to the Training Programs page.

▶ **3.** Click the **Go back one page** button to return to the home page.

▶ **4.** Click the **Go forward one page** button on the Navigation toolbar. The Training Programs page is redisplayed.

▶ **5.** Right-click the **Go forward one page** button, and then click **Pets -- Midland Pet Adoption Agency** to return to the Pets page.

▶ **6.** Click the **Reload current page** button on the Location bar to load a new copy of the Pets page. Because the content on the page hasn't been updated, you won't see any differences on the reloaded page.

Returning to Firefox's Home Page

When you click the Home button on the Navigation toolbar, the browser displays the home (or start) page for your installation of Firefox. You can select one or more pages to display as the default home page. If you select multiple pages, each page opens in a separate tab when you click the Home button. You can set the page or pages you want to use as the default home page in the Options dialog box, which you open by clicking the Firefox button, and then clicking Options.

REFERENCE

Changing the Default Home Page in Firefox

- Click the Firefox button, click Options to open the Options dialog box, and then if necessary click the General icon in the Options dialog box.
- To use the current page, use a bookmarked page, or use the default Mozilla Firefox start page, click the corresponding button in the Startup section. If you have more than one tab open, the Use Current Pages button saves all the open pages as your start page.
- To specify a home page, type the URL of that Web page in the Home Page box. To open multiple home pages on separate tabs, type the URL for each home page separated by commas in the Home Page box.
- Click the OK button.

You will use the Home button to return to your browser's home page, and then you will view the home page settings.

To view the settings for your browser's home page:

▶ **1.** Click the **Home** button on the Navigation toolbar. The home page for your browser appears in the browser window. This is the same page that opened when you started your browser at the beginning of this session.

▶ **2.** Click the **Firefox** button, and then click **Options**. The Options dialog box opens.

▶ **3.** If necessary, click the **General** icon to display the General panel with options for specifying your home page. See Figure 1-21.

TIP

Many organizations set the home page defaults on all of their computers and then lock those settings.

| Figure 1-21 | Options dialog box |

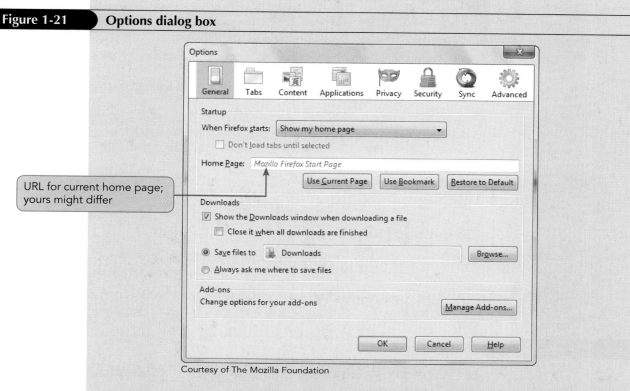

URL for current home page; yours might differ

Courtesy of The Mozilla Foundation

To use the currently loaded Web page as your home page, you would click the Use Current Page button. To use one of your bookmarks as your home page, you would click the Use Bookmark button. To use the default home page that was installed with Firefox, you would click the Restore to Default button. If you want to specify a home page other than the current, bookmarked, or default page, you would type the URL for that page in the Home Page box.

4. Click the **Cancel** button to close the dialog box without making any changes.

Using the Page Tabs

So far, all the Web pages you have visited have been displayed on the same tab. You can open additional page tabs on the tab strip next to the Firefox button, and load different Web pages on each tab instead of opening additional Web pages in separate browser windows. This tabbed browsing technique is especially useful when you need to open many pages or move frequently back and forth among multiple Web pages.

There are several methods for opening a Web page in a new tab. You can click the Open a new tab button on the tab strip, and then open a Web page as usual. You can right-click a link on a Web page, and then click Open Link in New Tab on the shortcut menu. Or, you can press the Ctrl key as you click a link. To close a tab, you click the Close Tab button on that page tab. If you have only one tab open, you must exit Firefox to close that tab. Conversely, if you try to exit Firefox when you have more than one tab open, a dialog box opens, confirming that you want to close all of the open tabs.

REFERENCE

Opening Web Pages in Tabs

- Click the Open a new tab button on the tab strip.
- In the Location bar, enter the URL for the Web page you want to open in the new tab.

or

- Right-click a link on the displayed Web page, and then click Open Link in New Tab on the shortcut menu.

or

- Press the Ctrl key as you click a link on the displayed Web page.

You'll use page tabs to open and navigate among multiple Web pages.

To use page tabs in Firefox:

1. On the tab strip, click the **Open in a new tab** button. A second tab, labeled New Tab, appears in the browser window and displays a blank page.

2. Type **www.midlandpet.com/pets.cfm** in the Location bar, and then press the **Enter key**. The Pets page opens on the page tab. See Figure 1-22.

Figure 1-22 New tab open

Courtesy of The Mozilla Foundation; © Cengage Learning

3. On the Pets page, right-click the **Home** link, and then click **Open Link in New Tab** on the shortcut menu. A third tab appears on the tab row labeled "Midland Pet Adoption Agency." To display this page in the browser window, you need to click the new tab.

4. Click the **Midland Pet Adoption Agency** tab on the tab strip. The home page is displayed in the browser window.

5. Press and hold the **Ctrl** key, click the **Training Programs** link, and then release the Ctrl key. The Training -- Midland Pet Adoption Agency page opens in a new tab.

6. Press and hold the **Ctrl** key, click the **Emergency Clinic** link, and then release the Ctrl key. The Clinic -- Midland Pet Adoption Agency page opens in a new tab.

7. Click the **Training -- Midland Pet Adoption Agency** tab. The tab for the training programs is displayed, as shown in Figure 1-23. The page tabs become smaller as you open additional tabs, and the text identifying the Web pages displayed on the tab becomes truncated.

TIP

To see the entire title of a Web page in a ScreenTip, point to its page tab.

Figure 1-23 Firefox with five tabs open

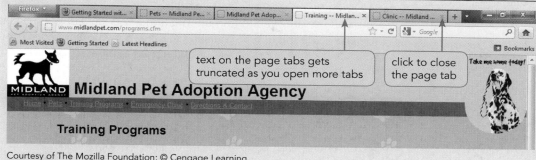

Courtesy of The Mozilla Foundation; © Cengage Learning

8. Point to the **Pets -- Midland Pet Adoption Agency** tab, and then click the **Close Tab** button. The tab closes.

9. On the Clinic -- Midland Pet Adoption Agency tab, click the **Close Tab** button. The tab closes.

10. On the Training -- Midland Pet Adoption Agency tab, click the **Close Tab** button.

11. Click the **Close Tab** button on the tab for your browser's home page. The Midland Pet Adoption Agency home page reappears in the browser window on the only open tab.

You like the format of the Midland Pet Adoption Agency's home page, so you want to make sure that you can go back to that page later if you need to review its contents. You can write down the URL so you can refer to it later, but Firefox makes it easier to return to previously visited Web pages using the Library.

Using the Library

The Library includes tools for managing and organizing a list of Web pages that you have visited so you can return to them easily. You open the Library by clicking the Bookmarks button on the Bookmarks toolbar or Navigation toolbar, and then clicking Show All Bookmarks; or by clicking the Firefox button, pointing to Bookmarks, and then clicking Show All Bookmarks. The Library tracks three items: History, Tags, and Bookmarks. A **bookmark** is a stored shortcut containing the URL of a Web page. A **tag** is a label or keyword you create to help you identify your bookmarks. History records your browsing activity by organizing and storing the URLs of the Web sites you have visited sorted in a variety of ways, including by date, name, visit count, location, and keyword.

Creating and Organizing Bookmarks

As you use the Web to find information, you can create bookmarks so you can easily return to sites of interest. To create a bookmark, you navigate to the page you want to bookmark, and then you click the Bookmark this page button on the Location bar. You might very quickly find yourself creating so many bookmarks that it is difficult to find a specific bookmark. When you start accumulating bookmarks, it is helpful to keep them organized so that you can quickly locate the site you need.

In the Library, you can add, delete, and organize bookmarks into folders that best suit your needs and working style. You can also create descriptive labels, called tags, and assign them to your bookmarks to help organize your bookmarks into categories. A bookmark can have more than one tag, and you can view the bookmarks associated with each tag in the Library. You can also add bookmarks that you want to access very frequently as buttons on the Bookmarks toolbar, which appears below the Navigation toolbar. Keep in mind that the bookmarks and folders you create are available only on the computer on which you are working.

As you use the Web to find information about pet adoption agencies and other sites of interest, you might find yourself creating many bookmarks so you can return easily to these sites. When you start accumulating bookmarks, it is helpful to create folders in the Library to keep them organized.

REFERENCE

Creating a Bookmark

- Open the Web page you want to save as a bookmark.
- Click the Bookmark this page button on the Location bar to bookmark the page.
- Click the Edit this bookmark button on the Location bar to open the Edit This Bookmark window.
- Click the Show all the bookmarks folders button to expand the Edit This Bookmark window.
- Click the Folder button, and then click Bookmarks Toolbar to add the bookmark as a button on the Bookmarks toolbar, or click a folder in which you want to store the bookmark in the Library.
- If you want to store the bookmark in a new folder, click the New Folder button, type a name for the new folder, and then press the Enter key.
- Click in the Tags box, and then type labels that are separated by commas.
- Click the Done button.

You will save the URL for the Midland Pet Adoption Agency Web page as a bookmark, and then create a Pet Adoption Agencies folder in which to store this favorite.

To create a bookmark and folder to store a link to the agency's home page:

1. With the Midland Pet Adoption Agency home page open, click the **Bookmark this page** button on the Location bar. The Bookmark this page button changes from gray to orange, indicating a bookmark for this page has been created in the Library, and the button becomes the Edit this bookmark button.

2. Click the **Edit this bookmark** button on the Location bar. The Edit This Bookmark window, as shown in Figure 1-24, opens with options for removing the bookmark, changing the bookmark name, changing the folder in which the bookmark is stored, and adding tags to the bookmark.

Figure 1-24   **Edit This Bookmark window**

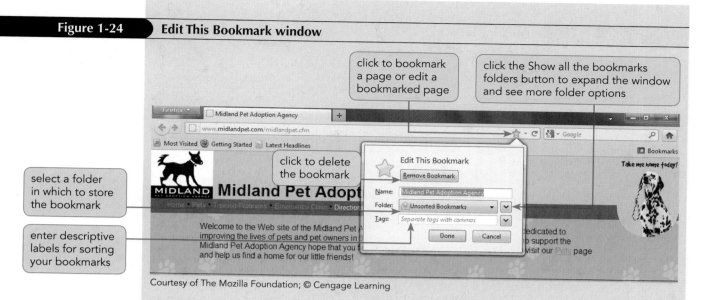

Courtesy of The Mozilla Foundation; © Cengage Learning

3. If the text selected in the Name box is not "Midland Pet Adoption Agency" (without the quotation marks), type **Midland Pet Adoption Agency**. You want to store the Midland Pet Adoption Agency bookmark in a new folder.

4. Click the **Show all the bookmarks folders** button to expand the window, and then click the **New Folder** button. A new folder is added in the Unsorted Bookmarks folder with its default name "New Folder" selected.

5. Type **Pet Adoption Agencies** as the new folder name, and then press the **Enter** key. The Pet Adoption Agencies folder is added as a folder in the Unsorted Bookmarks folder.

6. Click in the **Tags** box, and then type **pets, MN, pet adoption agencies** to create three tags for this bookmark, separated by commas.

7. Click the **Done** button to create the bookmark and close the Edit This Bookmark window. The bookmark is now saved in the Pet Adoption Agencies folder in the Library. You can test the bookmark by opening it from the Library.

8. On the Midland Pet Adoption Agency home page, click the **Emergency Clinic** link to open that page in your browser.

9. Click the **Firefox** button, point to **Bookmarks**, and then click **Show All Bookmarks**. The Library window opens.

10. Click the **expand** button to the left of the Unsorted Bookmarks folder in the left pane of the Library window to display a list of subfolders that have been stored in Firefox on the computer you are using, including the Pet Adoption Agencies folder you just created.

11. Click the **Pet Adoption Agencies** folder in the left pane to display the bookmark titled "Midland Pet Adoption Agency" that you just created. See Figure 1-25.

Figure 1-25 Library window

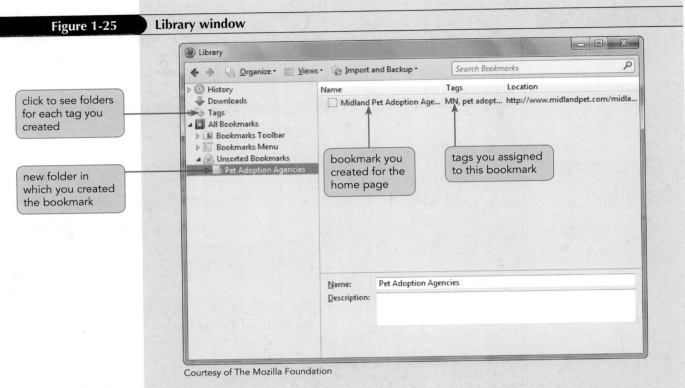

click to see folders for each tag you created

new folder in which you created the bookmark

bookmark you created for the home page

tags you assigned to this bookmark

Courtesy of The Mozilla Foundation

▶ **12.** Click **Tags** in the left pane to display the tags saved on your computer, including the three tags you just created: MN, pet adoption agencies, and pets. Notice that the tags are in alphabetical order.

▶ **13.** Double-click the **MN** tag folder in the right pane to display the bookmark you created for the Midland Pet Adoption Agency home page.

▶ **14.** Click the **pet adoption agencies** tag in the left pane to see that the bookmark also appears in that tag folder. As you see, one bookmark can appear in multiple tag folders, enabling you to sort and access your bookmarks in a wide variety of ways.

In the previous set of steps, you created a bookmark and a folder in which to store it. You can also create folders and move existing bookmarks into these folders in the Library. You can reorganize the favorites and folders stored in the Library at any point by creating new folders and rearranging bookmarks and folders within folders.

You saved the Midland Pet Adoption Agency's URL as a bookmark, which you stored in a new folder named Pet Adoption Agencies in the Library. Because Trinity might want you to collect information about adoption agencies in different states as you conduct your research, you will organize the information about adoption agencies by state. The Midland Pet Adoption Agency is located in Minnesota, so you will put information about the Midland Pet Adoption Agency in a separate folder named MN (the two-letter abbreviation for Minnesota) within the Pet Adoption Agencies folder. As you collect information about other agencies, you will add folders for the states in which they are located, too.

To move the Midland Pet Adoption Agency bookmark into a new folder:

1. In the left pane of the Library, right-click the **Pet Adoption Agencies** folder, and then click **New Folder** on the shortcut menu. The New Folder dialog box opens, with the default name "New Folder" selected in the Name box.

2. Type **MN** in the Name box, and then click the **Add** button. The MN folder appears in the right pane of the Library, as shown in Figure 1-26. Now that you have created a folder, you can move your bookmark for the Midland Pet Adoption Agency Web page into the new folder.

Figure 1-26	New folder created for bookmarks

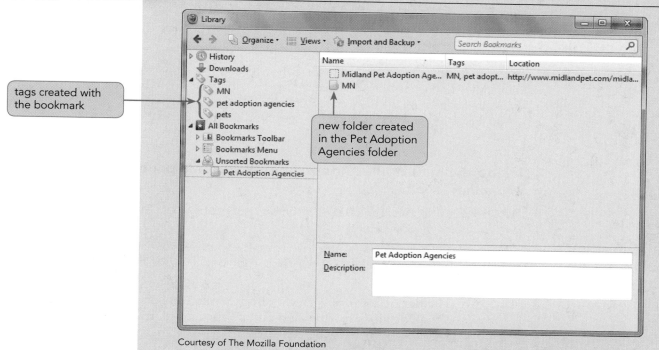

tags created with the bookmark

new folder created in the Pet Adoption Agencies folder

Courtesy of The Mozilla Foundation

3. Click and drag the **Midland Pet Adoption Agency** bookmark in the right pane down to the new MN folder, and then release the mouse button. The Midland Pet Adoption Agency bookmark moves into the MN folder.

4. Click the **Close** button on the Library window title bar to close the Library.

5. Click the **Bookmarks** button on the Bookmarks toolbar, point to **Recently Bookmarked** to see a list of recent bookmarks created on your computer, and then click **Midland Pet Adoption Agency**. The home page opens in the browser window.

Saving Bookmarks

Once you have a collection of bookmarks, you might want to use them on other computers in different locations. Firefox lets you save your bookmark file to a portable storage device or network disk drive so you can do this. When you save Firefox bookmarks to a device or drive, all of the bookmarks are saved. You cannot save just one bookmark or only selected bookmarks. To save your bookmarks, click the Import and Backup button on the Library window toolbar, and then click Export Bookmarks to HTML to open the Export Bookmarks File dialog box. Navigate to the location where you want to save the bookmark file, type a name for the bookmark file in the File name box, and then click the Save button. To open the bookmark file from your portable storage device on another computer, open the Firefox Library window, click the Import and Backup button on the toolbar, click Import Bookmarks from HTML to open the Import Bookmarks File dialog box, locate and select your bookmarks file, and then click the Open button.

You realize that you will need to go to the Midland Pet Adoption Agency home page frequently. Although it's easily available from the Library, it would be even faster to access that page from the Bookmarks toolbar.

You'll add the Midland Pet Adoption Agency's URL as a link on the Bookmarks toolbar.

To add the Midland Pet Adoption Agency home page to the Bookmarks toolbar:

1. Click the **Edit this bookmark** button on the Location bar. The Edit This Bookmark window opens.

    Trouble? If the Bookmarks toolbar doesn't appear on your screen, right-click the blank area to the right of the page tabs, and then click Bookmarks Toolbar on the shortcut menu.

2. Click the **Folder** button, and then click **Bookmarks Toolbar**. The bookmark moves to the Bookmarks toolbar as a button labeled with the Web page's title, as shown in Figure 1-27.

Figure 1-27	Bookmark added to the Bookmarks toolbar

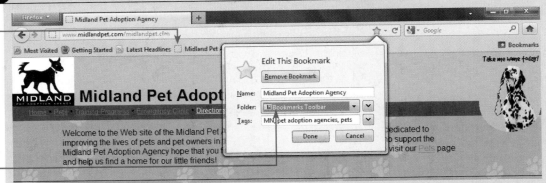

new bookmark on the Bookmarks toolbar

select to store the bookmark on the Bookmarks toolbar

Courtesy of The Mozilla Foundation; © Cengage Learning

3. Click the **Done** button.

4. Click the **Go back one page** button on the Navigation toolbar to return to the Emergency Clinic page.

5. Point to the **Midland Pet Adoption Agency** button on the Bookmarks toolbar. A ScreenTip displays the full title of the Web page and its URL.

6. Click the **Midland Pet Adoption Agency** button on the Bookmarks toolbar. The Midland Pet Adoption Agency home page opens in the browser.

Deleting Bookmarks and Folders from the Library

Creating bookmarks is a great way to keep track of sites you know you want to visit on a regular basis. However, sometimes you no longer want to visit a site, such as when you saved favorites related to a specific project. Other times, the URL for a site has changed or the site no longer exists. In all these instances, you'll want to delete the bookmarks and the folders in which they are stored. You can delete a specific bookmark, or you can delete a folder in the Library. When you delete a folder, the folder and all of its contents are moved to the Recycle Bin.

To delete the bookmark and folders you created:

TIP

You can also right-click a button on the Bookmarks toolbar, and then click Delete on the shortcut menu to remove the bookmark.

1. Click the **Edit this bookmark** button on the Location bar. The Edit This Bookmark window opens.

2. Click the **Remove Bookmark** button. The bookmark is deleted from Firefox, and the button disappears from the Bookmarks toolbar.

3. Click the **Bookmarks** button on the Bookmarks toolbar, and then click **Unsorted Bookmarks**. The Library window opens with the Unsorted Bookmarks folder selected in the left pane.

4. In the left pane, click **Tags**. As you can see, the three tags were also deleted when you deleted the bookmark.

5. In the left pane, click the **Pet Adoption Agencies** folder. The MN folder appears in the right pane.

6. Right-click the **Pet Adoption Agencies** folder in the left pane, and then click **Delete** on the shortcut menu. The folder and all of its contents are deleted from the Library.

7. Click the **Close** button on the Library window title bar to close the Library.

Navigating Web Pages Using the History List

Creating bookmarks is a great way to keep track of sites you know you want to visit on a regular basis. Another way to return to a site that you have visited recently is with the History list. The History list is useful when you know you visited a site recently, but you did not create a favorite and you cannot recall the URL of the site. You can see your recent browsing history by clicking the Firefox button, and then pointing to History to display a list of the last 15 Web pages that you visited on the History menu. You can see your complete History list by clicking the Firefox button and then clicking History to open the History list in the Library. From the History list, you can view a list of the sites that were visited on that computer during the last six months. You can display the history of visited sites organized by date, by site, by sites most visited, or by alphabetical order. You can also use the Search History box to search the History list for a specific site. To return to a specific Web page, just click its link in the History list.

Not every site that you visit as you research pet adoption sites for the Danville Animal Shelter will warrant being saved as a bookmark. The History list will be helpful if you want to show Trinity the breadth of sites you visited during your research. You will view the History list next.

To view the History list for this session:

1. Click the **Firefox** button, and then point to **History**. A list of the last 15 Web pages you viewed appears on the History menu.

2. Click **Show All History**. The Library window opens with History selected in the left pane. The right pane displays folders that contain the browsing history organized by date, with the most recent folder first. Usually, the folders will include Today, Yesterday, Last 7 days, and a list of the most recent five months followed by an Older than 6 months folder. You can change the way pages are organized in the History list by clicking the Views button on the Library window toolbar, pointing to Sort, and then clicking an option. For example, you can list the pages alphabetically by Web page title or by location (which groups all Web pages by the Web server from which they originated).

3. Double-click the **Today** folder in the right pane to open a list of Web sites visited most recently today in the order in which they were visited, including the Midland Pet Adoption Agency Web pages you visited in this session. Notice the home page for the site appears in the list more than once because you navigated back to that page from the other pages on the site. To return to a particular page, click that page's entry in the list.

4. Click **Midland Pet Adoption Agency**. The Web page's name, location, and tag information appear at the bottom of the Library window. See Figure 1-28.

TIP

If you are using a computer in a computer lab or a public computer, the History list will include sites visited by anyone who has used the computer, not just you.

| Figure 1-28 | History list in the Library |

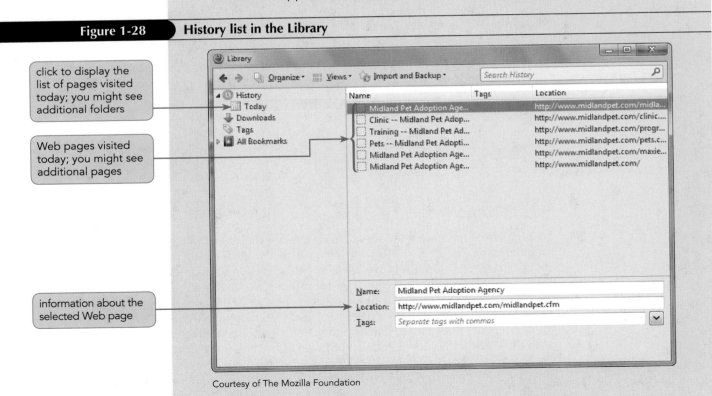

click to display the list of pages visited today; you might see additional folders

Web pages visited today; you might see additional pages

information about the selected Web page

Courtesy of The Mozilla Foundation

> **5.** Double-click **Training -- Midland Pet Adoption Agency** in the History list. The Training -- Midland Pet Adoption Agency page appears in the browser window, and the Library window is minimized.

> **6.** Point to the **Firefox** program button on the Windows taskbar, and then click the **Library** thumbnail to display the Library window.

> **7.** Click the **Close** button on the Library window title bar to close the Library.

INSIGHT

Erasing Your Browsing History

In some situations, such as when you are finishing a work session in a school computer lab or on any public computer, you might want to remove the list of Web sites that you visited from the History list of the computer on which you had been working. Erasing your browsing history helps protect your personal information and guard your privacy when working on a shared computer. You can delete your browsing history in Firefox by clicking the Firefox button, pointing to History, and then clicking Clear Recent History to open the Clear All History dialog box. You then click the Time range to clear arrow and select either a time range of browsing history to clear or Everything to clear the entire History list. If you select Everything, the dialog box will expand to show a list of items that will be deleted. Make sure the Browsing & Download History is the only check box selected in this list. If any other check boxes are selected, click each of them to clear the selections. After ensuring the Browsing & Download History is the only option checked, click the Clear Now button to erase the entire browsing history stored on the computer.

Managing Cookies

All Web browser users should know about the use of cookies. A **cookie** is a small text file that a Web server saves on the hard drive of the computer that is running the Web browser software. A cookie is used to store information about your visit to a specific Web site, such as your login name and password, which pages you viewed, and your shopping cart information. By storing this information on your computer, the Web server can retrieve the information when you return to that site, enabling it to perform functions such as automatic login, which makes it easier to sign in to Web pages you have visited before. However, the user often is unaware that cookie files are being written to the computer's hard drive.

When the site you are visiting places a cookie on your computer, it is called a **first-party cookie**. However, many cookies are written by companies that sell advertising on Web pages. The advertising elements of the Web page are delivered by the advertisers' Web servers, not the Web server of the site you are visiting. These cookies record which ads have appeared on Web pages you have viewed. Advertisers use these cookies to determine which ads they will deliver the next time you open a Web page. This can be beneficial because it prevents sites from showing you the same ads over and over again. On the other hand, many people believe that this sort of user tracking is an offensive invasion of privacy. Cookies that are placed by companies other than the company whose Web site you are visiting are called **third-party cookies**.

Most Web browsers, including Firefox, allow you to block cookies from your computer or to specify general categories of cookies (such as first-party or third-party) to block. In Firefox, you can specify privacy settings that control the writing of cookie files to your computer's hard drive. You can specify which types of cookies to block or you can block particular types of cookies from specific sites. These options are available on the Privacy panel in the Options dialog box. You will learn more about the different types of cookies, how they work, and how best to deal with them in Tutorial 6.

Firefox stores each cookie in a separate file. You can delete the cookies from your computer at any time or whenever you exit Firefox. To delete all of the cookies stored on your computer, click the Firefox button, click Options to open the Options dialog box, and then click the Privacy icon. You then can click the Show Cookies button to open the Cookies dialog box, and then click the Remove All Cookies button.

Because some cookies benefit users, you might not want to delete all of the cookies on your computer. For example, if you regularly visit a site that requires you to log in, the Web server can store your login information in a cookie on your computer so you do not have to type your user name each time you visit the site. You should always consider carefully whether the advantages of cookies outweigh the disadvantages for you before you delete all of your Firefox cookies.

Trinity wants you to view the cookies in Firefox on your computer.

To view cookies in Firefox:

▶ **1.** Click the **Firefox** button, and then click **Options** to open the Options dialog box.

▶ **2.** Click the **Privacy** icon to display the Privacy panel with the options for privacy settings.

▶ **3.** Click the **Firefox will** button, and then click **Use custom settings for history**. Options appear in the History section. See Figure 1-29.

Figure 1-29   **Options dialog box**

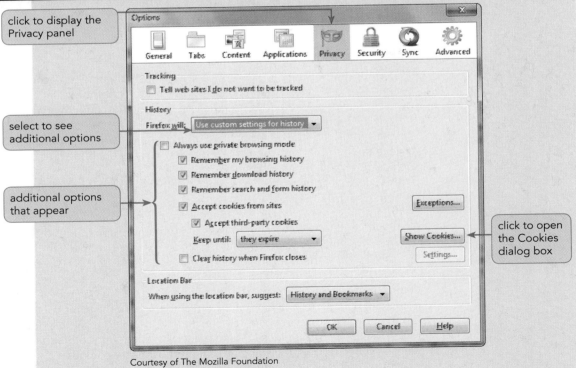

click to display the Privacy panel

select to see additional options

additional options that appear

click to open the Cookies dialog box

Courtesy of The Mozilla Foundation

▶ **4.** Click the **Show Cookies** button to open the Cookies dialog box.

You will examine the cookies for one of the Web sites that appears in the Cookies dialog box.

5. Click one of the Web site folders listed in the top section of the Cookies dialog box, and then click the arrow icon to the left of the folder.

6. Click one of the cookies placed on your computer by that Web site, and then read the cookie information that is displayed in the bottom panel of the dialog box. An example of a Cookies dialog box with several cookies appears in Figure 1-30. Your list of cookies will be different. Information about the selected cookie appears below the list of cookies.

Figure 1-30 Cookies dialog box

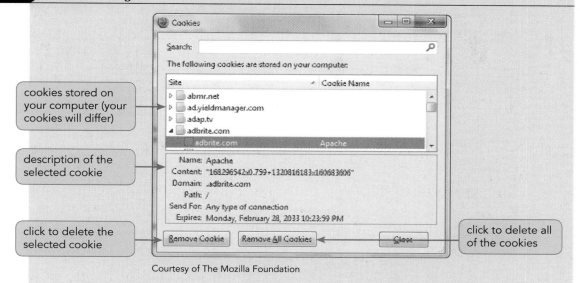

cookies stored on your computer (your cookies will differ)

description of the selected cookie

click to delete the selected cookie

click to delete all of the cookies

Courtesy of The Mozilla Foundation

7. Click the **Close** button to close the Cookies dialog box.

8. Click the **Cancel** button in the Options dialog box to close the Options dialog box without saving any changes.

Private Web Browsing

As you have learned, Firefox stores a considerable amount of information about your Web browsing activity. It stores a list of all the Web pages you have viewed in the History list, and it stores cookies that can contain information about your logins and passwords. It even stores information about which ads have been displayed on the Web pages you have viewed.

Firefox also stores copies of all or part of the Web pages you visit on whatever computer you are using. If you do not wish to have this information stored, you can use Firefox in Private Browsing mode. In **Private Browsing mode**, Firefox does not store your browsing history, cookies, or copies of the Web pages you visit. In other words, there is no record in Firefox of what sites you visited and what you looked at. When you are using a computer other than your own (such as a friend's computer or a computer at work, school, or another public location), Private Browsing mode can help protect your privacy and security.

To start a Private Browsing session, you click the Firefox button, and then click Start Private Browsing. The Private Browsing tab opens and displays a Private Browsing information page to confirm that you are in Private Browsing mode. In addition, the Firefox button changes from orange to purple and remains that way until you end the Private Browsing session. To end a Private Browsing session, you can click the Firefox button and then click Stop Private Browsing to return to the Web page you were viewing before the Private Browsing session, or you can simply close the browser window to exit Firefox.

As you visit Web pages in Private Browsing mode, the history list of the session, cookies from that session, and temporary Internet files will be tracked only during the Private Browsing session. When you end the Private Browsing session, the history list, the cookies, and temporary Internet files are removed from your computer.

REFERENCE

Opening a Private Browsing Session

- Click the Firefox button, and then click Start Private Browsing on the menu.
- If the Start Private Browsing dialog box opens, click the Start Private Browsing button.
- Enter a URL in the Location bar to navigate to a Web site, and navigate to other Web pages by clicking links or opening Web pages on other tabs as usual.
- To end a Private Browsing session, click the Firefox button, and then click Stop Private Browsing; or click the Close button on the Firefox title bar to close the browser window and all open tabs.

You will try an InPrivate Browsing session to see how it differs from the Web browsing you have done earlier in this session.

To start a Private Browsing session:

1. Click the **Firefox** button, and then click **Start Private Browsing**. The Start Private Browsing dialog box opens to confirm that you want to switch to Private Browsing mode.

2. Click the **Start Private Browsing** button in the Start Private Browsing dialog box. The Private Browsing page appears in the browser window, and the Firefox button changes to purple. See Figure 1-31.

Figure 1-31 **Private Browsing mode**

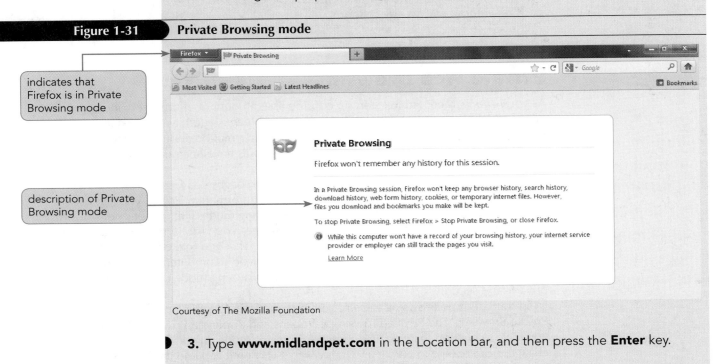

indicates that Firefox is in Private Browsing mode

description of Private Browsing mode

Courtesy of The Mozilla Foundation

3. Type **www.midlandpet.com** in the Location bar, and then press the **Enter** key.

4. Click the **Pets** link on the home page to visit the Pets page, click the **Training Programs** link to visit the Training page, and then click the **Directions & Contact** link to visit the Directions page. Notice that the links don't change color to show that they've been followed.

5. Click the **Firefox** button, and then click **Stop Private Browsing** to end the Private Browsing session. The Firefox button is once again orange, and the Midland Pet Adoption Agency Training page reappears on the only open tab in the browser window.

If you examine the browser's History, you will find that it includes no record of the Web pages you just visited. Although the browser does not record the pages you have visited (or other information, such as cookies), the network server that connects the computer to the Internet might have software that does. Therefore, it is best not to rely on Private Browsing mode to keep private the Web pages you visit while using a computer at work or another public location.

Getting Help in Firefox

Firefox has an online Help system that includes information about how to use the browser, getting started with Firefox, and troubleshooting information. You can also contact volunteers who can help find answers to your specific questions.

REFERENCE

Using Firefox Help

- Click the Firefox button, and then click Help to open the Firefox Support Home Page in a new tab.
- Type a question in the What do you need help with? box, and then click the Search button to display relevant topics or click a link to a Help topic listed on the page.
- Close the browser tab when you are finished.

Trinity wants you to learn more about Private Browsing. You will use Firefox Help to find more information about this feature.

To use Firefox Help:

1. Click the **Firefox** button, point to **Help** to see the different Help options, and then click **Help**. The Firefox Support Home Page opens in a new tab. See Figure 1-32. On this Web page you can enter a search topic in the What do you need help with? box. You also can click the links in the Top Issues section to find out information on current issues Firefox users are having, or you can click a link in the Explore Help Topics section.

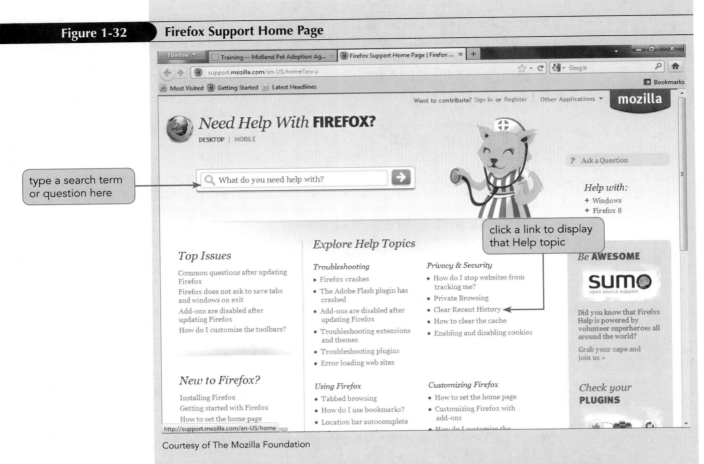

Figure 1-32 Firefox Support Home Page

type a search term or question here

click a link to display that Help topic

Courtesy of The Mozilla Foundation

2. Under the Privacy & Security heading, click the **Private Browsing** link. The Private Browsing Help page opens with a brief description of Private Browsing and a Table of Contents listing links to related content.

3. Click the **What does Private Browsing not save?** link under the Table of Contents heading, and then read the information on the page that appears.

4. Click other links and read the information provided. When you are finished reading, click the **Close Tab** button on the Private Browsing tab to close this tab and return to the Midland Pet Adoption Agency Training page.

Saving Web Page Content

At times you will want to refer to the information that you have found on a Web page without having to return to the site. In Firefox, you can save entire Web pages, particular graphics, or selected portions of Web page text.

Saving an Entire Web Page

When you save the entire Web page, you use the Save As dialog box, which is similar to the Save As dialog box in other programs. To open the Save As dialog box, click the Firefox button, and then click Save Page As.

Firefox by default saves the complete Web page, including the graphic page elements along with the Web page's text and the HTML markup codes. With the default format—Web Page, complete—Firefox saves each graphic element in its own file stored in a separate folder it creates with the same name as the HTML document. You can select a different format from the Save as type list in the Save As dialog box. The Web Page, HTML only format saves the Web page's text along with the HTML markup codes, but not any of the graphic page elements. When you open that file, the Web page will appear as it was originally formatted, but any graphics will be missing. The Text Files format saves the Web page's text without the HTML markup codes.

When you save to your computer from Firefox, the Downloads window opens to help you keep track of the files. The window shows information about the file, including its name, size, and original location. From the Downloads window, you can open a file or delete the record of that file among other actions.

You will save the Midland Pet Adoption Agency home page to show to Trinity. This Web site will provide Trinity an example of a well-designed site with appropriate text and graphics.

To save the Midland Pet Adoption Agency home page:

1. Return to the Midland Pet Adoption Agency home page.

2. Click the **Firefox** button, and then click **Save Page As**. The Save As dialog box opens.

3. Navigate to and select the **Tutorial.01\Tutorial** folder included with your Data Files. This is the location where you will save the Web page.

   Trouble? If you don't have the starting Data Files, you need to get them before you can proceed. Your instructor will either give you the Data Files or ask you to obtain them from a specified location (such as a network drive). In either case, make a backup copy of the Data Files before you start so that you will have the original files available in case you need to start over. If you have any questions about the Data Files, see your instructor or technical support person for assistance.

4. Type **Midland Pet Home Page FF** in the File name box.

5. Click the **Save as type** arrow, and then click **Web Page, complete** to select this format, if necessary.

6. Click the **Save** button. The Save As dialog box closes. The Web page for the Midland Pet Adoption Agency's home page is saved in the location you specified and appears in the Downloads window.

7. Click the **Close** button on the title bar of the Downloads window to close it.

Saving an Image from a Web Page

Most Web pages include graphics or pictures to provide interest, illustrate a point, or present information. You can save a graphic or picture instead of the entire Web page.

REFERENCE

Saving an Image from a Web Page

- Right-click the image on the Web page that you want to save, and then click Save Image As on the shortcut menu to open the Save Image dialog box.
- Navigate to the location in which you want to save the image, and change the default filename, if necessary.
- Click the Save button.

The Directions & Contact Web page also includes a street map that shows the location of the Midland Pet Adoption Agency. You will save this map to show Trinity as well.

To save the street map image:

▶ 1. Click the **Directions & Contact** link to open the Web page that has the address and phone number for the Midland Pet Adoption Agency.

▶ 2. On the Directions & Contact page, scroll the page as needed to display the map.

▶ 3. Right-click the **map**, and then click **Save Image As** on the shortcut menu to open the Save Image dialog box.

▶ 4. Navigate to and select the **Tutorial.01\Tutorial** folder included with your Data Files. This is the location where you will save the map graphic.

▶ 5. Type **Midland Pet Map FF** as the filename, and then click the **Save** button to save the graphic.

▶ 6. Click the **Close** button on the title bar of the Downloads window to close it.

INSIGHT

Understanding Copyright for Web Page Content

A **copyright** is the legal right of the author or other owner of an original work to control the reproduction, distribution, and sale of that work. A copyright comes into existence as soon as the work is placed into a tangible form, such as a printed copy, an electronic file, or a Web page. Copyright laws can place significant restrictions on the way that you can use information or images that you copy from another entity's Web site. Because of the way a Web browser works, it copies the HTML code as well as the graphics and media files to your computer before it can display them in the browser. Just because copies of these files are stored temporarily on your computer does not mean that you have the right to use them in any way other than having your computer display them in the browser window.

The United States and most other countries have copyright laws that govern the use of photocopies, audio or video recordings, and other reproductions of authors' original work. The copyright exists even if the work does not contain a copyright notice. If you do not know whether material that you find on the Web is copyrighted, the safest course of action is to assume that it is.

U.S. copyright law has a **fair use** provision that allows a limited amount of copyrighted information to be used for purposes such as news reporting, research, and scholarship. The source of the material used should always be cited. Commercial use of copyrighted material is much more restricted. You should obtain permission from the copyright holder before using anything you copy from a Web page. The copyright holder can require you to pay a fee for permission to use the material from the Web page. The steps in this tutorial are designed so that your use of copyrighted Web pages and elements of those pages falls within the fair use provisions of U.S. copyright law.

Copying Text from a Web Page

You can also copy and paste portions of a Web page to a file or email. This can be helpful when you want to save specific information from a Web page, such as a schedule of events, directions to a location, or information about a place.

Trinity plans to visit the Midland Pet Adoption Agency while she is traveling in Minnesota next week. She wants to contact Midland's director and schedule a meeting. You can copy and paste the agency's address and telephone number from its Web site into a document or email for Trinity.

To copy and paste text from the Midland Pet Adoption Agency Web site:

1. On the Directions & Contact page, select the name, address, and telephone number for Midland Pet Adoption Agency at the top of the page.

2. Right-click the selected text, and then click **Copy** on the shortcut menu to copy the selected text to the Clipboard, which is a temporary storage area in Windows.

3. Click the **Start** button on the taskbar, point to **All Programs**, click the **Accessories** folder, and then click **WordPad** to start the program and open a new document.

4. On the Home tab of the WordPad Ribbon, click the **Paste** button to paste the text into the WordPad document, as shown in Figure 1-33.

Figure 1-33	WordPad document with pasted text

click the Save button to open the Save As dialog box

click to paste the copied text

text copied and pasted from the Web page

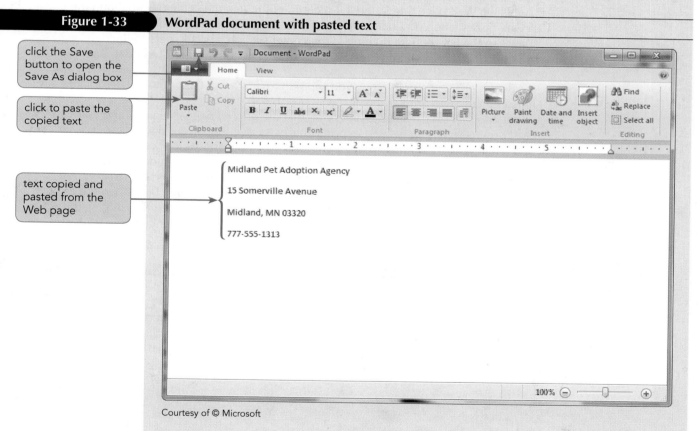

Courtesy of © Microsoft

5. Click the **Save** button on the WordPad Quick Access Toolbar to open the Save As dialog box.

6. Navigate to and select the **Tutorial.01\Tutorial** folder included with your Data Files. This is the location where you will save the WordPad document.

7. Click the **Save as type** button, and then click **Rich Text Format (RTF)**.

8. Type **Midland Pet Contact Info FF** in the File name box, and then click the **Save** button. The name, address, and phone number of the agency are now saved in a file for future reference.

9. Click the **Close** button on the WordPad title bar to close it.

Printing a Web Page

Sometimes you will want to print a Web page. This might occur when you want to keep a printed page for reference, save a record or receipt of an online purchase, or have a coupon to use at a local store or restaurant. You access the Print commands by clicking the Firefox button and pointing to Print on the menu to open a submenu of printing options. Clicking Print opens the Print dialog box, which includes options for selecting a printer, setting a page range, and specifying the number of copies to print.

You can also use the Page Setup dialog box to change aspects of a Web page printout, including the page orientation, print size, page background, margins, and headers and footers that print at the top and bottom of the page, respectively. The default header prints the Web page title in the left section, nothing in the center section, and the URL in the right section. The default footer prints the page number and the total number of pages in the left section, nothing in the center section, and the date in the right section. To open the Page Setup dialog box, click the Firefox button, point to Print, and then click Page Setup.

Before printing a Web page, you should preview what the printout will look like to ensure that it will print in the best way possible. For example, you want to ensure that extra or unnecessary pages won't print, that the printed page is legible, and that what will print is what you wanted to print. This extra step helps you to save resources, including paper and printer ink. To open the Print Preview window, click the Firefox button, point to Print, and then click Print Preview. The Print Preview window shows how the current Web page will look on the printed page. It also provides access to common printing options. From the toolbar, you can open the Print dialog box, open the Page Setup dialog box, adjust the scale, and change the page orientation. Changing the scale enables you to shrink the Web page to fit better on the page or enlarge the Web page on the printout so it's more legible.

REFERENCE

Printing the Current Web Page

- Click the Firefox button, and then click Print to open the Print dialog box.
- In the Print dialog box, select the printer you want to use, indicate the pages you want to print, and choose the number of copies you want to make of each page.
- Click the OK button.

You will preview a copy of the Midland Pet Adoption Agency home page, and then print it.

To preview and print the Midland Pet Adoption Agency home page:

▶ **1.** Return to the Midland Pet Adoption Agency home page.

▶ **2.** Click the **Firefox** button, point to **Print**, and then click **Print Preview** on the menu that appears. The Print Preview window opens. See Figure 1-34.

Figure 1-34   **Print Preview window**

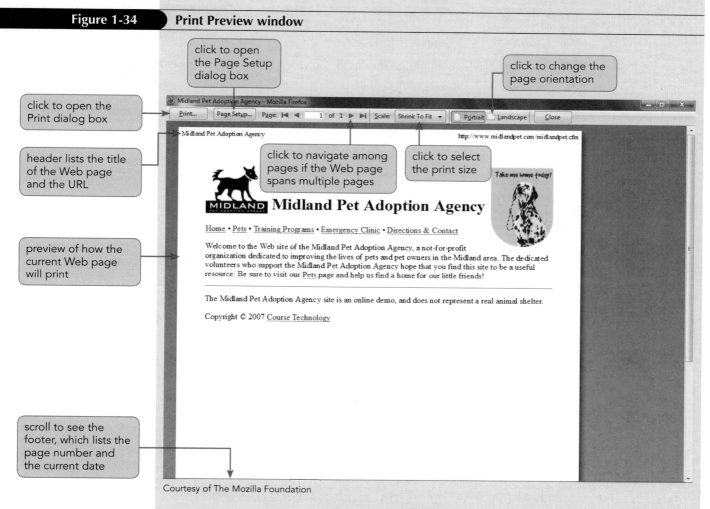

click to open the Page Setup dialog box

click to change the page orientation

click to open the Print dialog box

header lists the title of the Web page and the URL

click to navigate among pages if the Web page spans multiple pages

click to select the print size

preview of how the current Web page will print

scroll to see the footer, which lists the page number and the current date

Courtesy of The Mozilla Foundation

The preview looks fine, so you will print the page.

▶ **3.** Click the **Print** button on the toolbar. The Print dialog box opens.

▶ **4.** Make sure that the printer in the Name box is the printer you want to use; if not, click the **Name** button and select the appropriate printer from the list.

▶ **5.** Click the **Pages** option button in the Print range section of the Print dialog box, type **1** in the from box, press the **Tab** key, and then, if necessary, type **1** in the to box to specify that you want to print only the first page.

▶ **6.** Make sure that the Number of copies box displays **1**.

▶ **7.** Click the **OK** button to print the Web page, and then click the **Close** button on the Print Preview toolbar.

▶ **8.** Click the **Close** button on the Firefox title bar to close the Web browser.

You have copies of the Midland Pet Adoption Agency home page and map that will show Trinity how to get to the agency during her trip to Minnesota. Trinity will be able to use her Web browser or other software to open the files and print them.

In this session, you worked with Firefox as you browsed the Midland Pet Adoption Agency Web site. You navigated among pages, worked with favorites, reviewed the history list, saved and copied Web pages, and printed a Web page from the site.

REVIEW

Session 1.2 Quick Check

1. Briefly explain the difference between a network and the Internet.
2. What is a hypertext link?
3. What is a URL?
4. What is a bookmark?
5. If you have recently visited a Web site, but cannot recall the URL and didn't save it as a favorite, what feature can you use to return to that site?
6. Briefly explain what a cookie is.
7. What is Private Browsing mode?
8. Can you use an image you save from someone else's Web site on your Web site? Explain your answer.
9. Why should you preview what the printout will look like before printing a Web page?

Review Assignments

There are no Data Files needed for the Review Assignments.

Trinity is pleased with the information you gathered so far about the Midland Pet Adoption Agency's Web pages. In fact, she would like you to extend your research to other Web sites. She wants you to examine the Web sites of other charitable organizations that provide animal welfare services to their communities, and choose one site that would be a good example for the Danville Animal Shelter to follow as it updates its own Web site. She asks you to compile some information about the site you choose, including some specific files, by completing the following steps, using either Internet Explorer or Firefox:

1. Start your Web browser, and then enter the URL **www.cengagebrain.com** in your browser's Address or Location bar. On the CengageBrain home page that opens, enter the ISBN number for this book in the Search box at the top of the page, and then click the Find button. (*Hint:* The ISBN for your book can be found above the bar code located in the lower-right corner of the back cover of your book. You can use either the ISBN-13 or ISBN-10 number to locate this book on CengageBrain.) On the Web page for this book, click the Access Now button to open the Book Companion page.

2. Click the Weblinks link under the Book Resources heading, click the Download Now link for Tutorial 1, and then click the Review Assignments link.

3. Click one of the links listed under the Review Assignments heading and explore the Web site. These Web sites belong to organizations that have goals and activities similar to those of the Danville Animal Shelter. The list includes more links than you will need; however, Web sites can change their URLs and the organizations that created them can even close. If a link you have chosen does not lead you to an active site, or if it leads you to a site that you believe is not relevant to this assignment, simply click another link. Explore at least three more Web sites, opening each site on a separate page tab.

4. Choose one of the four sites that you think is well organized and has complete information presented concisely. Save a copy of the home page of your chosen Web site with the filename **Pet Home Page** to the Tutorial.01\Review folder included with your Data Files in the HTML only format.

5. Create a favorite (if you are using Internet Explorer) or a bookmark (if you are using Firefox) for the Web page of your chosen site, and accept the default name for the favorite or bookmark. Store it in a new folder in the Favorites Center or Firefox Library named **Pet Home Page**.

6. Using the links on the pages of your chosen site, navigate the site until you find a page that contains the organization's address and contact information (telephone number, email address, or similar information). Preview and print the Web page.

7. Navigate to a page that contains a photograph of a pet, and then save the photograph with the filename **Pet Picture** in the Tutorial.01\Review folder.

8. Navigate to a page that includes a statement about the site's copyright or restrictions on use of its content. (*Hint:* You can search a Web page using either Internet Explorer or Firefox for specific text, such as "copyright" or "content," by pressing the Ctrl + F keys to open the Find bar, typing the search text in the Find box that appears, and then clicking the Next button.) Copy and paste that text into a WordPad document and save it with the filename **Pet Web Site Copyright Page** in the Tutorial.01\Review folder.

9. Use your browser's Help system to find information on how cookies are tracked and managed in the browser. In a brief report to your instructor, summarize the Help information you find. Make sure your report identifies the title of the Help page you found, the definition of a cookie, the steps to view cookies if available, and the steps for deleting cookies.

10. Turn on InPrivate Browsing in Internet Explorer or start Private Browsing in Firefox. Repeat Steps 1 and 2 to access the Weblinks for the Review Assignments, and then click a link to another Web site you have not viewed. Click at least four links to explore the Web site and/or other sites it links to. When you are done, end the private browsing session.

11. View the history list to confirm that the Web pages you explored in the previous steps have not been recorded. Close the Internet Explorer Favorites Center or the Firefox Library when you are done.

12. If you are working in a computer lab or on a public computer, delete the folder and the favorite or bookmark you created in Step 5, and then close your Web browser.

Navigate to Web pages using tabbed browsing, collect favorites or bookmarks, and store them in appropriate folders.

APPLY

Case Problem 1

There are no Data Files needed for this Case Problem.

South High School Evening Program   You are the assistant to Angela Dixon, who is the new director of South High School's evening program for adult learners. The program offers lessons for students who are not native speakers of English in its English as a Second Language (ESL) course. It also offers a math refresher course for adults who need help brushing up on their high school math skills as they apply for better jobs or return to college after being out of high school for several years. Angela wants to add books to the school's library that will provide resources for students in these two courses, and she asks you to help her find suitable titles at Amazon.com. Complete the following steps using either Internet Explorer or Firefox:

1. Start your Web browser, and then enter the URL **www.cengagebrain.com** in your browser's Address or Location bar. On the CengageBrain home page that opens, enter the ISBN number for this book in the Search box at the top of the page, and then click the Find button. (*Hint:* The ISBN for your book can be found above the bar code located in the lower-right corner of the back cover of your book. You can use either the ISBN-13 or ISBN-10 number to locate this book on CengageBrain.) On the Web page for this book, click the Access Now button to open the Book Companion page.

2. Click the Weblinks link under the Book Resources heading, click the Download Now link for Tutorial 1, and then click the Case Problem 1 link.

3. Click one of the links under the Case Problem 1 heading to open the home page of a Web site for a bookseller.

4. Click the Search arrow, and then click Books or All Books. In the Search box, type **ESL books**, and then click the Go or Search button to open a list of links to books that could be useful to students in South High's ESL course.

5. Locate an ESL book that you believe would be useful for Angela, and then right-click the book's title and open the book's page on a new tab. Repeat this for two more books.

6. Create a folder titled **ESL Book Recommendations** in the Internet Explorer Favorites Center or in the Firefox Library in which you will store favorites or bookmarks to pages that Angela can examine as she reviews books for the library's collection.

7. Create shortcuts (as favorites if you are using Internet Explorer; as bookmarks if you are using Firefox) for the three books you have found, and place these in the ESL Book Recommendations folder you created in the previous step.

8. In the search box at the top of the page, type **high school math**, and then click the Go button to open a list of links to books that could be useful for students in South High's math refresher course.

9. Locate a math book that you believe would be useful for Angela, and then right-click the book's title to open the book's page on a new tab. Repeat this for two more books.

10. Create a folder titled **Math Book Recommendations** in the Internet Explorer Favorites Center or in the Firefox Library in which you will store favorites or bookmarks to pages that Angela can examine as she reviews books for the library's collection.

11. Create shortcuts (as favorites if you are using Internet Explorer; as bookmarks if you are using Firefox) for the three books you have found, and place these in the Math Book Recommendations folder you created in the previous step.

⊕ EXPLORE 12. In the Internet Explorer Favorites Center, expand the two folders you created so the favorites stored within them are displayed; or in the Firefox Library, click one of the two folders you created so the bookmarks stored within them are displayed. Press the Print Screen key to make a copy of the Web page, start WordPad, and then click the Paste button in the Clipboard group on the Home tab. If your instructor requests it, print a copy of the WordPad document.

13. Delete all of the folders and favorites or bookmarks you created in this Case Problem, and then close your Web browser.

Case Problem 2

Research competitors' Web sites to identify features to include in or omit from a new Web site design.

RESEARCH

There are no Data Files needed for this Case Problem.

Central Tools Central Tools is a company that sells woodworking tools to hobbyists, carpenters, and cabinetmakers in the South Valley metropolitan area. Most hardware stores sell a variety of hammers, saws, chisels, and other woodworking tools, but Central Tools focuses on the special needs of skilled woodworkers. These tools are of high quality, can be hard to find, and are expensive. Central Tools has developed an excellent reputation over the years throughout South Valley for its tool selection and fair prices. It also brings in famous woodworkers from time to time who conduct seminars on the latest techniques and traditional woodworking skills. Hal Porter, the owner of Central Tools, is thinking about selling tools online and has asked you to gather information about Web sites that would be Central Tools' competition on the Web. Complete the following steps using either Internet Explorer or Firefox:

1. Start your Web browser, and then enter the URL **www.cengagebrain.com** in your browser's Address or Location bar. On the CengageBrain home page that opens, enter the ISBN number for this book in the Search box at the top of the page, and then click the Find button. (*Hint:* The ISBN for your book can be found above the bar code located in the lower-right corner of the back cover of your book. You can use either the ISBN-13 or ISBN-10 number to locate this book on CengageBrain.) On the Web page for this book, click the Access Now button to open the Book Companion page.

2. Click the Weblinks link under the Book Resources heading, click the Download Now link for Tutorial 1, and then click the Case Problem 2 link.

3. Click the links listed under the Case Problem 2 heading and explore the Web sites of Central Tools' potential online competitors. Choose one of the listed sites that you believe would be a good example for Hal to follow as he takes his business online, and then save a copy of the site's home page as **Competitor Home Page** in the Tutorial.01\Case 2 folder included with your Data Files in the HTML only format. Perform the remaining steps for the Web site you have chosen.

4. Create a folder in the Internet Explorer Favorites Center or in the Firefox Library window named **Product Page Examples** in which you will store favorites or bookmarks to pages that Hal can examine.

◆ EXPLORE   5. Navigate the pages of your chosen site to find Web pages that include the following four types of woodworking tools: chisels, clamps, drills, and saws. Pick four pages, one for each type of tool, that you believe would be a good example for Hal. Create favorites in Internet Explorer or bookmarks in Firefox for each page, named **Chisels**, **Clamps**, **Drills**, and **Saws**, respectively. Store the four shortcuts in the folder you created in the preceding step.

◆ EXPLORE   6. Write a report that answers the following specific questions about each Web site you have chosen:

a. Does the site's home page include contact information or an easy-to-identify link to a page that contains contact information? What contact information is included?

b. List three things about the site that you would recommend including in the Central Tools Web site.

c. List three things about the site that you believe Hal should avoid when designing the Central Tools Web site.

d. Does the site include links to videos about the products for sale?

e. Does the site include information about how to use the tools or provide ideas for woodworking projects (including plans or drawings) that site visitors could build?

f. Provide one example of how the Web site provides focus in its presentation.

g. Provide one example of how the Web site is well organized.

7. Delete the folder and favorites or bookmarks you created in this Case Problem, and then close your Web browser.

Read Web pages to learn more about cookies and the risks they pose, and compare cookies' risks to their benefits.

RESEARCH

Case Problem 3

There are no Data Files needed for this Case Problem.

Nestor Analytics   Nestor Analytics is a financial market research firm in New York City. You have just started an internship working for Sally Nestor, the firm's director. Sally recently read an article that discussed potential security risks posed by Web servers that place cookie files on computers running Web browser software. She is concerned about this issue and asks you to research it for her. Sally explains to you that all employees of Nestor Analytics have laptop computers that they use to work from the office, their homes, and client locations. The firm's research analysts have powerful desktop computers at Nestor headquarters that store sensitive financial information about the firm's clients and details of their confidential trading strategies. All of these computers are connected to the Internet and run Web browser software. Sally is interested in learning more about any possible security issues that might arise from cookie files. She asks you to collect more information for her review by completing the following steps using either Internet Explorer or Firefox:

1. Start your Web browser, and then enter the URL **www.cengagebrain.com** in your browser's Address or Location bar. On the CengageBrain home page that opens, enter the ISBN number for this book in the Search box at the top of the page, and then click the Find button. (*Hint:* The ISBN for your book can be found above the bar code located in the lower-right corner of the back cover of your book. You can use either the ISBN-13 or ISBN-10 number to locate this book on CengageBrain.) On the Web page for this book, click the Access Now button to open the Book Companion page.

2. Click the Weblinks link under the Book Resources heading, click the Download Now link for Tutorial 1, and then click the Case Problem 3 link.

⊕ EXPLORE

3. Click the links listed under the Case Problem 3 heading and explore the Web sites to which they lead. These sites provide information about Web cookies that Sally might find helpful. As you read information on these sites, remember the distinction between first-party cookies and third-party cookies that you learned about in this tutorial.

4. Create favorites or bookmarks to any Web pages that you believe Sally should read in a folder titled **Nestor Analytics Cookie Research**.

5. Create a report to Sally that summarizes what you learned from your research. Make sure your report does the following:

a. Name and briefly describe two risks that cookie files might pose to Nestor Analytics.

b. Briefly describe the benefits that Nestor Analytics employees gain by allowing Web servers to write cookies to their computers.

c. Provide a general assessment of the level of risk posed to Nestor Analytics by cookie files, rating the risk high, medium, or low. Briefly state the reasons for your assessment.

d. Include the URLs for the Web pages you referenced during your research. (*Hint:* Select the URL in the Address bar or Location bar, and then copy and paste it as usual.)

6. Delete the folder and favorites or bookmarks you created in this Case Problem, and then close your Web browser.

Research and compare the features of the two leading Web browsers.

RESEARCH

Case Problem 4

There are no Data Files needed for this Case Problem.

Briar Lake Assisted Living Center   Nancy Francis is the events coordinator at Briar Lake Assisted Living Center. Recently, the center received a donation of five laptops and Nancy plans to make these available to residents. She knows that many of the residents are either new to computers or haven't used them recently, so she is considering offering small group workshops on basic computer skills. She wants to set these computers up with the necessary software for residents to be able to send and receive email, write letters, and browse the Internet. To help Nancy decide which browser software to install on the computers, you will research and compare the features of the two most prevalent browsers: Internet Explorer and Firefox. Complete the following steps:

1. Start your Web browser, and then enter the URL **www.cengagebrain.com** in your browser's Address or Location bar. On the CengageBrain home page that opens, enter the ISBN number for this book in the Search box at the top of the page, and then click the Find button. (*Hint:* The ISBN for your book can be found above the bar code located in the lower-right corner of the back cover of your book. You can use either the ISBN-13 or ISBN-10 number to locate this book on CengageBrain.) On the Web page for this book, click the Access Now button to open the Book Companion page.

2. Click the Weblinks link under the Book Resources heading, click the Download Now link for Tutorial 1, and then click the Case Problem 4 link.

3. If you completed Session 1.1 of this tutorial using Internet Explorer, then click the Firefox link under the Browsers heading to open the Firefox product page. If you completed Session 1.2 using Firefox, then click the Internet Explorer link under the Browsers heading to open the Internet Explorer product page.

4. Use the link on the browser's product page to familiarize yourself with the features and tools the browser offers. In your research, try to find answers to the following:

a. How are the tools and commands accessed in the browser?

b. Can you customize the browser window in any way?

c. Is there a way to keep track of your browsing activity, and if so, how?

   d. Are there any privacy tools, and if so, how easy are they to manage?

   e. Is there a search feature?

5. In a report, compare the information you found in Step 4 to your experience and knowledge of the Web browser you used in this tutorial. Be sure to compare and contrast the main features of the browsers. Identify features that might exist in one browser but not the other. If similar features exist in both browsers, assess whether you think one browser is easier or more difficult to use in that way. Conclude your report with a recommendation for Nancy as to which browser you think might work best for the residents at Briar Lake Assisted Living Center.

6. Close your browser.

Identify other Web browsers that are available and describe their features.

RESEARCH

Case Problem 5

There are no Data Files needed for this Case Problem.

West Shore Community Center Alex Jacoby is the youth coordinator at West Shore Community Center. Children come to the community center to play basketball, swim, learn crafts, and enjoy other activities. They can also use the community center's computer lab to complete school work and get help with assignments. Alex wants to update the Web browsers on the computers, and realizes that he can choose from a variety of browsers. To help Alex decide which browser or browsers to install, you will research and compare the features of two browsers. Complete the following steps:

1. Start your Web browser, and then enter the URL **www.cengagebrain.com** in your browser's Address or Location bar. On the CengageBrain home page that opens, enter the ISBN number for this book in the Search box at the top of the page, and then click the Find button. (*Hint:* The ISBN for your book can be found above the bar code located in the lower-right corner of the back cover of your book. You can use either the ISBN-13 or ISBN-10 number to locate this book on CengageBrain.) On the Web page for this book, click the Access Now button to open the Book Companion page.

2. Click the Weblinks link under the Book Resources heading, click the Download Now link for Tutorial 1, and then click the Case Problem 5 link.

3. Click one of the links under the Case Problem 5 heading to open the product page for a Web browser.

4. Use the links and videos on the browser's product page to familiarize yourself with the features and tools the browser offers. In your research, try to find answers to the following:

   a. What features are available in the browser?

   b. How are the tools and commands accessed in the browser?

   c. Can you customize the browser window in any way?

   d. Is there a way to keep track of your browsing activity, and if so, how?

   e. Are there any privacy tools, and if so, how easy are they to manage?

   f. Is there a search feature?

5. Repeat Steps 3 and 4 for a second browser.

6. In a report, compare and contrast the main features of the two browsers. Identify features that might exist in one browser but not the other. If similar features exist in both browsers, assess whether you think one browser is easier or more difficult to use in that way. Conclude your report with a recommendation for Alex as to which browser you think might work best at West Shore Community Center.

7. Close your browser.

OBJECTIVES

Session 2.1
- Learn how email works
- Understand basic email features and functions
- Learn about viruses, antivirus software, and spam

Session 2.2
- Create a Windows Live Hotmail email account
- Configure and use Windows Live Hotmail to send, receive, and print email messages
- Create and maintain contacts, and use them to address messages
- Explore Windows Live Web-based services

INTERNET

Basic Communication on the Internet: Email

Using Email and Sharing Files

Case | *Kikukawa Air*

Since 2001, Sharon and Don Kikukawa have operated a small hot air balloon service in Albuquerque, New Mexico. At first, Kikukawa Air employed only Sharon, who managed the office, reservations, and the company's financial records, and her husband Don, who served as pilot for the couple's brightly colored hot air balloon. After many successful years in business, Sharon and Don expanded their business to include longer scenic tours of the beautiful New Mexico mountains, special trips that feature meals or several balloons flying larger parties of clients to a specific destination, and participation in hot air balloon festivals and races. As a result of their expansion, Kikukawa Air now has 11 hot air balloons, 14 pilots, and a growing office staff of 10 people who coordinate reservations and accommodations for their clients.

Although most employees already use email to communicate with each other and with clients and vendors, they are not all using the same email provider. In addition, employees are currently having problems sending and receiving messages on their mobile devices while working across the state of New Mexico. Sharon believes that Kikukawa Air could benefit from the company's employees using the same email provider. This will make it easier to manage the accounts and troubleshoot connection problems on the mobile devices, and will streamline the company's operations.

Sharon asks you to investigate a solution for her employees to use Web-based email accounts to exchange email messages, and to share business documents and other files on their computers and mobile devices.

STARTING DATA FILES

Tutorial.02	Tutorial	Review	Cases	
	Timeline.pdf	KAir.gif	Bales.jpg	Paper.jpg
			Chance.jpg	Rocky.jpg
			Maple.jpg	Scout.jpg

SESSION 2.1 VISUAL OVERVIEW

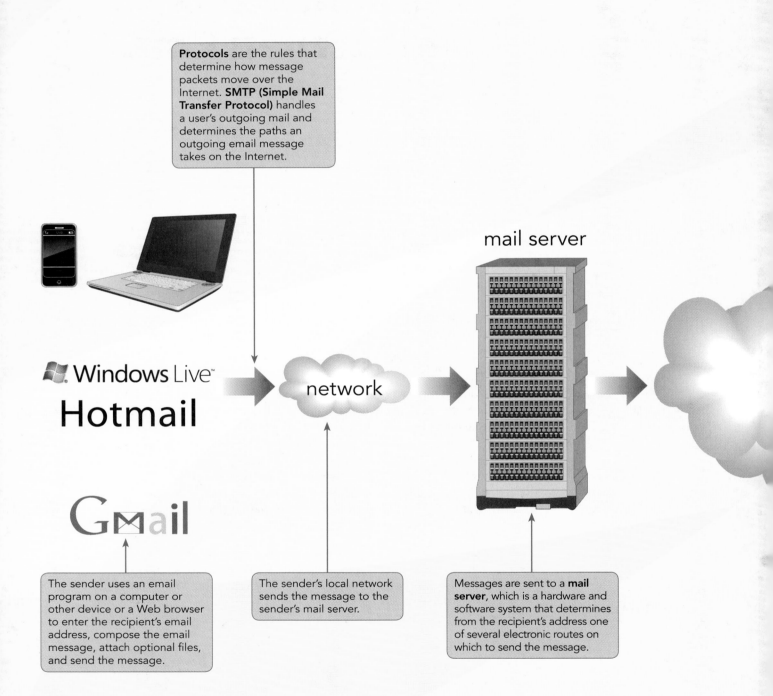

Protocols are the rules that determine how message packets move over the Internet. **SMTP (Simple Mail Transfer Protocol)** handles a user's outgoing mail and determines the paths an outgoing email message takes on the Internet.

mail server

Windows Live™
Hotmail

network

The sender uses an email program on a computer or other device or a Web browser to enter the recipient's email address, compose the email message, attach optional files, and send the message.

The sender's local network sends the message to the sender's mail server.

Messages are sent to a **mail server**, which is a hardware and software system that determines from the recipient's address one of several electronic routes on which to send the message.

HOW EMAIL WORKS

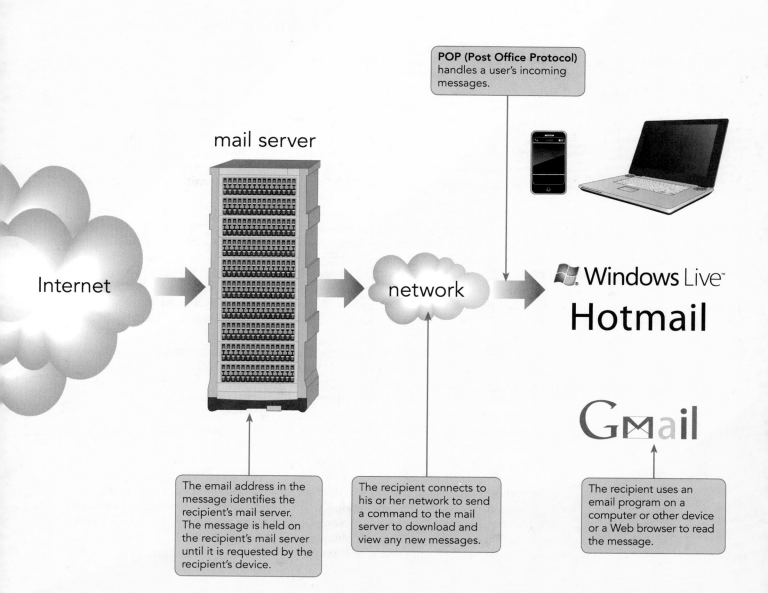

mail server

POP (Post Office Protocol) handles a user's incoming messages.

Internet

network

Windows Live™
Hotmail

Gmail

The email address in the message identifies the recipient's mail server. The message is held on the recipient's mail server until it is requested by the recipient's device.

The recipient connects to his or her network to send a command to the mail server to download and view any new messages.

The recipient uses an email program on a computer or other device or a Web browser to read the message.

What Is Email and How Does It Work?

Electronic mail, or **email**, is a form of communication in which electronic messages are created and transferred between two or more devices connected to a network. Email is one of the most popular forms of business communication, and for many people it is their primary use of the Internet. As shown in the Visual Overview for Session 2.1, email travels to its destination across the network to the recipient's account on a mail server. For many personal and business reasons, people rely on email as an indispensable form of written communication.

Similar to how Web pages and files move across networks, email messages also use protocols that send and receive them on networks. The two most common protocols for sending and receiving email messages are POP and SMTP, which are both described in the Session 2.1 Visual Overview. Two additional protocols, IMAP and MIME, also handle email messages. **IMAP (Internet Message Access Protocol)** retrieves mail messages from a remote server or messages stored on a large local network. **MIME (Multipurpose Internet Mail Extensions)** specifies how to encode nontext data, such as graphics and sound, so it can travel over the Internet.

When an email message arrives at its destination mail server, the mail server's software handles the details of distributing the message locally, in the same way that a mailroom worker opens a mailbag and places letters and packages into individual mail slots. To check for new email messages, you use a program stored on your Internet device—which might be a computer, cell phone, or other device, such as a tablet—to request the mail server to deliver any stored mail to your device. The software that requests mail delivery from the mail server to an Internet device is known as **mail client software**, or an **email program**.

An **email address** uniquely identifies an individual or organization that is connected to the Internet. To route an email message to an individual, you must identify that person by his or her account name, or **user name**, and also by the name of the mail server that manages email sent to the domain. The two parts of an email address—the user name and the domain name—are separated by an "at" sign (@). Sharon Kikukawa, for example, selected the user name "Sharon" for her email account. Kikukawa Air purchased the domain name "KikukawaAir.com" to use both as its Internet address (URL) and in the email addresses for Kikukawa Air employees. Therefore, Sharon's email address is Sharon@KikukawaAir.com.

A user name usually identifies one person's email account on a mail server. When you are given an email address from an organization, such as your school or an employer, the organization might have standards for assigning user names. Some organizations set standards so user names consist of a person's first initial followed by up to seven characters of the person's last name. Other organizations assign user names that contain a person's first and last names separated by an underscore character (for example, Sharon_Kikukawa). When you are given the opportunity to select your own user name, you might use a nickname or some other name to identify yourself. On a mail server, all user names must be unique.

The domain name is the second part of an email address. The domain name specifies the name of the server to which the mail is to be delivered on the Internet, just like the domain name identifies the name of the computer on which a Web site resides. Domain names contain periods, which are usually pronounced "dot," to divide the domain name. The most specific part of the domain name appears first in the address, followed by the top-level domain name. Kikukawa Air's Web site address, KikukawaAir.com (and pronounced "Kikukawa Air dot com"), contains only two names separated by a period. The *com* in the domain name indicates that this company falls into the large, general class of commercial organizations. *KikukawaAir* indicates the domain name associated with the IP address for KikukawaAir.com.

Most email addresses aren't case-sensitive; the addresses sharon@kikukawaair.com and Sharon@KikukawaAir.com are the same. It is important for you to type a recipient's address carefully; if you omit or mistype even one character, your message could be undeliverable or sent to the wrong recipient. When a message cannot be delivered, the receiving mail server might send the message back to you and indicate that the addressee is unknown. Sometimes mail that cannot be delivered is deleted on the receiving mail server without notifying the sender.

INSIGHT

Managing More than One Email Address

Keep in mind that an email account that was assigned to you by your school or employer is subject to the rules of use that the organization has established. Some schools and most employers have policies that dictate the permitted use of their equipment and email accounts. You should not use your employer's email address for personal correspondence unless your employer specifies that your personal use of the email account and your workplace computer is acceptable. In some cases, an employer might terminate employees who abuse the company's resources for personal use. In many cases, email is subject to monitoring by the organization, so messages you send with your organization-sponsored account are not guaranteed to be private.

For this reason, many people have more than one email address to manage their correspondence. It is very common for people to have a primary email address that they use for personal or business correspondence, and a secondary email address that they use for online subscriptions, online purchases, and mailing lists. If you are careful about how you distribute your primary email address, you might reduce the amount of unsolicited mail that you receive. When your secondary email address starts getting a lot of unwanted messages, you can discard it and create a new one. If you keep track of who has your secondary email address, it will be easy to update your contacts if you need to change your secondary email address.

Common Features of an Email Message

An email message consists of three parts: the message header, the message body, and an optional signature. The **message header** contains information about the message, and the **message body** contains the actual message content. A **signature** might appear at the bottom of an email message and contain standard information about the sender, which the recipient can use to contact the sender in a variety of ways.

Figure 2-1 shows a message that Don Kikukawa wrote to Jack Clancy, Margaret Durring, his pilots, and Sharon about an upcoming hot air balloon festival using an email program called Windows Live Mail, which you can download for free from the Windows Live Web site. The message contains an attached file named MealPlan.docx. Don created this file using Microsoft Word, saved it, and then attached it to the message. The primary features of this message are described in the next sections.

| Figure 2-1 | Common features of an email message |

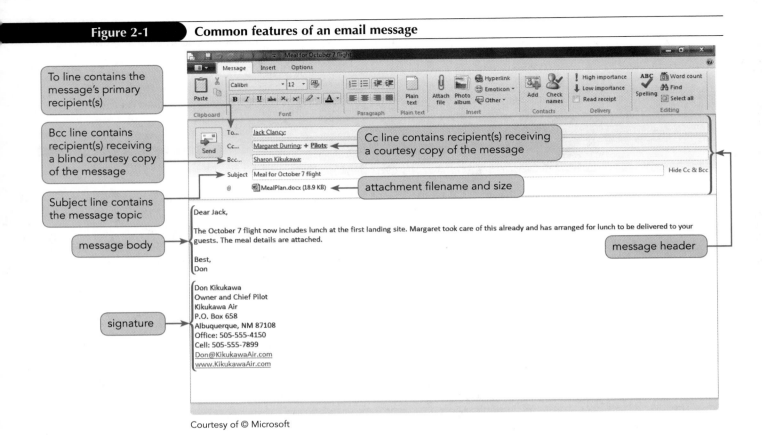

Courtesy of © Microsoft

To, Cc, and Bcc

You type the recipient's full email address in the **To line** of a message header. You can send the same message to multiple recipients by typing a comma or semicolon between the recipients' email addresses in the To line. If you have saved a recipient's email address in your address book—the feature of an email program that stores information about the people you exchange email with—the email program might display the address using the person's name, as shown in Figure 2-1, instead of the recipient's actual email address. The number of addresses you can type in the To line or in the other parts of the message header that require an address is not limited, but some mail servers will reject messages with too many recipients (usually 50 or more) as a way of controlling unsolicited mail. In Figure 2-1, Don used the To line to address his message to one recipient, Jack Clancy, whose email address was already stored in Don's address book.

You can use the optional **courtesy copy (Cc)** and **blind courtesy copy (Bcc)** lines to send mail to people who should be aware of the email message, but are not the message's main recipients. When an email message is delivered, every recipient (including Bcc recipients) can see the addresses of other recipients listed in the To and Cc lines. Because Bcc addresses are excluded from messages sent to addresses in the To and Cc lines, neither the primary recipients (in the To line) nor the Cc recipients can view the list of Bcc recipients. Bcc recipients are unaware of other Bcc recipients, as well. For example, if you send a thank-you message to a salesperson for performing a task especially well, you might consider sending a blind courtesy copy to that person's supervisor. That way, the supervisor knows a customer is happy and that the praise was unsolicited. In Figure 2-1, Don sent a courtesy copy of his email message to Margaret Durring and a blind courtesy copy to Sharon Kikukawa.

Sometimes an email address is not one person's address, but rather a special address called a **category** (also called a **group** in some email programs). In a category, a single email address can represent several or many individual email addresses. For example,

Don created a group named "Pilots" that includes the email addresses of the pilots who work for him so he can quickly address a new message to all pilots by typing the "Pilots" group name, instead of entering each pilot's email address individually. In Figure 2-1, Don included the Pilots group in the Cc line of the email message, so each member of the Pilots group will receive a copy of the message.

From

The **From line** of an email message includes the sender's name, the sender's email address, or both. Most email programs automatically insert the sender's name and email address in the From line of all outgoing messages. You usually do not see the From line in messages that you are composing, but you can see it in messages that you receive. Figure 2-1 does not show a From line because this is a message that Don is composing.

Subject

The content of the **Subject line** is very important. Often the recipient will scan an abbreviated display of incoming messages, looking for the most interesting or important message based on the content in the Subject line. If the Subject line is blank, then the recipient might not read the associated message immediately or at all. Including an appropriate subject in your message helps the reader determine its content and importance. For example, a Subject line such as "Just checking" is less informative and less interesting than "Urgent: New staff meeting time." The email message shown in Figure 2-1, for example, contains the subject "Meal for October 7 flight" and thus indicates that the message concerns food for an upcoming trip.

Attachments

You can send only text messages using SMTP, the protocol that handles outgoing email. When you need to send a more complex document, such as a Word document, an Excel workbook, a picture, or a PDF file, you send it along as an attachment. An **attachment** provides a simple and convenient way of sending files to one or more people. An attachment is encoded so that it can be carried safely over the Internet, to "tag along" with the message. Frequently, the attached file is the most important part of the email message, and the message body contains only a brief statement, such as "Here's the file that you requested."

Don's email message (see Figure 2-1) contains an attached file, whose filename and size in kilobytes appear in the message header. (A **kilobyte (KB)** is approximately 1,000 characters.) You can attach more than one file to an email message; if you include multiple recipients in the To, Cc, and Bcc lines of the message header, each recipient will receive the message and the attached file(s). However, keep in mind that an email message with many attachments quickly becomes very large in size, and it will take longer for the recipients to download the message. In addition, some Internet service providers (ISPs) place limits on the size of messages that they will accept; in some cases, an email message with file attachments larger than 10 megabytes in size might be rejected and returned to the sender.

Email programs differ in how they handle and display attachments. Some email programs identify an attached file with an icon that represents a program associated with the attachment's file type. In addition to an icon, some programs also display an attached file's size and filename. Other email programs display an attached file in a preview window when they recognize the attached file's format, and can start a program on the user's device to open the file. Double-clicking an attached file usually opens the file using a program on the user's device that is associated with the file type of the attachment. For example, if a workbook is attached to an email message, double-clicking the icon for the workbook attachment might start a spreadsheet program and open the workbook.

TIP

Before sending a message with a large attachment, ask the recipient for the best way to send it.

TIP

Before opening an attachment, be sure to scan it for viruses and other threats. You will learn more about detecting threats in this tutorial.

Similarly, a Word document opens in the Word program window when you double-click the icon representing the attached document, as long as you have the Word program, or a program that can open Word documents, installed on your device.

Viewing an attachment by double-clicking it lets you open a read-only copy of the file, but it does not save the file on your device. (A **read-only** file is one that you can view but that you cannot change.) To save an attached file on your device, you need to perform a series of steps to save the file in a specific location, such as on a hard drive. Some programs refer to the process of saving an email attachment as **detaching** the file. When you detach a file, you must indicate where to save it. You won't always need to detach an email attachment; if you simply keep the email message, you also keep a copy of the attachment for future use. You will learn how to attach and detach files later in this tutorial.

Message Body and Signature Files

Most often, people use email to write short, quick messages. However, email messages can be much longer. An email message is often less formal than a business letter that you might write, but it's still important to follow the rules of formal letter writing when composing an email message. You should begin your messages with a salutation, such as "Dear Jack," use proper spelling and grammar, and close your correspondence with a signature. After typing the content of your message—even a short message—you should check your spelling and grammar. You can sign a message by typing your name and other information at the end of each message you send, or you can create a signature file.

If you are using email for business communication, a **signature file** usually contains your name, your title, and your company's name. Signature files might also contain a mailing address, telephone numbers, a Web site address, and a company's logo. If you are using email for personal communication, signatures can be more informal. Informal signatures can include nicknames and graphics or quotations that express a more casual style found in correspondence between friends and acquaintances.

You can set your email account to insert a signature automatically into every message you send so you don't have to type its contents. You can modify your signature easily or choose not to include it in selected messages. You can usually create multiple signature files so you can choose which one to include when sending a message.

When you create a signature, don't overdo it: It is best to limit a signature to a few lines that identify ways to contact you. Figure 2-2 shows two examples of signatures. The first signature, which Don might use in his business correspondence to Kikukawa Air employees and friends, is informal. Don uses the second, more formal signature for all other business correspondence to identify his name, title, and contact information to make it easy for people to reach him.

| Figure 2-2 | Sample signatures |

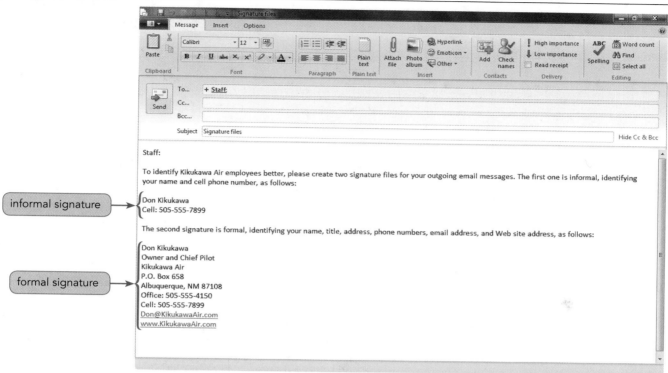

Courtesy of © Microsoft

Internet Etiquette (Netiquette)

Netiquette, a term coined from the phrase "Internet etiquette," is the set of commonly accepted rules that represent proper behavior on a network. Just as there are rules of proper conduct on networks that are owned or operated by schools and organizations, the Internet has its own set of acceptable rules. Unlike business networks on which administrators and webmasters set guidelines for acceptable use, and moderators are authorized to restrict usage of that network by users who don't follow those rules, the Internet is self-policing. Email has its own set of rules, which have evolved over time and will continue to evolve as it gains new users.

Because it sometimes takes so little time and effort to compose an email message, you might be tempted to take some shortcuts in your writing, such as omitting the salutation and using acronyms for commonly used phrases, such as the ones shown in Figure 2-3. These shortcuts are fine for informal messages that you might send to your friends and family members, but they are not acceptable in business communication.

| Figure 2-3 | Commonly used acronyms |

Acronym	Meaning
atm	At the moment
b/c	Because
btw	By the way
iac	In any case
iae	In any event
imho	In my humble opinion
imo	In my opinion
iow	In other words
jk	Just kidding
thx	Thanks

© Cengage Learning

An email message is a business document, just like a memo or letter, and you should treat it with the same level of formality. Sending a message containing spelling and grammatical errors to a colleague or a potential employer is a poor reflection on you and your work. Many employers seeking to fill open positions automatically disregard email messages that do not contain a subject line or information in the message body describing the contents of the attachment and the applicant's intention to apply for the position. In addition, some employers will not seriously consider applications that are sent with email messages that contain typos or demonstrate poor communication skills.

Because email can be an impersonal form of communication, some writers use emoticons to express emotion. An **emoticon** is a group of keyboard characters that when viewed together represent a human expression. For example, a smiley :-) looks like a smiling face when you turn your head to the left. Some writers use emoticons to show their readers a form of electronic body language. Figure 2-4 shows some commonly used emoticons that are used in email messages. The user can create these emoticons by using either typed characters or a feature of the email program that inserts an emoticon's picture equivalent. Just like acronyms, emoticons are appropriate in informal correspondence but not in business correspondence.

TIP

Some email programs let you insert emoticons as pictures instead of typing keyboard combinations.

| Figure 2-4 | Commonly used emoticons |

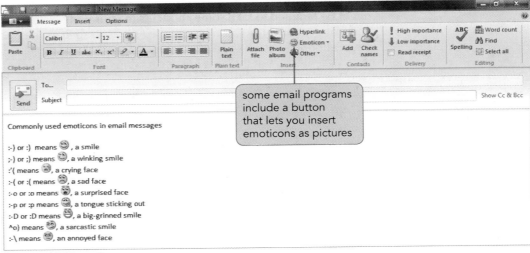

Courtesy of © Microsoft

You can learn more about netiquette by following the links in the Netiquette section of the Weblinks page for Tutorial 2.

PROSKILLS

Written Communication: Generally Accepted Rules for Email Messages

When composing email messages, keep the following generally accepted rules in mind, especially for business correspondence:

- Avoid writing your messages in ALL CAPITAL LETTERS BECAUSE IT LOOKS LIKE YOU ARE SHOUTING.
- Keep your messages simple, short, and focused on their topics.
- Don't use the "Reply All" feature when only the sender needs to know your response.
- Don't assume that everyone you know likes to receive jokes or family pictures. Check with the recipients first.
- When sending messages to a large group, use the Bcc field for the recipients' email addresses to protect their privacy and to prevent them from receiving additional responses from people who use the "Reply All" feature to respond.
- Include a descriptive subject in the Subject line and a signature, so the recipient knows the content of your message and how to get in touch with you.
- Use a spell checker, read your message, and correct any spelling or grammatical errors before sending it.
- Don't overuse formatting and graphics, which can make your email message difficult to read. The fonts you select on your device might not be available on the recipient's device and therefore the message might not display as you intended.
- Email is not private; don't divulge private or sensitive information in an email message. It's very easy for the recipient to forward your message to everyone he or she knows, even if it's by accident.
- Use caution when attempting sarcasm or humor in your messages, as the recipient might not appreciate the attempt at humor and might actually misunderstand your intentions. Without the sender's body language and tone of voice, some written statements are subject to misinterpretation.
- Use common courtesy, politeness, and respect in all of your written correspondence.
- When specifying a user name for your email address, select something that is appropriate for both professional and personal correspondence, and that clearly identifies you to recipients.

Email Programs

Different software companies that produce Web browsers might also produce companion email programs that you can use to manage your email. For example, when you install Microsoft Internet Explorer for Windows XP, the Outlook Express email program is also installed. Windows Vista and Windows 7 users might choose to install Windows Live Mail, and Mozilla Firefox users might choose to install the companion Thunderbird email program to manage their email messages. You can use these types of email programs to manage messages that are routed through a domain that sends email messages using the POP protocol. Messages that are routed through a domain in this way are called **POP messages** or **POP3 messages** because of the protocol used to send them. You might also have multiple email programs installed on your computer; in this case, the choice of which email program to use is up to you.

Before you can use an email program to send and receive your email messages, you must configure it to work with your email accounts. Before you decide which email program to use, you should be familiar with the different ones available. The Email Clients section of the Weblinks page for Tutorial 2 includes links to some popular email programs, some of which are free. You can explore these links to learn more about these programs and their features.

TIP

In Session 2.2, you will learn how to configure and use Windows Live Hotmail.

Common Features of Email Programs

Although there are many different ways to send and receive email messages, most email programs have common features for managing mail. Fortunately, once you learn the process for sending, receiving, and managing email with one program, it's easy to use another program to accomplish the same tasks.

Sending Messages

After you finish addressing and composing a message, it might not be sent to the mail server immediately, depending on how the email program or service is configured. A message can be **queued**, or temporarily held with other messages, and then sent when you either exit the program, connect to your ISP or network, or check to see if you have received any new email. Most email programs and services include a "Drafts" folder in which you can store email messages that you are composing but that you aren't ready to send yet. These messages are saved until you finish and send them.

Receiving and Storing Messages

When your mail server receives messages for your account, those messages are held on the mail server until you ask the server to retrieve your messages. Most email programs allow you to save delivered mail in any of several standard or custom mailboxes or folders on your Internet device. Once the mail is delivered to your device, one of two things can happen to it on the server: Either the server's copy of your mail is deleted, or it is preserved and marked as delivered or read. Marking mail as delivered or read is the server's way of distinguishing new mail from mail that you have read. For example, when Don receives mail on the Kikukawa Air mail server, he might decide to save his accumulated mail on the server—even after he reads it—so he can access the messages again from another device. On the other hand, Don might want to delete old mail to save space on the mail server. Both methods have advantages.

Saving old mail on the server lets you access your mail from any device that can connect to your mail server. However, if you automatically delete mail after reading it, you don't have to worry about storing and organizing messages that you don't need, which requires less effort. Some ISPs and email providers impose limits on the amount of data you can store, so you must occasionally delete mail from your mailbox to avoid interruption of service. In some cases, once you exceed your storage space limit, you cannot receive any additional messages until you delete existing messages from the server, or the service deletes your messages without warning to free up space in your mailbox.

Printing a Message

Reading mail on a computer or other device is fine, but there are times when you will need to print some of your messages. Most email programs let you print a message you are composing or that you have received. The Print command usually appears on the File menu or as a Print button on the toolbar.

Organizing Messages

Most email programs let you create folders in which to store related messages in your mailbox. You can create new folders when needed, rename existing folders, or delete folders and their contents when you no longer need them. You can move mail from the incoming folder to any other folder to file it. Some programs let you define and use a **filter** or rule to move incoming mail into a specific folder, or to delete it automatically based on the content of the message. Filters are especially useful for moving messages from certain senders into designated folders, and for moving **junk mail** (or **spam**), which

TIP

Filters aren't perfect. When using filters to move messages to specific folders or to the trash, it's a good idea to check your folders occasionally to make sure that your incoming messages are downloaded to the correct folder.

is unsolicited mail usually advertising or selling an item or service, to a trash folder. If your email program does not provide filters, you can filter the messages manually by reading them and moving them to the appropriate folders.

Forwarding a Message

You can forward messages that you receive to additional recipients. When you **forward** a message to another recipient, a copy of the original message is sent to the new recipient you specify without the original sender's knowledge. You might forward a misdirected message to another recipient, or forward a message to someone who was not included in the original message routing list.

When you forward a message, your email address and name appear automatically in the From line; most email programs amend the Subject line with the text "Fw," "Fwd," or something similar to indicate that the message has been forwarded. You simply add the new recipient's address to the To line and send the message. Depending on your email program and the preferences you set for forwarding messages, a forwarded message might be sent as an attached file or as quoted text. A **quoted message** is a copy of the sender's original message with your inserted comments. A special mark (a > symbol or a solid vertical line) sometimes precedes each line of the quoted message. Figure 2-5 shows a quoted message; the quoted message appears at the bottom of the message, and the "Fw:" text in the Subject line indicates a forwarded message.

Figure 2-5   Sample forwarded message

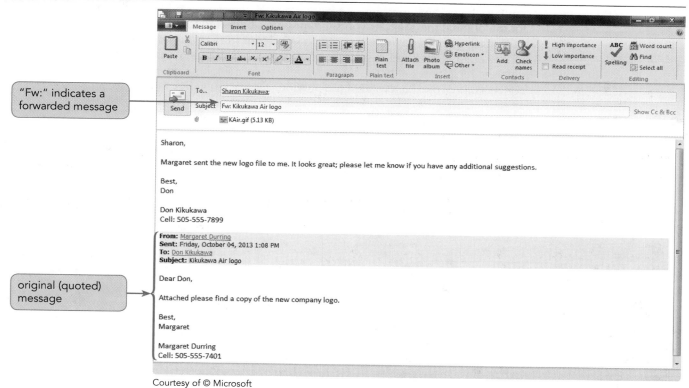

Courtesy of © Microsoft

"Fw:" indicates a forwarded message

original (quoted) message

Replying to a Message

Replying to a message sends a response to a message you have received. Most email programs provide two options for replying to a message: You can reply to only the original sender using the Reply option, or you can reply to the original sender and all other To and Cc recipients of the original message by using the Reply All option. When you **reply** to a message that you received, the email program creates a new message and automatically addresses it either to the original sender (when you select the Reply option), or to the original sender and all of the original To and Cc recipients of the message (when you select the Reply All option). Most email programs will add "Re:" to the beginning of the original subject text in the header and copy the contents of the original message and place it in the message body of the reply. Like forwarded messages, a special mark might appear at the beginning of each line to indicate the content of the original message. When you are responding to more than one question, you might type your responses below the original questions so the recipient can better understand the context of your responses. When you respond to a message that was sent to several people, make sure that you select the correct option when replying.

Some email programs display replies to messages as conversations, or **threads**. When you receive an email message as part of a conversation, it appears in your Inbox on a single line, instead of as stacked individual messages on separate lines. In Figure 2-6, the first message in Don's Inbox appears as a collapsed conversation, with a small arrow indicating that there are additional messages with the same subject line linked to the original message displayed in the Inbox. The second message in the Inbox is an expanded conversation; the selected message is displayed in the preview pane. If you reply to the original message as part of a thread, the reply is added to the conversation for the original message. As you send messages back and forth with the original sender, each subsequent reply from the original sender or from you is added to the conversation for the original message. Instead of needing to find and open multiple messages from different recipients, all of the messages related to a single original message appear in the conversation. To expand one of the previous replies, you click the sender's name.

| Figure 2-6 | Email messages viewed as a conversation, or thread |

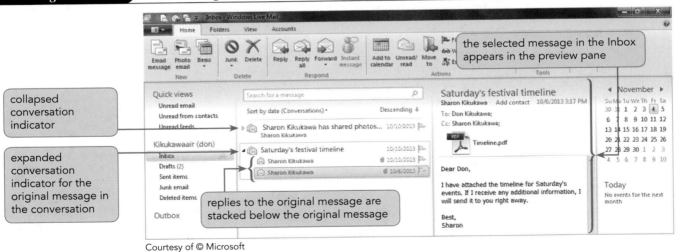

Courtesy of © Microsoft

Deleting a Message

Deleting a message is usually a two-step process. First, you temporarily delete a message by placing it in a "trash" folder or by marking it for deletion. Then you permanently delete the trash or marked messages by emptying the trash folder or indicating to the email program to delete the messages. It is a good idea to delete mail you no longer need because it takes up a lot of space on the drive or server on which your email messages are stored.

Managing Your Contacts

You use a **contact list** to save email addresses and other optional contact information about the people and organizations with which you communicate. The features of a contact list vary by email program. Usually, you can organize information about individuals and groups. Each entry in the contact list can contain an individual's full email address (or a group email address to represent several individual addresses), full name, and complete contact information. In addition, most email programs allow you to include notes for each contact. You can assign a unique nickname to each entry so it is easier to address your email messages. A **nickname** might be "Mom" for your mother or "Maintenance Department" to represent all the employees working in a certain part of an organization. Figure 2-7 shows the contact for Sharon Kikukawa in Don Kikukawa's address book. Notice that there are other options for storing a contact's personal, work, and other information.

Figure 2-7	Sharon's contact in Don's address book

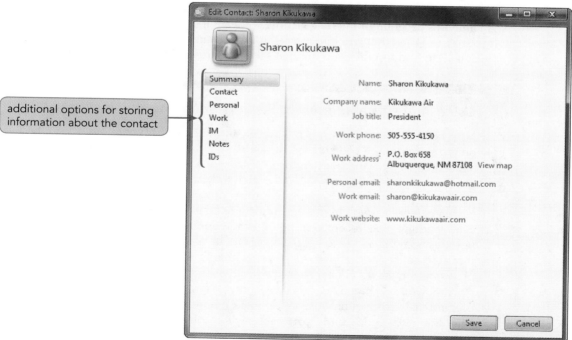

additional options for storing information about the contact

Courtesy of © Microsoft

After saving entries in the contact list, you can refer to them at any point while you are composing, replying to, or forwarding a message. You can review your contact list and sort the entries in many ways.

Protecting Your Computer from Viruses

Email attachments, just like any other computer files, can contain malicious programs called **viruses** that can harm your computer and its files. Some users send attachments containing viruses without realizing that they are doing so; other users send viruses on purpose to infect as many computers as possible. If you receive an email message from a sender that you don't recognize and the message contains an attached file, you should not open that file until you are sure that it doesn't contain a virus.

People create viruses by coding programs that hide by attaching themselves to other programs on a computer. Some viruses simply display an annoying or silly message on your screen and then go away, whereas others can cause real harm by reformatting your hard drive, changing the file extensions and their associations, or sending a copy of the virus to everyone in your email program's contact list. You must know how to detect and eradicate viruses if you plan to download anything, including data, programs, instant messages, or email attachments, from any Internet server.

Software that detects and eliminates viruses is called an **antivirus program**. The category of software that detects viruses and other common security threats on the Internet is called **Internet security software**. This software usually includes tools that eradicate specific Internet threats, including viruses. Internet security software and antivirus programs start automatically when you start the computer, regularly scan the files on your computer and the files being downloaded to your computer, and compare them to a signature that known viruses carry. A **virus signature** (also called a **virus pattern** or a **virus definition**) is a sequence (string) of characters that is always present in a particular virus.

An antivirus program can scan a single file or folder or your entire computer to search for infected files. When the antivirus program finds a virus signature, it might delete the file containing the virus or quarantine it and ask you how to proceed. Most antivirus programs can clean infected files by removing the virus. If your computer does not have an antivirus program or Internet security software installed on it, you can follow the links in the Virus Protection and Internet Security Software sections of the Weblinks page for Tutorial 2 to find resources on Internet security, viruses, and antivirus programs.

TIP

An antivirus program might be part of an Internet security suite that includes other programs that scan files for additional security threats and perform other tasks, such as blocking unwanted pop-up ads.

INSIGHT

Using Antivirus and Internet Security Software Effectively

Most computer manufacturers preload an antivirus program or Internet security suite on the system when you purchase it. Three popular choices for protecting computers are produced by Symantec (Norton), McAfee, and ZoneAlarm. These programs protect your computer from viruses, but only when they are turned on, are properly configured, and include current virus patterns and other program updates. When you first start the software, it will ask you to make a connection to its server, from which the program will download the most recent virus patterns and updates. You must regularly download updates from the server to keep your computer safe. Some programs include features that automatically download the patterns for you on a daily or weekly schedule; other programs require you to connect to the server and initiate the download.

When you purchase and install a security program, you usually receive a free or prepaid trial subscription—usually up to 12 months—for downloading current updates. After this initial period ends, you must pay the software producer a fee to continue downloading updates. In either case, security software can protect you only from viruses and other security threats that it recognizes. If you install a program to protect your computer and do not regularly download updates, your computer won't be protected from dozens of new threats that develop each month. In addition, if your software isn't turned on or set to scan downloaded files, it cannot protect your computer.

And, finally, keep in mind that you usually have to open or execute a file to run any virus it contains. By regularly scanning your computer for viruses, downloading regular updates, configuring the program to work automatically, and scanning all downloaded files, you can protect your computer from viruses and other threats.

Dealing with Unsolicited Messages

Spam, also known as **unsolicited commercial email (UCE)** or junk mail, includes unwanted solicitations, advertisements, or chain letters sent to an email address. For most Internet users, spam represents waste in terms of the time it takes to download, manage, and delete. Besides wasting people's time and their computers' disk space, spam can consume large amounts of network capacity. If one person sends a useless email message to hundreds of thousands of people, that unsolicited message consumes Internet resources for a few moments that would otherwise be available to users with legitimate communication needs.

Although spam has always been an annoyance, companies are increasingly finding it to be a major problem. In addition to consuming bandwidth on company networks and space on mail servers, spam distracts employees who are trying to do their jobs and requires them to spend time deleting unwanted messages. In addition, a considerable number of spam messages include content that is offensive or misleading to its recipients. According to the Messaging Anti-Abuse Working Group (MAAWG), approximately 88% to 91% of all email messages sent every day are spam. In real numbers, this is billions of email messages a day.

One way to reduce spam in your Inbox is to control the exposure of your email address in places where spammers look for them. Spammers use software robots to search the Internet for character strings that include the "@" character that appears in every email address. These robots search Web pages, discussion groups, and other online sources that might contain email addresses. If you don't provide your email address to these sources, you reduce the risk of a spammer getting it.

Some individuals use multiple email addresses to reduce spam. They use one address for display on a Web site, another to register for access to Web sites, another for shopping accounts, and so on. If a spammer starts using one of these addresses, the individual can stop using it and switch to another. Many Web hosting services include a large number of email addresses—often up to 10,000—as part of their service, so this is a good solution for people or small businesses with their own Web sites.

These strategies focus on limiting a spammer's access to, or use of, an email address. Other approaches use one or more techniques that filter email messages based on their contents. Many corporate organizations fight spam aggressively by blocking it on the mail server and preventing it from being downloaded to individual user accounts. Individual users can also set filters that analyze the content in their incoming messages, and move spam messages to a trash folder or other folder when they are downloaded. From the perspective of a corporation, ISP, or other organization, it is more effective and less costly to eliminate spam before it reaches users. The problem with this approach, however, is that it is difficult for a filter to accurately differentiate "real" messages from spam. In many cases, legitimate messages are prevented from reaching the recipient when a spam filter misdirects the message.

Because spam continues to be a serious problem for all email users and providers, an increasing number of approaches have been devised or proposed to combat it. Figure 2-8 shows the home page from the Spam site, sponsored by the Federal Trade Commission, which gives advice to consumers and businesses about combating spam.

Figure 2-8   **Federal Trade Commission Spam page**

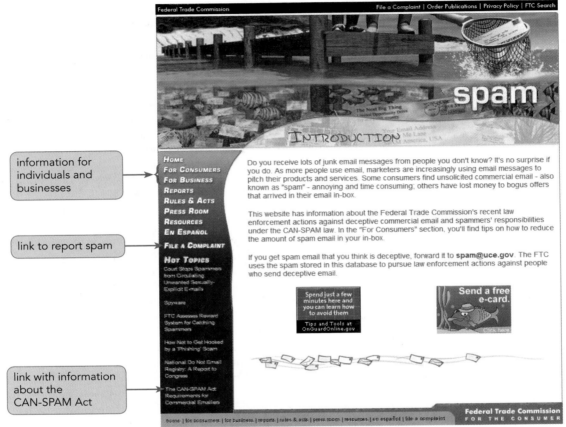

United States Federal Trade Commission, www.ftc.gov

Many U.S. jurisdictions have passed laws that provide penalties for sending spam. In January 2004, the U.S. CAN-SPAM Act (the law's name is an acronym for "Controlling the Assault of Non-Solicited Pornography and Marketing") went into effect. The CAN-SPAM Act was the first U.S. federal government effort to legislate controls on spam. It regulates all email messages sent for the primary purpose of advertising or promoting a commercial product or service, including messages that promote the content displayed at a Web site.

The law's main provisions are that unsolicited email messages must identify the sender, contain an accurate message subject and a notice that the message is an advertisement or solicitation, make it possible for the recipient to "opt out" of future mailings within 10 days of receipt of the request, include the sender's physical postal address, and prohibit the sender from selling or transferring an email address with an opt-out request to any other entity. Each violation of a provision of the law is subject to a fine of up to $16,000. Additional fines are assessed for those who violate one of these provisions and also harvest email addresses from Web sites, send messages to randomly generated addresses, use automated tools to register for email accounts that are subsequently used to send spam, and relay email messages through a computer or network without the permission of the computer's or network's owner.

To learn more about preventing spam, follow the links in the Fighting Spam section of the Weblinks page for Tutorial 2.

Now that you understand some basic information about email, you are ready to start using Windows Live Hotmail, which you will do in Session 2.2.

Session 2.1 Quick Check

REVIEW

1. The rules that determine how the Internet handles packets flowing on it are called _____.
2. What are the three parts of an email message?
3. True or False. On receipt, Bcc recipients of an email message are aware of other Bcc recipients who received the same email message.
4. Can you send a Word document with an email message? If so, how?
5. What are the two parts of an email address, and what information do they provide?
6. Why is it important to delete email messages that you no longer need?
7. What are two strategies for controlling the receipt of spam?

SESSION 2.2 VISUAL OVERVIEW

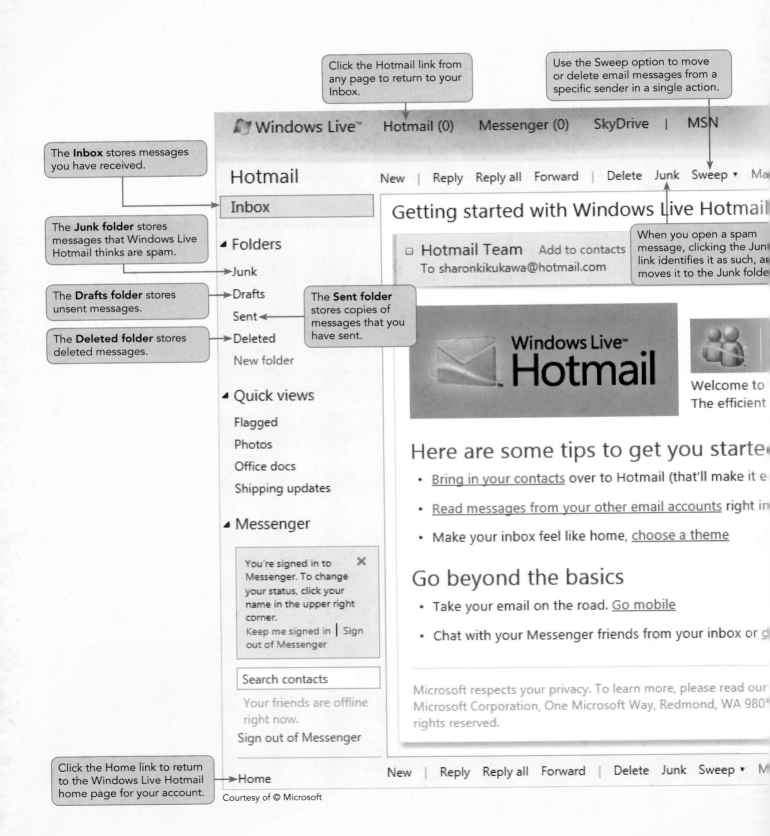

Click the Hotmail link from any page to return to your Inbox.

Use the Sweep option to move or delete email messages from a specific sender in a single action.

The **Inbox** stores messages you have received.

The **Junk folder** stores messages that Windows Live Hotmail thinks are spam.

The **Drafts folder** stores unsent messages.

The **Sent folder** stores copies of messages that you have sent.

The **Deleted folder** stores deleted messages.

When you open a spam message, clicking the Junk link identifies it as such, and moves it to the Junk folder

Click the Home link to return to the Windows Live Hotmail home page for your account.

Windows Live™   Hotmail (0)   Messenger (0)   SkyDrive | MSN

Hotmail

New | Reply   Reply all   Forward | Delete   Junk   Sweep ▾   Ma

Inbox

Getting started with Windows Live Hotmail

▾ **Folders**

☐ **Hotmail Team**   Add to contacts
To sharonkikukawa@hotmail.com

Junk

Drafts

Sent

Deleted

New folder

▾ **Quick views**

Flagged

Photos

Office docs

Shipping updates

▾ **Messenger**

You're signed in to Messenger. To change your status, click your name in the upper right corner.   ✕
Keep me signed in | Sign out of Messenger

Search contacts

Your friends are offline right now.

Sign out of Messenger

Home

Windows Live™ Hotmail

Welcome to
The efficient

Here are some tips to get you started

- Bring in your contacts over to Hotmail (that'll make it e
- Read messages from your other email accounts right in
- Make your inbox feel like home, choose a theme

Go beyond the basics

- Take your email on the road. Go mobile
- Chat with your Messenger friends from your inbox or g

Microsoft respects your privacy. To learn more, please read our
Microsoft Corporation, One Microsoft Way, Redmond, WA 980
rights reserved.

New | Reply   Reply all   Forward | Delete   Junk   Sweep ▾   M

Courtesy of © Microsoft

MESSAGE IN HOTMAIL

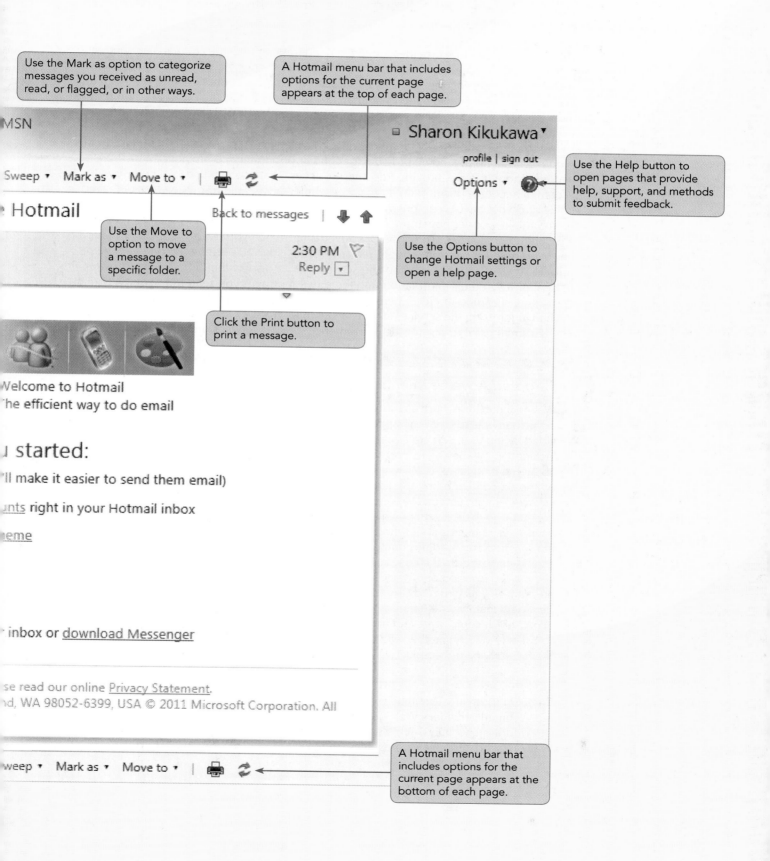

Use the Mark as option to categorize messages you received as unread, read, or flagged, or in other ways.

A Hotmail menu bar that includes options for the current page appears at the top of each page.

Use the Help button to open pages that provide help, support, and methods to submit feedback.

Use the Move to option to move a message to a specific folder.

Use the Options button to change Hotmail settings or open a help page.

Click the Print button to print a message.

MSN

Sharon Kikukawa

profile | sign out

Sweep ▾   Mark as ▾   Move to ▾ |

Options ▾

Hotmail   Back to messages |

2:30 PM
Reply ▾

Welcome to Hotmail
The efficient way to do email

u started:

'll make it easier to send them email)

nts right in your Hotmail inbox

eme

inbox or download Messenger

se read our online Privacy Statement.
d, WA 98052-6399, USA © 2011 Microsoft Corporation. All

A Hotmail menu bar that includes options for the current page appears at the bottom of each page.

weep ▾   Mark as ▾   Move to ▾ |

Webmail Providers

In Session 2.1, you learned about the basic features of an email message, and the basic commands and features in most email programs. You can also obtain and use an email address from a Webmail provider to send and receive your messages. A **Webmail provider** is a Web site that provides a free email address and features to manage, send, and receive email messages. Most Webmail providers also offer other Web-based services, such as online file sharing, to registered users. An email account that you have with a Webmail provider is also called **Webmail** because you access the email account through the Webmail provider's Web site. Two popular examples of Webmail providers are Windows Live Hotmail, which you'll use in this session, and Google's Gmail.

Most people who use Webmail providers have Internet access from their employer, school, public library, home provider, or cellular phone service provider. Many public and school libraries provide free Internet access that you can use to access your Webmail account. This portability makes Webmail a valuable resource for people who travel or do not have a computer or other device on which to send and receive email.

You might wonder how these companies can provide free services such as Webmail—after all, nothing is free. The answer is advertising. When you use a Webmail provider or any Web-based service, you might see advertising, such as a banner ad on the page or links to services sponsored by businesses that pay to display their information on your screen, or insert their information into the email messages you send from your Webmail account. Users must decide whether they are willing to endure this level of advertising in exchange for using the service. Most users of these free services agree that seeing some ads is a small price to pay for the convenience the free services provide.

INSIGHT

Targeted Advertisements in Webmail

Webmail providers, such as Microsoft and Google, are largely supported by adding advertisements to email messages based on message content and other information provided by the user. Ads are added to the user's messages based on predefined keywords included in the messages. For example, when your email message includes a discussion about meeting friends for Chinese food later, ads for local Chinese restaurants—based on the zip code or other geographical information you provided when you created your account—might automatically appear in your message window.

Although there is no human intervention to produce these advertisements, some users have concerns about the privacy of the email messages they receive because they are scanned and read by computers. Some people do not like the idea of seeing advertisements based on the content of the messages they send and receive because they see it as an invasion of privacy. Gmail has made efforts to ensure that its advertising appears only as targeted text ads. This strategy is different from those of other Webmail providers that include untargeted advertising in the form of banners and pop-up windows, which some users find to be more invasive. Just like any other free service, it is up to users to determine the level of advertising they are willing to endure in exchange for the free service provided.

To begin using any Webmail provider, you need to use your Web browser to connect to the Webmail provider's Web site and create an account. In this session, you will create a Windows Live ID, which also serves as your Windows Live Hotmail email address, so you can send and receive messages using Windows Live Hotmail.

Creating a Windows Live ID

The steps in this session assume that you have a Web browser and can connect to the Internet. Before you can use Windows Live Hotmail, you need to create a Windows Live ID. If you have an existing Hotmail email address, you can use it as your Windows Live ID and skip the following steps, which ask you to create a Windows Live ID.

x

TIP

Detailed directions for accessing the Weblinks for this book are printed on the inside front cover of this book.

To create a Windows Live ID:

1. Start your Web browser, go to **www.cengagebrain.com**, open the Tutorial 2 Weblinks page, click the **Session 2.2** link, and then click the **Windows Live** link to open the Windows Live Sign In page, which will look similar to Figure 2-9.

Figure 2-9   Windows Live Sign In page

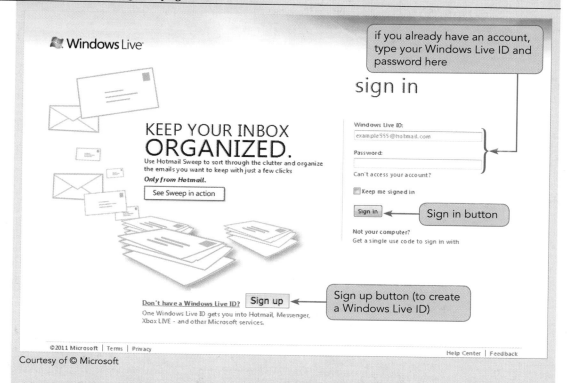

Courtesy of © Microsoft

Trouble? The Windows Live Sign In page and other Windows Live Hotmail pages might change over time. Check the Weblinks page for Tutorial 2 for notes about any differences you might encounter.

Trouble? If you already have a Windows Live ID, Windows Live Hotmail address, Messenger account, or Xbox LIVE account, use the "sign in" section to enter your user name and password, click the Sign in button, and then skip this set of steps.

2. Click the **Sign up** button. (If you do not see a Sign up button, Windows Live may have redesigned the Web site. Examine the page carefully until you find the button or tab that lets you create a Windows Live ID or Hotmail account.)

The Create your Hotmail account page shown in Figure 2-10 opens.

Figure 2-10	Create your Hotmail account page

Courtesy of © Microsoft

Trouble? The Create your Hotmail account page might change over time. If your page looks different, follow the on-screen instructions to create a Windows Live ID.

The first step in creating a Hotmail account is to create a **Windows Live ID** (Windows Live also calls this a sign-in name or a user name), which you will also use as your Windows Live Hotmail email address. A Windows Live ID can contain letters, numbers, or underscore characters (_), but it cannot contain any spaces. After creating a Windows Live ID, you must create a password containing letters and/or numbers, but no spaces. You type your password twice to ensure that you entered it correctly. Finally, to help remember your password in the event that you forget it, you enter a question and its secret answer so Windows Live can verify your identity in the future, as necessary.

3. Click in the **Hotmail address** box, and then type a user name, which you will use as your Windows Live ID and your Windows Live Hotmail address. Your user name must be unique. You can try typing your first and last names, separated by an underscore character, followed by your birth date or year of birth, such as sharon_kikukawa0616. A Windows Live ID can contain only letters, numbers, periods, hyphens, and underscores.

> **4.** If necessary, click the **arrow** on the box to the right of the Hotmail address box, and then click **hotmail.com**. (If the menu closes, click the arrow on the box to open the menu again.)

> **5.** Click in the **Create a password** box, and then type a password with at least six characters. The most effective passwords are ones that are not easily guessed and contain letters and numbers. As you type your password, dots or asterisks appear in the Create a password box to protect your password from being seen by other users. In addition, the Password strength indicator analyzes the password you typed to identify its strength. A weak password is one that contains only letters, such as "pencil." A stronger password includes letters and numbers, such as "pencil87." The strongest password is one that does not form a word and that includes mixed-case letters, numbers, and special characters, such as "p2nc1L%."

> **6.** Press the **Tab** key to move to the Retype password box, and then type your password again. Make sure to type the same password you typed in Step 5.

> **7.** Click in the **Alternate email address** box. If you have an existing email address, enter it in the Alternate email address box. This is the email address that Windows Live will use to send you your password in case you forget it.
>
> **Trouble?** If you don't have another email address, click the Or choose a security question for password reset link below the Alternate email address box, click the Question arrow that appears, select a question that you know the answer to, click in the Secret answer box, and then type the answer (using a minimum of five characters) to your question.

Now that you have entered a Windows Live ID and a password, you need to provide your account information.

To enter your account information:

> **1.** Click in the **First name** box, type your first name, press the **Tab** key to move to the Last name box, and then type your last name. Your first and last names will appear in all email messages that you send.

> **2.** If necessary, click the **Country/region** arrow, and then click the country or region where you live.

> **3.** If necessary, click in the **ZIP code** (or **Postal Code**) box, and then type your zip code or postal code. Windows Live will use this information to provide you with additional services, such as local weather forecasts, that you might request in the future.

> **4.** Click the appropriate option button in the Gender section to indicate your gender.

> **5.** Click in the **Birth date Month** box, click your birth month in the list, click in the **Birth date Day** box, click your birth day from the list, click in the **Birth date Year** box, and then click the four-digit year of your birth.

The last part of creating a Windows Live ID is to verify that you are a person and not an automated program, and also to read and accept the agreements that govern the use of a Windows Live ID account.

To finish creating a Windows Live ID:

1. Scroll down the page as necessary so you see characters in a box. Many Web sites use a collection of characters, called a **CAPTCHA** and shown in Figure 2-11, as a way of verifying that a person is using the form to create an account instead of a computer. Created by professors at Carnegie Mellon University, CAPTCHA stands for "Completely Automated Public Turing test to tell Computers and Humans Apart."

Figure 2-11	Required character entry to prevent abuse

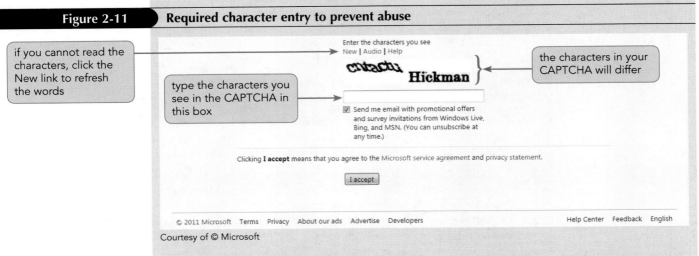

Courtesy of © Microsoft

Trouble? If you can't read the characters in the box, click the New link above the box to display a different collection of characters.

2. Click in the box, and then type the characters you see above it on the page. Be sure to type the characters shown on your screen; do not type the characters you see in Figure 2-11.

3. If you do not want to receive any emails with promotional offers, clear the check box that appears below the box in which you typed the characters.

4. Read the agreements, which appear as hyperlinks in the last paragraph on the page. After reading these agreements, click the **I accept** button. Your registration is complete when the page shown in Figure 2-12 (or a similar page) opens.

Figure 2-12	Windows Live Hotmail page

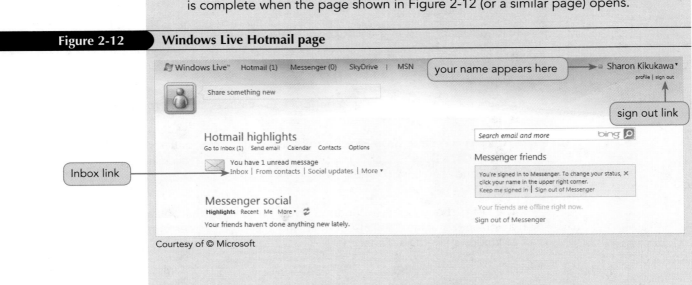

Courtesy of © Microsoft

Trouble? Windows Live might redesign its Web site, in which case your screen might not match the one shown in Figure 2-12.

Trouble? After clicking the I accept button, a page similar to the one shown in Figure 2-13 will appear if the user name you selected is already in use. Select the text in the Hotmail address box, type a new user name, repeat Steps 1 and 2, and then click the I accept button until you find a valid user name and see the page shown in Figure 2-12.

| Figure 2-13 | Message that appears when a user name is taken |

message indicating the user name you selected isn't available

Courtesy of © Microsoft

Now that you have created a Windows Live ID, Windows Live opens the Inbox for your Windows Live Hotmail address. So that you can practice signing in to your Windows Live account, you'll sign out. Signing out closes your account and logs you out of the system. You should always sign out of your account when you have finished working so that other users cannot access your email or send messages using your email address.

To sign out of your account:

1. In the upper-right corner of the page and below your name, click the **sign out** link. The MSN home page (or another page) appears in your browser.

2. Return to the Weblinks page for Tutorial 2, and then click the **Windows Live** link. The Windows Live Sign In page opens.

Accessing Your Windows Live Account

TIP

When choosing a sign-in method, select the one that provides the most security based on the level of privacy you expect to have on your computer.

Depending on your browser configuration, you might see your Windows Live Hotmail address in the Windows Live ID box on the Windows Live Sign In page. If you see your Windows Live Hotmail address, you can enter your password and then click the Sign in button to sign in to your Windows Live account. If you will be accessing your Windows Live account from your own computer, you might decide to click the Keep me signed in check box to select this option, so you won't need to enter your login information in the future. This option presents a security risk because other users with access to your computer can sign in to your account when they open the Windows Live Sign In page.

If you are having problems logging in to your account, you can enter your Windows Live ID and then click the Can't access your account? link to identify the problem you're having. The site will provide a method to correct the problem, which might involve asking you to answer the question you specified when you created your account, or sending information or instructions for resetting your password to your alternate email address, if you specified one.

Next, you'll sign in to your Windows Live account and open your Inbox.

To sign in to your Windows Live account:

1. If necessary, enter your Hotmail email address (your user name, the @ sign, plus hotmail.com) in the Windows Live ID box, type your password in the Password box, click the **Sign in** button, and then, if necessary, click the **Inbox** link to open your Hotmail Inbox, as shown in Figure 2-14. If you just created your Hotmail account, you might see one new message from the Hotmail Team, welcoming you to the service. (You might see other messages, as well.) You also might see an advertisement on the right side of the page.

| Figure 2-14 | Windows Live Hotmail Inbox |

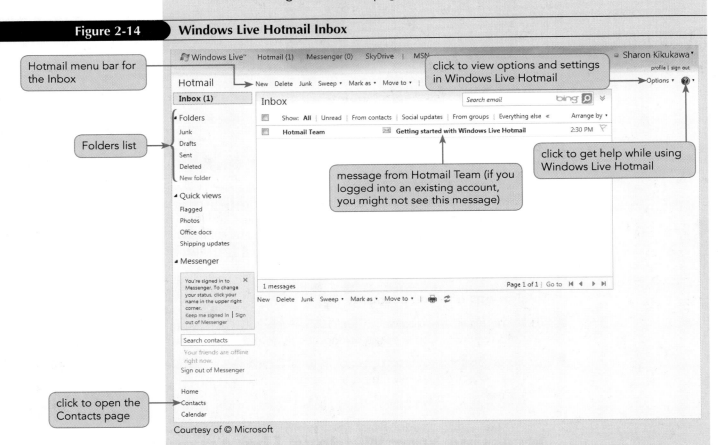

Courtesy of © Microsoft

Trouble? If you receive a message that your Windows Live ID or password is not found, clear the Windows Live ID and Password boxes, and then reenter your information. If you are still having problems, click the Can't access your account? link and follow the on-screen instructions. If you are still having problems, ask your instructor or technical support person for help.

Figure 2-14 displays the Home, Contacts, and Calendar links in the lower-left corner of the page. Clicking the Home link opens the home page that you see when you log in to your Windows Live Hotmail account. Clicking the Contacts link opens the **Contacts page**, which contains options for managing information about your contacts. Clicking the Calendar link opens the **Calendar page**, which contains options for organizing your scheduled appointments and daily calendar using **Windows Live Calendar**, another Windows Live service.

2. In the Inbox, click the subject for the message you received from the Hotmail Team (or any other message in your Inbox) to open the message. Depending on your browser's security settings, you might see advertisements when you view your email messages. See Figure 2-15.

Figure 2-15	**Message from Hotmail Team**

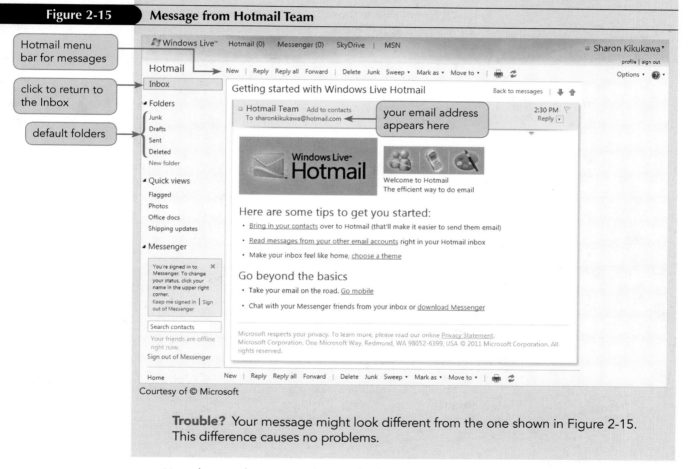

Hotmail menu bar for messages

click to return to the Inbox

default folders

your email address appears here

Courtesy of © Microsoft

Trouble? Your message might look different from the one shown in Figure 2-15. This difference causes no problems.

Now that you have created a Windows Live ID and a Hotmail email address, you are ready to send a message to Don.

Sending a Message Using Windows Live Hotmail

To send a message in Windows Live Hotmail, click the New link on the Hotmail menu bar, which opens the New Message page. The New Message page contains the message header and a place to type your message.

REFERENCE

Sending a Message Using Windows Live Hotmail

- On the Hotmail menu bar, click the New link to open the New Message page.
- In the To box in the message header, type the recipient's email address. To send the message to more than one recipient, use commas or semicolons to separate multiple email addresses.
- If you need to address the message to Cc and Bcc recipients, click the Show Cc & Bcc link on the right side of the message header, and then type the email address of any Cc or Bcc recipients in the appropriate boxes. Use commas or semicolons to separate multiple email addresses.
- If necessary, click the Attachments link in the message header, browse to and select the file to attach, and then click the Open button.
- Click in the message body, and then type your message.
- Check your message for spelling and grammatical errors.
- Click the Send link on the Hotmail menu bar.

When you use Windows Live Hotmail to send a message with an attached file to Don, you will also send a courtesy copy of the message to your own email address to simulate receiving a message.

To create a message with an attachment:

1. On the Hotmail menu bar, click the **New** link. The New Message page opens, and the insertion point appears in the To box in the message header. See Figure 2-16.

   Trouble? If you don't have the starting Data Files, you need to get them before you can proceed. Your instructor will either give you the Data Files or ask you to obtain them from a specified location (such as a network drive). In either case, make a backup copy of the Data Files before you start so that you will have the original files available in case you need to start over. If you have any questions about the Data Files, see your instructor or technical support person for assistance.

| Figure 2-16 | Creating a new message |

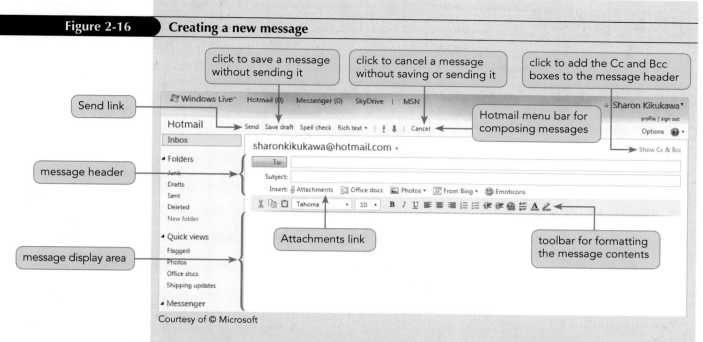

Courtesy of © Microsoft

Trouble? Your screen might look slightly different, depending on your computer's operating system, the browser you are using, and future changes to the site. These differences should not affect how Windows Live Hotmail functions.

2. In the To box, type **Don@KikukawaAir.com**.

Trouble? Make sure that you use the address Don@KikukawaAir.com or its lowercase equivalent, don@kikukawaair.com. If you type an email address incorrectly, your message will be returned as undeliverable.

3. In the upper-right corner of the message header, click the **Show Cc & Bcc** link to add the Cc and Bcc boxes to the message header.

4. Click in the **Cc** box, and then type your full email address. When you send this message, you and Don will both receive it.

Trouble? If you make a typing mistake on a previous line, use the arrow keys or click the insertion point to return to a previous line so you can correct your mistake. If the arrow keys do not move the insertion point backward or forward in the message header, press Shift + Tab or the Tab key to move backward or forward, respectively.

5. Click in the **Subject** box, and then type **Saturday's festival timeline**.

6. Click the **Attachments** link below the Subject box. The Open dialog box opens.

7. Navigate to the Tutorial.02\Tutorial folder provided with your Data Files, click **Timeline**, and then click the **Open** button. The message header now displays the attached file's name.

TIP

As you begin typing your email address, Windows Live Hotmail might open a menu with your complete email address in it. Pressing the Enter key adds the full email address to the Cc box and closes the menu.

Written Communication: Guidelines for Business Correspondence

Nearly all employees have some writing responsibility to communicate with colleagues, customers, and clients. Many corporate recruiters report that basic communication skills are one of the key items they assess when evaluating job candidates. A prospective employee's first contact with a company is often written and includes a cover letter and a résumé, sometimes submitted as an email message. A person's written communication skills are often a strong indicator of the type of employee that person might turn out to be.

Most busi ness professionals are busy and will only take time to read what is important and relevant to them at that point in time, especially when reading email. This means you must be succinct and to the point when composing email messages. When it comes to written precision, there are a few basic principles that will make your documents more polished. Because email messages are usually short and written quickly, it is easy to introduce grammatical mistakes that are more commonly found in oral communication, because the writer is "talking" while composing the message. The following guidelines will help you revise your messages to be grammatically correct:

- Avoid subject and verb disagreement. Pronouns must agree with the words they refer to in person, number, or gender.
- Don't change verb tenses within a sentence, paragraph, or written composition.
- Be sure to rewrite any run-on, incomplete, or unclear sentences.

Remember that the placement of commas, periods, apostrophes, and other punctuation marks can affect how the reader interprets your message. Before sending a message, verify that your punctuation is correct in the following situations:

- Use apostrophes to show possession ("The group's decision is to promote Gretchen.") or to indicate a contraction ("It's the best restaurant in town.").
- Do not use an apostrophe for plural nouns (DVDs, CDs), to reference a time period or numbers (the 1980s, "She is in her 20s."), or with possessive pronouns (yours, ours, hers, its).
- Use a colon to introduce a list of items or an explanation ("Campers should bring the following items: flashlight, sleeping bag, insect repellent, and water bottle."), in business letter salutations ("Dear Mrs. Robinson:"), and to maximize the impact of a word or phrase that follows ("There is only one word to describe the event: magnificent.").
- Use a comma to indicate a brief pause in a sentence, or to join or separate sentence parts. Use a comma before "and" in a list or series ("Steven, Hannah, and Annie went to the beach."), between two or more adjectives that describe a noun ("Please bring a new, unused gift for the toy drive."), to separate an introductory phrase or word ("However, the team won."), to separate clauses that won't change the meaning of a sentence if they are omitted ("The airport, which is located 30 miles south of town, has off-site parking."), between names and titles or degrees (John F. Kennedy, Jr. or Susan Marino, Ph.D.), and inside a quotation mark in a sentence ("I'll be there soon," replied Juan.).
- Use a period in certain abbreviations (J.D., Jr., Mrs.) or to end a sentence. If a sentence ends with an abbreviation that ends in a period, no additional period is needed. When a sentence ends with a quote, the period goes inside the quotation mark.
- Use a semicolon to join independent, closely related thoughts ("My favorite activity is reading; I read at least three books a week.").

You can learn more about business correspondence by following the links in the Business Writing section on the Weblinks page for Tutorial 2.

Next, you will type, proofread, and send a brief message to Don.

To type, proofread, and send the message:

1. Click in the message display area, type **Dear Don,** (including the comma), and then press the **Enter** key twice to insert a blank line.

2. In the message display area, type **I have attached the timeline for Saturday's events. If I receive any additional information, I will send it to you right away.**

3. Press the **Enter** key twice, type **Best,** (including the comma), press the **Enter** key, and then type your first name to sign your message. See Figure 2-17.

Figure 2-17	Completed message

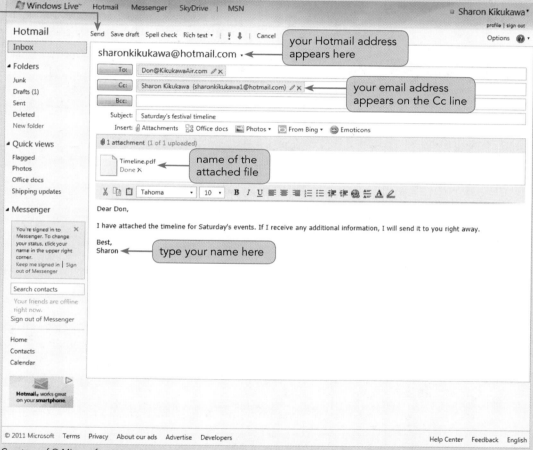

Courtesy of © Microsoft

Before sending your message, you can click the Spell check link on the Hotmail menu bar to check the message for spelling errors. Misspelled words and words not in the dictionary (such as proper names) will appear with a red, wavy underline. When you right-click one of these words, you have the choice of selecting a word from a menu, ignoring the word, or adding it to the dictionary. If you don't see the correct word in the menu, you can correct the misspelled word directly.

4. Click the **Spell check** link on the Hotmail menu bar, review your message for typing or grammatical errors, and, if necessary, correct any errors.

TIP

Even when you use the spell checker to find spelling errors, it is still important to proofread your message and make any necessary corrections before sending it.

Trouble? If you are using Firefox, a dialog box might open and tell you that the browser is checking the spelling automatically. Click the OK button, and then check the message for spelling errors by looking for words with red, wavy lines under them. Make any necessary corrections, and then continue with Step 5.

Trouble? Google Chrome doesn't include a Spell check link. Check your message for spelling and grammatical errors, and then continue with Step 5.

5. Click the **Send** link on the Hotmail menu bar to send the message. A message confirmation page opens and shows that your message has been sent. See Figure 2-18.

Trouble? If you see a yellow message bar asking you to enter characters to stop spammers, click the "enter characters before sending your message" link on the yellow message bar, enter the characters shown on the Help us fight junk email page that opens, click the Continue button, and then close the tab to return to your message. Repeat Step 5 to send the message.

| Figure 2-18 | Message confirmation page |

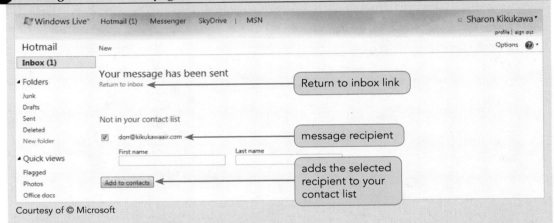

Courtesy of © Microsoft

If the email addresses you include in your messages are not already saved in your contact list, Windows Live Hotmail provides an option on this page for you to add new contacts to your contact list by selecting the email address and clicking the Add to contacts button. If the contact already exists, you'll see an "Already a contact" note. You will add contacts to your contact list later, so no action is necessary now.

Next, you'll return to the Inbox, which checks for new email messages.

Receiving and Opening a Message

When you receive new email messages, messages that you have not opened are displayed in the Inbox with closed envelope icons, and messages that you have opened are displayed with open envelope icons. You will check for new mail next.

To check for new mail:

1. Click the **Return to inbox** link. The Saturday's festival timeline message appears in the Inbox.

   Trouble? If you don't see the message, click the Inbox link on the left side of the page. It might take a few seconds for the message to arrive.

   Because you haven't read this message yet, it appears in bold in the message list. After you read the message, it will appear in a normal font. To read a message, you click its sender or subject.

2. Click the **Saturday's festival timeline** subject in the message. The message opens and displays the message header and content. See Figure 2-19.

Figure 2-19	Message received

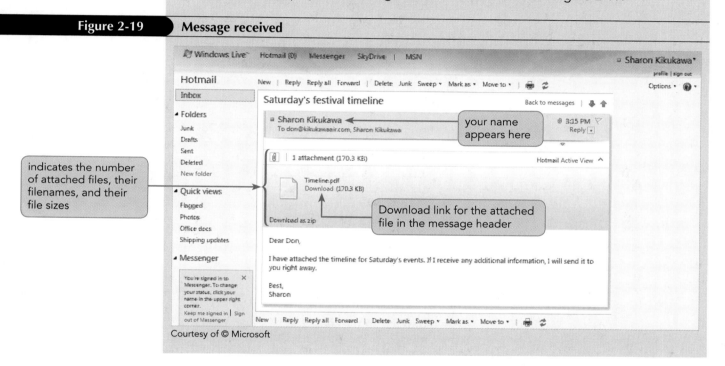

indicates the number of attached files, their filenames, and their file sizes

your name appears here

Download link for the attached file in the message header

Courtesy of © Microsoft

Viewing and Saving an Attached File

If a message includes an attachment, the attachment information appears in the message header. When you receive a message with one or more attachments, you can open the attachment or save it.

REFERENCE

Viewing and Saving an Attached File in Windows Live Hotmail

- In the Inbox, click the message that contains the attachment.
- To open the file using a program on your computer, click the attached file's Download link in the message header, and then click the Open button on the message bar in Internet Explorer. If you are using Firefox, click the Open with option button, choose the program to use to open the file, and then click the OK button. If you are using Chrome, click the Keep button on the message bar at the bottom of the screen, and then click the Timeline.pdf button to open the file.
- To save the file using Internet Explorer, click the attached file's Download link in the message header, click the Save button arrow on the message bar, click Save as to open the Save As dialog box, browse to the drive and folder where you want to save the attached file, click the Save button, and then click the Close button on the message bar.
- To save the file using Firefox, click the attached file's Download link in the message header, click the Save File option button in the dialog box that opens, and then click the OK button. Depending on your browser's settings, you might also need to specify the location in which to save the file; otherwise, the file will be saved automatically in the Downloads folder. Click the Close button if necessary to close the Downloads window.
- To save the file using Chrome, click the attached file's Download link in the message header, click the Show all downloads link on the right side of the message bar at the bottom of the screen, click the Show in folder link for the attachment that you want to save, and then move the file in the Downloads folder to the folder in which you want to save it.

You want to make sure that your attached file was sent properly, so you decide to open it. Then you will save the file.

To view and save the attached file:

1. Click the **Download** link in the message header. The message bar opens at the bottom of the browser window and asks if you want to open or save the file, or cancel the operation.

   Trouble? If you are using Firefox, the dialog box that opens is named Opening Timeline.pdf. Click the Open with option button in the Opening Timeline.pdf dialog box, click the OK button, and then continue with Step 3.

   Trouble? If you are using Chrome, click the Keep button on the message bar at the bottom of the screen, click the Timeline.pdf button, and then continue with Step 3.

2. Click the **Open** button. Adobe Reader or another program on your computer starts and opens the attached file. If necessary, maximize the program window that opens.

3. Review the page, and then click the **Close** button on the program window's title bar to close the program window that opened the attachment. Now that you have viewed the attachment, you can save it.

   Trouble? If a Downloads dialog box is open, click the Close button on its title bar to close it.

▶ **4.** Click the **Download** link in the Attachment section, click the **Save button arrow** on the message bar at the bottom of the browser window to open a menu, click **Save as**, navigate to the **Tutorial.02\Tutorial** folder provided with your Data Files, click the **Save** button, and then click the **Yes** button to replace the existing file with the same name.

Trouble? If you are using Firefox, the Opening Timeline.pdf dialog box opens. Click the Save File option button, and then click the OK button. Depending on your browser settings, you might need to specify a location in which to save the file. In this case, browse to and select the Tutorial.02\Tutorial folder, click the Save button, click the Yes button to overwrite the existing file with the same name, and then skip Step 5. If you don't need to specify a file location, click the Close button on the Downloads dialog box to close it.

▶ **5.** If you are using Internet Explorer, click the **Close** button on the message bar at the bottom of the window to close it.

When you receive a message with an attached file, you can view and save the attachment for as long as you store the message. When you delete the message, you delete the file attached to the message. When you detach a file from an email message and save it on a disk or drive, it is just like any other file that you save. Be sure to save any important attachments soon after receiving them so you do not inadvertently delete the messages containing them.

Replying to and Forwarding Messages

Replying to and forwarding messages are common tasks for email users. You can forward any message you receive to one or more email addresses. Similarly, you can respond to the sender of a message quickly and efficiently by replying to a message.

Replying to an Email Message

To reply to a message, click the Reply link on the Hotmail menu bar to reply only to the sender, or click the Reply all link on the Hotmail menu bar to reply to the sender and other people who received the original message (all email addresses listed in the To and Cc boxes). Windows Live Hotmail opens a reply message page and places the original sender's address in the To box; other email addresses that received the original message appear in the To and Cc boxes as appropriate. You can leave the Subject box as is or modify it. Most programs, including Windows Live Hotmail, copy the original message and place it in the reply window. Figure 2-20 shows a reply to a message.

Figure 2-20	**Replying to a message**

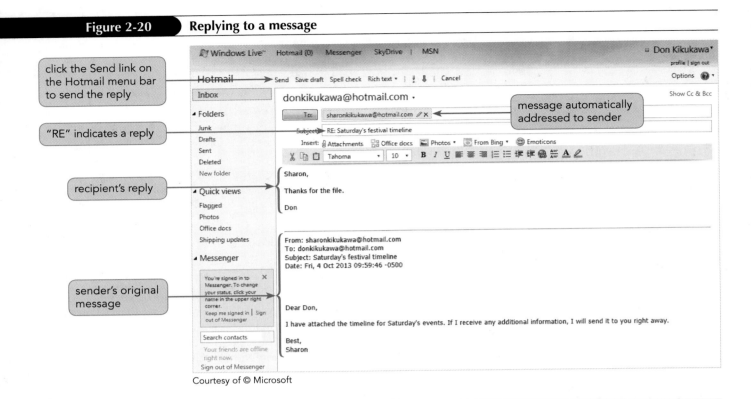

click the Send link on the Hotmail menu bar to send the reply

"RE" indicates a reply

recipient's reply

sender's original message

message automatically addressed to sender

Courtesy of © Microsoft

Replying to a Message Using Windows Live Hotmail

REFERENCE

- Open the message you want to reply to.
- Click the Reply link on the Hotmail menu bar to reply to the sender, or click the Reply all link on the Hotmail menu bar to reply to the sender and other To and Cc recipients of the original message.
- Type other recipients' email addresses in the message header as needed.
- Change the text in the Subject box if necessary.
- Edit the message body as necessary.
- Click the Send link on the Hotmail menu bar.

Forwarding an Email Message

When you forward a message, you are sending a copy of the message, including any attachments, to one or more recipients who were not included in the original message. (If you do not want to forward the original sender's attached file to the new recipients, click the Close button next to the name of the attached file in the message header to remove it from the message.) To forward an existing mail message to another user, open the message you want to forward, and then click the Forward link on the Hotmail menu bar. A Forward message page opens, in which you can type the address of the recipient in the To box. If you want to forward the message to several people, type their addresses, separated by commas, in the To box (or Cc or Bcc boxes). Windows Live Hotmail includes the original message in the message display area and adds a blank line above it so you can add an optional message to provide context for the recipient. Figure 2-21 shows a forwarded copy of a message.

Figure 2-21   **Forwarding a message**

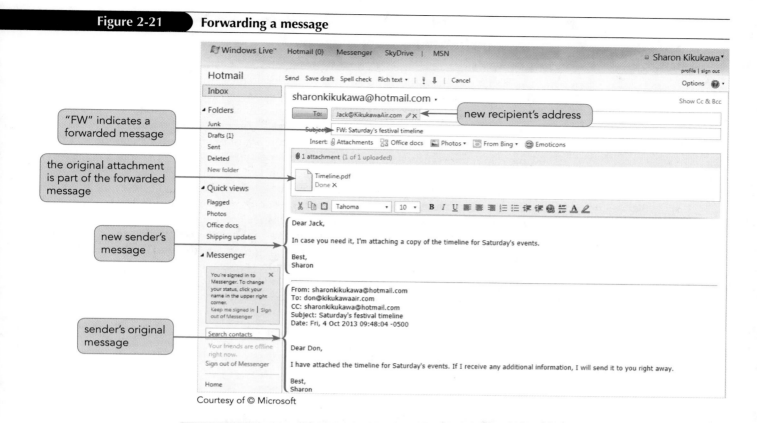

"FW" indicates a forwarded message

the original attachment is part of the forwarded message

new sender's message

sender's original message

new recipient's address

Courtesy of © Microsoft

Forwarding an Email Message Using Windows Live Hotmail

REFERENCE

- Open the message that you want to forward.
- Click the Forward link on the Hotmail menu bar.
- Click the To box, and then type one or more email addresses, separated by commas. Add Cc and Bcc email addresses as necessary.
- Click the blank line above the quoted message, and then type an optional message to add context for the recipient(s).
- Click the Send link on the Hotmail menu bar.

INSIGHT

Forwarding Messages Appropriately

When forwarding a message to a new recipient, and especially when forwarding a message that was forwarded originally to you, keep in mind that a forwarded message includes the email addresses of all the message's previous recipients and senders. When you need to forward a message to a new recipient and it's not important for the new recipient to know who sent you the original message, you can use the Copy and Paste commands in your email program to paste the content of the forwarded message into a new message, thus protecting the privacy of the message's original recipients and making the message easier to read for its new recipients.

Some people routinely send information about Internet viruses and hoaxes, or about emotional or charitable causes, such as cancer research, to everyone they know in an attempt to "spread the word." Often, these messages contain incorrect information. Before being alarmed by information about viruses or hoaxes, contributing to any charity that you learn about in this way, or forwarding the message to other users, be sure to check one of the many reputable Internet resources for more information. The Email Hoaxes and Rumors section of the Weblinks page for Tutorial 2 contains links to sites that contain information about viruses, hoaxes, and fraudulent schemes.

Occasionally, Don receives messages he wants to keep for later reference. In Windows Live Hotmail, you can file email messages so you can refer to them later or print them as needed.

Filing and Printing an Email Message

You can use the Windows Live Hotmail folders to file your email messages by category. When you file a message, you move it from the Inbox to a folder. You will file your message in a new folder named "Festivals" for safekeeping.

To create the new folder:

1. Click the **Inbox** link, and then click the **New folder** link in the Folders list on the left side of the page. The New folder page opens, and the insertion point appears in the Folder name box. See Figure 2-22.

Figure 2-22	Creating a new folder

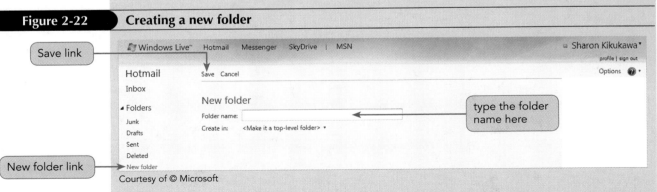

Courtesy of © Microsoft

2. With the insertion point in the Folder name box, type **Festivals**.

> **3.** Click the **Save** link on the Hotmail menu bar. The page changes to show the list of folders and details about the folders' contents. The Festivals folder appears in the list of folders.

After you create a folder, you can transfer messages to it. Besides transferring messages from the Inbox, you can select messages in any other folder and then transfer them to a different folder. You will move the Saturday's festival timeline message from the Inbox to the newly created Festivals folder.

To file a message in the Festivals folder:

> **1.** Click the **Inbox** link.

> **2.** Click the **check box** to the left of the Saturday's festival timeline message to add a check mark to it.

> **3.** Click the **Move to** link on the Hotmail menu bar to open a list of folders, and then click **Festivals** in the list. The message is transferred to the Festivals folder.

> **4.** Click the **Festivals** link in the Folders list on the left side of the page. The message appears in the **Festivals** folder.

You might want to print certain messages for future reference. You can print a message at any time—when you receive it, before you send it, or after you file it. You will print the Saturday's festival timeline message next.

To print the email message:

> **1.** Click the subject for the **Saturday's festival timeline** message to open it.

> **2.** Click the **Print** button on the Hotmail menu bar. A new window opens and displays a "printer-friendly" version of the message, and the Print dialog box opens.

> **3.** If necessary, select your printer in the list, and then click the **Print** button (or the **OK** button). The message is printed.

> **4.** Close the window with the printer-friendly version of the message, and then click the **Inbox** link.

TIP

A "printer-friendly" version of a message excludes ads and other content on the page, such as links.

When you no longer need a message, you can delete it.

Deleting a Message and a Folder

When you don't need a message any longer, you can delete it by opening the message or selecting the message in the Inbox, and then clicking the Delete link on the Hotmail menu bar. You can delete a folder by selecting it and then clicking the Delete link on the Hotmail menu bar. When you delete a message or folder, you are simply moving it to the Deleted folder. The default setting for Windows Live Hotmail accounts is for the system to delete all messages in the Deleted folder periodically. However, if you want to remove items permanently, you can delete them from the Deleted folder.

REFERENCE

Deleting a Message in Windows Live Hotmail

- Open the folder that contains the message you want to delete.
- Click the check box to the left of the message you want to delete to add a check mark to it, and then click the Delete link on the Hotmail menu bar.
- To delete items permanently, click the Deleted link in the Folders list on the left side of the page, click the Delete link or the Empty link on the Hotmail menu bar, and then, if necessary, click the OK button.

Now you will delete the Saturday's festival timeline message.

To delete the message:

1. Click the **Festivals** link in the Folders list on the left side of the page.

2. Click the **check box** that appears to the left of the Saturday's festival timeline message to add a check mark to it and select the message.

3. Click the **Delete** link on the Hotmail menu bar. The message is deleted from the Festivals folder and is moved to the Deleted folder.

4. Click the **Deleted** link in the Folders list on the left side of the page. The Saturday's festival timeline message appears in the folder.

5. Click the **check box** to the left of the Saturday's festival timeline message to add a check mark to it, and then click the **Delete** link on the Hotmail menu bar. The message is permanently deleted from your Windows Live Hotmail account.

You will delete the Festivals folder using the Manage folders link.

REFERENCE

Deleting a Windows Live Hotmail Folder

- Point to Folders on the left side of the page to display the More actions for folders button, click the More actions for folders button to open a menu of options, and then click Manage folders to open a page showing the folders for your account and the details of each folder's contents.
- Click the check box to the left of the folder you want to delete.
- Click the Delete link on the Hotmail menu bar.
- Click the OK button.

Windows Live Hotmail won't let you delete the default system folders, but you can delete folders that you created. You'll delete the Festivals folder next.

To delete the Festivals folder:

1. Point to the **Folders** link on the left side of the page to display the More actions for folders button to the right of the word "Folders."

2. Click the **More actions for folders** button to open a menu of options, and then click **Manage folders**. A page opens and displays the folders in your Windows Live Hotmail account, along with the number of messages in each folder and their combined file sizes.

3. Click the **check box** to the left of the **Festivals** folder to select it.

4. Click the **Delete** link on the Hotmail menu bar. A dialog box opens and warns that deleting the folder also deletes any messages stored in the folder.

5. Click the **OK** button. The Festivals folder is deleted.

6. Click the **Inbox** link.

Maintaining Your Contact List

As you use email to communicate with business associates and friends, you might want to save their contact information in your contact list to make it easier to enter addresses into the header of your email messages.

Adding a Contact to the Contact List

You can open your contact list by clicking the Contacts link on the left side of the page. To create a new contact, click the New link on the Hotmail menu bar, and then enter the contact's information in the appropriate boxes.

REFERENCE

Adding a Contact to the Contact List

- Click the Contacts link to open the All contacts page.
- Click the New link on the Hotmail menu bar to open the New contact page.
- Enter the contact's information in the appropriate boxes on the New contact page.
- Click the Save link on the Hotmail menu bar.

Now you can add contacts to your contact list. You begin by adding Jack Clancy's contact information.

To add a contact to your contact list:

1. On the left side of the page, click the **Contacts** link (you might need to scroll down the page to see this link). The All contacts page opens.

2. Click the **New** link on the Hotmail menu bar. The New contact page opens and displays boxes for entering a contact's first name, last name, nickname, personal email address, Windows Live ID, and other information.

3. Click in the **First name** box, and then type **Jack**.

4. Press the **Tab** key to move the insertion point to the Last name box, and then type **Clancy** in the Last name box.

5. Scroll down the page to the Work info section, click in the **Work email** box, and then type **Jack@KikukawaAir.com**. See Figure 2-23.

Figure 2-23 **Adding a contact to the contact list**

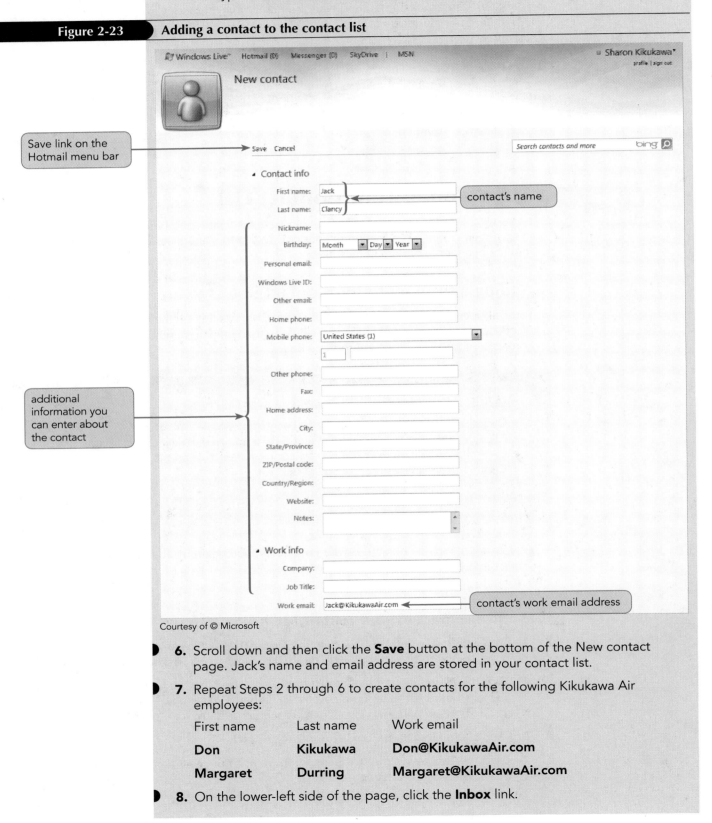

Courtesy of © Microsoft

6. Scroll down and then click the **Save** button at the bottom of the New contact page. Jack's name and email address are stored in your contact list.

7. Repeat Steps 2 through 6 to create contacts for the following Kikukawa Air employees:

First name	Last name	Work email
Don	**Kikukawa**	**Don@KikukawaAir.com**
Margaret	**Durring**	**Margaret@KikukawaAir.com**

8. On the lower-left side of the page, click the **Inbox** link.

Now that you have stored the names and email addresses for Jack, Don, and Margaret in your contact list, you can click the To, Cc, or Bcc button that appears to the left of a To, Cc, or Bcc box in a new message, and then click one of their names in the contact list to enter that person's email address in the message header.

Creating a Category

You can create a group of contacts, called a category or distribution list, and use the category to address messages to a group of recipients. For example, Sharon frequently sends messages to Jack, Don, and Margaret as a group because they work as a team when participating in hot air balloon festivals and racing events. You will create a category in your contact list so you can type one nickname for the group of email addresses, instead of having to type each address separately.

REFERENCE

Creating a Category in the Contact List

- Click the Contacts link on the left side of the page to open the All contacts page.
- Click the Categories link on the Hotmail menu bar, and then click New category to open the New category page.
- Type a name for the category in the Name box.
- Click in the Members box, and then type the names of existing contacts to add to the category or the email addresses of contacts who are not in your contact list.
- Click the Save link on the Hotmail menu bar.

You'll create a category next.

To create a category in your contact list:

1. If necessary, scroll down the page, and then click the **Contacts** link to open the All contacts page.

2. Click the **Categories** link on the Hotmail menu bar to open a menu of options, and then click **New category**. The New category page opens. The insertion point appears in the Name box.

3. In the Name box, type **Race Team**.

4. Click in the **Members** box, and then type **Jack**. As you type Jack's first name, his name appears in a box that opens. Press the **Enter** key to add Jack's name to the category.

5. With the insertion point in the Members box, type **Don**. When Don's name appears in the box, press the **Enter** key to add Don's name to the category.

6. With the insertion point in the Members box, type **Margaret**. When Margaret's name appears in the box, press the **Enter** key to add Margaret's name to the category. The category contains three contacts. See Figure 2-24.

TIP

To remove a contact from the category, click the Close button on the contact name.

Figure 2-24 **Category added to contact list**

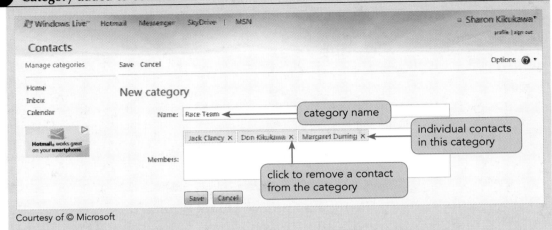

Courtesy of © Microsoft

▶ **7.** Click the **Save** link on the Hotmail menu bar to save the category.

Now, you will test the category by creating a new message.

To address a message to a category:

▶ **1.** Click the **Inbox** link, which appears on the left side of the page, and then click the **New** link on the Hotmail menu bar to open the New message page.

▶ **2.** Click the **To** button to the left of the To box. A pop-up window opens and displays your individual contacts on the People tab. To see the Race Team category, you need to display the Categories tab.

▶ **3.** Click the **Categories** tab. The Race Team category appears in the list. The notation "3 people" indicates the number of individual contacts stored in the category.

▶ **4.** Click the **check box** to the left of the Race Team category to add a check mark to it. The Race Team category name is added to the To box. The pop-up window stays open until you close it, so you can add additional recipients to the message if necessary.

▶ **5.** Click the **Close** link on the pop-up window to close it. The Race Team category appears in the To box.

▶ **6.** Click the **Show Cc & Bcc** link to add the Cc and Bcc boxes to the message header.

▶ **7.** Click the **Cc** button in the message header, click the **People** tab, click the **check box** for your email address, and then click the **Close** link. Your email address is added to the Cc box. See Figure 2-25.

TIP

Clicking the plus sign to the left of a category in the To box displays the individual email addresses in the category so you can delete a receipient or confirm the recipients by name.

Figure 2-25   **Using the contact list to address a message**

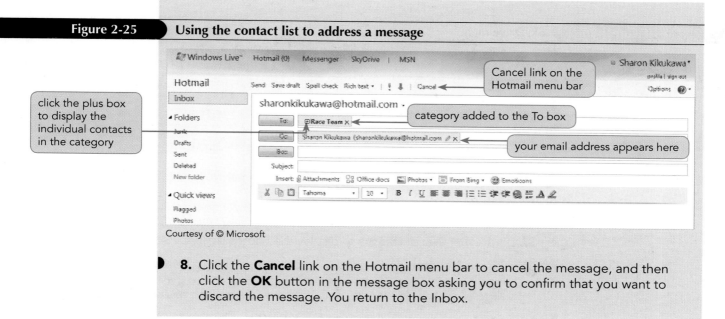

click the plus box to display the individual contacts in the category

Cancel link on the Hotmail menu bar

category added to the To box

your email address appears here

Courtesy of © Microsoft

> **8.** Click the **Cancel** link on the Hotmail menu bar to cancel the message, and then click the **OK** button in the message box asking you to confirm that you want to discard the message. You return to the Inbox.

When you need to modify a category's contacts, you can do so by clicking the Contacts link on the left side of the page, clicking the Manage categories link on the left side of the page, and then clicking the category's name on the Manage categories page to add or remove individual contacts in the category, or edit the category name. To delete the category (but not the individual contacts), select the check box for the category on the Manage categories page, click the Delete link on the Hotmail menu bar, and then click the OK button. Deleting a category does not delete the individual contacts it stores; it only deletes the category.

Using SkyDrive to Share Files

In this session, you learned how to use email to send and receive messages with files attached to them. When you need to send multiple files or large files to other users, it is often impractical to attach them to an email message because your mail server or the recipient's mail server might reject the message due to the number or size of its attachments. In other cases, you might need to collaborate on a document, workbook, or other file with multiple users, or simply share the content of a document with multiple users. In these situations, you can use another Windows Live service, called **SkyDrive**, to post your files to a server and then use your Windows Live Hotmail account to share access to these files with users that you specify.

Sharon might want to post pictures of balloon races or tours using her Windows Live account, so she asks you to explore the options for posting photos on SkyDrive.

To view the SkyDrive options for sharing photos:

> **1.** At the top of the page, click the **SkyDrive** link. The SkyDrive page opens.

> **2.** Point to the **SkyDrive** link at the top of the page to open a menu. See Figure 2-26. The menu includes options for sharing existing files and photos with other users. You can also use the "New" links to create a new Word document, Excel workbook, PowerPoint presentation, or OneNote notebook and store it in your SkyDrive account.

Figure 2-26

SkyDrive menu

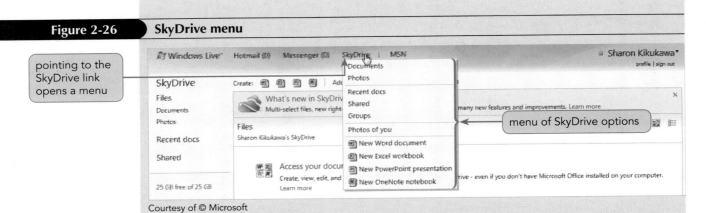

pointing to the
SkyDrive link
opens a menu

menu of SkyDrive options

Courtesy of © Microsoft

3. On the menu, click **Photos** to display the Photos page for SkyDrive.

4. Click the **New folder** link on the SkyDrive menu bar to create a new photo album folder. You can assign a name to the album and change the settings to control how to share the album. The default folder (album) name is selected.

5. Type **My photos** and then press the **Enter** key. The folder name is updated.

6. Click the **My photos** folder to select it, and then click the **Add files** link on the SkyDrive menu bar. A window opens and includes a link to add files to the folder. Clicking the "select them from your computer" link opens the Open dialog box, where you can browse to and select one or more photos to upload. (You will not upload any photos at this time.)

7. Click the **Close** button on the Add files window to close it.

8. On the right side of the page, click the **Share folder** link to display the options for sharing your photos. Notice that you can choose to restrict access to your photos by sharing them only with people you specify using their email addresses. You can also choose to restrict who can edit your photos or require people to log in before viewing your photos.

9. Click the **Close** button to close the Share box.

10. Click the **SkyDrive** link near the top of the page to return to the SkyDrive page.

Sharon might also like to use SkyDrive to create and post files, such as Word documents and Excel workbooks, to make it easy for employees to access and collaborate on their work. She asks you to explore the feature that lets you create a file next.

To view the SkyDrive options for creating a file:

1. At the top of the page, point to the **SkyDrive** link. The SkyDrive menu opens.

2. On the menu, click **New Excel workbook**. The New Microsoft Excel workbook window opens.

3. Click the **Create** button to accept the default filename, Book1, for the file. The Microsoft Excel Web App window opens the Book1 workbook that you created. Notice that the Excel Web App includes a Ribbon with features similar to what is available in the full Microsoft Excel program. These features let you create and edit a worksheet. See Figure 2-27.

Figure 2-27   **Microsoft Excel Web App window**

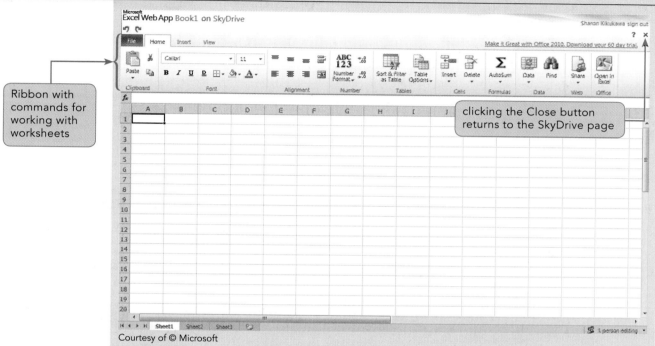

Courtesy of © Microsoft

4. In the upper-right corner of the page, click the **Close** button to close the Excel Web App window and to return to the SkyDrive page. The Book1 workbook appears on the Files page for your SkyDrive account.

5. If necessary, click your name in the Last modified by column for the Book1 file to open the details pane for the Book1 workbook on the right side of the screen. See Figure 2-28. The details pane includes options for working with the selected file. Notice that you can rename or delete the file, or click the Share link in the Sharing section to change the settings for who can access the file.

| Figure 2-28 | **SkyDrive Files page for Sharon** |

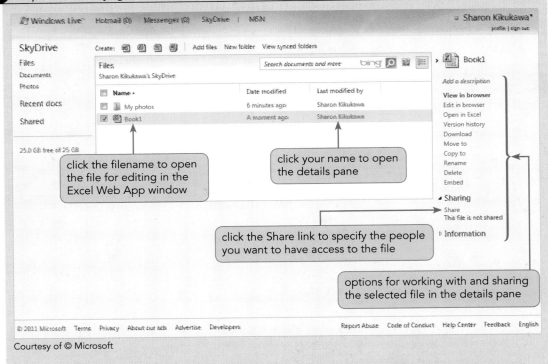

Courtesy of © Microsoft

Trouble? If you see the Excel Web App window instead of the page shown in Figure 2-28, you clicked the Book1 filename and opened it. Click the Close button to close the Excel Web App window, and then repeat Step 5, making sure to click your name in the Last modified by column and not the filename.

Trouble? If the Sharing section is collapsed, click the arrow to the left of the word "Sharing" to expand the section so you can see its options.

After uploading a file to SkyDrive, you can add comments to it, rename it, or move it into a folder that you create. As with most file-sharing sites, part of the user and terms of service agreements that you must accept when creating a Windows Live account prohibit you from uploading copyrighted material to the Windows Live site without authorization from the copyright's owner. SkyDrive also puts other restrictions on file uploads; for example, you cannot upload a file that is larger than 100 megabytes or a file that has the same name as a file that you already uploaded to SkyDrive. For more information about SkyDrive and other file-sharing services, you can follow the links in the File Sharing section of the Weblinks page for Tutorial 2.

Signing Out of Your Windows Live Account

You are finished evaluating Windows Live, so you need to sign out of your Windows Live account and close your browser. It is important that you sign out before closing the browser to ensure the security of your email and to prevent unauthorized access. If you do not sign in to your Windows Live Hotmail account within a specified time period after creating it, Microsoft might deactivate your email address or delete it.

To sign out of Windows Live and close your browser:

1. Click the **sign out** link below your name near the upper-right corner of the page. The MSN.com home page (or another Web page) opens.

2. Click the **Close** button on the browser's title bar to close your browser.

In this session, you learned how to use Windows Live Hotmail to create, send, receive, and manage email messages. You also learned how to create and use the contact list to manage information about contacts. Finally, you learned about using SkyDrive to share photos and other files.

REVIEW

Session 2.2 Quick Check

1. What information is required when you create a Windows Live account?
2. True or False. When using a computer in a public library to access your Windows Live Hotmail account, you should sign out of your account when you are finished viewing your messages to protect your privacy.
3. When you receive a message with an attachment in Windows Live Hotmail, what two options are available for the attached file?
4. When you delete a Hotmail message, can you recover it? Why or why not?
5. What information can you store about a person in the contact list?
6. What are three types of files you can create using Windows Live SkyDrive?

*Practice the skills
you learned in
the tutorial using
the same case
scenario.*

PRACTICE

Review Assignments

Data File needed for the Review Assignments: KAir.gif

Now that you have learned how to use Windows Live Hotmail to manage your email messages, Sharon asks you to submit a review of your experience using the Webmail provider and a recommendation about whether Kikukawa Air should continue using it. Sharon also wants to see how graphics are sent over the Internet, so she asks you to send her the Kikukawa Air logo to simulate how it appears when sent by Kikukawa Air employees.

1. Start your Web browser, go to **www.cengagebrain.com**, open the Tutorial 2 Weblinks page, and then click the Review Assignments link. Click the Windows Live link.
2. Sign in to your Windows Live Hotmail account.
3. Add your instructor's full name and email address and Sharon Kikukawa's full name and email address (Sharon@KikukawaAir.com) to your contact list.
4. Create a category named **Classmates** using the full names and email addresses of three of your classmates.
5. Create a new message. Address the message to Sharon and to your instructor. Add your email address to the message header so you will receive a courtesy copy of the message, and so the members of the Classmates category will receive a blind courtesy copy of the message. Use the subject **Hotmail review** for the message.
6. In the message body, type three or more sentences describing your overall impressions about Windows Live Hotmail. Be sure to evaluate the program's features, ease of use, and other important considerations that you determine.
7. In the message body, press the Enter key twice, and then type your full name and email address on separate lines.
8. Attach the **KAir.gif** file, which is saved in the Tutorial.02\Review folder included with your Data Files, to the message.
9. Check the spelling of your message before you send it, and correct any mistakes. Proofread your message and verify that you have created it correctly, and then send the message.
10. Wait a few seconds, check for new messages, and then review the message you sent to Sharon and your instructor.
11. Forward the message and the attached file to your instructor. In the message body, describe the appearance of the file you attached to the message and explain your findings in terms of attaching a graphic to a message. Send the message.
12. Create a new folder named **Reviews**, and then file the Hotmail review message in the Reviews folder.
13. Sign out of your Windows Live Hotmail account.

*Apply the skills
you learned to
send an email
message with
attached files.*

APPLY

Case Problem 1

Data Files needed for this Case Problem: Bales.jpg and Paper.jpg

Greenfield County Recycling   Greenfield County boasts a 98% compliance rate in the county's extensive recycling program from residential, business, and government customers. Separate facilities process all types of paper, glass, cans, plastics, household goods and appliances, and yard waste. The county just opened its eighth paper facility and needs you to send some pictures to the media liaison and to two managers in the county's technology office for an upcoming press release. Complete the following steps:

1. Start your Web browser, go to **www.cengagebrain.com**, open the Tutorial 2 Weblinks page, and then click the Case Problem 1 link. Click the Windows Live link.

2. Sign in to your Windows Live Hotmail account.

3. Create individual contacts using the full name and email address of your instructor and two classmates.

4. Create a category named **Managers** using the two classmates you added in Step 3.

5. Create a new message addressed to your instructor. Add the Managers category to the message header so its members will receive a courtesy copy of the message. Add your email address to the message header so you will receive a blind courtesy copy of the message. Use the subject **Facility pictures**.

6. In the message display area, type a short note telling the recipients that you are attaching two pictures of the new recycling facility, and ask them to respond to you when they receive your message. Sign your message with your first and last names.

7. Attach to the message the files named **Bales.jpg** and **Paper.jpg**, which are saved in the Tutorial.02\Cases folder included with your Data Files.

8. Send the message, wait a few seconds, and then check your Inbox for new messages.

9. Create a new folder named **Paper Facility**, and then file the message you received in the Paper Facility folder.

10. Sign out of your Windows Live Hotmail account.

Use Windows Live Hotmail to learn how to manage unsolicited messages.

RESEARCH

Case Problem 2

There are no Data Files needed for this Case Problem.

Estancia Ridge Estate   Bridget Estancia owns and operates the Estancia Ridge Estate, a small, private, family-owned olive grove specializing in locally grown olives that are pressed into olive oil on the premises. Bridget manages the gardens, the historic estate where she also lives, tours of the home and grove, and a gift shop. Olive oil sales are Bridget's largest income item, but she has seen a rise in tourism over the past year at her unique estate. Because of this rise in tourism, Bridget is advertising in local tourism publications and other publications that might attract people to visit the estate. As part of the advertisements, she includes the estate's phone number, its Web site address, and her email address. Although she receives many email messages from interested tourists, she has also started to receive many unsolicited messages as her email address is added to different mailing lists, some of which distribute information that she does not want to receive. Bridget asks you to research how she can use Windows Live Hotmail to manage the messages she receives by blocking senders from whom she does not want to receive messages, deleting junk mail, and filtering messages into categories or different views so she receives fewer messages in her Inbox. Complete the following steps:

1. Start your Web browser, go to **www.cengagebrain.com**, open the Tutorial 2 Weblinks page, and then click the Case Problem 2 link. Click the Windows Live link.

2. Sign in to your Windows Live Hotmail account, and then open your Inbox.

3. Click the Options button in the upper-right corner of the page, and then click More options to open the Hotmail Options page. The Hotmail Options page displays general help topics for Windows Live Hotmail.

4. Click the links on the page that deal with topics such as preventing junk email, using filters, and setting safe and blocked senders. Review the information you find to learn more about the tools Bridget can use to reduce or prevent junk email messages. If you would like to do so, set one or more options for your account, and then click the Save button. If you do not make any changes, click the Cancel button to return to the previous page without making any changes, or click the Options or Hotmail link on the left side of the page to return to the Hotmail Options page.

5. On the Hotmail Options page, click a link that lets you create rules for sorting new messages, and then examine the page that opens. Review the options on the page and consider how Bridget could use a rule to limit or reduce messages she receives from specific senders. If you would like to do so, set one or more options for your account, and then click the Save button. If you do not make any changes, click the Options or Hotmail link on the left side of the page to return to the Hotmail Options page.

6. Click the Hotmail link near the top of the page. Create a new message addressed to your instructor. Add your email address to the message header so you will receive a courtesy copy of the message. Use the subject **Filter and junk mail options**.

⊕ EXPLORE
7. In the message display area, explain how Bridget can use Windows Live Hotmail to manage the mail she receives better in two or three paragraphs. Use information from the Hotmail Options page in your response, and cite specific features and steps for your recommendations. Sign your message with your first and last names.

8. Send the message to your instructor.

9. Sign out of your Windows Live Hotmail account.

Use Windows Live Hotmail to learn how to create a signature for your outgoing email messages.

CREATE

Case Problem 3

There are no Data Files needed for this Case Problem.

Trinity Cablevision　You have just been hired as an installation contractor for Trinity Cablevision, which provides digital cable television, digital phone service, and high-speed Internet services to residential and business customers. Because you are a contractor, you will need to use your Windows Live Hotmail account for your business correspondence. To identify yourself to email recipients, you decide to create a signature for your outgoing messages that identifies your name, city, email address, and contractor license number. Complete the following steps:

1. Start your Web browser, go to **www.cengagebrain.com**, open the Tutorial 2 Weblinks page, and then click the Case Problem 3 link. Click the Windows Live link.

2. Sign in to your Windows Live Hotmail account.

3. Click the Options button in the upper-right corner of the page, and then click More options to open the Hotmail Options page. The Hotmail Options page displays general help topics for Windows Live Hotmail.

4. Locate and click a link on the page that deals with creating a signature (or a signature file).

⊕ EXPLORE
5. Use the page that opens to create a signature with your first and last names on the first line, your city and state on the second line, and your email address on the third line. On the fourth line, type **Contractor number** and any six-digit number. When you are finished, click the Save button.

6. Click the link to return to the Inbox.

7. Create an individual contact using the full name and email address of your instructor.

8. Create a new message addressed to your instructor. Add your email address to the message header so you will receive a courtesy copy of the message. Use the subject **Contractor cable services**.

⊕ EXPLORE
9. Use the toolbar to change your name in your signature for the current message to a blue, bold font.

10. Send the message, wait a few seconds, and then check for new messages.

⊕ EXPLORE
11. Create a second message, address it to your instructor, and add your email address to the message header so you will receive a courtesy copy of the message. At the top of the message, explain the steps you need to take to send a message that does not

include your signature. Delete your signature from the message, sign the message with your first and last names, and then send the message.

12. Sign out of your Windows Live Hotmail account.

Use SkyDrive to create a photo album.

CHALLENGE

Case Problem 4

Data Files needed for this Case Problem: Chance.jpg, Maple.jpg, Rocky.jpg, and Scout.jpg

Rescue Me Canine   Amy Brask works as a volunteer for Rescue Me Canine, an agency that places healthy puppies and dogs that have been picked up by animal control officers with people who agree to care for these pets either as foster or adoptive families. Amy receives many email messages from local vets and community leaders who refer potential foster and adoptive families to her. Amy had been sending pictures of dogs to prospective families, but she would rather post them in one place. She decides to investigate using a SkyDrive photo album to see if this might make distributing photos of pets easier and more efficient.

1. Start your Web browser, go to **www.cengagebrain.com**, open the Tutorial 2 Weblinks page, and then click the Case Problem 4 link. Click the Windows Live link.

2. Sign in to your Windows Live account.

3. Create individual contacts using the full name and email address of your instructor and two classmates.

4. Open the SkyDrive page, point to the SkyDrive link at the top of the page to open a menu of options, and then click the Photos option.

✦ EXPLORE

5. Near the top of the page, click the New folder link on the SkyDrive menu bar to create a new folder (album) named **Dogs**, press the Enter key, and then click the Dogs folder. Click the Add files link on the SkyDrive menu bar; click the link to select photos from your computer; browse to and select the Tutorial.02\Cases folder with your Data Files; press and hold the Ctrl key; click the files **Chance.jpg**, **Maple.jpg**, **Rocky. jpg**, and **Scout.jpg**; release the Ctrl key; and then click the Open button. Four files are uploaded to the album. (*Note:* Depending on your Internet connection speed, it might take a minute or longer to upload the files.)

✦ EXPLORE

6. After the files have been uploaded, click the Share folder link in the Sharing section on the right side of the page. In the To box, type the names of the recipients you created in Step 3, and then type your own email address in the To box. (Be sure to press the Enter key after typing an address to add it to the To box.) Click the Share button.

7. Click the Hotmail link at the top of the page and check for new messages. Examine the message that you sent to yourself, use the option in the message to view the photos in the album you created, and then examine the page that displays your photos and its features as you review the photos you posted.

8. Sign out of your Windows Live Hotmail account.

Expand the skills you learned in this tutorial to create a document using the tools available in SkyDrive.

CHALLENGE

Case Problem 5

There are no Data Files needed for this Case Problem.

Mangietti's Pizza Garden   Mangietti's Pizza Garden serves pizza and other Italian specialties. Its claim to fame is its coal-fired pizza oven and homemade, hand-tossed pizza dough. Customers are asked for their email addresses when they pay their bills so Mangietti's can send them coupons and follow-up surveys. You are working on an advertisement for the local newspaper and want to use actual customer comments in the ad, so you decide to gather these comments using a survey that you will send to customers with an email message that includes a 10% discount off their next meal. Because you need to coordinate the survey's questions with the owner and a few other staff members, you decide to post it on SkyDrive so the group can collaborate on the document before it is finalized and sent to customers. Complete the following steps:

1. Start your Web browser, go to **www.cengagebrain.com**, open the Tutorial 2 Weblinks page, and then click the Case Problem 5 link. Click the Windows Live link.

2. Sign in to your Windows Live Hotmail account.

3. Create individual contacts using the full name and email address of your instructor and two classmates. Then create a category named **Ad Survey Group** and add these three contacts to the group.

4. On the SkyDrive page, point to the SkyDrive link at the top of the page to open a menu, and then click the New Word document option.

5. In the Name box, type **Customer Survey** as the name of the document to create, and then click the Create button. The Word Web App window opens a blank document. The Ribbon contains options that let you work with documents, similar to how you work with documents in the Microsoft Word program.

✦ EXPLORE 6. Use Figure 2-29 and the options on the Ribbon to create the content and formatting in the document.

Figure 2-29 **Content for SkyDrive document**

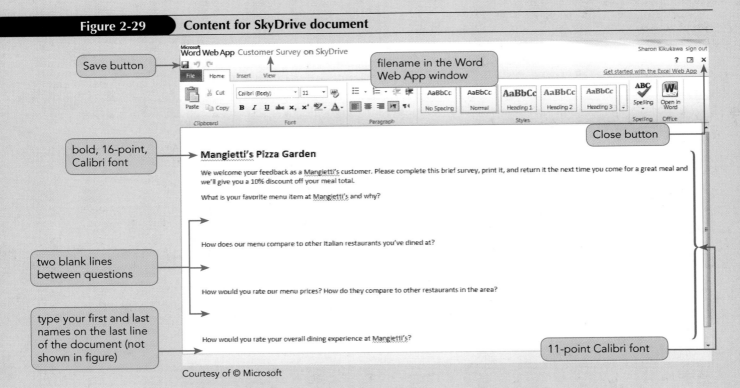

Courtesy of © Microsoft

7. At the bottom of the document, type your first and last names.

8. When you are finished, click the Save button above the File tab on the Ribbon. Then click the Close button in the upper-right corner of the page, below the sign out link, to close the Word Web App window. The Customer Survey document appears in your list of files in SkyDrive.

9. If necessary, click your name in the Last modified by column for the Customer Survey document to open the details pane for the document you created. If necessary, expand the Sharing section.

⊕ EXPLORE   10. In the details pane, click the Share link in the Sharing section to open the Share window for the document. In the To box, enter the Ad Survey Group category you created in Step 3, type your own email address, and then click the Share button to send a notification to your instructor and the two classmates you entered in Step 3 that your document is finished, along with a link to view it.

11. Check your Hotmail account for the message you sent to yourself, and then use it to open the document you shared.

12. Close the Word Web App window, and then sign out of your Windows Live Hotmail account.

Searching the Web

Using Search Engines and Directories Effectively

INTERNET

OBJECTIVES

Session 3.1
- Determine whether a research question is specific or exploratory
- Formulate an effective Web search strategy to answer research questions
- Use Web search tools including search engines, Web directories, metasearch engines, and Web bibliographies effectively

Session 3.2
- Apply Boolean logic and filtering techniques to improve your Web searches
- Perform complex searches in search engines
- Use advanced search options in Web search engines
- Assess the validity and quality of Web research resources

Case | *International Executive Reports*

International Executive Reports (IER) is a company that publishes a variety of weekly newsletters, monthly reports, and annual reviews of major trends in economic conditions and management developments. IER's clients are top-level managers and other people who serve on the governing boards of large companies and not-for-profit organizations. IER publications are mailed or emailed to subscribers. The subscription rates range from $300 to $900 per year.

The IER writing staff provides content for all of its publications. In some cases, content that is developed for one publication is edited and used in other publications. Anne Hill, the managing director for content at IER, has recruited an excellent staff of editors, writers, and researchers who work together to create a wide variety of content. Anne has hired you to fill an intern position on the research staff. Your job will involve conducting online research and fact-checking for two of the staff writers, Dave Burton and Ranjit Singh. Dave is an international business specialist, and Ranjit is an economist who writes about current economic trends.

STARTING DATA FILES

There are no starting Data Files needed for this tutorial.

SESSION 3.1 VISUAL OVERVIEW

A search engine includes a database of URLs and keywords, and several types of software for processing requests and returning results.

Search Engine

The search engine's Web formatting software converts the results of a database query to a Web page, which it sends to the user's Web browser.

Web page formatting software

The user formulates a question into a search expression, enters it into the search engine's Web page, and then the user reads the search results returned by the search engine.

Search expression query processing software

The search engine's search expression query software converts the user's search expression into a database-readable query.

Valua Vitaly/Shutterstock.com; © Cengage Learning

HOW A SEARCH ENGINE WORKS

Indexing and page ranking software manages the content of the search engine's database, and determines which pages will be listed first (page ranking) in the search results Web page.

Indexing and page ranking software

Database of URLs and keywords

The Web

Web robot/spider software

The URLs, keywords (or full text), page rankings, and links to other URLs for each Web page are stored in the search engine's database.

The search engine's robot crawls the Web, searching for new Web pages, and adds URLs and keywords (or full text) to the database.

Types of Search Questions

Searching the Web is a challenging task. No one knows exactly how many pages exist on the Web, but the number is now in the billions. Each of these pages might have thousands of words, images, or links to downloadable files. Thus, the content of the Web is far greater than that of any library. Unlike the content of a library, however, the content of the Web is not indexed in any standardized way. So to successfully locate specific information for Dave and Ranjit, you will need to develop appropriate search strategies for their research questions.

Dave and Ranjit will need different kinds of help because of their different writing goals. Dave will need quick answers to specific questions. Dave writes about business opportunities and developments in almost every country in the world. His writing requires background research on most major businesses and industries. To support Dave, you need to be able to "get the facts" using the Web. For example, he might need to know the population of Bolivia or the languages spoken in Thailand.

Ranjit writes longer, more thought-provoking pieces about broad economic and business issues. The Web is a good place to find unusual and interesting views on the economy and general business practices. Ranjit needs you to use the Web as a source for locating information on interesting concepts and new angles on old ideas, rather than as a place to find fast answers to specific questions. For example, he might need you to find Web sites that contain collections of research papers that discuss the causes of the Great Depression.

You can use the Web to obtain answers to both of these question types—Dave's specific questions and Ranjit's exploratory questions—but each requires a different search strategy. A **specific question** is a question that you can phrase easily and one for which you will recognize the answer when you find it. In contrast, an **exploratory question** is an open-ended question that can be harder to phrase; it is also difficult to determine when you find a good answer.

Finding Answers to Specific Questions

The characteristics of a specific question are that the question can be answered with a single fact or set of information, and that the search for the answer involves a process of narrowing down the range of potential answers you examine in each step. Examples of specific questions include:

- Who was the prime minister of the United Kingdom during World War II?
- What is the second-highest mountain peak in the world?
- Who discovered radium?
- What is the chemical formula for table salt?
- In what year did Magellan circumnavigate the globe?

You will always know when you have completed the process of answering a specific question because you have the answer or you have determined that the question *cannot* be answered. In some cases, your answer will not be in the form you expected. For example, in a search to answer the specific question "In what year did Magellan circumnavigate the globe?," you might learn that Magellan's circumnavigation took almost three years, from 1519 to 1522. You would also likely learn that Magellan was killed in the Philippine Islands, so he did not complete the circumnavigation personally; and that the purpose of the voyage was not to circumnavigate the globe, but to find a trading route to Asia.

When searching for the answer to a specific question, you need to start with broad categories of information and gradually narrow the search until you find the answer to your question. Figure 3-1 shows this process of sequential, increasingly focused questions.

| Figure 3-1 | Specific research question search process |

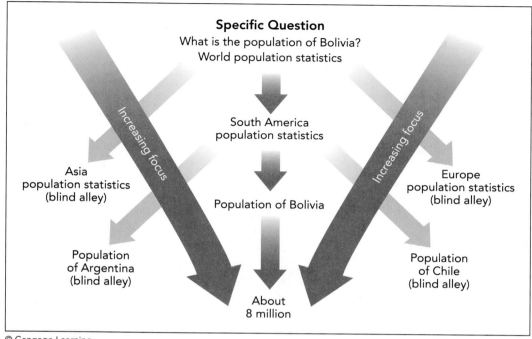

© Cengage Learning

As you narrow your search, you might find that you are heading in the wrong direction or down a blind alley. In that case, you need to get back on track by moving back inside the funnel defined by the two large red arrows shown in Figure 3-1. You can keep searching for increasingly narrow elements of information until you find the exact answer to your question. In the example shown, you might first find sources of population statistics for the entire world, and then narrow your search to the specific continent (South America) and the specific country (Bolivia).

Finding Answers to Exploratory Questions

An exploratory question cannot be answered with a single fact or set of information. Examples of exploratory research questions include:

- What workplace conditions increase the risk of cancer?
- What is the best way to measure intelligence?
- Why did the Japanese maintain an isolationist policy in the 17th and 18th centuries?
- What are the safest and most effective ways to lose weight?
- How did jazz evolve as an American musical form?

An exploratory search starts with general questions that lead to other, less general questions. The answers to the questions at each level should lead you to more information about the topic in which you are interested. This information then leads you to more questions. Figure 3-2 shows how this questioning process leads to a broadening scope as you gather information pertinent to the exploratory question.

Figure 3-2 **Exploratory research question search process**

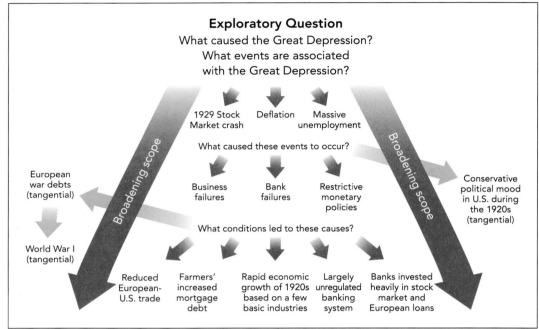

© Cengage Learning

In Figure 3-2, you can see that a search for causes of the Great Depression resulted in five distinct facts or sets of information. Further research would tell you that the relative importance and validity of each of these causes is still debated by economists today. As you expand an exploratory search, you might find yourself collecting tangential (secondary or nonessential) information that is somewhat related to your topic but does not help answer your exploratory question.

INSIGHT

Determining Useful Information

The boundary between useful and tangential information can be difficult to identify for exploratory search questions. Sometimes, what appears to be tangential information at first can later turn out to be useful information that leads you to expand your exploratory search in a fruitful direction. Do not be too quick to classify information as tangential. Remember, an exploratory search involves examining an increasingly wider range of information and identifying new insights in that information as you continue to search.

Formulating Effective Web Search Strategies

Once you have established the type of question you need to answer, you can implement an effective search strategy for finding the information you need.

If your question is specific, the first step in your search strategy is to formulate and state your question. Next, you select the appropriate tool or tools to use in your search and translate your question into a search query that will work with your chosen search tool. (Web search tools will be discussed in the next section.) You then run the query and evaluate your results to determine whether they provide a specific answer to your question. If your results do not answer your question, you can continue the search by deciding whether a different search tool might produce useful results using your original question. If you do not believe a different search tool will help, you can revise and narrow your question and repeat the process.

If your question is exploratory, you begin your search strategy by formulating and stating questions that will yield information related to the area of your inquiry. Then you select appropriate search tools and translate each of your questions into search queries that will work in each search tool. After running the queries, you review your results and determine whether the information you have gathered is related to your question and whether you have collected sufficient information to answer your question. If not, you can formulate and state additional questions and repeat the process until you do have sufficient information to answer your original question.

Note that the first four steps are quite similar for both specific and exploratory questions, but the determination of when your search process is completed is different for the two types of questions. Figure 3-3 illustrates the search strategies for both types of questions so you can compare the processes used for each.

Figure 3-3 **Effective Web search strategies**

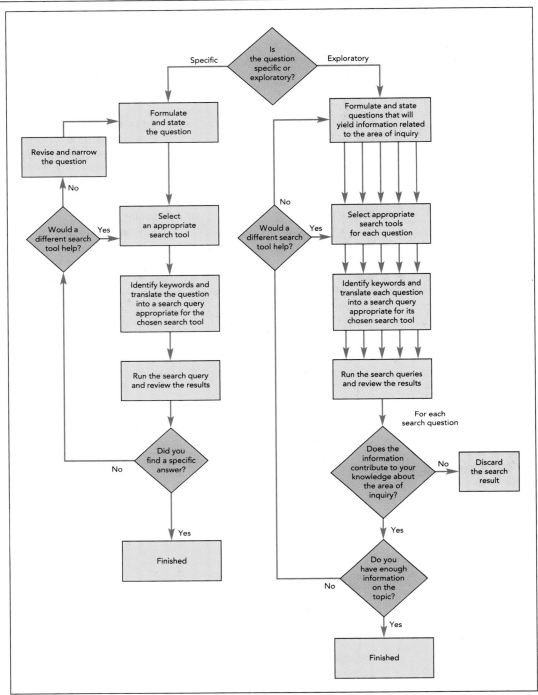

© Cengage Learning

Problem Solving: Repeating the Search Process

What happens if you conduct a Web search and you do not find an answer to your question? You can repeat the search process as many times as necessary until you obtain either the specific answer you seek or a satisfactory range of information regarding your exploratory topic. Sometimes, you might find that the nature of your original question is different than you had originally thought. You also might find that you need to reformulate, or more clearly state, your question. As you restate your question, think of synonyms for each word. Unfortunately, many words in the English language have multiple meanings. For example, the word "mogul" can mean an influential businessperson, an Indian person of Mongolian or Persian descent, or a small bump in a ski run. If you use a word in your search that is common and has many meanings, you can be buried in irrelevant information or be led down many blind alleys. Identifying unique phrases that relate to your topic or question is a helpful way to avoid some of these problems. For example, if you are searching for sites that discuss ways to ski safely over a mogul, you could include the word "skiing" or "slope" in your search expression to reduce the chances of obtaining results that link to Web pages about Indian people or business magnatesds.

An important part of any search is evaluating the quality of the search results you obtain. You will learn how to assess the validity and reliability of Web pages you find during your searches in the next session.

Web Search Tools

To implement any Web search strategy, you will use one or more Web search tools. **Web search tools** include four broad categories of sites: search engines, directories, metasearch engines, and other Web resources such as Web bibliographies. The Additional Information section of the Tutorial 3 Weblinks page at www.cengagebrain.com includes links to many of these Web search tools.

In this section, you will learn how to use each type of search tool.

Understanding Search Engines

A Web **search engine** is a Web site (or part of a Web site) that finds other Web pages that match a word or phrase you enter into the search engine's search page. This word or phrase is called a **search expression** or a **query**. A search expression or query might also include instructions that tell the search engine how to search; you will learn how to formulate search expressions that include additional search instructions later in this tutorial. The basic search page for Bing, a popular search engine site, is shown in Figure 3-4.

Figure 3-4   Bing basic search page

A basic search page includes a text box for entering a search expression and a command button to begin the search. The basic search page for Google, one of the most popular search engines, appears in Figure 3-5.

Figure 3-5   Google basic search page

© Google

When a user enters a search query into a search engine, the search engine does not search the Web to find a match; it searches only its *own* database of information about Web pages that it has collected, indexed, and stored. A search engine's database includes the URL of the Web page (recall from Tutorial 1 that a Web page's URL, or Uniform Resource Locator, is its Web address). The Session 3.1 Visual Overview shows how a search engine works. Most search engines use Web robots to build their databases of links to Web pages. A **Web robot**, also called a **bot** or a **spider**, is a program that automatically searches the Web to find new Web sites and update information about old Web sites that are already in the database. One of a Web robot's more important tasks is to delete information in the database when a Web site no longer exists. The main advantage of using an automated searching tool is that it can examine far more Web sites than an army of people ever could. However, the Web changes every day, and even the best search engine sites cannot keep their databases completely updated.

People who create Web pages want their sites to be found by people who are interested in the content of those pages. Therefore, many search engines allow Web page creators to submit the URLs of their pages to the databases of search engines. This gives search engines another way to add Web pages to their databases. Most companies that operate search engines screen Web page submissions to prevent a Web page creator from submitting a large number of duplicate or similar Web pages. When the search engine receives a submission, it sends its Web robot out to visit the submitted URL and collect data about the site.

INSIGHT

Varying Results from Search Engines

If you enter the same search expression into different search engines, you will often get different results because each search engine has collected a different set of information in its database, and each search engine uses different procedures to search its database. Some search engines do not collect their own information to build their databases. These search engines buy the right to use the database of another search engine. However, because each search engine uses different procedures to retrieve information from its database, a search engine that uses another search engine's database can still yield different results even though it uses the same database.

After you enter your search query into the search page, the search engine returns a series of **results pages**. These are Web pages that list hyperlinks to the Web pages in the search engine's database that contain text that matches your search expression. An example of a search results page (for a search on the word "car") from the Google search engine appears in Figure 3-6.

Figure 3-6   **Google search results for the search term "car"**

number of hits

sponsored links

search results

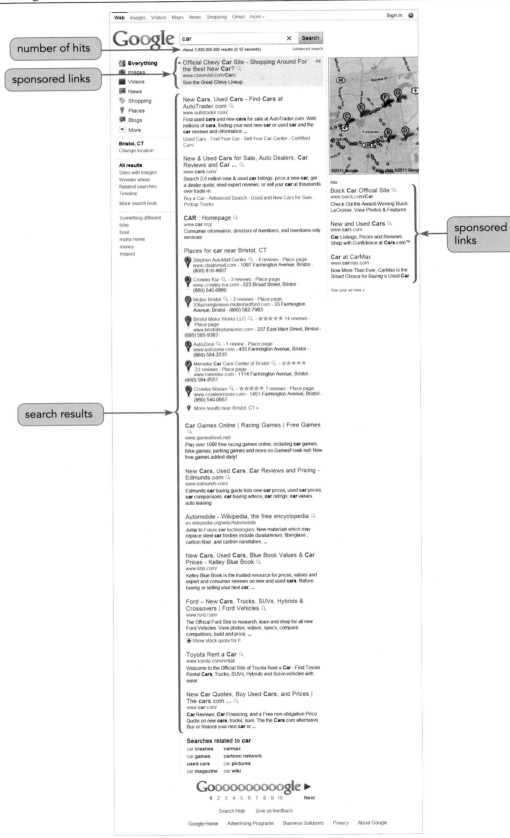

sponsored links

Most search engines report the number of hits they find on the results page. A **hit** is a Web page that is indexed in the search engine's database, and that contains text that matches a specific search expression. When you click hyperlinks on a search engine results page, you might find that some of the Web pages no longer exist. A hyperlink to a Web page that no longer exists or has been moved to another URL is called a **dead link**. Web pages or Web sites that have a number of dead links are said to suffer from **link rot**.

The organizations that operate search engines often sell advertising space on the search engine Web page and on the results pages. An increasing number of search engine operators also sell paid placement rights on results pages. A **paid placement** is the right to have a link to your Web site appear on the search results page when a user enters a specific search term. For example, Toyota might want to purchase the right to have its site listed on the search results page whenever a user enters the search term "car." When you enter a search expression that includes the word "car," the search engine creates a results page that will have a link to Toyota's Web site at or near the top of the results page. Most, but not all, search engines label these paid placement links as "sponsored," and they are usually called **sponsored links**. Figure 3-6 shows sponsored links to advertisers that have paid for placement on this page. If the advertising appears in a box on the page (usually at the top, but sometimes along the side or at the bottom of the page), it is usually called a **banner ad**. Banner ads usually include pictures and other graphic elements in addition to the text of the ad.

Search engines use the revenue from sponsored links and banner ads to generate profit after covering the costs of maintaining the computer hardware and software required to search the Web, and the costs to create and search the database. The only price users pay for access to these useful search tools is being exposed to banner ads on the search results pages and having to scroll through a few sponsored links at the top of results pages.

Your first research assignment is to find the amount of average rainfall in Belize for Dave. This search question is a specific question, not an exploratory question, because you are looking for a fact and you will know when you have found that fact. You can use the process shown earlier in Figure 3-3 as follows:

- Formulate and state the question. In this case, the question can be formulated as "What is the average rainfall amount in Belize?"
- Because the question is very specific, you decide that a basic search engine would be a good tool to use.
- To translate the question into a search query, you can use the keywords "Belize," "annual," and "rainfall" from your question to create an appropriate search query. These terms should appear on any Web page that includes the answer to the question. The term "Belize" should be especially useful in narrowing the search to relevant Web pages.
- When you obtain the results, review and evaluate them, and then decide whether they provide an acceptable answer to your question.
- If the results do not answer the question to your satisfaction, you can redefine or reformulate the question so it is more specific, and then conduct a second search using a different tool, question, or search expression until you find the fact you seek.

To find the average annual rainfall in Belize:

1. Start your Web browser, go to **www.cengagebrain.com**, open the Tutorial 3 Weblinks page, and then click the **Session 3.1** link.

2. Click a link to one of the search engines in the Basic Search Engines section to open that search engine's Web site.

3. Type **Belize annual rainfall** in the search box.

4. Click the appropriate button to start the search. The search results appear on a new page. This page should indicate that there are hundreds, perhaps even thousands, of Web pages that might contain the answer to your question.

5. Scroll down the results page and examine your search results. Click some of the links until you find a page or several pages that provide annual rainfall information for Belize. If you do not find any useful links on the first page of search results, click the link to view more search results pages (usually located at the bottom of the first results page).

6. Click your browser's **Back** button to return to the results page. You should find that Belize has several climate zones and that the annual rainfall ranges from 60 to 160 inches.

When you formulated and stated your question, you probably expected that you would find one rainfall amount that would be representative of the entire country; but that is not the case. Web searches often disclose information that helps you adjust the assumptions you made when you formulated the original research question.

Because you are fact-checking for a story that IER will publish, you will confirm what you have found by searching again using a different search engine.

To conduct the same search to confirm your results:

1. Return to the Tutorial 3 Weblinks page, and then click a link to another of the search engines in the Basic Search Engines section.

2. Type **Belize annual rainfall** in the search box.

3. Click the appropriate button to start the search. You will most likely see a completely different set of links on your search results page.

4. Scroll down the results page and examine your search results, and then click some of the links until you find a page that provides the average annual rainfall for Belize.

5. Return to the Tutorial 3 Weblinks page. Once again, you should find that Belize has several climate zones and that the annual rainfall ranges from 60 to 160 inches, confirming the information you found in your first search. If this was not the case, you can conduct additional searches to determine the reason your answers are not consistent.

You might notice your second search returned a different set of links because each search engine includes different Web pages in its database, and because different search engines use different rules to evaluate search expressions. Some search engines will return hits for pages that include *any* of the words in the search expression. Other search engines return hits only for pages that include *all* of the words in the search expression. You might also have noticed that many of the links on the results pages led to Web sites that have no information about Belize rainfall at all. This is why most researchers routinely use at least two search engines; answers that are difficult to find using one search engine are often easy to find with another.

The best way to determine how a specific search engine interprets search expressions is to read the Help pages on the search engine Web site. As you become an experienced Web searcher, you will find that you use two or three particular search engines for most of your work. Read the Help pages on those Web sites regularly because search engines do change the way they interpret search expressions from time to time. You should also get in the habit of checking other search engines occasionally because new search engines are launched and old search engines often make changes to stay competitive.

Understanding Search Engine Databases

Search engine databases store different collections of information about the pages that exist on the Web at any given time. Many search engine robots do not search all of the Web pages at a particular site. Further, each search engine database uses its own approach to index the information it has collected from the Web. Some search engine robots collect information only from a Web page's title, description, keywords, or HTML tags; others read only a certain number of words from each Web page. Figure 3-7 shows the first few lines of HTML from a Web page that contains information about developments in climate change research.

Figure 3-7   **Meta tags in a Web page**

```
<head>

<title>
Current Developments in Climate Change Research
</title>

<meta name="description" content="Current news and
reports about climate change research.">

<meta name="keywords" content="climate change, global
warming, greenhouse gas, GHG, emissions, CO2, carbon
dioxide, ozone layer, fossil fuels">

</head>
```

© Cengage Learning

The description and keywords tags are examples of HTML meta tags. A **meta tag** is HTML code that a Web page creator places in the page header for the specific purpose of informing Web robots about the content of the page. Meta tags do not cause any text to appear on the page when a Web browser loads it; rather, they exist solely for the use of search engine robots.

The information contained in meta tags can become an important part of a search engine's database. For example, the "keywords" meta tag shown in Figure 3-7 includes the phrase "climate change." These keywords could be a very important phrase in a search engine's database because the two individual words "climate" and "change" are common terms that often are used in search expressions that have nothing to do with climate change research. A search engine that includes the full phrase "climate change" in its database will greatly increase the chances that a user interested in that topic will find this particular page.

Some search engines store the entire content of every Web page they index; but most search engines store only parts of Web pages. Search engines that store a Web page's full content are called **full text indexing** engines. If you use a search engine that is not full text indexing, and the terms you use in your search expression are not in the part of the Web page that the search engine stores in its database, the search engine will not return a hit for that page. Many search engines, even those that claim to be full text indexed search engines, omit common words such as "and," "the," "it," and "by" from their databases. These common words are called **stop words**. For example, if you enter a search expression of "Law and Order" (without the quotes) while looking for pages related to the television show of that name, a search engine that omits stop words will return a large number of irrelevant links because it will search on the two words "law" and "order." Most search engines will include stop words if you include them as part of a phrase enclosed in quotes. You can find out how a particular search engine handles stop words by examining the search engine Web site's Help pages; many search engines include information about their search engines, robots, and databases on their Help or About pages.

Search Engine Features

Page ranking is one technique that search engines use to find Web pages that might be relevant to a specific search expression. **Page ranking** is a way of grading Web pages by the number of other Web pages that link to them. The URLs of Web pages with high rankings are presented first on the search results page. A page that has more Web pages linking into it (these connections are called **inbound links**) is given a higher ranking than a page that has fewer pages linking into it. In complex page ranking schemes, the value of each link varies with the linking page's rank.

For example, a Web page with many inbound links might have a lower ranking than another Web page that has fewer inbound links if the second page's inbound links are from Web pages that, in turn, have a large number of inbound links themselves. As you can imagine, calculating page ranks can be complex; but the rankings can effectively identify pages that are likely to meet the needs of users. Although Google was the first search engine to use page ranking, and continues to lead in the development of highly sophisticated page ranking algorithms, most other search engines now use page ranking and are constantly working to refine the effectiveness of their algorithms.

Most search engines automatically use **stemming** to search for variants of keywords. For example, if you search using the keywords "Canada travel guide," most search engines will return hits that include the keywords "Canadian" and "Canada" along with pages containing variants of the words "travel" and "guide." Figure 3-8 shows how a search engine can use stemming to create multiple combinations of these terms and their variants to expand the results it will return for this query.

Figure 3-8   **How a search engine uses stemming to expand its results**

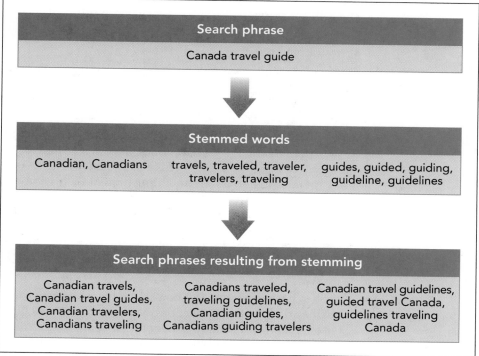

© Cengage Learning

Another feature that some search engines have attempted to include in their pages is natural language querying. A **natural language query interface** allows users to enter a question exactly as they would ask a person that question. For example, using a natural language query, you might phrase the Belize rainfall search as "How much rain does Belize get each year?" You could ask the same question in various ways. The search engine analyzes the question using knowledge it has been given about the grammatical structure of questions, and then uses that knowledge to convert the natural language question into a search query. This procedure of converting a natural language question into a search expression is called **parsing**.

Although no major search engine has yet been able to make a truly successful natural language query interface, the mathematical software company Wolfram has a Web site that offers a natural language interface to a database of collected facts. This site, Wolfram Alpha, lets users ask questions in natural language that relate to the facts in its database. You will use Wolfram Alpha to find out what the life expectancy is for people living in Belize.

To use the Wolfram Alpha natural language interface:

1. Return to the Tutorial 3 Weblinks page, and then in the Basic Search Engines section, click the **Wolfram Alpha** link to open the Wolfram Alpha search engine page.

2. Type **what is the life expectancy in Belize** in the box near the top of the page.

3. Click the **Compute** button to run the search. Instead of a results page listing links to Web sites related to your query, the site returns an actual answer to the question.

4. Examine the results and notice that, in addition to returning the answer as a value in years for the life expectancy in Belize, the site returns a good bit of information about the population of Belize and its characteristics. Although Wolfram Alpha is a search engine, it was built by a mathematics software company and advertises itself as being a computational engine, too. When you run a search with Wolfram Alpha, it will try to identify additional calculations that a person entering your search expression might want to perform. It performs those calculations and reports their results along with the search results.

Search engines provide a powerful tool for executing keyword searches of the Web, but they do have their limitations. Most search engine URL databases are built by computers running programs that perform the search automatically, so they can miss important classification details that a human searcher would notice instantly. For example, if a search engine's robot found a Web page with the title "Test Data: Do Not Use," it would probably not recognize the text as a warning and would include content from the page in the search engine database. If a person were to read such a warning in a Web page title, that person would know not to include the page's contents. However, with billions of Web pages on the Internet today, it is impossible to have people screen every Web page.

Using Directories and Hybrid Search Engine Directories

Web directories use a completely different approach from search engines to build useful indexes of information on the Web. A **Web directory** is a listing of hyperlinks to Web pages that is organized into hierarchical categories. The difference between a search engine and a Web directory is that the Web pages included in a Web directory are selected and organized into categories before visitors use the directory. In a search engine, the database is searched in response to a visitor's query, and results pages are created in response to each specific search.

Most Web directories have human editors who decide which Web pages will be included in the directory and how they will be organized; however, some Web directories use computers to perform these tasks. Web directory editors, who are knowledgeable experts in one or more subject areas and skilled in various classification techniques, review candidate Web pages for inclusion in the directory. When these experts decide that a Web page is worth listing in the directory, they determine the appropriate category in which to store the hyperlink to that page.

The main weakness of a directory is that users must know which category is likely to yield the information they desire. If users begin searching in the wrong category, they might follow many hyperlinks before they realize that the information they seek is not in that category. Some directories overcome this limitation by including hyperlinks in category levels that link to lower levels in other categories.

TIP

Most Web directories allow a Web page to be indexed in several different categories.

One of the oldest and most respected directories on the Web is Yahoo! Directory. David Filo and Jerry Yang, two Stanford University doctoral students who wanted a way to keep track of interesting sites they found on the Web, started Yahoo! Directory in 1994. Yahoo! Directory currently lists hundreds of thousands of Web pages in its categories—a sizable collection, but only a small portion of the billions of pages on the Web. Although Yahoo! Directory does use some automated programs for checking and classifying its entries, it relies on human experts to do much of the selection and classification work. The Yahoo! Directory home page appears in Figure 3-9.

Figure 3-9	Yahoo! Web directory home page

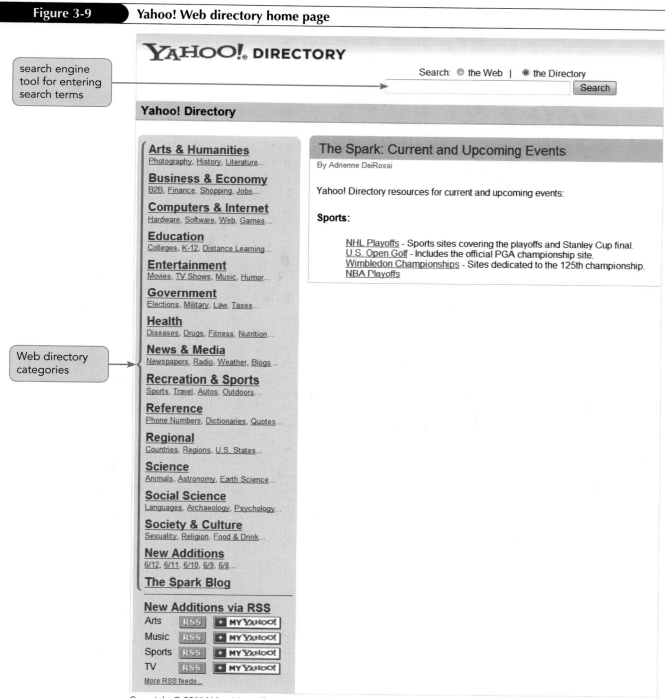

The search tool that appears near the top of the page is a search engine within Yahoo! Directory. You can enter search terms into this tool, and Yahoo! Directory will search its listings to find a match. This combination of search engine and directory is sometimes called a **hybrid search engine directory**; however, most directories today include a search engine function, so many people simply call these sites Web directories. No matter what it is called, the combination of search engine and directory provides a powerful and effective tool for searching the Web. Using a hybrid search engine directory can help you identify which category in the directory is likely to contain the information you need. After you select a category, the search engine is useful for narrowing a search even further; you can enter a search expression and limit the search to that category.

Yahoo! Directory includes 16 main categories, each with several subcategories. These are not the only subcategories; they are just a sample of those that are the largest or most used. You can click a main category hyperlink to see all of the subcategories under that category.

The Open Directory Project is different from most other Web directories because the editors volunteer their time to create the directory's entries. The home page for the Open Directory Project is shown in Figure 3-10. The Open Directory Project uses the services of more than 40,000 volunteer editors who maintain listings in their individual areas of interest. The Open Directory Project offers the information in its Web directory to other Web directories and search engines at no charge. Many of the major Web directory, search engine, and metasearch engine sites regularly download and store the Open Directory Project's information in their databases. For example, AltaVista, Dogpile, and Google all include Open Directory Project information in their databases.

Figure 3-10   **Open Directory Project home page**

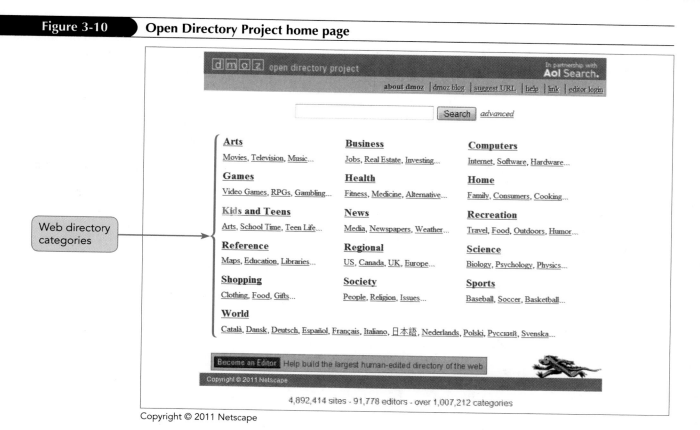

Copyright © 2011 Netscape

Another Web directory, About.com, hires people with expertise in specific subject areas to create and manage its Web directory entries in those areas. Although both Yahoo! and Bing use subject matter experts this way, About.com takes the idea one step further and identifies its experts. Each About.com expert, called a Guide, hosts a page with hyperlinks to related Web pages, moderates discussion areas, and provides an online newsletter. This creates a community of interested persons from around the world that can participate in maintaining the Web directory.

Dave is working on an article about current trends in corporate governance. He knows that The Conference Board is an organization that conducts research on business issues related to governance. Dave would like you to give him a list of organizations similar to The Conference Board so he can do more extensive background reading before he writes the article. You will try to find The Conference Board in a Web directory to learn in what category the directory has placed it. Then, you can search the other listings in that category to find similar organizations.

To find organizations similar to The Conference Board using a Web directory:

1. Return to the Tutorial 3 Weblinks page, and then click a link in the Web Directories section to open a Web directory site.

2. In the search box near the top of the page, type **The Conference Board**, and then click the appropriate button to start the search.

3. Examine the page that loads in your browser. In the text for the link to The Conference Board, the directory will include a link to the category (or categories) in which that directory has placed The Conference Board.

4. Click a link to a category to open the category page and identify links to organizations' Web pages that might be helpful for Dave.

5. If you do not find links that might be helpful to Dave, you can search another category if one is listed. You can also search similar categories or try a different Web directory. Figure 3-11 shows the category in which The Conference Board is included in the Yahoo! Directory (Organizations within Business and Economy). This category includes links to several organizations' Web sites that could be helpful to Dave.

Figure 3-11	Yahoo! Web directory search results page

YAHOO!® DIRECTORY

○ Web | ● Directory | ○ Category

[   ] [Search]

Business Organizations   Email this page   Suggest a Site   Advanced Search

Directory > Business and Economy > Organizations

CATEGORIES (What's This?)

category →

Top Categories

- **By Region** (10623)

Additional Categories

- **African American@**
- **Christian@**
- **Consumer Economy@**
- **Economic Development@**
- **Education@**
- **Finance and Investment@**

- **Islamic@**
- **Lesbian, Gay and Bisexual@**
- **Professional** (134)
- **Small Business@**
- **Trade Associations** (190)
- **U.S. Hispanic@**

SITE LISTINGS By Popularity | Alphabetical   (What's This?)   Sites 1 - 14 of 14

- **Better Business Bureau (BBB)** (21)
  Provides reports on businesses and charities to help consumers and donors make informed decisions, helps resolve consumer complaints, and promotes ethics in business. Browse a list of regional bureaus.
  dir.yahoo.com/.../Organizations/Better_Business_Bureau__BBB_

- **Service Corps Of Retired Executives (SCORE)**
  Nonprofit association dedicated to entrepreneur education and the formation, growth, and success of small businesses nationwide.
  www.score.org

- **U.S. Chamber of Commerce**
  Federation of businesses, chambers of commerce, American chambers overseas, and trade and professional associations.
  www.uschamber.com

link to The Conference Board Web site →

- **Conference Board, The**
  Nonprofit business membership and research organization for senior executives internationally; produces the Consumer Confidence Index, and Leading Economic Indicators.
  www.conference-board.org

- **World Chamber of Commerce Directory**
  Features a directory of U.S. and international chambers of commerce, tourism boards, and economic development agencies.
  www.chamberofcommerce.com

- **Indus Entrepreneurs (TiE)**
  Global network of entrepreneurs and professionals, established to support entrepreneurship.
  www.tie.org

- **Fabless Semiconductor Association**
  Stimulates technology and foundry capacity by communicating the future needs of the fabless semiconductor segment, and provides interactive forums for the benefit of its members.
  www.fsa.org

- **Business Committee for the Arts**
  Works across the United States to help businesses establish alliances with the arts that meet business objectives.
  www.bcainc.org

- **Business Council for International Understanding**
  International business and trade association that facilitates dialogue between the American business community and U.S. and foreign government leaders.
  www.bciu.org

Now that you have seen how to use a search engine and a hybrid search engine directory, you are ready to use an even more powerful combination of Web research tools: the metasearch engine.

Using Metasearch Engines

You have already seen how the differences in how search engines work cause the various search engines to return significantly different results for the same search expression. As stated previously, to perform a complete search for a particular question, you might need to use several individual search engines. A **metasearch engine** is a tool that combines the power of multiple search engines. Some metasearch tools also include directories.

Using a metasearch engine lets you search several engines at the same time, so you need not conduct the same search multiple times. Metasearch engines do not have their own databases of Web information; instead, a metasearch engine transmits your search expression to several search engines. These search engines run the search expression against their databases of Web page information and return results to the metasearch engine. The metasearch engine then reports consolidated results from all of the search engines it queried.

Dogpile was one of the first metasearch engines on the Web. Dogpile forwards search queries to a number of major search engines and Web directories. The specific search engines and directories that Dogpile uses change from time to time because newer and better search tools become available and older tools disappear. Each item on the search results page is labeled to indicate the search engine or Web directory that found it. When more than one source provides the same result, that entry is labeled with all of the sources. Figure 3-12 shows the Dogpile metasearch engine home page.

Figure 3-12	Dogpile metasearch home page

Courtesy of Copyright 2011 InfoSpace, Inc. All rights reserved.

You want to learn how to use metasearch engines so that you can access information faster. You decide to test a metasearch engine using Dave's Belize rainfall question.

To use a metasearch engine:

▶ **1.** Return to the Tutorial 3 Weblinks page, and then click a link in the Metasearch Engines section to open the Web site.

▶ **2.** Type **Belize annual rainfall** in the search box, and then click the appropriate button to start the search.

▶ **3.** Examine and evaluate your search results. If you did not find the information you were seeking, repeat your search using a different metasearch engine.

As with the other search tools, you will notice that the various metasearch engines can return differing results.

Using Web Bibliographies

In addition to search engines, Web directories, and metasearch engines, the Web includes **Web bibliographies**, another category of search tools. As their name suggests, Web bibliographies are similar to print bibliographies; but instead of listing books or journal articles, they contain lists of hyperlinks to Web pages. Just as some bibliographies are annotated, many of these resources include summaries or reviews of Web pages. Web bibliographies are also called **resource lists**, **subject guides**, **clearinghouses**, and **virtual libraries**. Sometimes they are called Web directories, which can be somewhat confusing. Web bibliographies are usually more focused on specific subjects than Web directories, and Web bibliographies usually do not include a tool for searching within their categories.

Web bibliographies can be very useful when you want to obtain a broad overview or a basic understanding of a complex subject area. Using a search engine to locate broad information on a complex subject is likely to turn up a narrow list of references that are too detailed and that assume a great deal of prior knowledge. For example, using a search engine or directory to find information about quantum physics will probably give you many results that link to technical papers and Web pages devoted to current research issues in quantum physics. However, your search probably will yield very few Web pages that provide an introduction to the topic, and those few pages will be hard to find in the large number of Web pages that deal with advanced details of the subject. In contrast, a Web bibliography search results page can offer hyperlinks to information regarding a particular subject that is presented at various levels. Many of these resources include annotations and reviews of the sites they list. This information can help you identify Web pages that fit your level of knowledge or interest.

Some Web bibliographies, such as Awesome Library and the Librarian's Internet Index, are general references. Most are more focused, such as Martindale's The Reference Desk, which emphasizes science-related links. Some Web bibliographies, such as the Internet Scout Archive, are no longer actively updated, but they are maintained on the Web as useful information resources.

Many Web bibliographies are created by librarians at university and public libraries. You can find Web bibliographies on specific subjects by entering a search term along with the words "subject guide" into a search engine. The results of an example search on the words "Native American subject guide" conducted in the Google search engine appear in Figure 3-13.

Figure 3-13   **Results of a search on "Native American subject guide"**

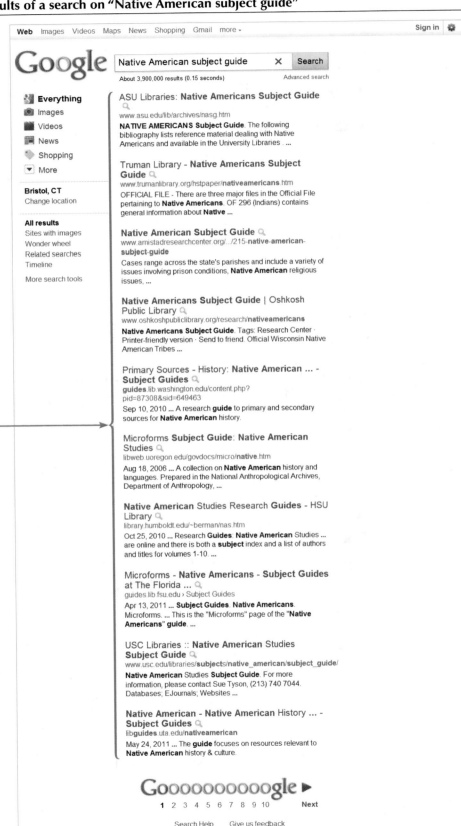

search results include several links to Web bibliographies about Native Americans

TIP

If you regularly conduct research in a specific field, it can be helpful to ask other researchers who work in the field if they know of useful Web bibliographies that specialize in relevant subjects.

Another way to find Web bibliographies is to use a Web directory site. Many Web directories include links to subject-specific Web bibliographies within the category listings for those subjects. For example, the Yahoo! Web directory includes a link titled "Web Directories" within its Social Science category. This link leads to a list of Web bibliographies on the subject of social science. It also has similar links in many of the social science subcategories, such as Economics. Other Web directories include similar links.

Ranjit is planning a series of articles on the business and economic effects of current trends in biotechnology, including information about the potential effects of genetic engineering research. You need to find some Web sites that Ranjit can use to learn more about biotechnology trends in general and genetic engineering research in particular. An exploratory search will locate the required information, and you can use a Web bibliography site for your research. Biotechnology is a branch of the biological sciences, so you will use the three category terms "biotechnology," "genetic engineering," and "biology" as your search terms.

To use a Web bibliography to conduct an exploratory search:

1. Return to the Tutorial 3 Weblinks page, choose one of the sites in the Web Bibliographies section, and then click a link in the Web Bibliographies section to open a Web bibliography's Web site. The home page for most Web bibliography sites provides a search box and a list of subject categories you can choose from to narrow your search.

2. Use the search tool in the Web bibliography you chose to find links to general information about biotechnology, genetic engineering, or biology. Follow those links to gather information relative to your search.

3. Examine your search results and determine whether you have gathered sufficient useful information to provide to Ranjit. If you have not, repeat the search using a different Web bibliography.

4. Close your browser.

You have completed your research for Dave and Ranjit using various search tools to obtain different results. In the next session, you will learn how to structure your search queries to achieve more precise results using Boolean logic and filtering techniques.

REVIEW

Session 3.1 Quick Check

1. What are the key characteristics of an exploratory search question?
2. True or False. The Web is indexed in a standardized way, as is a library's collection of books.
3. The part of a search engine site that is a program that automatically searches the Web to find new Web sites is called a(n) _____.
4. A search engine that uses page ranking will list a Web page near the top of search results pages if the page has many _____.
5. True or False. Most search engines index all Web page contents in their databases.
6. Name one advantage and one disadvantage of using a Web directory instead of a Web search engine to locate information.
7. How does a hybrid search engine directory overcome the disadvantages of using either a search engine or a directory alone?
8. How does a metasearch engine process the search expression you enter into it?
9. How can you find Web bibliographies about a specific subject area?

SESSION 3.2 VISUAL OVERVIEW

A quality site will disclose the author's qualifications and will identify the owner of the site so you can determine any bias that might result from the owner's interests.

Read the content to identify its connection to your research question, and any bias in point of view. You should also check other Web sites to confirm the accuracy of the information presented.

Identify the content's author and the Web site owner

Determine accuracy, relevance, scope, and objectivity of content

Yuri Arcurs/Shutterstock.com; © Cengage Learning

EVALUATING WEB SITES

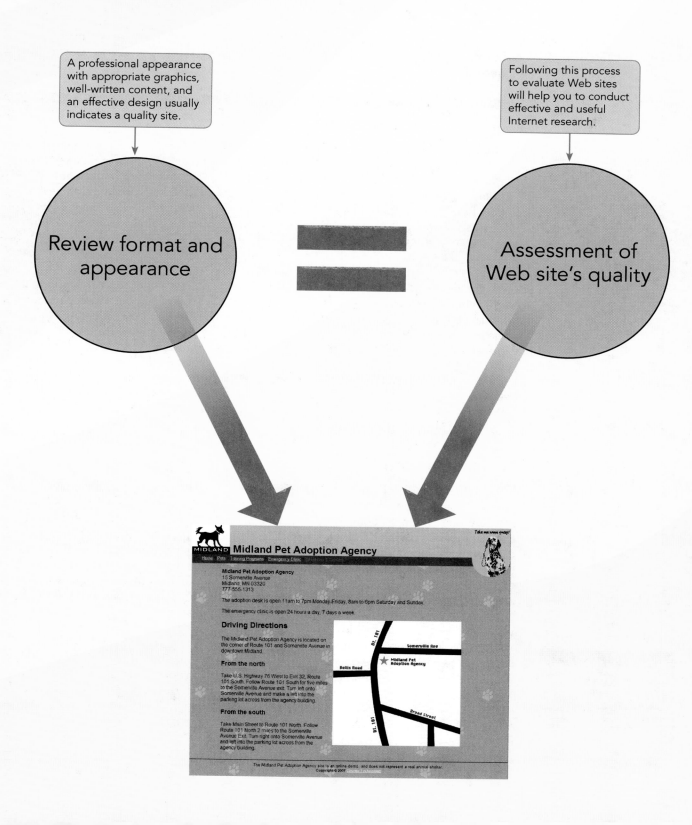

A professional appearance with appropriate graphics, well-written content, and an effective design usually indicates a quality site.

Following this process to evaluate Web sites will help you to conduct effective and useful Internet research.

Review format and appearance

=

Assessment of Web site's quality

Midland Pet Adoption Agency

Home Pets Training Programs Emergency Clinic

Midland Pet Adoption Agency
15 Somerville Avenue
Midland, MN 03320
777-555-1313

The adoption desk is open 11am to 7pm Monday-Friday, 8am to 6pm Saturday and Sunday.

The emergency clinic is open 24 hours a day, 7 days a week.

Driving Directions

The Midland Pet Adoption Agency is located on the corner of Route 101 and Somerville Avenue in downtown Midland.

From the north

Take U.S. Highway 76 West to Exit 32, Route 101 South. Follow Route 101 South for five miles to the Somerville Avenue exit. Turn left onto Somerville Avenue and make a left into the parking lot across from the agency building.

From the south

Take Main Street to Route 101 North. Follow Route 101 North 2 miles to the Somerville Avenue Exit. Turn right onto Somerville Avenue and left into the parking lot across from the agency building.

The Midland Pet Adoption Agency site is an online demo, and does not represent a real animal shelter.
Copyright © 2007

Using Logical Operators and Filtering Techniques in Complex Searches

The most important factor in obtaining good results from a search engine, a metasearch engine, or a search tool within a hybrid search engine directory is careful selection of the search terms you use. When the object of your search is straightforward, you can usually choose one or two words that will work well. More complex search questions require more complex queries, which you can use along with Boolean logic, search expression operators, wildcard operators, or filtering techniques, to broaden or narrow your search expression.

INSIGHT

Searching Library Databases

The Boolean operators and filtering techniques you will learn to use in this session can also be helpful when you are doing searches in library databases. These databases, which can be very expensive to purchase, provide much information that cannot be found on the Internet and are often available at school libraries, company libraries, or your local public libraries. Each database has its own implementation of Boolean operators and filtering tools, but the principles you learn here will help you in formulating your searches of these library databases.

When you enter a single word into a Web search tool, it searches for matches to that word. When you enter a search expression that includes more than one word, the search tool makes assumptions about the words that you enter. You learned in Session 3.1 that some search engines assume that you want to match *any* of the keywords in your search expression, whereas other search engines assume that you want to match *all* of the keywords. These alternative assumptions can result in dramatic differences in the number and quality of hits returned. Some search engines are designed to offer both options because users might want to match all of the keywords in one search and any of the keywords in a different search. One way of implementing these options is to use logical operators in the search expression.

Logical Operators

Logical operators specify the relationship between the elements they join, just as the plus sign in arithmetic specifies the mathematical relationship between the two elements it joins. The most commonly used logical operators in complex Web searching are **Boolean operators**, named for George Boole, a nineteenth-century British mathematician who developed a system of logic called **Boolean algebra**. Boolean algebra allows two values, usually *true* and *false*. Although Boole did his work a hundred years before computers became commonplace, his algebra is still useful to computer engineers and programmers. Unlike the algebra you might have learned in your math classes, Boolean algebra does not use numbers or arithmetic operators. Instead, Boolean algebra uses words and logical relationships.

Three basic Boolean operators—AND, OR, and NOT—are recognized by most search engines. You can use these operators in many search engines by simply including them with search terms. For example, the search expression "exports AND France" returns hits for pages that contain both the words "exports" and "France." The expression "exports OR France" returns hits for pages that contain either word, and "exports NOT France" returns hits for pages that contain the word "export" but not the word "France."

TIP

Some search engines use "AND NOT" to indicate the Boolean NOT operator.

Some search engines recognize variants of the Boolean operators, such as "must include" and "must exclude" operators. For example, a search engine that uses the plus sign to indicate "must include" and the minus sign to indicate "must exclude" would respond to the expression "exports + France - Japan" with hits that include pages with the words "exports" and "France" but only if those pages did not also include the word "Japan."

Figure 3-14 shows several ways to use Boolean operators in more complex search expressions that contain the words "exports," "France," and "Japan." The figure shows the matches that a search engine will return if it interprets the Boolean operators correctly. Figure 3-14 also describes information-gathering tasks in which you might use these expressions.

Figure 3-14   **Using Boolean operators in search expressions**

Search Expression	Search Returns Pages that Include	Use to Find Information About
exports AND France AND Japan	All of the three search terms	Exports from France to Japan or from Japan to France
exports OR France OR Japan	Any of the three search terms	Exports from anywhere, including France and Japan, and all kinds of information about France and Japan
exports NOT France NOT Japan	Exports, but not if the page also includes France or Japan	Exports to and from any countries other than France or Japan
exports AND France NOT Japan	Exports and France, but not Japan	Exports from France to anywhere but Japan or to France from anywhere but Japan

© Cengage Learning

Other Search Expression Operators

When you are creating a search query that combines three or more search terms with Boolean operators, the complexity of the query can make it hard to construct properly. One way to simplify the process is to use precedence operators along with the Boolean operators. A **precedence operator**, also called an **inclusion operator** or a **grouping operator**, establishes specific grouping levels within a complex expression and is usually indicated by the parentheses symbols. You might have used precedence operators (parentheses) in your math or algebra classes in a similar manner to group mathematical expressions. Logical precedence operators work the same way. They establish grouping levels within which the Boolean operators function.

For example, the Boolean search expression "red AND green OR blue" would return results that include red and green along with all results that include blue. Using precedence operators could change the outcome of that search. For example, the expression "red AND (green OR blue)" would return any results that include red and either green or blue. Figure 3-15 shows several ways to use precedence operators with Boolean operators in search expressions.

Figure 3-15   Using Boolean and precedence operators in search expressions

Search Expression	Search Returns Pages that Include	Use to Find Information About
Exports AND (France OR Japan)	Exports and either France or Japan	Exports from or to either France or Japan
Exports OR (France AND Japan)	Exports or both France and Japan	Exports from anywhere, including France and Japan, and all kinds of other information about both France and Japan
Exports AND (France NOT Japan)	Exports and France, but not if the page also includes Japan	Exports to and from France, except those going to or from Japan
(Exports OR Imports) AND (France NOT Japan)	Either exports or imports, along with France, but not if the page also includes Japan	Exports and imports to and from France, except those to or from Japan

© Cengage Learning

Some search engines use double quotation marks to indicate precedence grouping; however, most search engines use double quotation marks to indicate search terms that must be matched exactly as they appear within the double quotation marks. Using an exact match search phrase can be particularly useful because most search engines ignore stop words by default. You can force most search engines to include a stop word (that they would, by default, otherwise ignore) in a search expression by enclosing it in double quotation marks (or by including it in an exact search phrase that is enclosed in double quotation marks). This technique can be especially helpful when searching a specific topic that includes several stop words. For example, if you were searching for information about J.D. Salinger's novel, *The Catcher in the Rye*, and used those words in your search expression, most search engines would ignore the three stop words included in the title and would search for pages containing "Catcher" and "Rye" only. By using the double quotes to force the search engine to include the stop words, "The Catcher in the Rye," you would be more likely to see search results in which you were interested.

Another useful search expression operator is the location operator. A **location operator**, or **proximity operator**, lets you search for terms that appear close to each other in the text of a Web page. The most common location operator offered in Web search engines is the NEAR operator. If you are interested in French exports, you might want to find only Web pages in which the terms "exports" and "France" are close to each other; for example, "exports NEAR France." Unfortunately, each search engine that implements this operator uses its own definition of "NEAR." One search engine might define NEAR to mean "within 10 words," whereas another search engine might define NEAR to mean "within 20 words." To use the NEAR operator effectively, you must read the search engine's Help pages to determine its definition of NEAR.

Wildcard Characters

Some search engines support the use of a wildcard character in their search expressions. A **wildcard character** allows you to omit part of a search term. The search engines that include this function most commonly use the asterisk (*) as the wildcard character. For example, the search expression "export*" would return pages containing the terms "exports," "exporter," "exporters," and "exporting" in many search engines.

As you learned earlier in this tutorial, many search engines automatically use stemming to search for additional word endings. Using the search term "import" in one of those search engines is exactly the same as using a wildcard character at the end of the search term ("import*") in a search engine that supports wildcard characters. However, a search engine that uses wildcard characters is more flexible than one that uses simple stemming because the wildcard character can be inserted in the middle or at the beginning of the search term, as well as at the end. For example, the expression "wom*n" would return pages containing both "woman" and "women."

Search Filters

Many search engines allow you to restrict your search by using search filters. A **search filter** eliminates Web pages from search results. The filter criteria can include such Web page attributes as language, date, domain, host, or page component (URL, hyperlink, image tag, or title tag). For example, many search engines provide a way to search for the term "exports" in Web page titles and ignore pages in which the term appears in other parts of the page.

Performing Complex Searches

Most search engines implement many of the operators and filtering techniques you have learned about in this session. The way in which various search engines apply these techniques can differ; some search engines provide separate advanced search pages for these techniques, while others allow you to use advanced techniques such as Boolean operators on their simple search pages. When formulating a strategy for a complex search, it is important for you to understand the operators and filtering options available in the search engine you are using, so you can use these tools most effectively to formulate and run your search query.

This section describes how to conduct complex searches in several specific search engines. The steps are correct as this book is printed, but the Web changes constantly. When you perform these steps, the screens you see might look different and you might need to modify the steps. If you encounter difficulties, ask your instructor for assistance or read the Help pages on the search engine site. If major changes occur, the Tutorial 3 Weblinks page at www.cengagebrain.com will be updated to indicate how to make the searches work.

Using Exalead to Perform a Boolean Search

Ranjit is writing about the role that trade agreements play in limiting the flow of agricultural commodities between countries. His current project concerns the German economy. Your job is to find some Web page references that might provide useful background information. Ranjit is especially interested in learning more about the German perspective on trade issues.

This is an exploratory question. You can use the Boolean search capabilities of the Exalead search engine to conduct a complex search for Web pages. Exalead is a search engine that allows the use of several Boolean and precedence operators.

To create an effective search expression, you must identify search terms that might lead you to appropriate Web pages. Some terms you might use for the search are "Germany," "trade," "treaty," and "agriculture." You want to locate a reasonable number of hyperlinks to Web pages, but you do not want to search through thousands of URLs, so you will combine the search terms using Boolean logic to increase the chances that the search engine will return only useful sites. You want your search results to include only Web pages that have the words "Germany" and "trade," along with either of the words "treaty" or "agriculture." Figure 3-16 shows how to use the Boolean operators AND and OR, combined with parentheses as precedence operators, to formulate an appropriate search query.

Figure 3-16   Combining the Boolean AND and OR with precedence operators

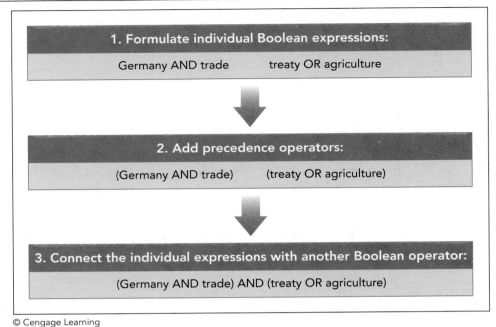

© Cengage Learning

To perform a Boolean search using Exalead:

1. Start your Web browser, open the Tutorial 3 Weblinks page at www.cengagebrain.com, click the **Session 3.2** link, and then click the **Exalead** link.

2. Click the **Web** link on the Exalead home page, if necessary.

3. Type **(Germany AND trade) AND (treaty OR agriculture)** into the search box.

4. Click the **Search** button to start the search. The results page includes a number of useful links that meet the search criteria along with links to search results that contain related terms. The results page also provides links to search results categorized by file type and Web site type.

Filtered Search in Google

Dave is writing an item about Finland and would like to interview a professor he once met who taught graduate business students there. He does not remember the professor's name or the name of the university at which the professor teaches, but he does remember that the professor taught business subjects at a university in Finland. Dave is confident that he would recognize the university's name if he saw it again. He asks if you can search the Web to find the names of some Finnish universities.

You will use the Google search engine for this task. To create a useful search expression, you must identify search terms that might lead you to appropriate Web pages. In this case, you will include "Finland" as a search term. Also, Dave told you that graduate schools of business in Europe are often called Schools of Economics, so you will include the exact phrase "School of Economics" in your search. The country code for Finland is ".fi," so you will limit the search to Web pages in this top-level domain using the Google filter options. Because Dave reads English only, you also will filter the search to return pages that are in English.

To perform a filtered search using Google Advanced Search:

1. Return to the Tutorial 3 Weblinks page, and then click the **Google Advanced Search** link.

2. Click in the **Find web pages that have all these words** box at the top of the page, and then type **Finland**.

3. Click in the **Find web pages that have this exact wording or phrase** box, and then type **School of Economics**.

4. Click the **Language** arrow, and then click **English**.

5. Click in the **Search within a site or domain** box, and then type **.fi**. Figure 3-17 shows the Google Advanced Search page with the search expressions entered and the filters set.

Figure 3-17	Google Advanced Search page

search expression entered by Google as you type in other fields

language filter

top-level domain filter

Web Images Videos Maps News Shopping Gmail more ▾   Sign in 🔧

Google Advanced Search   Advanced Search Tips | About Google

Finland "School of Economics" **site:** .fi

Find web pages that have...

all these words: Finland

this exact wording or phrase: School of Economics   tip

one or more of these words: [ ] OR [ ] OR [ ]   tip

But don't show pages that have...

any of these unwanted words: [ ]   tip

Need more tools?

Reading level: no reading level displayed ▾

Results per page: 10 results ▾   This option does not apply in Google Instant.

Language: English ▾

File type: any format ▾

Search within a site or domain: .fi
    (e.g. youtube.com, .edu)

➕ Date, usage rights, numeric range, and more

Advanced Search

©2011 Google

© Google

6. Click the **Advanced Search** button to start the search. The top portion of the search results page appears in Figure 3-18 and includes a number of links to Finnish universities.

Figure 3-18 **Google Advanced Search results page**

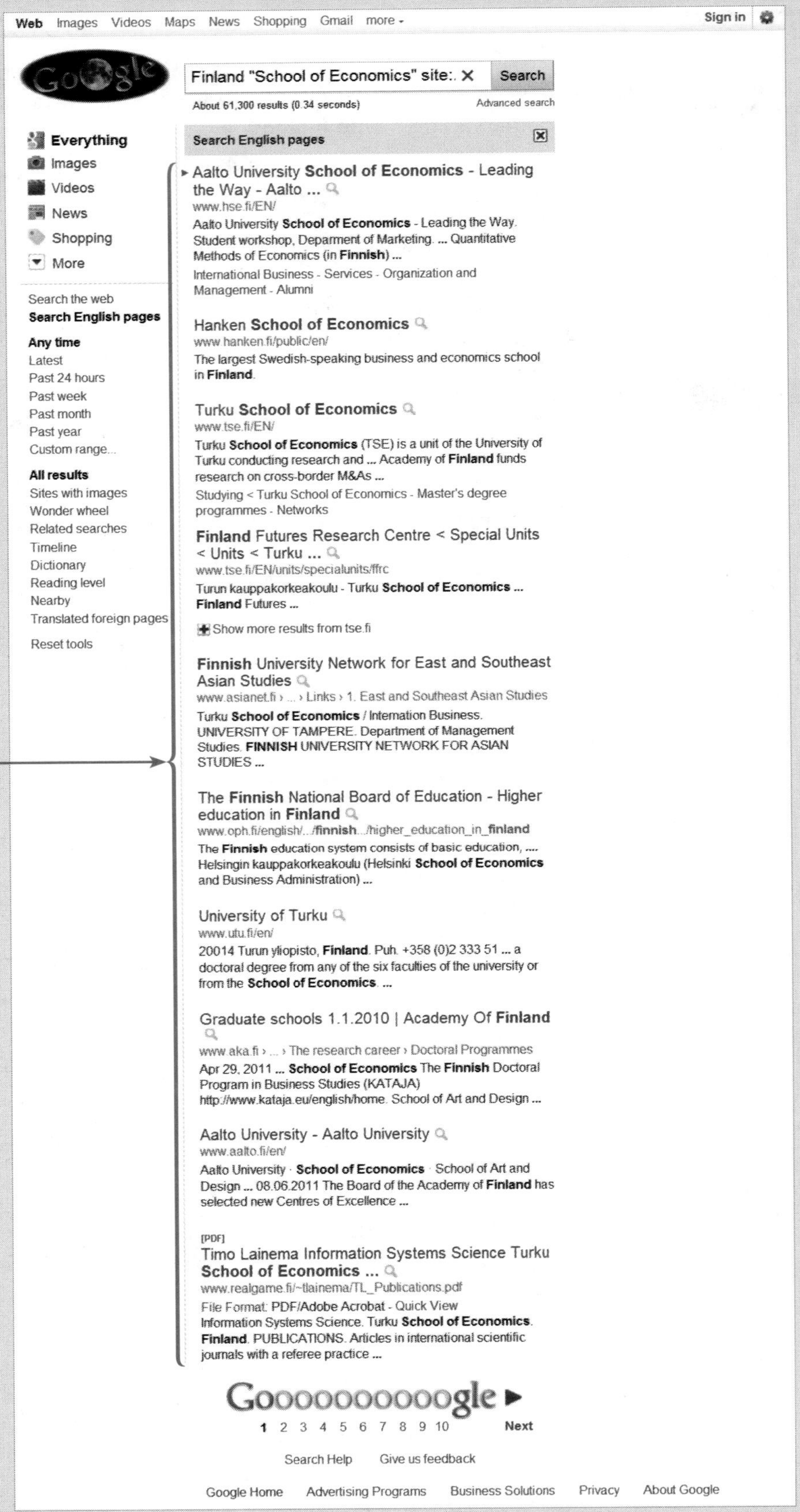

search results list; your search results will differ

© Google

7. Examine your search results and determine which of the hyperlinks in the search results lead to Finnish universities. Remember that you might need to examine several pages of search results to find exactly what you need.

Using Search Engines with Clustering Features

You have seen how Boolean operators and filters can help target the search to return pages that will more likely meet your needs. However, these pages might still number in the tens of thousands (or even millions). Scrolling through hundreds of results pages looking for useful resources is not very efficient. Some search engines group their search results into clusters. The clustering of results is similar to a filtering effect; however, the filtering is done automatically by the search engine after it runs the search. Another difference is that none of the search results are discarded; they are simply sorted into multiple categories, or clusters. Clustering can be especially effective when a word in the search expression has multiple meanings. For example, the word "java" can mean the name of an island, the name of a programming language, or a slang term for coffee. Clustered results place each of these meanings in separate categories.

Search engines that include a clustering feature use one of two strategies to implement clustering. One approach is to create categories as the search engine database is built. Each Web page that is stored in the database is placed into one or more categories. A second approach creates the categories after the search expression is run against the database. The search engine constructs the categories on the fly and uses information about all the words in the search expression (and their relations to each other and keywords in the Web pages selected). For example, the Yippy search engine collects search results into clusters and runs the clustering algorithms as the search results are returned. That is, instead of classifying Web pages into categories in its database, it creates the categories dynamically after it processes the search expression. Yippy defines its clusters using artificial intelligence. The clustering is done in real time for each search and depends on the search expression and the clustering algorithm, which is continually revised.

Ranjit is writing about fast-food franchises in various developing countries. He needs information on this industry's experience in Indonesia. You can run this search using a search engine with a clustering feature such as Yippy. As you know, to create a useful search expression, you must identify search terms that might lead you to appropriate Web pages. Some terms you might use include "Indonesia," "fast food," and "franchise." You are not interested in Web pages that contain the individual terms "fast" and "food," so you will use double quotation marks to specify the phrase "fast food." The Yippy search engine uses its clustering feature as a substitute for Boolean logic, so you will enter a simple expression and let it filter your results into searchable categories.

To obtain clustered search results using Yippy:

1. Return to the Tutorial 3 Weblinks page, and then click the **Yippy** link in the Search Engines with Clustering Features section.

2. Click in the Search box if necessary, and then type **Indonesia "fast food" franchise**. Make sure that you type the quotation marks so that you find the phrase "fast food" instead of the individual terms "fast" and "food."

3. Click the **Search** button to start the search. Figure 3-19 shows the search results page, which includes links to a number of promising Web pages.

Figure 3-19   Yippy search results page

search expression

search results collected into clusters of related hyperlinks

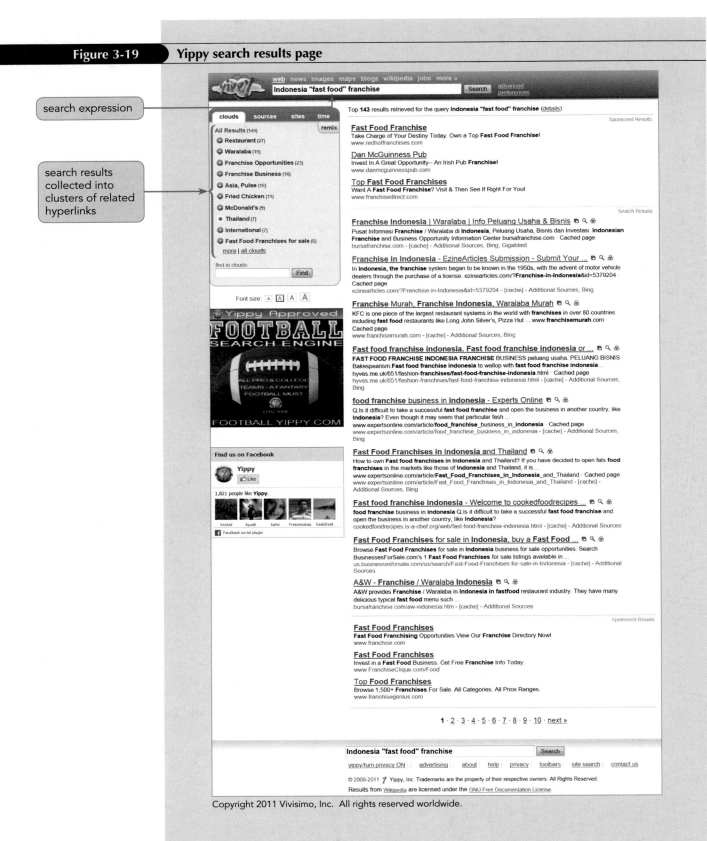

On the left side of the page, you will see a heading, "clouds," which is the term this search engine uses for its clusters. You can click the plus sign to the left of a cloud heading to open any cluster that looks like it is related to your search topic.

4. Click the plus sign next to one of the cloud headings and examine its sub-categories that open. Notice the list of links on the page changes to pages contained in that category.

Exploring the Deep Web

Many different companies and organizations are working on ways to make searching the Web easier and more successful for the increasing numbers of people who use the Web. One weakness of most current search engines and Web directories is that they only search static Web pages. A **static Web page** is an HTML file that exists on a Web server computer. The robots used by search engines to build their databases can find and examine these files.

An increasing number of Web sites do not store information as HTML files. Instead, they store information in a database; and when a user submits a query using the search tools on the site, the site's Web server searches the database and generates a Web page on the fly that includes information from the database. These generated Web pages are called **dynamic Web pages**. For example, if you visit Amazon.com and search for books about birds, the Amazon.com Web server queries a database that contains information about books and generates a dynamic Web page that includes that information. This Web page is not stored permanently on the Web server and cannot be found or examined by search engine robots. Much of the information stored in these databases can only be accessed by users who have a login and password to the Web site that generates dynamic pages from the database.

Several researchers have explored the difficulties that search engine robots face when trying to include information contained in the databases that some Web sites use to generate their dynamic pages. Some researchers call this information the **deep Web**; other researchers use the terms **hidden Web** and **invisible Web**. Many of these researchers are working at universities and research institutes. One team working at the University of Utah has created an experimental Web site that allows visitors to search the deep Web. The home page of this site, called DeepPeep, is shown in Figure 3-20.

Figure 3-20   DeepPeep home page

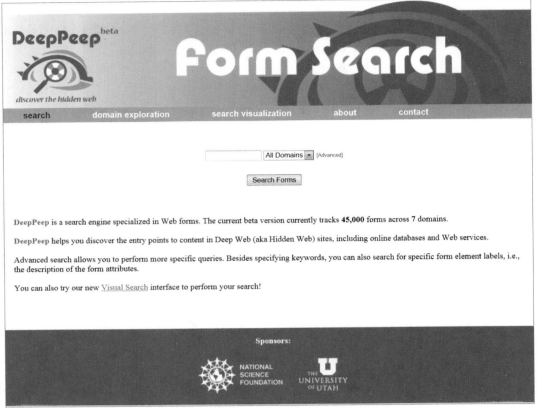

Courtesy of the National Science Foundation and the University of Utah

Evaluating Web Research Resources

One of the most important issues in conducting research on the Web is assessing the validity and quality of the information provided on the Internet. Because the Web has made publishing information so easy and inexpensive, virtually anybody can create a Web page on almost any subject. Research published in scientific or literary journals is subjected to peer review. Similarly, books and research monographs are often reviewed by peers or edited by experts in the appropriate subject area. However, information on the Web is seldom subjected to the review and editing processes that have become a standard practice in print publishing.

When you search the Web for entertainment or general information, you most likely will not suffer significant ramifications from gathering inaccurate or unreliable information. When you are searching the Web for an answer to a serious research question, however, the risks of obtaining and relying on inaccurate or unreliable information can be significant.

You can reduce your risks by evaluating carefully the quality of any Web resource on which you plan to rely for information related to an important judgment or decision. To develop an opinion about the quality of the resource, you can evaluate four elements of any Web page: the Web page's authorship, ownership, content, and appearance. The Session 3.2 Visual Overview summarizes the process for effectively evaluating Web pages.

Authorship, Expertise, and Objectivity

The first step in evaluating a Web research resource is to determine who authored the page. If you cannot easily find authorship information on a Web site, you should question the validity of the information included on the site. A Web site that does not identify its author has very little credibility as a research resource. Any Web page that presents empirical research results, logical arguments, theories, or other information that purports to be the result of a research process should identify the author *and* present the author's background information and credentials so you can evaluate the author's expertise. The information on the site should be sufficient to establish the author's professional qualifications.

You can also check secondary sources for corroborating information. For example, if the author of a Web page indicates that he or she is a member of a university faculty, you can find the university's Web site and confirm that the author is listed as a faculty member. The Web site should also provide author contact information, such as a street address, email address, or telephone number, so that you can contact the author or consult information directories to verify the addresses or telephone numbers. This allows you to determine that the author is an actual person, and is the person depicted as the author of the Web site content.

You also should consider whether the qualifications presented by the author pertain to the material that appears on the Web site. For example, the author of a Web site concerned with gene-splicing technology might list a Ph.D. degree as a credential. However, if the author's Ph.D. is in history, it would not suggest sufficient expertise to support the credibility of the gene-splicing technology Web site. If you cannot determine the specific areas of the author's educational background from the Web site itself, you can look for other examples of the author's work on the Web. By searching for the author's name and terms related to the subject area, you should be able to find other sites that include the author's work. The fact that a Web site author has written extensively on a subject can provide some evidence—although not necessarily conclusive evidence—that the author has expertise in the field.

In addition to identifying the author's identity and qualifications, author information should include details about the author's affiliations—either as an employee, owner, or consultant—with organizations that might have an interest in the research results or other information included in the Web site. Information about the author's affiliations will help you determine the level of independence and objectivity that the author has with respect to the topics presented on the Web site. For example, research results supporting the contention that cigarette smoke is not harmful presented in a site authored by a researcher with excellent scientific credentials might be less compelling if you learn that the researcher is the chief scientist at a major tobacco company. By reading the page content carefully, you might be able to identify a potential bias in the author.

Web Site Ownership and Objectivity

The author of a Web page is seldom the owner of the Web site. In some cases, it can be difficult to determine who owns a specific Web site. Most Web sites include information about ownership on their About pages; however, some sites do not. In some cases, the owner might be an organization with an intentionally misleading name.

You can make a rough assessment of what type of entity a Web site's owner is by examining the domain identifier in the URL. If the site claims affiliation with an educational institution, the domain should be .edu. A not-for-profit organization would most likely have the .org domain, and a government unit or agency would have the .gov domain. These are not hard-and-fast rules, however. For example, some perfectly legitimate not-for-profit organizations have URLs with a .com domain.

Once you have determined who or what entity owns the Web site, you can assess whether they are likely to have a bias regarding the content of the site. A for-profit company, for example, would be unlikely to provide unbiased evaluations of products or services provided by their competitors.

Accuracy, Relevance, Scope, and Objectivity of Content

When evaluating the actual content on the Web page, you want to assess its accuracy, its relevance to your research question, the depth of the topic's coverage, and the objectivity of the material's presentation.

When considering accuracy, you might first determine the timeliness of the content. If the material was not published recently, the information might no longer be accurate. Check the Web page for a clearly stated publication date or updated date. You can also search other Web sites to confirm that factual information presented is similar to factual information presented on these other sites. However, this does not guarantee that the information is correct because it is possible for a number of sites to have incorrect information.

The relevance of a site's content to your research question can be more difficult to judge; after all, people often search the Web to learn about topics with which they are not familiar. However, some characteristics of the content on a Web page can help you determine whether that content will help you answer your research question.

You can read the content with a critical eye and evaluate whether the included topics are relevant to your research question. You might be able to evaluate the scope of the site by determining whether important topics or considerations are omitted from the sites content. You can do this by comparing the content to what you find on other Web pages devoted to the topic. Comparisons to other Web pages can help you assess the depth of treatment the author gives to the subject.

Finally, to ensure you are getting complete information on your topic, you will want to confirm the Web page content's objectivity—in other words, whether it acknowledges its own bias. Some Web pages present a balance of viewpoints, but many are created for the specific purpose of supporting a particular position. This is especially true if the issue is contentious. The best Web sites with information on contentious issues always make clear which side they are taking in the argument and show respect for the position taken by the other side.

Form and Appearance

A Web site that is a legitimate source of accurate information usually presents its information in a professional form that helps convey its validity. Many Web pages that contain low-quality or incorrect information are poorly designed and not well edited. For example, a Web page devoted to an analysis of Shakespeare's plays that contains spelling errors is likely to be a low-quality resource. Loud colors, graphics that serve no purpose, and flashing text are all Web page design elements that often indicate that the Web page is a low-quality resource. However, these indicators are not infallible. The Web does contain pages full of misinformation and outright lies that are nicely laid out, include professionally produced graphics, and have grammatically correct and properly spelled text.

Evaluating the Quality of a Web Page

Now that you understand the principles of assessing Web page quality, you will apply these principles as you analyze a Web page.

REFERENCE

Evaluating a Web Page

- Open the Web page in your Web browser.
- Identify the author, if possible. If you can identify the author, evaluate his or her credentials and objectivity.
- Examine the content of the Web site for accuracy, relevance, scope, and objectivity.
- Evaluate the site's form and appearance to determine quality and appropriateness.
- Draw a conclusion about the site's overall quality.

Anne Hill has been doing research for IER on how companies can appeal to children on the Web by promoting products while not taking advantage of the children who visit their sites. Anne would like you to evaluate the quality of a Web page titled "Children's Websites" that she has found.

To evaluate the quality of the Children's Websites Web page:

1. Return to the Tutorial 3 Weblinks page, and then click the **Children's Websites** link in the Evaluating Web Research Resources section.

   The browser loads the Web page that appears in Figure 3-21. To evaluate the page, examine the content of the Web page, read the text, examine the titles and headings, and consider the page's appearance.

| Figure 3-21 | Children's Websites Web page |

Web site owner's name

date of publication

author's name

useit.com → Alertbox → Sept. 2010 Websites for Kids   [Search]

Jakob Nielsen's Alertbox, September 13, 2010:

Children's Websites: Usability Issues in Designing for Kids

Summary:
New research with users aged 3–12 shows that older kids have gained substantial Web proficiency since our last studies, while younger kids still face many problems. Designing for children requires distinct usability approaches, including targeting content narrowly for different ages of kids.

Millions of children use the Internet, and millions more are coming online each year. Many websites specifically target children with educational or entertainment content, and mainstream websites often have specific "kids' corner" sections — either as a public service or to build brand loyalty from an early age.

Despite this growth in users and services, little is known about how children actually use websites or how to design sites that will be easy for them to use. Website design for kids is **typically based purely on folklore** about how kids supposedly behave — or, at best, on insights gleaned when designers observe their own children, who hardly represent average kids, typical Internet skills, or common knowledge about the Web.

To **separate design myths from usability facts**, we turn to empirical user research: observations of a broad range of children as they use a wide variety of websites.

This research covers **users aged 3–12 years**. (Guidelines for sites targeting 13- to 17-year-olds are available in a report from our separate research with teenagers.)

User Studies

We conducted **two separate rounds of usability studies**, testing a total of 90 children (41 girls and 49 boys):

- Study 1 (9 years ago). In this study, we tested **27 sites with 55 children**, aged 6–11. We conducted about a third of the study in Israel, and the rest in the United States.
- Study 2 (new research). In this study, we tested **29 sites with 35 children**, aged 3–12 years. All of these user sessions were in the U.S.

In Study 1, we conducted sessions in participants' homes, at schools, and in a usability lab. All of Study 2 sessions were run in a lab. We tested some users in friendship pairs, and other individually. Pair sessions worked best for 6- to 8-year-old users. In contrast, for children younger than 6 or older than 8, individual sessions were just as good (and are obviously cheaper, as we had to recruit only one user per session).

Although it can be difficult for shy or very young kids, we encouraged users to think out loud while they were using the sites. We told the children that **they were the experts**, and that we wanted them to teach us how kids use and think about websites. We then explained that, in order for us to learn, they had to explain what they were thinking at all times.

We conducted look at more specific . . . the . . . between . . . is vast.)

Finally, it's important to **retain a consistent user experience** rather than bounce users among pages targeting different age groups. In particular, by understanding what attracts children's attention, you can "bury" the links to service content for parents in places that kids are unlikely to click. Text-only footers worked well for this purpose.

Advice for Parents and Educators

We conducted this research in order to generate usability guidelines for companies, government agencies, and major non-profit organizations that want to design websites for children. Even so, some of our findings have personal **implications for parents, teachers, and others** who want to help individual children succeed on the Internet:

- The main predictor of children's ability to use websites is **their amount of prior experience**. We also found that kids as young as 3 can use websites, as long as they're designed according to the guidelines for this very young audience. Together, these two findings lead to the advice to start your children on the Internet at an early age (while also setting limits; too much computer time isn't good for kids).
- Campaigns to sensitize children to **the Internet's potential dangers** and to teach them to be wary of submitting personal information are meeting with success. Keep up this good work.
- On a more negative note, kids still don't understand the Web's commercial nature and **lack the skills needed to identify advertising** and treat it differently than real content. We need much stronger efforts to teach children about these facts of new media.

Learn More

Our 275-page report with 130 design guidelines for designing websites for children is available for download.

- Other Alertbox columns (complete list)
- Sign up for newsletter that will notify you of new Alertboxes

You can see that the author of the page is Jakob Nielsen and that the page has a clear, simple design. You note that the grammar and spelling are correct and the content is neither inflammatory nor overly argumentative, although it does reflect a strong specific viewpoint on the issue. The date on which the page was published is clearly stated at the top of the page. You note that this page appears to be part of a Web publication called "Alertbox" by looking at the page's URL and by noting the link at the top of the page.

2. Click the **Alertbox** link near the top of the Web page to learn more about the Web publication.

   You see that the full title of the publication is "Alertbox: Current Issues in Web Usability" and that it is written by Dr. Jakob Nielsen, a principal of the Nielsen Norman Group. You can also see that the site offers a free email newsletter, and that it has a clearly stated privacy policy that governs the use of any email addresses submitted. Although some sites state policies that they do not follow, the existence of a clearly stated policy is a good indicator of a high-quality site.

3. Click the **Jakob Nielsen** link that appears under the publication title near the top of the page to open a biography page on which you can learn more about Dr. Nielsen.

4. Click your browser's **Back** button to return to the Alertbox page, and then click the **Nielsen Norman Group** link to open the Nielsen Norman Group information page. Reviewing the information on these pages helps you to evaluate the quality of the Children's Websites page.

5. Close your Web browser.

The information you examined should lead you to conclude that the Children's Websites page is of high quality. Dr. Nielsen and his organization are both well respected in the field of Web site usability research. If you would like to do an additional exploration regarding this topic, you could use your favorite search engine to conduct searches on combinations of terms such as "Nielsen" and "Web usability."

Evaluating Wikipedia Resources

Wikipedia is a Web site that hosts a community-edited set of online encyclopedias in more than a dozen different languages. The concept behind Wikipedia is similar to that behind the Open Directory Project you learned about in Session 3.1. Instead of hiring experts to review and edit entries, which is what all print encyclopedias do, Wikipedia relies on contributions from anyone for its entries. Those entries then can be edited by anyone who reads them and thinks they should be changed in some way. The idea is that with enough people reading, editing, and re-editing the entries, the information on the site will evolve to a higher degree of accuracy.

Some of the articles on Wikipedia are well written, authoritatively referenced, and show the benefit of the multiple reviews by qualified volunteer editors. Other articles, especially those about subjects that are not of interest to a large number of readers, are written by authors of questionable qualifications and have not been edited at all. Although unsourced material can be challenged and ultimately removed, this does not occur unless someone who is interested in the topic takes the time and effort to challenge the material. A large number of Wikipedia articles include a dated disclaimer stating that they need additional citations or verification. In many cases, the disclaimer is several years old. Figure 3-22 shows parts of the Wikipedia article on internal rate of return, a topic in corporate finance.

Figure 3-22   Wikipedia article on internal rate of return

disclaimer noting
the need for
additional citations

references and
links to related
research resources
on the topic

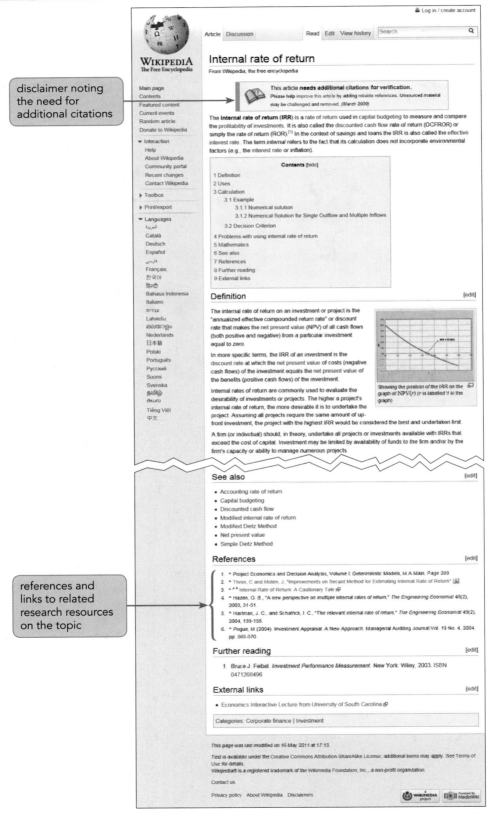

As you can see, the article includes a disclaimer at the top noting that it needs additional citations. The article does provide a few citations (near the bottom of the page) and includes a reference for readers who want to learn more about the topic. However, most people who wanted to learn how to compute the internal rate of return in a specific context would find this article hard to read and incomplete.

The end result of Wikipedia's open nature is that it contains a great deal of useful information, and much of that information is valid. However, Wikipedia's content is only as good as its contributors; and consequently, some of the information on the site is inaccurate, incomplete, or biased.

One of the most important tools you can use to assess the quality of information on the Web is the author's identity. On Wikipedia, contributors may post and edit articles anonymously, in which case the author is identified only by the IP address of his or her connection to the Internet. Even when the author or editor of an article chooses to be identified, it is through a Wikipedia account name and the biographical information included on the user page is entered by the account holder. That information can be limited or incorrect if the account holder so chooses.

PROSKILLS

Aa Written Communication: Using Wikipedia in Web Research

Some researchers have found Wikipedia to be a useful tool for doing preliminary background reading when they are investigating a subject that is new to them. They find that Wikipedia can often give them a general introduction to the subject that they can use to search intelligently for authoritative materials relevant to their information search. However, few researchers would rely on Wikipedia as their sole source of information on a topic, even if the article were well-referenced, written by a credible author, and subjected to multiple edits. Few teachers or employers would accept a research project that referenced Wikipedia as a primary source. In fact, it is always a good idea to check with your instructor for guidance before using online resources, such as Wikipedia, in your research.

In this session, you have learned the process for evaluating Web results when researching the Web. The determination of Web site quality is not an exact science; but with practice, you can develop your skills in this area.

REVIEW

Session 3.2 Quick Check

1. The three basic Boolean operators are _____, _____, and _____.
2. Write a search expression using Boolean and precedence operators that returns Web pages containing information about wild mustang horses in Wyoming, but not information about the Ford Mustang automobile.
3. True or False. The NEAR location operator always returns phrases that contain all keywords within 10 words of each other in a search expression.
4. True or False. In most search engines, the wildcard character is a * symbol.
5. Name three kinds of filters you can include in a Google search run from its Advanced Search page.
6. What function do parentheses serve in an advanced or Boolean search expression?
7. Why is the deep Web so difficult to search?
8. List three factors to consider when evaluating the quality of a Web site.

Practice the skills you learned in the tutorial using the same case scenario.

PRACTICE

Review Assignments

There are no Data Files needed for the Review Assignments.

Anne, Dave, and Ranjit are keeping you busy at IER. You have noticed that Dave and Ranjit frequently need information about the economy and economic forecasts. Your internship will be over soon, so you would like to leave them with links to some resources that they might find useful after you leave. To create the links, complete the following steps:

1. Start your Web browser, go to www.cengagebrain.com, open the Tutorial 3 Weblinks page, and then click the Review Assignments link. The Review Assignments section of the Tutorial 3 page contains links organized under three headings: Search Engines, Web Directories, and Metasearch Engines.
2. Choose at least one search tool from each category and conduct searches using combinations of the search terms "economy," "economics," "forecasts," "conditions," and "outlook."
3. Expand or narrow your search using each tool until you find five Web sites that you believe are good Web research resources that Anne, Dave, and Ranjit should include in their bookmarks or favorites lists to help them locate information about international business stories.
4. For each Web site, record the URL and write a paragraph that explains why you believe the site would be useful to an international business news writer. Identify each site as a guide, directory, or other resource.
5. Evaluate the quality of each Web site. Write a paragraph for each site rating the site's quality as low, medium, or high, and explain the reasons for your rating.
6. When you are finished, close your Web browser.

Apply the skills you learned in this tutorial to choose a search tool and use it to find geographic information.

APPLY

Case Problem 1

There are no Data Files needed for this Case Problem.

Midland University Earth Sciences Institute   You are an intern at the Midland University Earth Sciences Institute. The Institute conducts research on the primary effects of earthquakes on land stability, soil composition, and water redirection, as well as secondary effects such as changes in plant and animal life. When an earthquake strikes, the Institute sends a team of geologists, soil chemists, biologists, botanists, and civil engineers to the site to examine the damage to structures, land formations, and rivers. An earthquake can occur without warning nearly anywhere, so the Institute needs quick access to information on local conditions in various parts of the world, including temperature, money exchange rates, demographics, and local customs. In early July, you receive a call that an earthquake has occurred in northern Chile. To obtain information about local midwinter conditions there, complete the following steps:

1. Start your Web browser, go to www.cengagebrain.com, open the Tutorial 3 Weblinks page, and then click the Case Problem 1 link. The Case Problem 1 section contains links to lists of search engines, directories, and metasearch engines.
2. Choose one of the search tools you learned about in this tutorial to conduct searches for information on local conditions in northern Chile. When searching for information on weather conditions, be sure to obtain information about conditions during the month of July. (*Hint:* You might need to conduct preliminary searches to identify terms that you can use to limit your searches to northern Chile.)

3. Prepare a short report that includes the daily temperature range, average rainfall, current exchange rate for U.S. dollars to Chilean pesos, and any information you can obtain about the characteristics of the local population.

4. When you are finished, close your Web browser.

Apply the skills you learned in this tutorial to find information about companies that sell a specific product.

APPLY

Case Problem 2

There are no Data Files needed for this Case Problem.

Lightning Electrical Generators, Inc.   You work as a marketing manager for Lightning Electrical Generators, Inc. John Delaney, the firm's president, has asked you to investigate new markets for the company. One market to consider is the uninterruptible power supply (UPS) business. A UPS unit supplies continuing power to a single computer or to an entire computer system if the regular source of power fails. Most UPS units provide power only long enough for an orderly shutdown of the computer. John wants you to study the market for UPS units in the United States. He wants to know which firms make and sell UPS products. He would also like to know the power ratings and prices of individual units. To provide John with the information he needs, complete the following steps:

1. Start your Web browser, go to www.cengagebrain.com, open the Tutorial 3 Weblinks page, and then click the Case Problem 2 link. The Case Problem 2 section contains links to lists of search engines, directories, and metasearch engines.

2. Use one of the search tools to conduct searches for information about specific UPS products for John. You should design your searches to find the manufacturers' names and information about the products that they offer. (*Hint:* Try searching on the full term, "uninterruptible power supply," in addition to the acronym, "UPS.")

3. Prepare a short report that includes the information you have gathered for at least five UPS products, including the manufacturer's name, model number, product features, and suggested price.

4. When you are finished, close your Web browser.

Apply the skills you learned in this tutorial to find and evaluate the quality of specific Web page content.

APPLY

Case Problem 3

There are no Data Files needed for this Case Problem.

Eastern College English Department   You are a research assistant in the Eastern College English Department. The department head, Professor Garnell, has an interest in Shakespeare. She has spent years researching whether William Shakespeare actually wrote the plays and poems attributed to him. Some scholars, including Professor Garnell, believe that most of Shakespeare's works were written by Christopher Marlowe. Professor Garnell wants to include links on the department Web page to other researchers who agree with her, but she is concerned that many Web pages that discuss this matter are not reputable. Professor Garnell wants to include links to high-quality sites only. To gather the URLs, complete the following steps:

1. Start your Web browser, go to www.cengagebrain.com, open the Tutorial 3 Weblinks page, and then click the Case Problem 3 link. The Case Problem 3 section contains links to lists of search engines, directories, and metasearch engines.

2. Use one of the search tools to find Web sites that contain information about the Shakespeare-Marlowe controversy.

3. Use the procedures outlined in this tutorial to evaluate the quality of the sites you found in the previous step. (*Hint:* Most useful sites will have some connection to a university or research library.)

4. Choose at least five Web sites that Professor Garnell might want to include on her Web page. For each Web site, record the URL and write at least one paragraph in which you describe the evidence you have gathered about the site's quality.

5. When you are finished, close your Web browser.

Research the Web to find specific information, and then evaluate the information.

RESEARCH

Case Problem 4

There are no Data Files needed for this Case Problem.

Glenwood Employment Agency   You work as a staff assistant at the Glenwood Employment Agency. Eric Steinberg, the agency's owner, wants you to locate Web resources for finding open positions in your geographic area. Eric would like this information to gauge whether his own efforts are keeping pace with those of the competition. He wants to monitor a few good pages but does not want to conduct exhaustive searches of the Web every week. To help Eric find current employment information, complete the following steps:

1. Start your Web browser, go to www.cengagebrain.com, open the Tutorial 3 Weblinks page, and then click the Case Problem 4 link. The Case Problem 4 section contains links to lists of search engines, directories, and metasearch engines.

2. Use one of the search tools to find Web sites containing information about job openings in your geographic area. (*Hint:* You can use search expressions that include Boolean and precedence operators to limit your searches.)

3. Prepare a list of at least five URLs of pages that you believe would be good candidates for Eric's monitoring program.

4. For each URL that you find, write a paragraph that explains why you selected it, and then identify any particular strengths or weaknesses of the Web site based on Eric's intended use.

5. When you are finished, close your Web browser.

Create a report that evaluates the effectiveness of a search tool you chose to find specific information.

CREATE

Case Problem 5

There are no Data Files needed for this Case Problem.

Lynda's Fine Foods   For many years, Lynda Rice has operated a small store that sells specialty foods, such as pickles and mustard, and related gift items. Lynda is thinking about selling her products on the Web because they are small, inexpensive to ship relative to their product prices, and easy to package. She believes that people who buy her products might appreciate the convenience of ordering over the Web. Lynda would like to find some specialty food store sites on the Web to learn about possible competitors and to obtain some ideas that she might use when she creates her own Web site. To research selling specialty food items on the Web, complete the following steps:

1. Start your Web browser, go to www.cengagebrain.com, open the Tutorial 3 Weblinks page, and then click the Case Problem 5 link. The Case Problem 5 section contains links to lists of search engines, directories, and metasearch engines.

2. Use one of the search engines to find Web sites that offer gift items such as pickles or mustard. You can use search expressions that include Boolean and precedence operators to limit your searches.

3. Repeat your search using one of the Web directory tools.

4. Compare the results you obtained using a search engine and using a Web directory. Explain in a report of about 100 words which search tool was more effective for this type of search. Your instructor might ask you to prepare a presentation to your class in which you summarize your conclusions.

5. When you are finished, close your Web browser.

OBJECTIVES

Session 4.1
- Find current news
- Get up-to-date weather information
- Obtain maps and destination information
- Locate people and businesses
- Purchase items online

Session 4.2
- Understand copyrights, fair use, public domain, and plagiarism
- Learn how to cite Web resources
- Find library and text resources on the Web
- Locate multimedia elements on the Web, including images, audio, and video

Information Resources on the Web

Finding Specific Information Online

Case | *Cosby Promotions*

Marti Cosby is the president of Cosby Promotions—a growing booking agency that handles promotion and concert contract negotiations for musicians and bands. Cosby Promotions works with a wide variety of music acts, including bands that play pop, Latin, heavy metal, techno, industrial, and urban styles of music. Marti wants to use Web searching techniques to help Cosby Promotions' staff stay current on entertainment news and trends that might affect the agency's clients.

The agency does not currently handle many country music acts, but Marti wants to expand its country music business during the next few years. To this end, she is planning a trip to Nashville, Tennessee, home of the Grand Ole Opry. In this tutorial, you will use the Internet to find information for Marti as she prepares for her trip to Nashville, where she will visit a new venue, meet with new clients, and learn more about the country music genre.

INTERNET

STARTING DATA FILES

There are no starting Data Files needed for this tutorial.

SESSION 4.1 VISUAL OVERVIEW

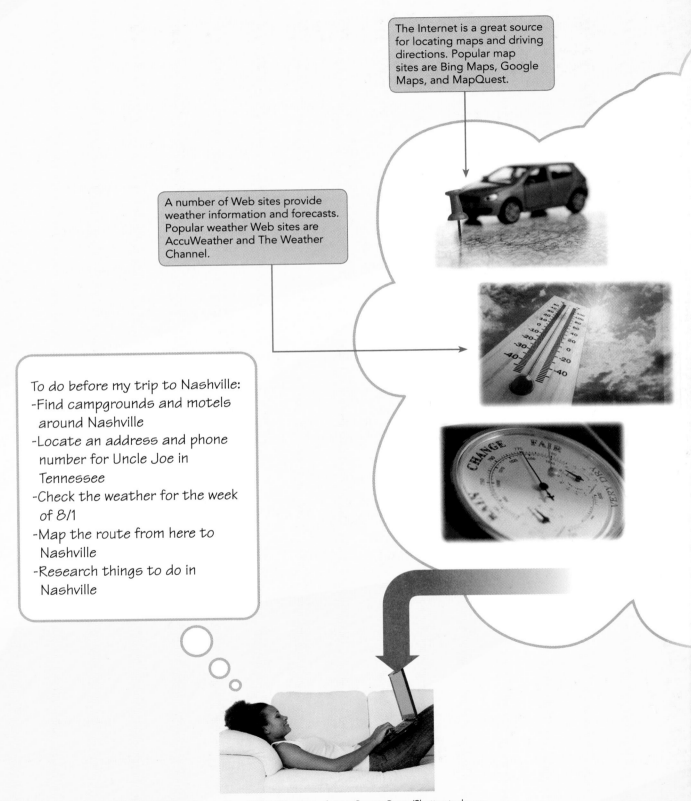

The Internet is a great source for locating maps and driving directions. Popular map sites are Bing Maps, Google Maps, and MapQuest.

A number of Web sites provide weather information and forecasts. Popular weather Web sites are AccuWeather and The Weather Channel.

To do before my trip to Nashville:
- Find campgrounds and motels around Nashville
- Locate an address and phone number for Uncle Joe in Tennessee
- Check the weather for the week of 8/1
- Map the route from here to Nashville
- Research things to do in Nashville

TYPES OF INFORMATION ON THE INTERNET

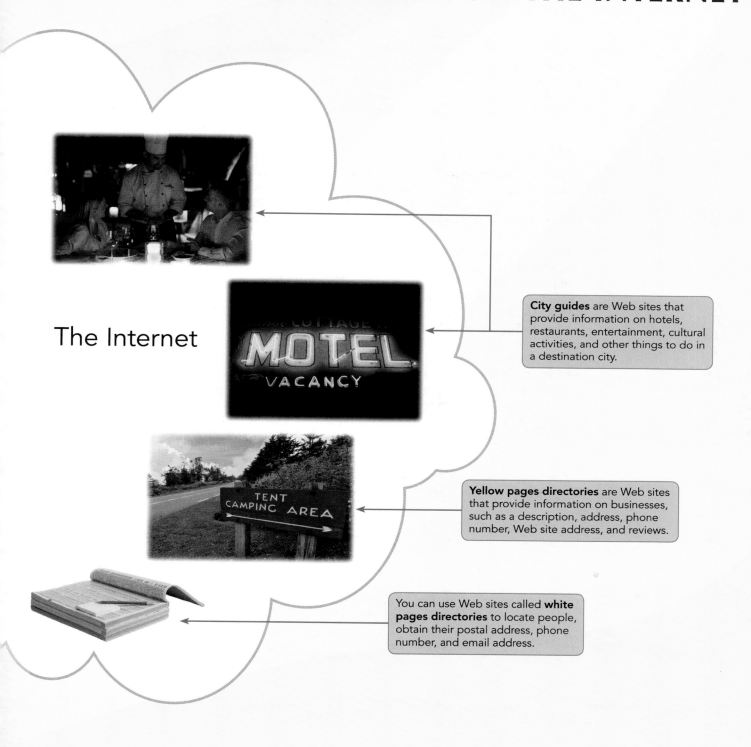

The Internet

City guides are Web sites that provide information on hotels, restaurants, entertainment, cultural activities, and other things to do in a destination city.

Yellow pages directories are Web sites that provide information on businesses, such as a description, address, phone number, Web site address, and reviews.

You can use Web sites called **white pages directories** to locate people, obtain their postal address, phone number, and email address.

Finding Current and Specific Information on the Web

In Tutorial 3, you learned how to use search engines, directories, and other resources to find information on the Web. In many instances, your goal was to find facts about a topic. Often, these facts don't change over time. Sometimes, however, you will need to find the most up-to-date information on a particular subject or event. For example, Marti's work at Cosby Promotions involves finding the most recent news and information about clients, potential sponsors, performance venues, and trends in the music industry.

Finding Recent Information

When you are searching for recent news, you could go directly to the Web sites of local and national newspapers, magazines, television stations, and radio stations. But the news sources you choose to visit might not have articles on the information you want. Instead of this hit-or-miss approach, you can conduct a search to determine which sources have the information you want. Before conducting a search, you should consider which search tool would be the best option: a search engine or a directory. Search engines usually include more recent listings because the editorial review process of many Web directories takes time to complete. In addition, a Web directory might not include listings for the topic you want to find.

Most search engines enable you to search for Web sites that have been modified recently. This feature is usually included as a filter option on the sites' advanced search pages. The filtering options for selecting recently modified Web pages will be different on the various search engines. For example, the Google Advanced Search page allows a search to be filtered based on when the page was last updated, as shown in Figure 4-1. You choose from among the most recent 24 hours, week, month, or year. Exalead includes an advanced search option so you can specify a particular date and search before or after that date, or you can include two date arguments in an Exalead search expression and search for Web pages modified after one date but before another date.

Figure 4-1	Date filter options on the Google Advanced Search page

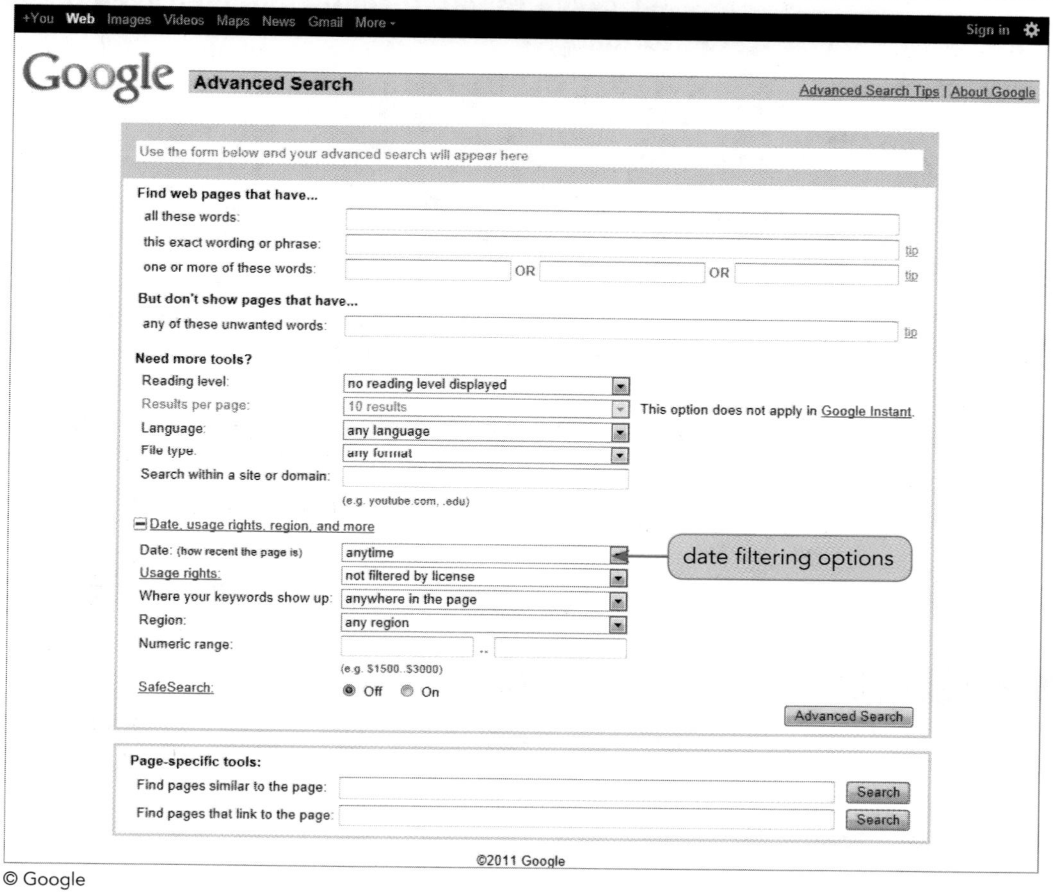

© Google

How Search Engines Filter Results by Date

Search engines can perform date-filtered searches because when Web servers send a Web page to a browser (or a search engine's Web robot), they include a header that contains information about the Web page, such as the date it was last modified. Search engines then store this information in their databases and use it to create date-filtered results.

Marti wants to book several of her newest clients to play at Ryman Auditorium in Nashville, Tennessee, and she needs to find current information about the auditorium to help her prepare for an upcoming meeting with the venue's manager. Although Web directories will collect many useful sites that include the name "Ryman Auditorium" in their databases, a search engine would provide more recent listings. In this case, you will use Google to search for information on Ryman Auditorium from the past month.

To use Google to find recently modified Web pages about Ryman Auditorium:

1. Start your Web browser, go to **www.cengagebrain.com**, open the Tutorial 4 Weblinks page, and then click the **Session 4.1** link.

2. Click the **Google** link to open the Google home page.

3. Click the **Options** button in the upper-right corner of the page, and then click **Advanced search**. The Google Advanced Search page opens.

4. Click in the **all these words** box at the top of the search form, and then type **Ryman Auditorium**. This search expression will locate Web pages that include the search term. You want the search to return pages that have been modified in the last month.

5. Click the **Date, usage rights, region, and more** link near the bottom of the page to display options that allow you to filter the search results.

6. Click the **Date** arrow, and then click **past month** to limit your search to pages that have been modified within the past month.

7. Click the **Advanced Search** button. Figure 4-2 shows a part of the date-filtered results page generated by the Google search engine for this query.

Figure 4-2	Google date-filtered search results

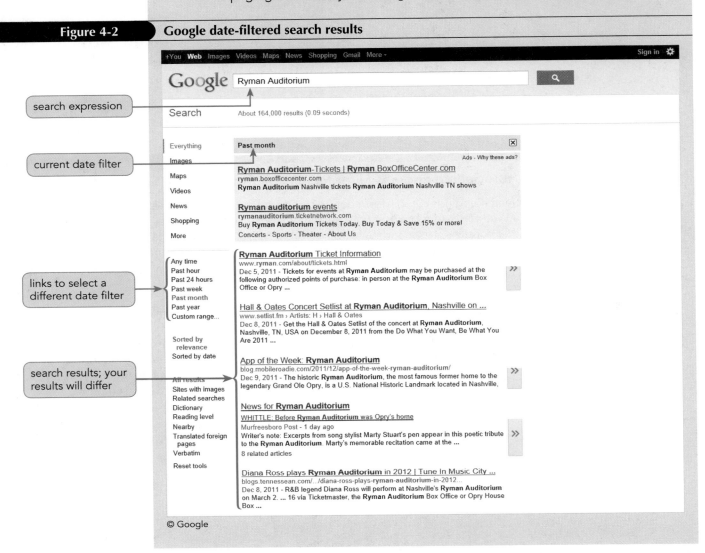

© Google

Search engines' date filtering capabilities are only as good as the information they collect. These databases store the date each Web page was last modified. A page gets a new modification date no matter how large or small the change is. So, even if most of the content on the page did not change, the modification date would still be updated. Because of this, a date-filtered search doesn't always provide the results you want. Another good way to find recent information about companies, people, or events is to look for current news about them.

Getting Current News

TIP

In many instances, you can search the site's archives for older articles.

The Web has a variety of sources for current news stories. Some news outlets are available only online. Others are available both online and offline. Traditional news outlets—including print and broadcast media—often post news stories on the Web in addition to their usual distribution in newspapers and magazines or on the radio and television. These Web sites include search features so you can search the site for specific news stories. Also, search engines and Web directories include links to these types of sources.

PROSKILLS

Written Communication: Evaluating Sources of Information

On the Internet and the Web, information is now disseminated rapidly and extensively, and updated frequently. The quantity of information available is astounding in part because of the low investment required, and in part because of the new sources of information that are easily available. This means that you as the reader need to evaluate the material you are reading.

The cost of publishing on the Web is very low. A Web-based publication can be financially successful with few advertisers, no subscribers, and relatively few readers. As a result, online publications can focus on the specialized, narrow interests of relatively small audiences. Online-only publications such as Slate, Salon.com, and The Huffington Post have become established parts of the media industry.

The low cost of Web publishing also means that anyone with the interest and the financial means can use the Web to promote his or her views—commonly in the form of a Web log (also called a Weblog or blog). A **blog** is a written commentary on current events, personal experiences, or anything else an individual wants to expound upon. Blogs are usually written by a single person (called the blogger) who wants to express a particular point of view. Some blogs allow readers to add comments or reactions to the blogger's statements, which may be edited or deleted by the blogger. Although blogs exist on a wide variety of topics, many blogs focus on political, religious, or other issues about which people have strong opinions. Because the blog owner writes the main content and decides which comments posted by readers will be included in the blog, the content and direction of the blog are controlled by its owner. (You will learn more about blogs in Tutorial 5.)

An alternative form of interactive online writing is the wiki. A **wiki** is a Web site that is designed to allow multiple users to contribute content and edit existing content. "Wiki" is a Hawaiian word that means "fast," and wikis are set up to allow many different users to add and edit content quickly and easily. Most wikis are focused on facts or collaborative work. Wikipedia, the online encyclopedia that you learned about in Tutorial 3, is probably the most famous wiki in the world. A wiki that has received a lot of attention in recent years is WikiLeaks, which provides a way for anonymous sources to leak information to its journalists, including secret government information.

You must also determine whether the content is opinion or fact. And, if you see the same information repeatedly at several sites, you need to determine the original source of that information. For example, various sites could reprint information from the same source, making it seem that the information is being corroborated by multiple sources when in actuality it is all from one source. With the wide variety of information available on the Web, you must be diligent in evaluating the accuracy of the information you are reading.

One of the simplest ways to find a wide selection of current news reports is to use a news aggregation Web site. A **news aggregation Web site** collects and displays content from a variety of online news sources, including wire services, print media, broadcast outlets, and even blogs, and displays it in one place. You can then quickly access news stories on a topic from multiple sources.

One example of a news aggregation Web site is Yahoo!, which provides links to different topical sites on its home page. The News link opens the Yahoo! News site, shown in Figure 4-3, with access to the latest news and headlines—both in print and broadcast. You can access the day's top stories, latest news, and stories published by a particular news outlet. The page also features links to different aspects of the news—such as World, Business, Entertainment, Sports, Tech, and Politics—that include corresponding types of news stories. Other news aggregation Web sites include Bing News, Google News, Drudge Report, The Huffington Post, and NewsNow. Keep in mind that news aggregation Web sites, like any other media, may show a bias toward certain points of view.

Figure 4-3   **Yahoo! News home page**

tabs display other filters or sorts of the current news

top stories compiled by the news aggregation site

Courtesy of Yahoo! Inc. © 2011 by Yahoo! Inc. YAHOO! and the YAHOO! logo are trademarks of Yahoo! Inc.

You will use a news aggregation Web site to locate current news stories about Ryman Auditorium that might not have appeared in the results of your search of recently modified Web pages.

To find recent news stories on the Web that mention Ryman Auditorium:

1. Return to the Weblinks page for Tutorial 4, locate the heading News Aggregation Web Site in the Session 4.1 section, and then click the **Yahoo!** link to open the search engine Web site.

2. Click the **News** link to open Yahoo! News, the news aggregation Web site.

3. Scroll down to locate the News Search box, type **Ryman Auditorium** in the News Search box, and then click the **News Search** button. The search results show the current headlines along with the source where they were published, as well as the date and time they were published. Figure 4-4 shows a part of the results page generated by Yahoo! News for this search.

Figure 4-4   **Yahoo! News search results page**

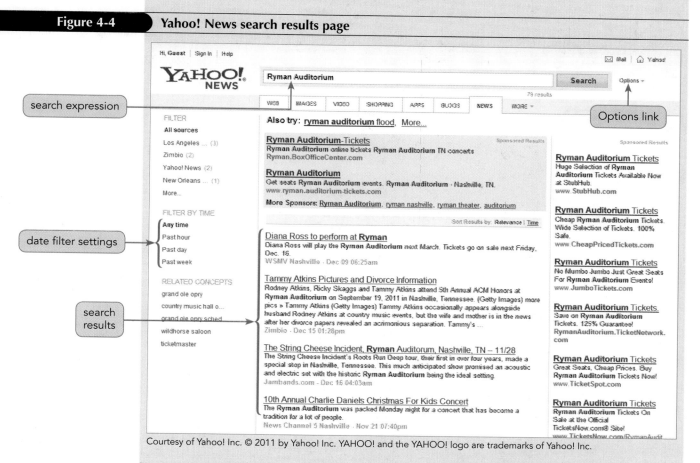

Courtesy of Yahoo! Inc. © 2011 by Yahoo! Inc. YAHOO! and the YAHOO! logo are trademarks of Yahoo! Inc.

4. Click the **Options** link next to the search box at the top of the page, and then click **Advanced Search**. The Advanced News Search page opens with options for narrowing your search. See Figure 4-5.

| Figure 4-5 | Yahoo! Advanced News Search page |

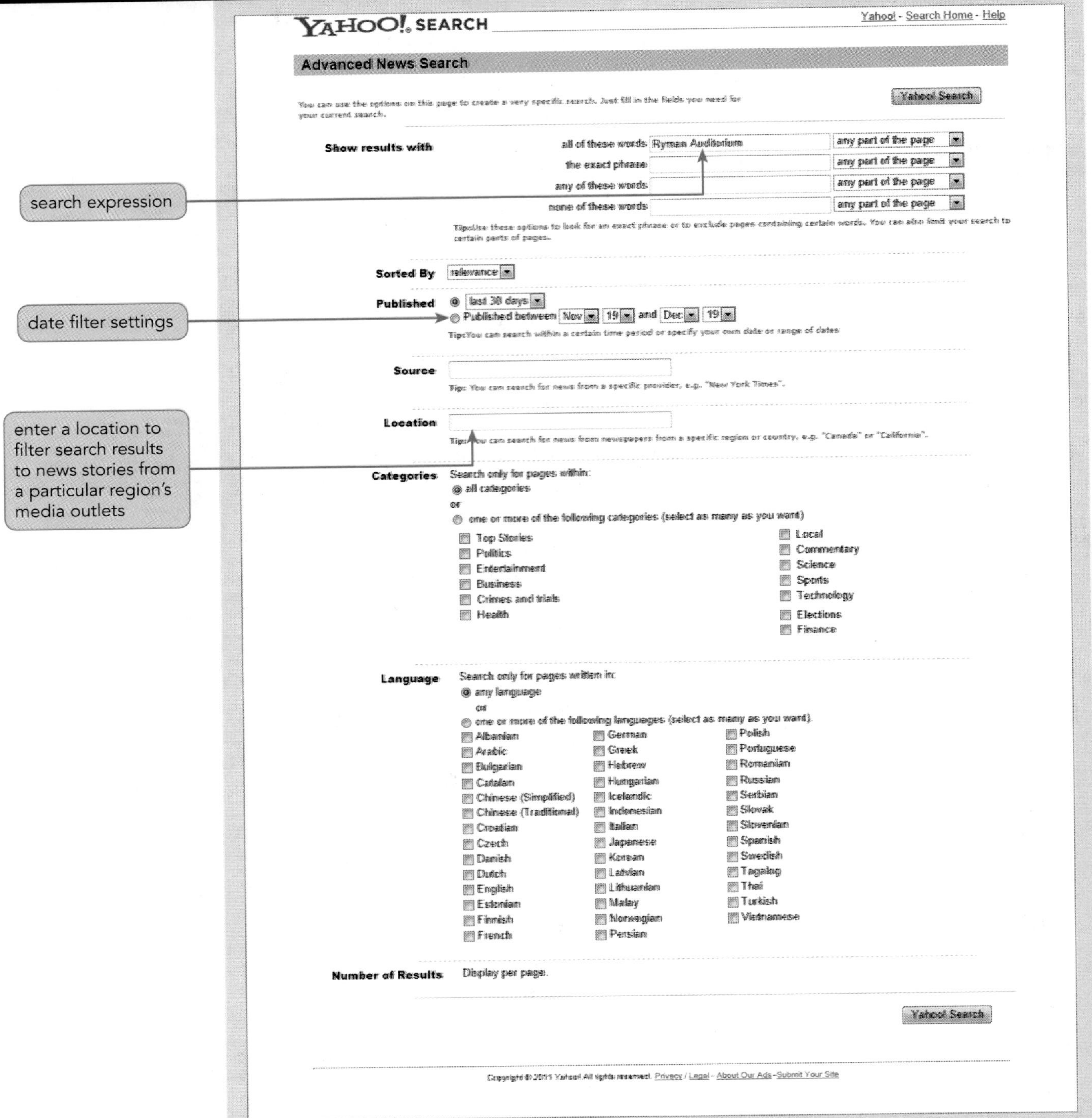

search expression

date filter settings

enter a location to filter search results to news stories from a particular region's media outlets

5. Click the **Location** box, and then type **Nashville, TN** to narrow the search results to local Nashville newspapers.

6. Click the **Yahoo! Search** button. The search results show news about Ryman Auditorium that was published by Nashville news media.

To visit additional news aggregation Web sites, you can use the links in the News Aggregation Web Sites section of the Additional Information section of the Weblinks page for Tutorial 4.

INSIGHT

Understanding How News Gets Distributed Electronically

The content for news outlets comes from wire services, newspapers, and broadcast networks. A **wire service** (also called a press agency or news service) is an organization that hires reporters to gather and write news stories, which it then distributes to newspapers, magazines, broadcasters, Web sites, and other organizations that pay a fee to the wire service.

Although there are hundreds of wire services around the world, most news comes from the four largest wire services: United Press International (UPI) and the Associated Press (AP) in the United States, Thomson Reuters in Great Britain, and Agence France-Presse (AFP) in France. In addition to selling stories to print, broadcast, and online news outlets around the world, these major wire services all publish current news stories on their own Web sites.

Likewise, print, broadcast, and online news outlets hire reporters to write news stories, which might also be distributed or sold to affiliates or other news outlets. Major newspapers, such as *The New York Times*, *Washington Post*, and the *Los Angeles Times*, have Web sites that include current news and many other features from their print editions. All of the major U.S. broadcast networks, including ABC, CBS, CNN, FOX, MSNBC, NBC, and NPR, have Web sites that carry news features. Broadcasters in other countries, such as the BBC in Great Britain, also provide news reports on their Web pages. Local radio and television stations often have their own Web sites where they offer selected news, sports, and weather information for their local market areas.

Because many newspapers, magazines, broadcasters, and news aggregation sites obtain stories from the major wire services and from each other, you often find the same news stories in your search results. Sometimes one news source will edit a story to shorten it or add information that appeals to its local audience. In many cases, different news outlets will just republish the original story without changes. Keep in mind that finding the same story published in multiple places doesn't mean that it is accurate or current. Be sure to evaluate the content as you learned in Tutorial 3 for accuracy and currency.

Finding Up-to-Date Weather Information

Many people consult a weather forecast daily because they want to know the weather conditions before dressing and venturing out for the day. When planning a vacation, they can review weather patterns for their intended destination. Before packing for a trip, they can obtain detailed weather information to guide their clothing choices. Some people enjoy seeing the weather conditions for family and friends who live elsewhere. Many also want to follow current weather conditions when there is a major storm—whether snow, wind, rain, hurricane, etc. These weather forecasts, conditions, and other information are available on the Web.

A number of companies, such as AccuWeather, The Weather Channel, National Oceanic and Atmospheric Administration's National Weather Service, and Weather Underground, provide weather conditions and forecasts on their Web sites. These Web sites also offer a wealth of other features and information, including live radar, graphs,

10-day forecasts, trip planners, severe weather reports, satellite views, desktop weather apps, and video forecasts for different areas. Many sites let you enter your zip code so the page always opens with weather for your area. You can also install a gadget on your desktop or an app on your smartphone to display the current weather conditions for your area.

Some weather sites sell their information to other companies that then include it on their Web sites. So you might see an AccuWeather forecast or weather map on many other Web sites, such as Yahoo! or your local newspaper's site. These same weather sites are also available as a gadget for your Windows desktop or an app for your smartphone.

Local television and radio stations offer weather information on their Web sites. Some of these sites purchase weather information from other outlets such as AccuWeather or The Weather Channel, but larger stations usually employ their own meteorologists and have their own weather prediction equipment. These local weather forecasts can be more accurate and detailed than those provided by the major weather Web sites for your area.

Marti plans to travel to Nashville later in the week to meet with some country music artists whom she hopes to sign as clients for the agency. You will check the weather for the Nashville area.

To find weather information for the Nashville area:

▶ **1.** Return to the Weblinks page for Tutorial 4, and then click one of the links under the Weather Information Web Sites heading in the Session 4.1 section. The weather site opens in your browser. You can search for the weather forecast for a specific location by entering the city and state or a zip code.

▶ **2.** In the search box, type **Nashville, TN** and then click the **Go, Search, Find Weather**, or similar button. The local Nashville forecast appears on the page. Depending on the site you chose, there might be links to the extended local forecast, radar, satellite, and videos or webcams. Figure 4-6 shows the Nashville Weather Forecast and Conditions on The Weather Channel's Web site.

Figure 4-6 The Weather Channel local forecast page for Nashville

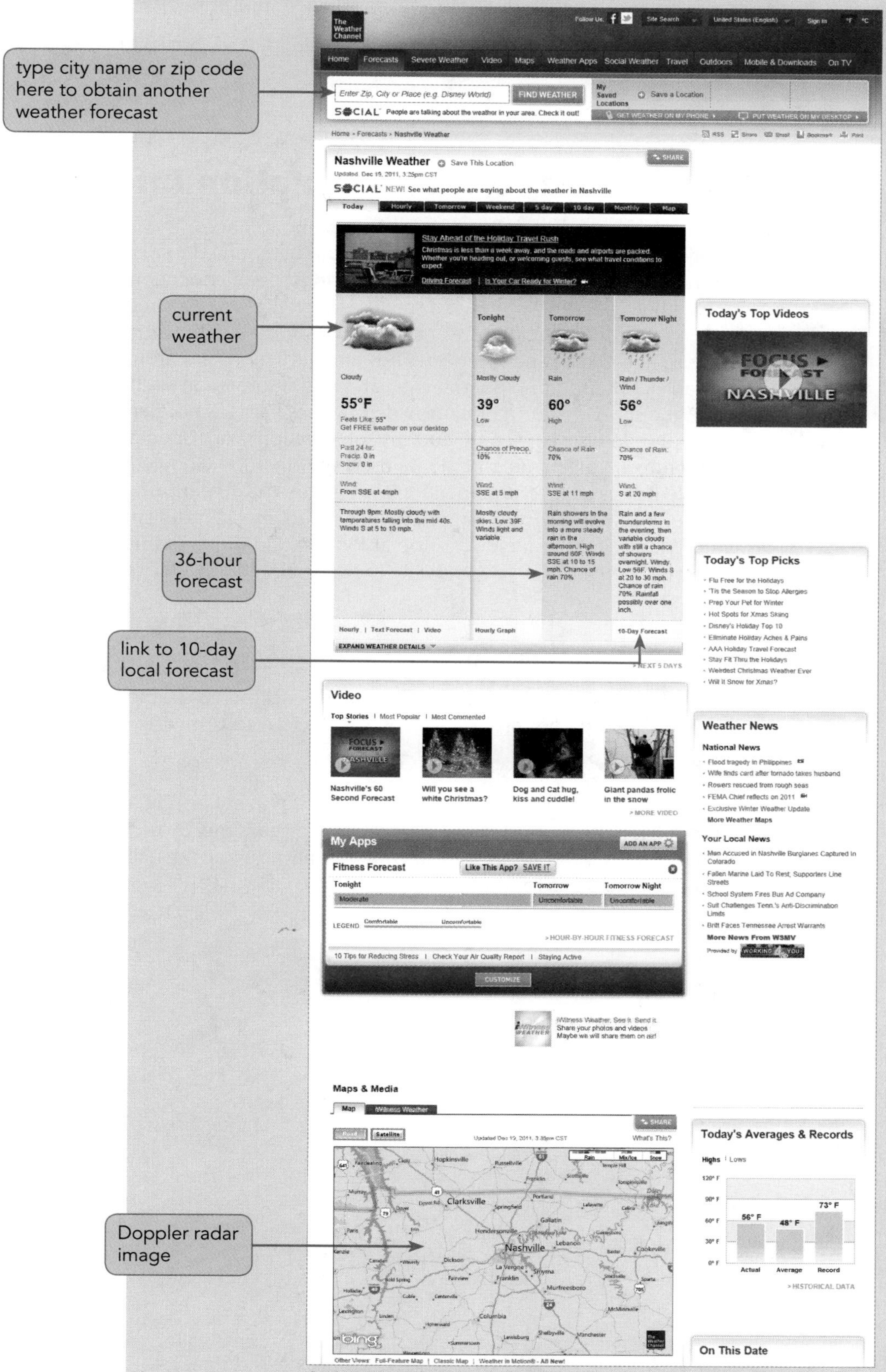

type city name or zip code here to obtain another weather forecast

current weather

36-hour forecast

link to 10-day local forecast

Doppler radar image

3. Click a link to see an extended forecast for Nashville.

4. If available, play the video of the Nashville weather forecast.

5. Click a link to see a satellite map of Nashville, and then click the **Play** button if necessary.

Obtaining Maps and Destination Information

Map sites provide an abundance of information about places. The maps can show a broad overview of a region or state, and they can be zoomed to display detailed maps of a city or neighborhood. You can get directions to a specific location, observe current traffic and weather conditions, look at a satellite view instead of a street map, and in some cases see photos of the location. You can find businesses in the area, including restaurants, hotels, and shops; see what activities and attractions are around; identify services such as banks, libraries, and pharmacies; and find information such as gas prices and parking. Although the information provided by these sites is not perfect (for example, new roads and detours caused by current construction work often are not included), they are helpful travel aids. Some commonly used sites include Google Maps and MapQuest.

Nashville has been a central location for country music performers for many years. In fact, the Grand Ole Opry, a long-running country music radio show, is based in Nashville. Marti wants to include a stop at Ryman Auditorium, which is the home of the Grand Ole Opry. You will use a map site to determine the location of Ryman Auditorium.

To locate Ryman Auditorium using Google Maps:

1. Return to the Weblinks page for Tutorial 4, and then click the **Google** link under the Map Site heading in the Session 4.1 section to open the Google home page.

2. Click the **Maps** link to open the Google Maps search page.

3. In the Search box, type **Ryman Auditorium, Nashville, TN**, and then click the **Search Maps** button. A map of Nashville appears marked with the location of Ryman Auditorium. Figure 4-7 shows the map that appears in Google Maps. The map includes tools for adjusting your view of the map.

Figure 4-7   Ryman Auditorium area map in Google Maps

search expression

drag to map to switch to Street view

drag to zoom in or out

search location

click to display traffic information

© Google

4. Click the **Zoom In** button three times, or until you can clearly see that Ryman Auditorium is located on 5th Avenue North. The Google Maps Web site offers views other than Map view, including Street view, which is a group of photos of the location and surrounding area.

5. Drag the **yellow person** icon at the top of the Zoom bar onto the map to display blue lines, and then release the mouse button when the green pointer under the person icon is pointing to the location of Ryman Auditorium on the map. As you drag the person icon to the location, a ScreenTip appears over the person icon's head giving the address of Ryman Auditorium. A photo of the street view of Ryman Auditorium appears in place of the map. Figure 4-8 shows the photo that appears in Google Maps.

Figure 4-8   **Street view of Ryman Auditorium on Google Maps**

click to exit Street view

picture of Ryman Auditorium (you might see a different picture)

Map view of the current picture

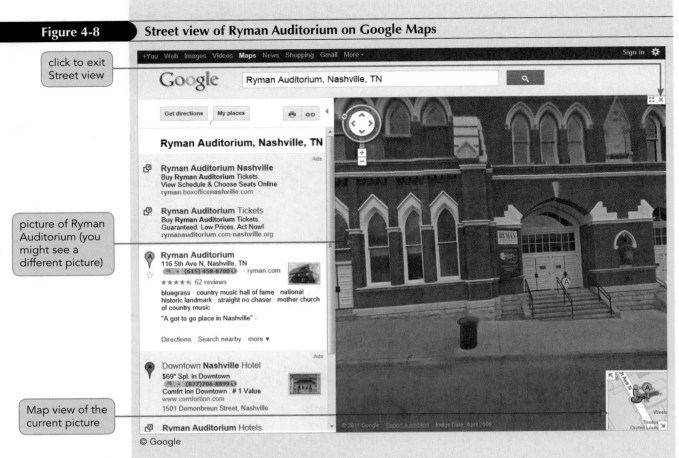

© Google

6. In Google Maps, click the **Exit street view** button in the upper-right corner of the street view photo to return to Map view.

7. Point to the **Satellite** button to open a menu of options for additional information you can display for this location, such as Traffic, Photos, Weather, and Webcams.

8. Click **Traffic** on the menu. Depending on the current traffic conditions, red, yellow, and green lines appear on the map indicating the current traffic status around Ryman Auditorium.

9. Click the **Ryman Auditorium** link next to the letter "A" in the pane to the left of the map. A Web page appears showing a photograph of the auditorium, its address, its phone number, links to printed directions, links to reviews, a description of the venue, and a list of upcoming events.

To visit additional map sites, you can use the links in the Map Sites section of the Additional Information section of the Weblinks page for Tutorial 4.

Although map sites often provide basic listings and information about lodging, restaurants, attractions, and entertainment opportunities for a particular location, you can often find more detailed information and reviews using travel guide sites. These sites include descriptive and comprehensive information about a location, reviews of hotels and restaurants, trip ideas, travel deals, and calendars of events, as well as discussions, photos, and blogs. People often use these sites to plan a trip from selecting a destination to learning about the history and attractions, finding hotels and restaurants, and making flight and hotel reservations. Some common travel guide sites are Fodor's Travel Guides, Frommer's Travel Guides, Let's Go Travel, Lonely Planet Travel Guides and Travel Information, and TripAdvisor.

To further help Marti prepare for her Nashville trip, you want to find some general historical information about Nashville, locate a restaurant for dinner, and get information on a hotel.

To obtain information about Nashville restaurants and entertainment:

▶ **1.** Return to the Weblinks page for Tutorial 4, and then click a link under the Travel Guides Web Sites heading in the Session 4.1 section.

▶ **2.** In the search box, type **Nashville, TN**, and then click the search or go button. The search results show a list of links related to Nashville.

▶ **3.** Click the **Nashville travel guide** link (the specific wording of this link will change depending on the site you use). A variety of information is available about Nashville. Figure 4-9 shows Frommer's Guide to Nashville.

| Figure 4-9 | Frommer's Guide to Nashville |

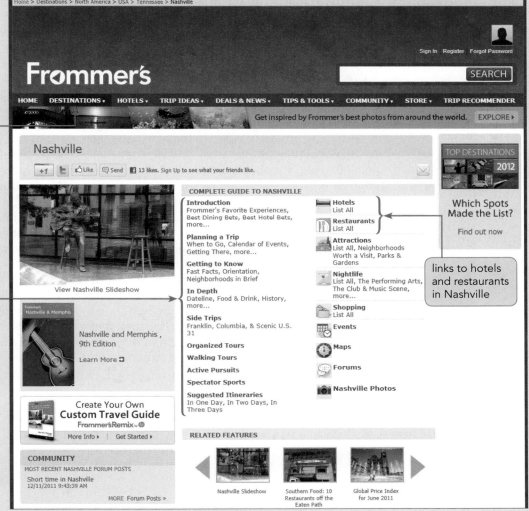

links to categories of information included in the travel guide

details about Nashville

links to hotels and restaurants in Nashville

> **4.** If there is an overview or introduction to Nashville, read the information provided.

> **5.** Locate and click a link that provides a list of Nashville restaurants, and then find a restaurant to recommend to Marti.

> **6.** Locate and click a link that provides a list of Nashville hotels, and then find a top-rated hotel where Marti can stay during her visit.

Marti should have enough information now to solidify her travel plans for her business trip to Nashville. To visit additional Travel Guide sites, you can use the links in the Travel Guides section of the Additional Information section of the Weblinks page for Tutorial 4.

Finding People and Businesses

Online directory Web sites include listings of businesses and people, much like the printed telephone books that were used for decades to find phone numbers and contact information as well as businesses and services. Traditionally, white pages directories store individuals' names, addresses, and telephone numbers, and yellow pages directories store information about businesses. Today, however, the line between yellow and white pages directories is blurred. Most big name online directories provide access to both people and business contact information. Some common online directories are Superpages.com, Yellowbook, YP.com – Yellow Pages, Switchboard, Internet Address Finder, White Pages, and Yahoo! People Search.

When looking for a person, you can search for an individual by name, by postal address, by email address, or by phone number (called a reverse lookup). In some cases, you can find the contact information for people at both home and at work. When looking for a business, you can search for a specific business by name or you can look at businesses in a specific category for a geographic area.

Some sites provide a variety of other features, including maps and driving directions, reviews of businesses, area code and zip code lookup, name popularity, a person's age, and information about his or her relatives. Some provide a resource to perform a background check that looks at a person's criminal history, address history, personal assets, lawsuits, and other legal entanglements. Another resource might be available to find property value, sales history, property details, and neighborhood information. However, most directory sites charge a fee to access this level of detailed information about a person.

Some Web sites make unpublished and unlisted telephone numbers available for public use. Other sites group individual listings by categories, such as religious or political affiliation. Many people expressed concerns about privacy violations when this type of information became easily accessible on the Web. In response to these privacy concerns, most directory sites provide a way for people to remove their listings. For example, Switchboard will accept a list removal request made on its Web page or sent by email. You might want to verify that white pages directories have a correct listing for you and decide whether you want your listing to appear on a white pages site.

TIP

Many online white pages and yellow pages directories are also available as mobile apps for smartphones.

These online directories compile information in several ways. Individuals and businesses can submit new entries as well as update or correct existing entries. Directory sites can also collect information from publicly available sources, published telephone directories, and the Web, such as data provided when signing up for a social network like Facebook. Directory sites also purchase information from third-party sources, such as personal information individuals provided to a business or provided when filling out a form to enter a contest or start a subscription. Businesses then share this information with online directories. All of this information is indexed by the directory so that it can be quickly accessed during a search.

How Directories Fund Their Services

INSIGHT

Business directories provide ads and listings that appear in response to relevant search queries on search engines such as Google or Yahoo!. The ads can be static advertisements like you would see in a print directory, or interactive multimedia ads that include sound and video. And many directory sites provide sponsored results to searches, which means that businesses pay a fee to have their contact information and ads placed higher in the search results. The business pays a fee each time its advertisement is clicked.

Marti is planning to develop reciprocal relationships with local booking agencies in Nashville. She wants to make some initial contacts during this trip and asks you to search the Web to find a list of booking agencies in Nashville. You can use an online directory to find music agencies located in Nashville.

To search online directories for a music agency:

1. Return to the Weblinks page for Tutorial 4, locate the Online Directories heading in the Session 4.1 section, and then click the link to one of the sites listed to open its home page.

2. Click the appropriate link to search for a person (the exact link will vary, but could be labeled People Search, Find People, or Find a Person). Figure 4-10 shows the Find People tab at Superpages.com. Before looking for a music agency, use the site to find your own listing.

| Figure 4-10 | Superpages.com Find People |

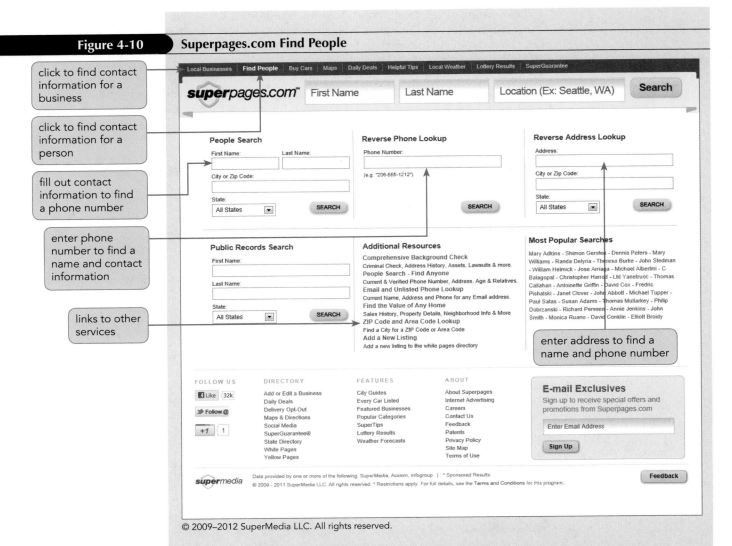

click to find contact information for a business

click to find contact information for a person

fill out contact information to find a phone number

enter phone number to find a name and contact information

links to other services

enter address to find a name and phone number

3. In the corresponding boxes, enter your first name, last name, city and state, or your zip code, and then click the **Search** or **Find** button. Examine your listing that appears.

> **Trouble?** If you do not find your listing, your telephone number might be listed under another person's name, such as a parent or roommate. Repeat Step 3 using that person's name to find your listing. If you still cannot find a listing for yourself, try searching for a friend's listing or a relative's listing, or try your search in a different directory.

4. Click the appropriate link to search for a business (the exact link will vary, but could be labeled Local Businesses, Find a Business, or Business).

5. In the corresponding boxes, enter **Music Agents** as the category of the business you want to find and **Nashville, TN** as the location, and then click the **Find** or **Search** button. The results page shows information about music booking agencies in Nashville. This search can be challenging because no single category description is universally used by companies that book performing musicians. Figure 4-11 shows the results page for a search using the term "Music Agents" on the Superpages.com site.

TIP

You also can type Music Agent, Nashville TN in the search box to return results for music agents in that city.

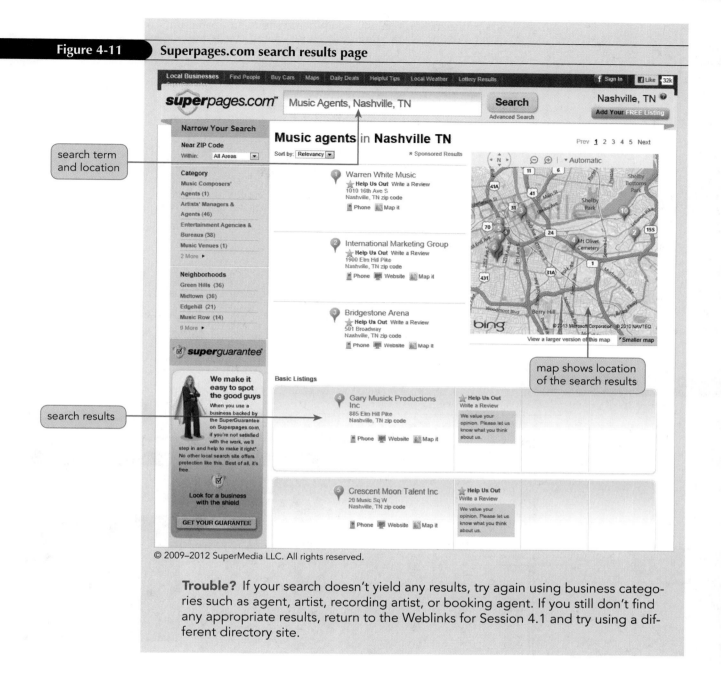

Figure 4-11   Superpages.com search results page

© 2009–2012 SuperMedia LLC. All rights reserved.

Trouble? If your search doesn't yield any results, try again using business categories such as agent, artist, recording artist, or booking agent. If you still don't find any appropriate results, return to the Weblinks for Session 4.1 and try using a different directory site.

Finding Products and Services Online

Many items are available for purchase on the Web: food, clothing, books, computers, software, games, music, specialty items, office supplies. Pretty much anything you can think of is available. Retailers—big and small as well as international, national, and local—have a presence on the Web. Some retailers have both a physical location and a Web site; others such as Amazon.com are online only without a storefront/brick-and-mortar store. In addition, individuals have flocked to the Web to sell their products and services. **E-commerce**, or electronic commerce, refers to the process of developing, marketing, selling, delivering, servicing, and paying for products and services online. You'll learn more about e-commerce in Tutorial 9.

TIP

Retail business that occurs online is also sometimes called e-tail.

Perhaps the most prevalent e-commerce site is Amazon.com. Amazon.com was founded by Jeff Bezos in 1995 to sell books on the Web. Since then, Amazon has expanded to sell a wide variety of products and services in the categories of books, movies, music, games, electronics and computers, home, garden, tools, groceries, health and beauty, toys, kids and babies, clothing, shoes, jewelry, sports, automotive, and industrial. All items are shipped directly to the purchaser or to another recipient specified by the purchaser. Since 2000, individuals as well as retailers have been able to partner with Amazon to sell their products, creating an online marketplace.

So, today, when you search for an item on Amazon.com, you can select the department you want to search, enter keywords for your search, and then view the results sorted in the order you prefer, such as relevance, popularity, price, or average customer review. When searching for books, you can also filter the search results by the book format you want, such as paperback, hardcover, Kindle e-reader edition, HTML, or audio.

Marti wants to find out more about the Grand Ole Opry. You'll search Amazon for a suitable book.

To find a book about the Grand Ole Opry on Amazon.com:

1. Return to the Weblinks page for Tutorial 4, and then click the **Amazon** link under the Online Shopping heading in the Session 4.1 section to open that Web site's home page. See Figure 4-12.

Figure 4-12	Amazon home page

click the Search in arrow to select the department to search in

enter the search term

departments available on Amazon

2. At the top of the page, click the **Search in** arrow, and then click **Books**. Your search will be limited to books rather than all departments.

3. Type **Grand Ole Opry** in the Search for box, and then click the **Go** button. The results show books about the Grand Ole Opry sorted by relevance.

4. At the top of the page, click the **Kindle Edition** link to filter the books to only those that are available for the Kindle e-reader.

5. Click the **Sort by** arrow, and then click **Popularity**. The books are reordered to show the most popular title first.

6. Scroll through the items to get a sense of which books are available and how much they cost.

Individuals can also sell items on the Web using sites such as eBay and craigslist. eBay identifies itself as the world's online marketplace where buyers and sellers come together to trade almost anything. Pierre Omidyar founded the auction site in 1995 as AuctionWeb, creating a marketplace for individuals to exchange goods. The site's name was changed to eBay in 1997. Today, eBay boasts more than 97 million users around the world. It has sites throughout the globe and has acquired or launched a variety of businesses, including PayPal (a global online payment company), Shopping. com (an online comparison shopping site), Half.com (a marketplace for used books, movies, music, and games), Rent.com (a listing site for rental housing in the United States), Milo.com (a product search company), brands4friends (an online shopping club for fashion and lifestyle), and eBay Classifieds (a listing site for classified advertisements). In 2011, it launched Fashion Outlet, the first virtual outlet mall in the United States.

You can find a variety of items on eBay, ranging from autographs to toys to antiques to books. Individuals place items for sale, choosing either to create an auction listing and accept only bids for the item, or to allow people to purchase the item right away for a set amount. For the online auction, the seller sets the minimum bid and the length of the auction; then, at the end of the allotted time, the highest bid wins. For a Buy It Now listing, the first person willing to pay the indicated price gets the item. Payment for an item is made through PayPal, which is a global online payment company people can use to send or receive secure payments without sharing their personal financial information. Anyone can view the items up for auction, but you must register with eBay to post or bid on an item.

Another popular site where individuals can buy and sell items is craigslist. In 1995, Craig Newmark started sending emails to friends about events in the San Francisco Bay Area. The following year, he changed his email distribution list into a Web-based service that included additional categories. In 2000, craigslist started expanding to other cities in the United States.

Today, craigslist is a network of more than 700 local sites in 70 countries that features free online classified advertisements with sections devoted to jobs, housing, personals, for sale, services, community, gigs, resumes, and discussion forums. See Figure 4-13. To buy or sell an item, a seller posts an ad following the site's guidelines, and buyers contact the seller to arrange the purchase, payment, and delivery of that item.

Figure 4-13   craigslist Nashville home page

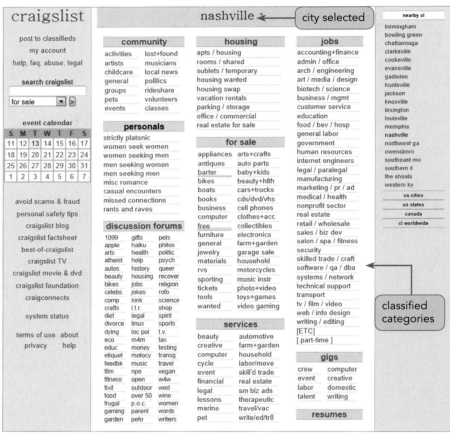

© 2010 Craigslist

Marti is considering creating a contest to promote her country music clients, and she wants to find an autograph of a country music star that she can use as the prize. You'll see what is available on eBay.

To search for an autograph of a country musician on eBay:

1. Return to the Weblinks page for Tutorial 4, and then click the **eBay** link under the Online Shopping heading in the Session 4.1 section to open that Web site's home page. See Figure 4-14.

| Figure 4-14 | eBay home page |

enter item you
want to search for

select a category
of items to search

Copyright © 1995–2012 eBay Inc. All Rights Reserved.

2. Type **country music autographs** in the Search box, and then click the Search button. The results show all of the autographs available.

3. Scroll through the items to get a sense of which autographs are available and how much the cost to purchase them could be. Notice that you can see how many bids were made for the item, the minimum bid accepted, whether you can buy the item immediately, and how much time is left in the auction.

4. Return to the Weblinks page for Tutorial 4.

In the next session, you will learn about multimedia resources on the Web and the copyright issues that arise when you use them.

REVIEW

Session 4.1 Quick Check

1. How can you find Web pages that contain news published during the past week?
2. What is a news aggregation Web site?
3. What types of information are provided on weather sites?
4. What types of information are provided on map sites?
5. What types of information are provided on travel guide sites?
6. What kind of Web site would you use to find contact information for people or businesses?
7. True or False. Some Web sites make unpublished and unlisted telephone numbers available for public use.
8. _____ refers to the process of developing, marketing, selling, delivering, servicing, and paying for products and services online.

SESSION 4.2 VISUAL OVERVIEW

Note the Web site URL in the address or location bar.

The Web site title is usually located prominently on the page.

Make sure you locate and note the name of the publisher or institution that maintains the Web site on which the page is stored.

The Web page title will usually appear directly above the main content of the page.

The author of this Web page is Norman Paskin.

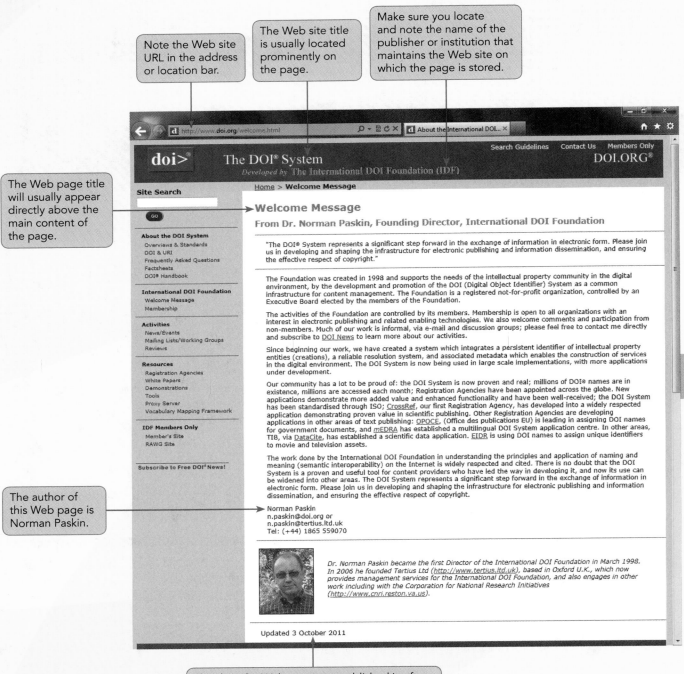

The date the Web page was published is often found at the bottom of the Web page. Also remember to document the date you access the Web page because its content might be changed or updated when someone else views the page at a later date.

WEB PAGE CITATION GUIDELINES

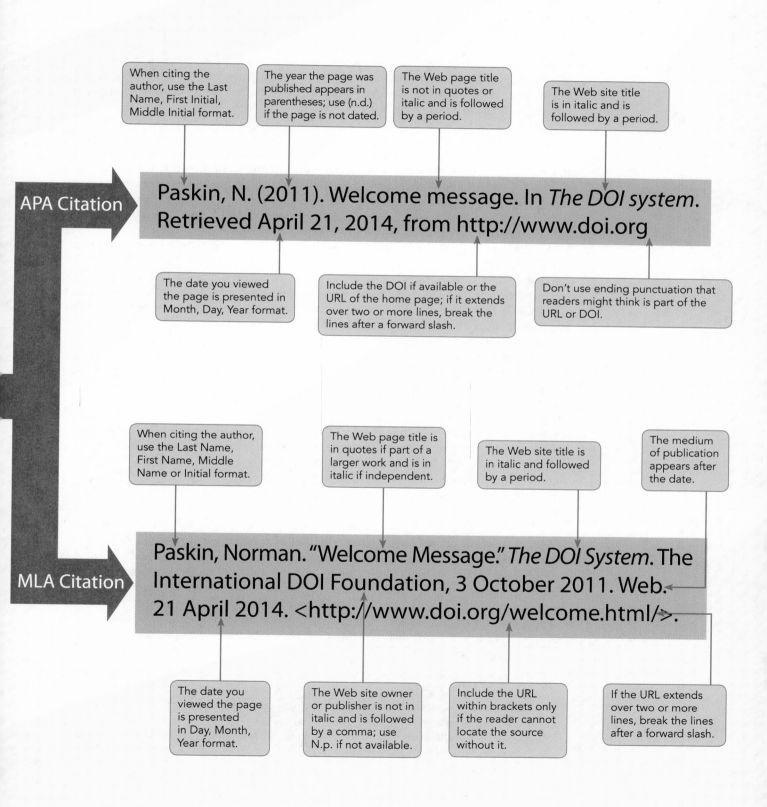

When citing the author, use the Last Name, First Initial, Middle Initial format.

The year the page was published appears in parentheses; use (n.d.) if the page is not dated.

The Web page title is not in quotes or italic and is followed by a period.

The Web site title is in italic and is followed by a period.

APA Citation

Paskin, N. (2011). Welcome message. In *The DOI system*. Retrieved April 21, 2014, from http://www.doi.org

The date you viewed the page is presented in Month, Day, Year format.

Include the DOI if available or the URL of the home page; if it extends over two or more lines, break the lines after a forward slash.

Don't use ending punctuation that readers might think is part of the URL or DOI.

When citing the author, use the Last Name, First Name, Middle Name or Initial format.

The Web page title is in quotes if part of a larger work and is in italic if independent.

The Web site title is in italic and followed by a period.

The medium of publication appears after the date.

MLA Citation

Paskin, Norman. "Welcome Message." *The DOI System*. The International DOI Foundation, 3 October 2011. Web. 21 April 2014. <http://www.doi.org/welcome.html/>.

The date you viewed the page is presented in Day, Month, Year format.

The Web site owner or publisher is not in italic and is followed by a comma; use N.p. if not available.

Include the URL within brackets only if the reader cannot locate the source without it.

If the URL extends over two or more lines, break the lines after a forward slash.

Understanding Copyright

Many Web page elements and other items you find online are a form of **intellectual property**, which includes all creations of the human mind, such as original ideas and creative works presented in a form that can be shared or that others can recreate, emulate, or manufacture. On a Web page, intellectual property includes the images, videos, and text on the page, as well as the design of the page itself. Intellectual property as a tangible expression of an idea is protected just like other tangible forms of property, such as houses, and cars. Each country has its own rules and laws governing intellectual property rights and protection. In the United States, intellectual property is protected through patents, trademarks, trade secrets, and copyrights.

As you learned in Tutorial 1, a copyright is literally the right of a person to make copies of his or her work. Copyrights are granted by a government to the author or creator of an original work who creates a tangible expression of that work or creation. Creations that can be copyrighted include virtually all forms of artistic or intellectual expression, such as books, music, artwork, audio and video recordings, architectural drawings, choreographic works, product packaging, and computer software. The tangible form of the work can be words, numbers, notes, sounds, pictures, and so forth. Copyright protection exists whether the work is published or unpublished.

A collection of facts can be copyrighted, but only if the collection is arranged, coordinated, or selected in a way that causes the resulting work to rise to the level of an original work. For example, the Yahoo! Directory is a collection of links to URLs. These URLs existed before Yahoo! selected and arranged them into the form of its directory. However, most intellectual property experts would argue that the selection and arrangement of the links into categories probably makes the directory copyrightable.

The copyright is in effect for the length of time specified in the copyright law and gives the author or creator the exclusive right to reproduce, adapt, distribute, publicly perform, publicly display, or sell the work. In the United States, under the 1976 Copyright Act, works created after 1977 are protected for the life of the author (or the last surviving author in the case of a "joint work" with multiple authors) plus another 70 years. Works made for hire and anonymous or pseudonymous works are protected for 95 years from the date of publication or 120 years from the date of creation, whichever is earlier. The copyright holder can transfer, license, sell, donate, or leave the copyright to his or her heirs. Works created before 1978 are protected under the 1909 Copyright Act and have more complex and variable terms of copyright.

Determining Fair Use

U.S. copyright law allows people to use portions of copyrighted works without obtaining permission from the copyright holder if that use is a fair use. Section 107 of the 1976 Copyright Act lists criticism, comment, news reporting, teaching, scholarship, and research as examples of uses that may be eligible for fair use. However, the circumstances surrounding a particular use determine whether that use is considered fair. Keep in mind that the legal definition of fair use is intentionally broad and can be difficult to interpret. As a result, many disputes about whether a use is fair have landed in court. Courts generally consider the following four factors when determining fair use:

1. The purpose and character of the new work. This factor considers such issues as whether the use adds something new to the body of knowledge and arts or just reproduces the work, and whether the use is commercial or for nonprofit educational purposes.
2. The nature of the copyrighted work. In general, more creative works have stronger protection than factual works. Keep in mind that an unpublished work has the same copyright protections for fair use as a published work.

3. The amount and substantiality of the portion used in relation to the copyrighted work as a whole; in other words, how much of the copyrighted work was used. The less work that is used, the more likely it falls under fair use. However, using even a small amount of the work can be copyright infringement if it is the heart of the work. This is especially true with musical compositions. The use of even a small portion of a copyrighted song can be an infringing use.

4. The effect of the use on the potential market, or value, of the copyrighted work. For example, does the use of the copyrighted material hurt the market for the original work, and does it impair or limit the ability of the copyright owner to earn income or otherwise benefit from the work?

Again, no hard-and-fast rule determines fair use. If you are unsure whether your use is indeed fair use, the safest course of action is to contact the copyright owner and ask for permission to use the work.

One area where fair use disputes are prevalent is videos being posted on YouTube. Consider that any one video can include both original and copyrighted material. A video that includes even a small clip from a movie or television show or part of a song written or performed by someone else can constitute copyright infringement. This means that the copyright owner can sue the person who created and posted the video.

To learn more about fair use, you can use the links in the Fair Use section of the Additional Information section of the Weblinks page for Tutorial 4.

Works in the Public Domain

Once the term of the copyright has expired, the work moves into the **public domain**, which means that anyone is free to copy the work without requesting permission from the last copyright holder. Older literary works, such as *A Tale of Two Cities* by Charles Dickens that was published in 1859, are in the public domain and may be reproduced freely. Songs or musical works published earlier than 1922, such as the Star Spangled Banner written by Francis Scott Key in 1814, are also in the public domain in the United States, although sound recordings are not in the public domain.

A copyright can protect a particular expression of a creative work in addition to the work itself. For example, a Mozart symphony is in the public domain because it was written hundreds of years ago and is no longer protected by Austrian copyright law. But Mozart's creative work was writing the notes of the symphony down on paper in a particular form. If the Cleveland Orchestra makes an audio recording of that public domain Mozart symphony, its performance is a separate work that can be copyrighted by the Cleveland Orchestra and protected under current copyright laws.

Authors or creators can place their work into the public domain voluntarily at any time. For example, some Web sites provide graphics files that visitors can use free of charge. You can include public domain content on a Web page, in a paper, or in any other form of creative expression. However, you should still acknowledge the source of the public domain material and not represent the work as your own, which is plagiarism.

TIP

Web sites that offer free files for noncommercial use often carry a restriction against selling or redistributing those files.

INSIGHT

The Digital Millennium Copyright Act

When Congress passed the 1976 Copyright Act, personal computers, the Internet and Web, email, digital photos, and other electronic content did not exist. However, with these newer technologies and media came new copyright concerns and issues.

In 1998, Congress passed the Digital Millennium Copyright Act (DMCA) to help protect copyright owners from online infringement or piracy. The DMCA addresses the following common issues: circumvention of copyright protection systems, fair use in a digital environment, and online service provider liability. The DMCA prohibits individuals from bypassing technologies that the copyright holders have added to their works to prevent others from using them even if that use would be considered a fair use. However, since 2010, the Librarian of Congress has said that accessing a small portion for educational uses by college professors and students would no longer be prohibited. Finally, the DMCA protects online service providers that act as "mere conduits" to provide transitory digital communications or that host third-party material on their servers and networks such as YouTube. As long as the service providers respond to copyright owners' claims, take down the material, and cancel accounts of repeat offenders, they are protected from some copyright infringement liability.

One Nashville country music band that Marti wants to sign has the same name as a band in another part of the country. You will find out whether it is possible to copyright the name of a band.

To find information about copyrights:

1. Start your Web browser, go to **www.cengagebrain.com**, open the Tutorial 4 Weblinks page, click the **Session 4.2** link, and then click the **United States Copyright Office** link to open the U.S. Copyright Office home page. The Copyright Office Web site provides basic information on copyright laws and the application of the law. At this site you can also register a work for copyright and record a copyright document. See Figure 4-15.

Figure 4-15   **U.S. Copyright Office home page**

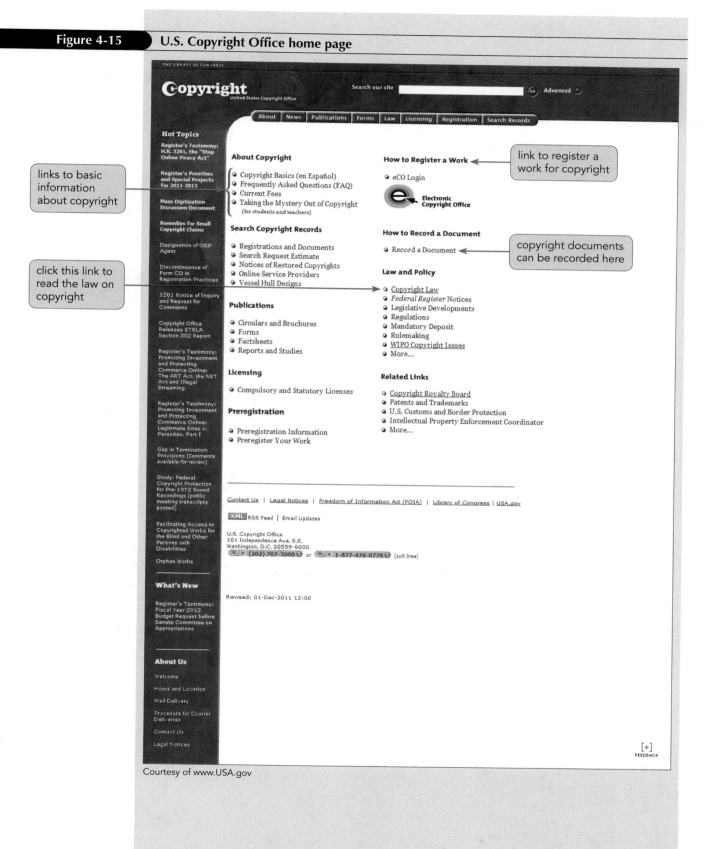

Courtesy of www.USA.gov

2. In the About Copyright section, click the **Frequently Asked Questions (FAQ)** link. The Frequently Asked Questions about Copyright page opens.

3. Read some of the questions, and then click the **Can I copyright the name of my band?** link in the What Does Copyright Protect? section.

4. Read the answer to find out that names are not protected by copyright law, although some names may be protected under trademark law.

Understanding Plagiarism

The Internet makes it very easy to copy someone else's work. If you use someone else's work, whether the work is in the public domain or protected by copyright, you must cite the source of the material. Failure to cite the source of material that you use is called **plagiarism**. Claiming someone else's work as your own is a serious legal violation that can lead to a failing grade, being expelled from school, being fired from a job, or being subjected to a hefty fine or prosecution.

Plagiarism can be as simple as including a sentence or two from someone else's work without using quotation marks or attribution. It can be as blatant as duplicating substantial parts of someone else's work and claiming it as your own. It can be more subtle, such as paraphrasing someone else's content without the proper citation of the source. Another form of plagiarism is when students purchase essays, term papers, and even theses or dissertations from commercial services and then pass them off as their own.

To combat the growing issue of plagiarism, academic instructors, researchers, publishers, and others have turned to Web resources. A number of plagiarism checker sites are available for free or for a fee to detect plagiarism in written content. These sites compare the submitted work against archived student papers; publications including articles in journals, periodicals, and newspapers; books; databases; and Web page content. These sites can check for exact duplication or a paraphrase of someone else's work.

For example, Turnitin is a Web site that checks a submitted paper against 14 billion Web pages, 150 million student papers, and millions of articles from leading library databases and publications, and then determines how much of the paper is unoriginal. Figure 4-16 shows the home page for Turnitin.

To ensure that you don't unintentionally plagiarize someone else's work, be sure to properly reference the sources of works that you use. Keep in mind that just including a source citation is not enough if you plan to use the finished product commercially. You must also obtain the copyright holder's permission if you want to use the work in a way that falls outside of fair use.

To learn more about sites that check your writing for plagiarism, you can use the links in the Plagiarism Checkers section of the Additional Information section of the Weblinks page for Tutorial 4.

Figure 4-16   Turnitin home page

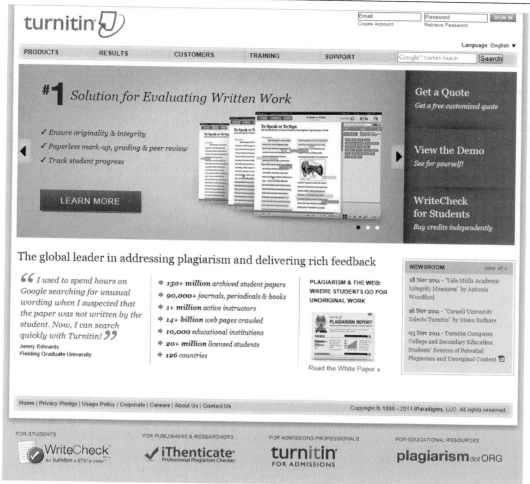

Citing Web Resources

To avoid charges of plagiarism, all works you reference in a report or paper—whether they are protected by copyright, in the public domain, or considered fair use—need to be documented. This gives proper credit to the original authors as well as provides readers with the information they need to find and review the works you used.

However, documentation can become a challenge when you are referencing a Web page. Because the Web is a dynamic medium that changes constantly, the content of any given page can change in an instant. Also, its URL can change or disappear from day to day. Unlike published books and journals, which have a physical existence, a Web page exists only in an HTML document on a Web server computer. If the file's name or location changes, or if the Web server is disconnected from the Internet, the page is no longer accessible.

To address this issue, digital intellectual content such as online journals, articles, reports, and white papers are assigned a unique alphanumeric string of characters, called a **digital object identifier (DOI)**, to identify that content and provide a persistent link to its location (or locations) as long as the content exists somewhere on the Internet.

All DOI numbers begin with *10.* followed by a prefix of a unique combination of four or more digits, then a slash, and finally a suffix that is any alphanumeric combination that identifies the publisher. The International DOI Foundation issues prefixes to DOI Registration Agencies, such as CrossRef.org, which then assign them to publishers and others. The publisher assigns the suffix using a unique identifier such as the book's ISBN. The DOI usually appears near the copyright notice. Unlike a URL, a DOI does not change when the content moves to a new location. If the content exists in multiple forms on the Web—for example, in one location as an Adobe PDF file and in another as a Microsoft Word file—all forms will have the same DOI.

For academic research, the two most widely followed standards for citations are those of the American Psychological Association (APA) and the Modern Language Association (MLA). The APA and MLA formats for Web page citations are similar. Both include the information shown in the Visual Overview for Session 4.2, which shows both APA and MLA citations for a specific Web page and how that information is obtained from the Web page. Figure 4-17 shows examples of other Web page citations that conform to the APA citation style. Be aware, however, that both the APA and MLA standards change from time to time. Consult these organizations' Web sites as well as the APA and MLA style guides for the latest rules and updates to these styles before using them. Also, always check to see if your instructor or editor (for work you are submitting for publication) has established other guidelines.

Figure 4-17	APA Web page citations

Web page with a title and an author, undated

Norman, D. (n.d.). Welcome to jnd.org. In *Don Norman's jnd website*. Retrieved April 21, 2014, from http://www.jnd.org

Web page with a title and authors, dated

Koeppel, D. (2011, August 19). The future of light is the LED. In *Wired*. Retrieved April 23, 2014, from http://www.wired.com/magazine/2011/08/ff_lightbulbs

Web page with a title but no author, undated

Pew Environment Group. (n.d.). In *The PEW Charitable Trusts*. Retrieved April 23, 2014, from http://www.pewenvironment.org

Web page with no title and no author, undated

United States Postal Service [Home page]. (n.d.). Retrieved April 23, 2014, from http://www.usps.com

INSIGHT

Formatting URL Line Breaks

One difficulty of including long URLs or DOIs is typesetting them in printed documents. However, if you must include one and it does not fit on one line, you should break the URL or DOI only after a slash that occurs in the address. Also, you should not add a hyphen at the line break because a reader might mistakenly type the hyphen as part of the URL.

To learn more about format styles for citing sources, use the links in the Citation Formats section of the Additional Information section of the Weblinks page for Tutorial 4.

Accessing Text-Based Resources Online

Over the past decades, many reference materials that were once available only in print have become available electronically, and in many cases on the Web. Before that, anyone wanting to learn more about a topic had to go to a library to perform research using print resources. For example, encyclopedias were one of the first types of resources made available in electronic format; cross-references to other topics were made into hyperlinks, glossary definitions were changed to pop-up windows, and the entire encyclopedia became searchable by keyword. Unlike the print editions, digital versions could include audio and video clips. One of the earliest and most popular digital encyclopedias was Microsoft Encarta, which was available starting in 1993 on CD-ROMs. Dictionaries, thesauri, and almanacs soon followed. As access to the Web became more widespread, these sources were placed online.

Today, libraries offer content (books, periodicals, journals, and so forth) in a wide variety of formats. With the huge number of books being published every year, libraries don't have enough shelf space to store print versions of every resource. As a result, libraries are buying fewer printed books and offering more content electronically. Publishers are encouraging this trend by making digital content cheaper and easier to access. Consequently, an increasing number of books are available as e-books, which are electronic versions of books that are read on electronic readers (also called e-readers) such as the Kindle and the iPad as well as computers, tablets, and smartphones.

In addition, libraries can subscribe to huge databases that offer a wealth of information, which individuals cannot usually afford. For example, Dow Jones Factiva is a comprehensive global news and business information and research tool that provides access to top media outlets, trade and consumer publications, and business Web sites along with in-depth company, executive, and industry profiles; expert analysis; market data; and detailed reports. ProQuest Dialog is a combination of online research tools that provides online-based information services in subject areas such as business, science, engineering, finance, and law, in a format designed to meet the specific needs of a wide range of users, including information professionals and end users at business, professional, scientific, academic, and government organizations in more than 100 countries.

Likewise, other print resources—such as periodicals, scholarly journals, and government resources—have become available on the Web. This has helped these resources to remain current and easily accessible to their audiences. In addition, it means that these resources are now available day and night, regardless of whether the business or library in which they are housed is open.

Online References

TIP

In many instances, virtual libraries and online reference sites overlap and/or link to one another.

The Web contains many online references, including dictionaries, thesauri, encyclopedias, atlases, almanacs, quotations, grammar checkers, rhyming dictionaries, and language-translation sites to name just a few. These online references range in quality from very low to very high, so be sure to consider the results for accuracy. Some online reference resources require a subscription fee, but many free online reference tools also exist. Some common free online reference sites include Dictionary.com, Thesaurus.com, Merriam-Webster Online dictionary and thesaurus, World Sites Atlas, Enclopedia.com, Britannica Online Encyclopedia, BrainyQuote, and The Quotations Page. To learn more about online references, use the links in the Online References section of the Additional Information section of the Weblinks page for Tutorial 4.

The Web also includes sites that offer full-text copies of works that are no longer protected by copyright. Two well-known full-text sites are the Project Gutenberg and Bartleby.com Web sites. These volunteer efforts have collected the contributions of many people throughout the world who have spent enormous amounts of time entering or converting printed text into electronic form. The Project Gutenberg site currently offers more than 36,000 free e-books and is supported by donations. The Bartleby.com site, which is named for the main character in Herman Melville's famous short story "Bartleby the Scrivener," was converted into a privately held corporate site in 1999. Since then, it has used advertising to generate revenue to support its operations. The Bartleby.com home page is shown in Figure 4-18.

Figure 4-18   **Bartleby.com home page**

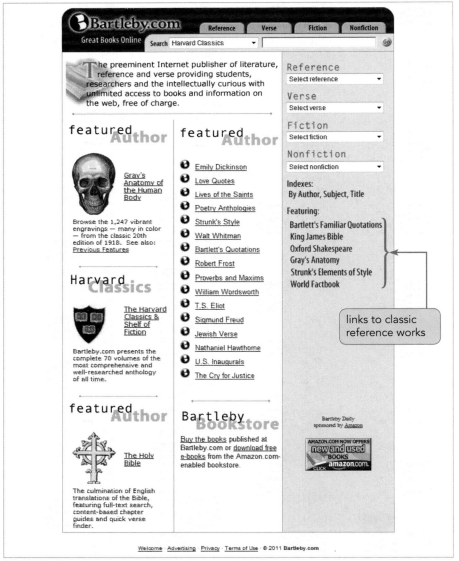

© 2011 Bartelby.com

The Web itself has become the subject of archivists' attention. The Internet Archive's Wayback Machine provides researchers with a series of snapshots of Web pages as they were at various points in the history of the Web. The site has archived more than 150 billion Web pages since 1996. The Internet Archive site also stores text, moving image, audio, and other files that have been contributed to the site. The wide array of information at the Internet Archive site makes it a valuable resource for a variety of research projects. The Internet Archive home page is shown in Figure 4-19.

| Figure 4-19 | Internet Archive home page |

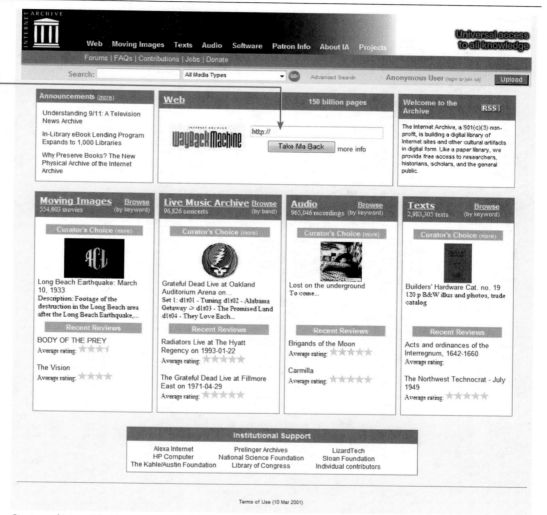

enter a URL to search for an archived Web page

Courtesy of Internet Archive.com

The Weblinks page for Tutorial 4 includes links to Web sites that offer electronic texts and archives in the Additional Information section under the Electronic Texts and Archives heading.

Before her trip to Nashville, Marti wants to find more information about country music. You'll search an online encyclopedia to learn more about this type of music.

To search an online encyclopedia for information about country music:

1. Return to the Tutorial 4 Weblinks page for Session 4.2, and then in the Encyclopedias section, click one of the encyclopedia links to open the home page. Figure 4-20 shows the Encyclopedia.com home page.

| Figure 4-20 | Encyclopedia.com home page |

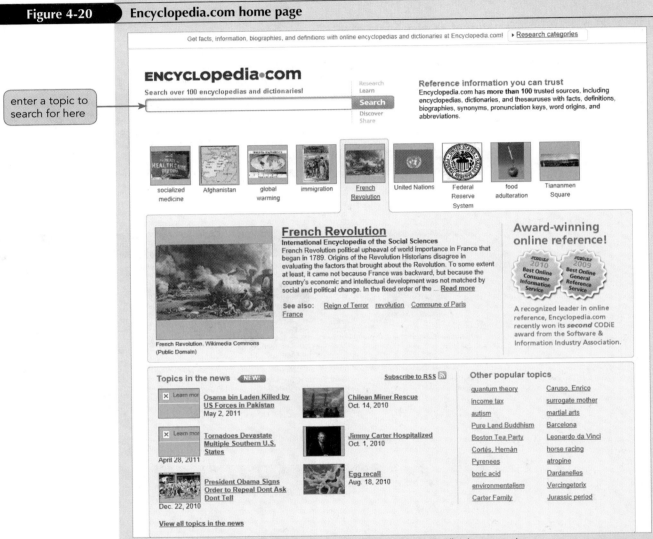

enter a topic to search for here

2. Type **country music** in the search box, and then click the appropriate button to start the search. A list of topics related to your search term appears.

3. Click a link that is most related to the keywords "country music" or "country and western music" to display an entry with information about country music along with links to related topics.

4. Read the information, and when you are finished, return to the Weblinks page for Tutorial 4.

Periodical Databases

Periodicals—magazines, journals, and other articles—related to almost any industry, field, or topic abound. Originally periodicals were available only in printed format at libraries, but now thousands of periodicals are available on the Web. If you know what periodical you want to search, you could go directly to its Web site. If you are more interested in articles related to a particular topic, then you can use a periodical database to locate them. For example, MagPortal.com is a search engine and directory for finding online magazine articles. It has indexed articles from hundreds of magazines. You can browse the indexed articles by topic or you can search for articles based on a keyword you supply.

Marti wants to find current information about digital music and how it is affecting the music industry. You will see what information you can find using MagPortal.com.

To find information about digital music in magazine articles:

1. On the Weblinks page for Session 4.2 in the Periodical Database section, click the **MagPortal.com** link to open the MagPortal.com home page. On MagPortal you can search articles by quality of match, date, publication, or category.

2. In the Search for Magazine Articles box, type **digital music rights** in the Search box, and then click the **Search** button. As shown in Figure 4-21, the Search Results box lists articles related to your search expression. Each result shows the name of the magazine, the publication date, the article's author in the left column, and the article's title followed by a brief description in the right column and two icons. The My Articles icon lets you mark articles you find interesting so you can find them later. The Similar Articles icon opens a list of articles that are similar to the original article.

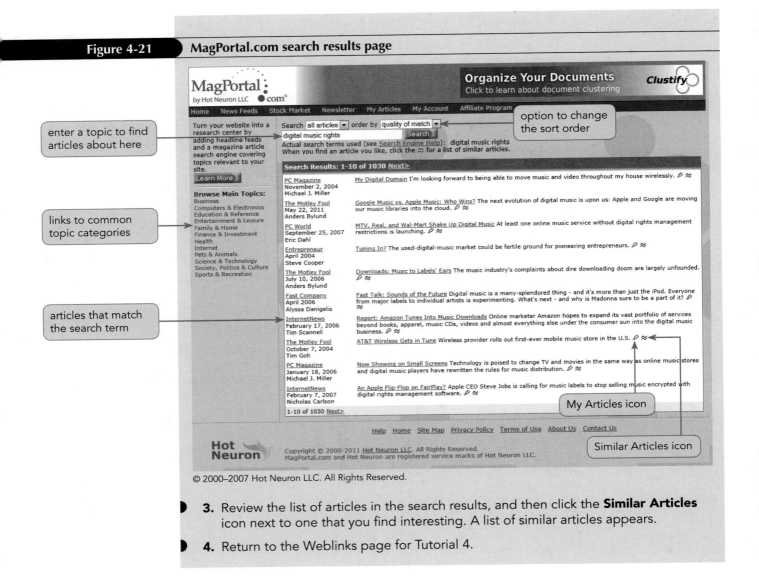

Figure 4-21   MagPortal.com search results page

3. Review the list of articles in the search results, and then click the **Similar Articles** icon next to one that you find interesting. A list of similar articles appears.

4. Return to the Weblinks page for Tutorial 4.

Online and Virtual Libraries

Most libraries now provide online access to their collections and services. You can search the library catalog and reserve books or place books on hold. You can access articles from newspapers and magazines, and search databases to which the library subscribes. You can also access general reference resources, including encyclopedias, almanacs, dictionaries, thesauri, language dictionaries, quotations, time and calendar information, world facts, population, and statistics. Many libraries also provide access to Web-based books and videos, as well as make available e-books, e-journals, and digital audiobooks for download to use on a computer, an e-reader such as a Kindle or an iPad, or a mobile device.

Another way to access library information is through a **virtual library**, which is a Web site that provides online access to library information services. Some virtual libraries are also portal sites that link to a variety of library and reference sites on the Web. A **portal site** is a Web site that you use as a gateway or entry to other sites on the Web. The portal site can be general and provide access to a wide variety of Web sites, or it can be specialized and provide access to related sites.

One virtual library, ipl2, describes itself as a global information community that offers a collaborative research forum, and supports and enhances library services by providing authoritative collections, information assistance, and instruction for the public. From its Web site, you can access resources by subject, newspapers and magazines, featured collections on specific topics that were created by ipl2 contributors, references, and topical resources specifically for kids and teens. Another free virtual library resource is LibrarySpot.com. It includes many of the same materials you would find in a public or school library. You can access reference materials, electronic texts, and other library Web sites from one central Web page. Unlike a brick-and-mortar library, these libraries are open 24 hours a day and seven days a week.

Marti has never visited Tennessee before and she wants to learn more about that state before she travels there. You'll explore a virtual library and see what you can find.

To find information about Tennessee using a virtual library:

1. In the Virtual Libraries section of the Tutorial 4 Weblinks page, click the **LibrarySpot** link to open the home page for this virtual library. See Figure 4-22.

Figure 4-22	LibrarySpot home page

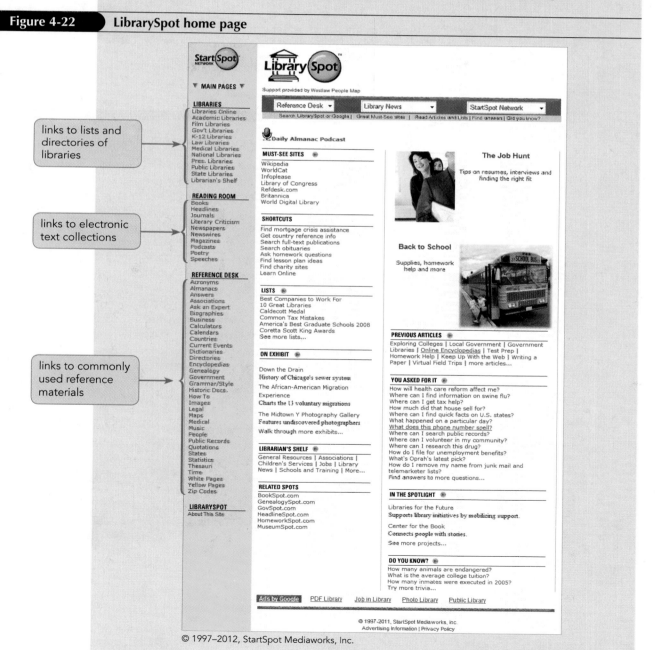

links to lists and directories of libraries

links to electronic text collections

links to commonly used reference materials

2. On the LibrarySpot home page, click the **States** link listed under the Reference Desk heading to open the State Information page, and then click the **TN** state on the map. A page listing links to information about the state of Tennessee opens.

3. Click some of the links to find facts about Tennessee that might be of interest to Marti.

4. Return to the Tutorial 4 Weblinks page, and then click the **ipl2** link under the Virtual Libraries heading. The home page for ipl2, another virtual library, opens. On ipl2, you can search for a topic by entering a search term or phrase in the search box, or you can browse the site, which is organized by subject, newspapers and magazines, special collections, and information for kids and teens.

5. On the ipl2 home page, click in the **search** box, type **Tennessee**, and then click the **Search ipl2** button. A Web page listing links to information about Tennessee displays.

6. Scroll the list of links and select one that looks appropriate for Marti's needs. Read the information on the page that opens.

7. When you are finished, return to the Weblinks page for Tutorial 4.

PROSKILLS

Written Communication: Summarizing Research Results

Research is the first step toward conveying information and facts in a written report. When you summarize your research results, how you organize the information and write the report is just as important as the quality of the research that you have done. If you do an excellent job gathering the facts, be sure to deliver a report that is clear and easy to understand. This ensures that your audience benefits from your hard work and gets the information they need. A lack of clarity can introduce noise into the communication and prevent readers from getting the message you intend to convey.

As you research a topic, be sure to take accurate notes about what you learn. Remember to include complete information about your sources so you can cite them as needed in your report. After you finish your research, you should organize your notes into a logical order so that you can present the information clearly and logically.

As you begin writing, make sure it's apparent why you are writing in the first place. Are you writing to inform, to entertain, or to express your opinion? When writing a factual report, your opinions are not relevant and should not be included. Next, determine the appropriate writing style: formal or informal. If you are writing for a professor or supervisor, you usually use a more formal tone than you would in a casual email to a colleague, friend, or family member.

When you have finished your report, be sure to read it carefully, keeping the recipient's viewpoint in mind. Make sure your points are clear and are presented in a logical order. Also, check your spelling and grammar, and correct any errors that you find. However, do not rely only on spelling and grammar checkers because they do not always find all errors. You might find it helpful to read what you have written out loud to determine whether your intended message and tone are coming through clearly. As a final step, you could ask a friend or colleague to read your final report and provide feedback.

Government Sites

The United States government collects and creates a wide variety of information and provides many services—from laws, tax codes, and Supreme Court rulings, to data on the census, the environment and energy, commerce, jobs, education, public safety, science and technology, travel and transportation, health and nutrition, and voting and elections.

Much of this information is available on the Web. You can go to local, state, and federal government agency sites to locate specific information, such the U.S. Census Bureau, the U.S. Government Printing Office, NASA, and the U.S. Library of Congress. For example, the U.S. Library of Congress Web site includes links to a huge array of research resources, ranging from the THOMAS legislative information site to the Library of Congress archives. The home page for the THOMAS section of the Library of Congress Web site is shown in Figure 4-23. The THOMAS Web site is a serious research tool that provides access to the full text of bills that are before the U.S. Congress, the *Congressional Record*, and Congressional Committee Reports. News reporters, investigative journalists, and civic-minded citizens all use this site to find detailed information about how the U.S. government operates.

Figure 4-23	U.S. Library of Congress THOMAS home page

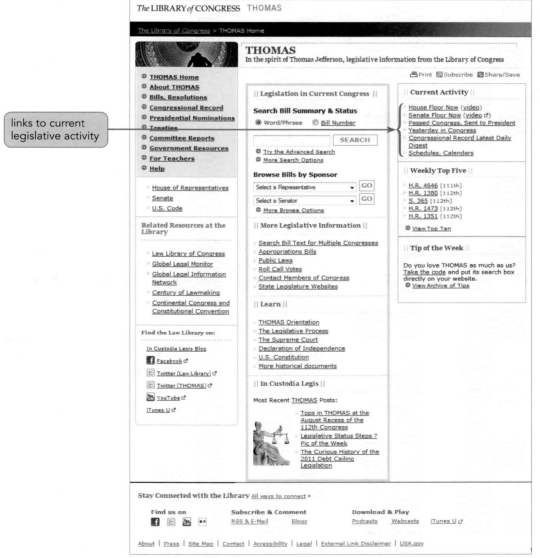

links to current legislative activity

Courtesy of www.USA.gov

You can also use a portal site to access any government-related information from a central place. USA.gov is the official Web portal for the U.S. government. It provides access to all official U.S. government services and information in one place so you can easily find all U.S. government information that has been posted on the Internet.

To learn more about government sites and portals, use the links in the Government Sites section of the Additional Information section of the Weblinks page for Tutorial 4.

Marti wants to know more about the demographic statistics for Nashville. You will use the USA.gov Web portal to track down this data.

To find demographic information about Nashville:

1. In the Government Portal section of the Tutorial 4 Weblinks page, click the **USA.gov** link to open the USA.gov home page. See Figure 4-24.

Figure 4-24	USA.gov home page

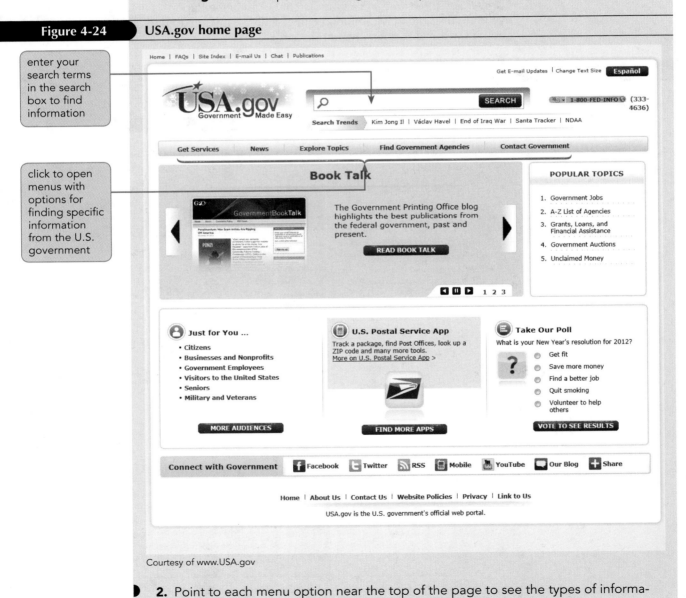

Courtesy of www.USA.gov

2. Point to each menu option near the top of the page to see the types of information and resources available on this portal site.

3. Type **Nashville demographics** in the search box, and then click the Search button. The search results show relevant Web pages. See Figure 4-25.

Figure 4-25   **Search results**

USA.gov | FAQs | E-mail USA.gov | Chat | Publications

GOVERNMENT > Web   Images   Recalls   Forms   Change Text Size   **Buscador.USA.gov**

Search.**USA**.gov   🔍 Nashville demographics   **SEARCH**

Advanced Search | Busque en español

Results 1-10 of about 59,300 for 'Nashville demographics'

Web

Images

Recalls

Forms

Nashville-Davidson (balance) QuickFacts from the US **Census** Bureau
Frequently requested statistics for **Nashville**-Davidson (balance). ... People QuickFacts **Nashville**-Davidson Tennessee; Population, 2010 : 601,222: 6,346,105
quickfacts.census.gov/.../4752006.html - Cached

Tennessee QuickFacts from the US **Census** Bureau
Source U.S. **Census** Bureau: State and County QuickFacts. Data derived from Population Estimates, American Community Survey, **Census** of Population and Housing, ...
quickfacts.census.gov/qfd/.../47000.html - Cached

Davidson County QuickFacts from the US **Census** Bureau
Nashville-Davidson--Murfreesboro--Franklin, TN Metro Area : 1: Includes data not distributed by county. ... Source U.S. **Census** Bureau: State and County QuickFacts.
quickfacts.census.gov/qfd/.../47037.html - Cached

Nashville.gov - Planning Department - **Demographics**
US **Census** Bureau; US **Census** Bureau Data Profile - Davidson County, TN; US **Census** American Community Survey (Estimates) **Demographic** Data Profile; Social Data Profile
www.nashville.gov/mpc/maps/census.asp - Cached

Nashville-Davidson, TN (balan Tennessee QuickLinks from the US ...
[Excel] or the letters [xls] indicate a document is in the Microsoft® Excel Spreadsheet Format (XLS). To view the file, you will need the Microsoft® Excel Viewer
quickfacts.census.gov/.../4752006lk.html - Cached

Nashville-Davidson (balance), Tennessee - Population Finder ...
Population Estimates and Trends for **Nashville**-Davidson (balance), Tennessee
factfinder.census.gov/.../SAFFPopulation?_event=Search... - Cached

Welcome to the City of LaVergne - LaVergne, TN - **Demographics**
Demographics City of La Vergne The City of La Vergne, incorporated in 1972, is a general-law charter municipality. ... **Nashville** Area Chamber of Commerce, 743-3000
www.lavergnetn.gov/.../demograph.shtml - Cached

Williamson County, TN - Official Site - **Demographics**
Nashville Region Info. Who's Hiring. **Demographics** Williamson County **Demographic** Reports Please click on the links below to find out about population, education, ...
www.williamsoncounty-tn.gov/index.asp?NID=712... - Cached

Local **Census** Office Map - 2010 **Census** Jobs
Columbia, TN 38401 Phone: 🔲 ▾ 931-922-5030 ℹ **Census** takers start at: $11.75/hour. **Nashville** McGavock Pike **Nashville**, TN 37214 Phone: 🔲 ▾ 615-234-5760 ℹ **Census** takers start at: $17.00/hour.
2010.census.gov/.../local-office-map.php?x=1492... - Cached

City of Lebanon, Tennessee **Demographics**
To link to the US **Census** Bureau's American Community Survey page for the City of Lebanon ... **Nashville** Area Metropolitan Planning Organization ...
www.lebanontn.org/demographics.aspx - Cached

1 2 3 4 5 6 7 8 9 ... 99 100 Next   results by **bing**

Connect with USASearch   📧 Twitter   📱 Mobile   💬 Our Blog   ➕ Share

USA.gov | Website Policies | Privacy

ABOUT USASearch >   USASearch Program | Affiliate Program | APIs and Web Services | Search.USA.gov

Search.USA.gov is the U.S. government's official search engine.

links to information about Nashville demographics

Courtesy of www.USA.gov

4. Click a link to a Web page that provides census data for Nashville, and then find the population data for the city.

5. Return to the Weblinks page for Tutorial 4.

In addition to the vast text-based material on the Internet, you can find graphics such as clip art, animations, and photos, as well as audio and video clips.

Multimedia on the Web

Most Web pages include a variety of multimedia elements. **Multimedia** is anything you can see or hear, including text, pictures, audio/sound, videos, films, or animations. These multimedia elements are used to enhance the information presented on Web pages. The use of multimedia elements on Web sites has, in many instances, improved the functionality and usefulness of the Web. Retail sites can show multiple images of an item for sale, providing different views or showing an item such as a shirt in different colors. News sites can provide videos of unfolding events as they happen. Music sites can include audio clips to let customers listen to parts of songs before they buy them. Do-it-yourself help sites can provide videos that show demonstrations, such as a master plumber installing a new sink. The use of multimedia on the Web is limited only by the Web designer's imagination and creativity.

The Web is also a great resource for users seeking specific multimedia such as graphics, photos, videos, and music to use for their own purposes and entertainment.

Finding Graphic Images on the Web

"Graphic" is a generic term that can refer to a variety of still images, including photographs, clip art, and line drawings. An abundance of graphic images are available in electronic form on the Web. These are commonly in one of three file formats: JPEG images for photographs, GIF images for line drawings, and PNG images for more complex graphics. You'll learn more about these file formats in Tutorial 8.

There are a variety of ways to find graphic images on the Web. You can use a search engine such as Google or Bing to locate images related to your search term. You can filter the search results to show only images, and then further refine the filter to show only images of a certain size; full-color or black-and-white images; a specific type of image such as a face, a photo, clip art, or a line drawing; as well as images posted during a certain time frame such as the past week. When you click an image in the search results, a larger version of that image appears along with information about the image, including the Web site where it originated, the size of the image, the file type, the date, and sometimes the camera and settings specifications used to create that image.

You can also search stock photography sites, which are devoted to providing stock images for sale and licensing. **Stock images** are professional photographs, line drawings, and other graphics that are available for purchase. Stock images are immediately available, can be sold to multiple customers, and are usually affordable. Companies that offer stock photographs and images for sale include Shutterstock, Bigstock, iStockphoto, Corbis Images, and Getty Images. You can also license specific uses of the images, such as displaying an image on a Web page. Some sites permit downloading of at least some files for personal use. You can also contribute your own photos and images to the sites.

You can also find photographs to use through photo-sharing sites such as Yahoo! Flickr and Google Picasa. Flickr has partnered with Getty Images to make its members' photographs available for licensing to others. You can either submit specific photos to Getty Images for review, or you can allow other Flickr members to make a request to license any of your images. Getty Images reviews requests and handles the permissions, releases, and pricing details. You'll learn more about Flickr and photo-sharing sites in Tutorial 5.

To learn more about finding images, use the links in the Stock Images and Photo Sharing Sites section of the Additional Information section of the Weblinks page for Tutorial 4.

Marti wants to find some photos of Nashville bands to use in promotional literature about her agency's latest venture into signing country music artists.

To find images of Nashville bands:

1. In the Image Search Engines section of the Tutorial 4 Weblinks page, click a link to open the home page for a search engine.

2. Click the **Images** link to open the images search page.

3. Type **Nashville TN bands** in the search box, and then click the search button. The search results appear on the results page. The search results page shows thumbnails of images of bands with a connection to Nashville. Depending on the image search engine you used, you might see links to filter the search results by size, color, type, and so forth.

4. Click a thumbnail image on the results page. A Web page opens, showing a larger version of the image you selected. Again, depending on the image search engine you used, you might see a description of the image, detailed information about the image such as file size and type, and a note about any copyright restrictions. Figure 4-26 shows the enlarged image on the Google Images page.

Figure 4-26	Google Images details

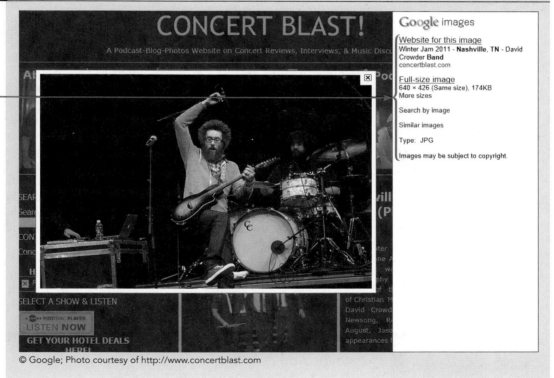

© Google; Photo courtesy of http://www.concertblast.com

Finding Audio Files on the Web

In addition to images, you can find audio files on the Web. The term "audio" refers to sounds of any type: instrumental music, songs with vocals, speeches, audio books, sound effects such as a creaky door or a barking dog, and so forth. Audio searches are most commonly conducted to find music and books. Other popular searches include special effects and sounds that might be used on a Web site.

Audio files are available in a variety of formats. Most music is now available in the MP3 file format. MP3 (MPEG Audio Layer 3) files can hold information about the music they store, such as the title, the artist's name, and even a photo of the album cover. Other sounds might be in WAV, MIDI, or AU formats, which are described in Figure 4-27.

Figure 4-27   **Audio file formats**

Format File	Extension	Description
MP3 (MPEG Audio Layer 3)	.mp3	The audio portion of the MPEG file format; most popular for music and audio books.
WAV (Wave)	.wav	Jointly developed by Microsoft and IBM; stores digital audio and can be played on any Windows computer that supports sound; can be recorded at different quality levels, which results in different size files (higher quality means a larger file).
MIDI (Musical Instrument Digital Interface)	.midi or .mid	The standard adopted by the music industry for controlling devices that create and read musical information; much smaller than WAV files.
AU (audio UNIX) format	.au	The original audio format because much of the Internet was originally constructed on computers running the UNIX operating system; stores sound at various quality levels, creating files that are approximately the same size as WAV files recorded at similar quality levels.

© Cengage Learning

Music CDs are recorded in the WAV format at a very high-quality level. A standard CD has a capacity of about 650 MB and can hold about 74 minutes of high-quality stereo music. Files in the MP3 format are somewhat lower in quality than WAV format files, but they are 90% smaller. This means that a CD that holds 15 popular songs in high-quality WAV format (about 40 megabytes per song) could instead hold 150 popular songs in MP3 format (about 4 megabytes per song).

The MIDI format records information about each element of the sound—including its pitch, length, and volume—in a digital format. Most keyboard synthesizers and other electronic instruments use MIDI so that music recorded on one instrument can be played on other instruments. MIDI files can also be played on computers that have a MIDI interface or MIDI software. It is much easier to edit music recorded in the MIDI format than music recorded in the WAV format because the individual characteristics of the sound can be manipulated with precision. MIDI files are much smaller than WAV files and are used when storage space is at a premium. Many mobile phone ringtones, for example, are in the MIDI format.

Although very few new audio files are created in the AU format today, this format still appears on the Web and most Web browsers can read it. The AU format can store sound at various quality levels, and the resulting files are approximately the same size as WAV files recorded at similar quality levels.

INSIGHT

Downloading Plug-Ins

Unlike graphic files, audio and video files appear on the Web in many different formats. In order for your Web browser to play these different formats, you might need to install additional software extensions. These software extensions, or **plug-ins**, are usually available as free downloads. The companies that offer media players as free downloads earn their profits by selling encoding software to developers who want to include audio and video files in that format on their Web sites. Each company that creates a format has an incentive to promote its use, so a variety of audio and video formats are used on the Web today. You will learn more about plug-ins in Tutorial 8.

You can find audio on the Web in a variety of places. A growing number of recording artists and bands sell and distribute their music on their own Web sites. Many online stores, such as Amazon.com, also sell digitized music. These sites have obtained the legal right to distribute the musical works they offer for sale. Some of these sites charge a download fee per song, whereas others charge a monthly fee that allows subscribers to download as many songs as they wish. There are also digital music subscription services such as Rhapsody, Pandora, and Rara Music that you can subscribe to and create custom playlists from millions of songs that are available on the service. Sometimes referred to as Internet radio stations, you can listen to the music on most connected devices, including computers, smartphones, and tablets.

Digital audio books are also popular download items. Like music, you can purchase audio books directly from publishers, from etailers such as Amazon.com, or on sites devoted to audio books, such as LibriVox, Audible, and Audiobooks.com. Some books are in the public domain and have been recorded so that people can listen to them for free. Others are still protected by copyright and must be purchased or used as part of a subscription service. Some libraries also offer digital audio books for checkout just like printed books in their catalog.

To learn more about digital audio books, use the links in the Digital Audio Books Sites section of the Additional Information section of the Weblinks page for Tutorial 4.

Some sites that sell downloadable music place restrictions on the number of copies you can make of each song. A few of these sites restrict you from converting downloaded song files into other formats, or they restrict the types of devices on which you are permitted to play the song. The restrictions are implemented in the files themselves, using systems of encoding called **digital rights management (DRM)**. Because different online music vendors use different DRM systems, their files might not be compatible with each other. Because of these differing DRM systems and because you can incur legal liability by using or copying downloaded files (even those you have purchased) in ways that the vendor prohibits, you should always check the site carefully for details about file formats and copying restrictions before you buy songs or sign up for a subscription.

Marti wants to listen to some classic country music before meeting with potential clients in Nashville. You will find songs by Johnny Cash that can be purchased and downloaded.

> **TIP**
>
> Make sure that the files from a particular site are compatible with your portable music player before you sign up for a download subscription.

To search for country music songs to purchase online:

1. Return to the Weblinks page for Tutorial 4, and then click a link under the Online Music Stores heading in the Session 4.2 section to open that Web site's home page. Figure 4-28 shows the eMusic home page.

Figure 4-28 eMusic home page

select whether to search all the music on the site or search by artist, album, tracks, labels, etc.

enter search expression

2. In the search box, type **Johnny Cash** and then click the **Search** button (or something similar) to display the results.

   Trouble? Some online music stores require you to sign up for a trial membership before you can search for music. Many of these trial memberships are free. If you do not want to sign up for a membership, try another music store.

3. Click one of the songs or albums to see more information about that item, if necessary.

4. Make sure your speakers are turned on or your headphones are connected and the sound is unmuted, and then click a song to play a preview of the song.

Storing Multimedia Files in the Cloud

Image, music, and audio books are more commonly being stored in the cloud. The **cloud** is a group of technologies and services that provide computing over the Internet so people can interact with programs and data using any device that can access the Internet, including computers, tablets, and smartphones. People are using cloud computing to share software and networking resources. More sites are providing cloud storage in which you can save and access files. This allows users to store their files remotely and access them from any device with the appropriate software and Internet access. For example, in 2011 Apple launched iCloud, which provides subscribers with space to store digital content, including music, photos, books, and documents. It also keeps changing content such as email, calendars, and contacts up to date on all your devices running iCloud. So you can use your iPhone, iPad, iPod touch, and computer to access the same files and information.

Finding Video Files

The term **video** refers to content that has a progression of visual images and can include audio as well. Video clips are commonly included in a variety of different types of Web sites, including news sites to show events that have occurred, retail sites to demonstrate how a product works, broadcasting sites to play television shows, and music sites to show bands performing their songs.

High-quality audio files and video files of any significant length can be very large, especially if the files are in a digital format. Therefore, all online video is compressed to make it faster to download or play. Although a video file can be completely downloaded and then played, streaming transmission lets users watch the video file in real time.

In a **streaming transmission**, the Web server sends the first part of the file to a Web browser or a media player program such as RealPlayer or Windows Media Player, which uncompresses and then plays the file. While the first part of the file plays, the server is sending the next segment of the file. Streaming transmission allows you to access large audio or video files in less time than the download-then-play procedure because the streamed file begins playing before it finishes downloading. RealNetworks, Inc. pioneered streaming technology. Video files on the Web are available in a variety of formats, including Flash, MPEG, AVI, and 3GP formats. Figure 4-29 describes some of the more common formats.

Figure 4-29	Video file formats

Format File	File Extension	Description
RealAudio	.ra	The original formats for streaming audio and video files, developed by RealNetworks.
RealVideo	.rv	
WMV (Windows Media Video)	.wmv	A streaming video format developed by Microsoft to compete with RealVideo.
Flash Video	.flv	A common streaming video format; requires the Adobe Flash Player plug-in to play Flash video files. Flash files can include video, high-resolution moving graphics, and graphic elements that interact with the user's mouse movements.
Moving Picture Experts Group (MPEG)	.mp2, .mpe, .mpeg, .mpv2, .mpg, .3gp, .mpg4	A series of standards for compressed file formats created by the International Organization for Standardization. The file extension identifies the version of the MPEG standard with which the file was encoded.
AVI (Audio Video Interleaved)	.avi	An older video file format created by Microsoft.
QuickTime	.mov	An older video file format created by Apple; usually requires a plug-in to play the files.

© Cengage Learning

You can find videos on the Web in a variety of ways. Some sites are devoted to video distribution, such as YouTube and Hulu. You will learn more about video-sharing sites such as YouTube, which allows users to upload video files that they have created and view videos that others have created, in Tutorial 5. Other sites provide stock videos, including Shutterstock Footage, iStock Video, and Thought Equity Motion. You can also use a search engine, such as Google Videos and Bing Videos, to find video files on the Web.

Because Marti will be visiting Ryman Auditorium when she travels to Nashville, she wants to see a video that features the auditorium.

To search for videos about Ryman Auditorium:

1. Return to the Weblinks for Session 4.2, click a link in the Video Search Engines section to open the search engine's home page, and then click the **Video**, **Videos**, or **Footage** link at the top of the page.

2. Type **Ryman Auditorium** in the search box, and then click the search button. Videos that feature Ryman Auditorium appear on the search results page. Depending on the search engine you are using, filters might appear so you can narrow the search results to show videos of a specific duration, from a certain time frame, of a specific quality, and from a specific source. Figure 4-30 shows the search results and filter options for videos on Google Videos.

| Figure 4-30 | **Google Videos search results** |

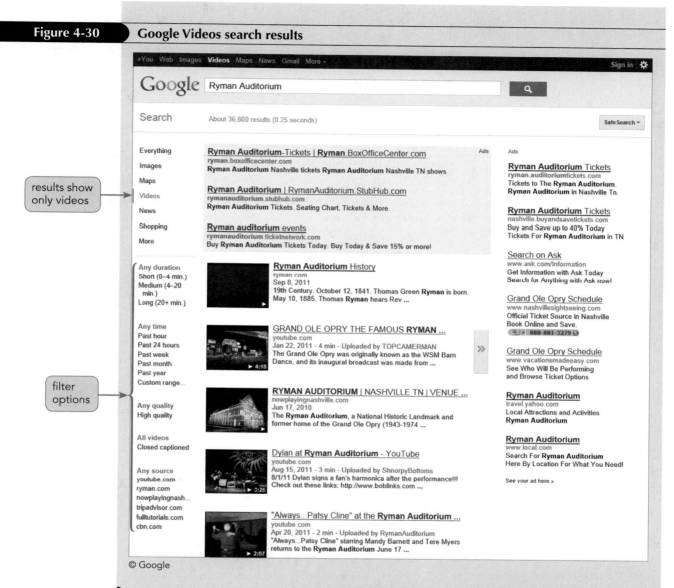

© Google

results show only videos

filter options

3. Click the link to a video that shows the history of the auditorium, a travel video that features the auditorium, or a performance that was recorded at the auditorium, and then watch the video.

Trouble? If you cannot hear the audio portion of the video, you might need to turn on the computer's speakers or unmute the sound.

Trouble? If the video doesn't play, you might need to install a plug-in to play that video format. Return to the search results and select a different video.

4. Close your Web browser.

Marti is now up to date on copyright issues and information about Nashville, Ryman Auditorium, and country music. She's ready for her trip to Nashville.

REVIEW

Session 4.2 Quick Check

1. What is intellectual property?
2. What types of books do Bartleby.com and Project Gutenberg legally provide online in their entirety without paying royalties to the authors of those books?
3. Briefly explain the concept of fair use.
4. If you use material that is in the public domain or that qualifies for fair use without citing the source, you might be guilty of _____.
5. What is a virtual library?
6. What kinds of elements can a multimedia file include?
7. What are stock images?
8. Most music is now available in what file format?
9. _____ transmission begins to play an audio or video file before it finishes downloading.

Practice the skills you learned in the tutorial using the same case scenario.

PRACTICE

Review Assignments

There are no Data Files needed for the Review Assignments.

Marti is preparing to visit a new techno band in Chicago, Illinois, that she would like to sign. While in Chicago, she wants to visit several clubs that feature blues artists. You'll find information for Marti's upcoming trip and then write a report summarizing your findings. You'll need to include citation information for each site you visit. Complete the following steps:

1. Start your Web browser, go to **www.cengagebrain.com**, open the Tutorial 4 Weblinks page, and then click the Review Assignments link.

2. Use one or more of the links in the News Search Engines section of the Weblinks page to find an article in a Chicago-area newspaper from the past month that discusses a local blues band or an area blues club that features live music. Summarize the article in a short report to your instructor and include a citation to the article in the report.

3. Return to the Tutorial 4 Weblinks page to obtain a local weather forecast for the Chicago area for the coming week using one of the links in the Weather Sites section for the Review Assignments (or consult your favorite weather sites). Record the upcoming forecast and the citation information in your report.

4. The techno band is renting practice space in a warehouse near the corner of West 35th Street and South Morgan Street in Chicago's South Side. Return to the Tutorial 4 Weblinks page, and then use one of the links in the Map Sites section for the Review Assignments to find a map that shows the location. View a street-level map and switch between map view and aerial, satellite, or street view of the location. In your report, describe what you learned and record the citation information for the Web pages you visited.

5. Return to the Tutorial 4 Weblinks page, and use one of the links in the Travel Guides Web Sites section for the Review Assignments to locate three restaurants in the Chicago area that you would recommend to Marti for entertaining clients. Include this information in your report along with the appropriate citation information.

6. Return to the Tutorial 4 Weblinks page, and use one of the Travel Guide sites listed in the Travel Guides Web Sites section for the Review Assignments to locate at least two blues clubs that Marti can visit while she is in Chicago. Describe these clubs in your report along with the citation information for the Web pages you visited.

7. Return to the Tutorial 4 Weblinks page, and use one of the links listed in the Online Directories section for the Review Assignments to find the address of the House of Blues. Record the information in your report along with a citation to the Web page where you found the information.

8. Return to the Tutorial 4 Weblinks page, and use one of the links listed in the Online Shopping section for the Review Assignments to locate blues memorabilia that Marti can purchase. Include a description of a memorabilia item you find and its cost in your report, along with the citation information for the Web pages you visited.

9. Return to the Tutorial 4 Weblinks page, and use one of the links in the Encyclopedias section for the Review Assignments to find out the history of blues music. Include a brief summary of what you learned in your report along with citations of the Web pages you visited.

10. Return to the Tutorial 4 Weblinks page, and use one of the links in the Online Music Stores section for the Review Assignments to find recordings of blues music. Listen to the previews of three songs. In your report, list the songs you listened to and your opinion of them. Include citations for the Web pages you visited.

11. Return to the Tutorial 4 Weblinks page, and use a link in the Video Search Engines section for the Review Assignments to find video clips of blues musicians playing their songs. View two videos. List the videos you watched along with your opinion of the performances in your report. Include citations for the Web pages you visited.

12. Close your Web browser.

Apply the skills you learned in this tutorial to prepare for a business trip.

APPLY

Case Problem 1

There are no Data Files needed for this Case Problem.

Davenport Trenchers, Inc.   You are a sales representative for Davenport Trenchers, Inc., a company located in Davenport, Iowa. The company sells trenchers, which are machines used for digging small trenches in the ground that hold water lines, drainage pipe, and electrical conduit. Davenport's customers include builders, landscape contractors, and stores that rent the trenchers to other businesses and individuals for short-term use. You have been promoted to manage the company's office in St. Louis, Missouri, and are planning your first sales trip there. Because you will drive to St. Louis, you need information about the best route as well as a map of St. Louis. Because you hope to generate new customers on this trip, you need to identify sales prospects in the area. Complete the following steps:

1. Start your Web browser, go to **www.cengagebrain.com**, open the Tutorial 4 Weblinks page, and then click the Case Problem 1 link.
2. Use one of the Web sites provided in the Map Sites section to obtain driving directions from Davenport, Iowa (your starting address) to St. Louis, Missouri (your destination address). Record the information in a report along with a citation for the Web page you used to obtain the directions.
3. To identify sales prospects in the St. Louis area, return to the Tutorial 4 Weblinks page, and use one or more of the directories listed in the Online Directories section for Case Problem 1 to search for builders, landscape contractors, and equipment rental stores in the St. Louis area that sell concrete. The results pages for your searches should include contact information for a number of companies that would be good prospects. In a report to your instructor, document at least three sales prospects. Include a citation for the Web pages that provided the information.
4. Return to the Tutorial 4 Weblinks page and use the link in the Government Site section for Case Problem 1 to explore QuickFacts from the U.S. Census Bureau to find out the latest population of St. Louis. Record this information in your report along with a citation for the Web page where you found this information.
5. Return to the Tutorial 4 Weblinks page. Using one of the links in the Stock Images Sites section for Case Problem 1, find an image of a trencher that might be good to use in your sales material. Document the image you found along with the site where you found it.
6. Return to the Tutorial 4 Weblinks page. Using one of the links in the Video Search Engines section for Case Problem 1, find footage that shows a trencher in action. Again, document the video and the Web page where you found it.
7. Close your Web browser.

Find MIDI files and copyright restrictions on downloaded music files.

RESEARCH

Case Problem 2

There are no Data Files needed for this Case Problem.

Midland Elementary School Music Classes   You are a third-grade language skills teacher at Midland Elementary School. The school has closed its music program because of budget cuts. However, you believe that it is important to expose your students to the music of the great composers, such as Beethoven and Mozart. You do not have a budget for buying CDs, but you do have a computer with an Internet connection in the classroom as well as a small electronic piano that can play audio files in MIDI format. You want to find music files to play on the computer and the electronic piano, but you need to make sure that any use of these files complies with U.S. copyright law. Some musical instruments, particularly pianos, sound realistic when synthesized in MIDI format. You would, therefore, like to find some music in this format to begin your collection for the class. Complete the following steps:

1. Start your Web browser, go to **www.cengagebrain.com**, open the Tutorial 4 Weblinks page, and then click the Case Problem 2 link.

2. Use one of the links in the Search Engines section to locate resources for elementary music teachers that you can use to prepare your class lessons. In preparation for writing a report to your instructor, document the sites you visited and identify the sites that you think will be helpful.

3. Return to the Tutorial 4 Weblinks page. Click one or more of the links provided in the MIDI Files Sites section for Case Problem 2 to find sources of MIDI files of classical music that you could play on the classroom computer or piano. Read the Web pages you find that include downloadable MIDI files, and then evaluate their terms and conditions of use. In particular, look for copyright statements and any restrictions on the use of downloaded files. (*Hint*: The copyright restrictions might not be listed on the page from which you download the files, so be sure to look for links to pages with titles such as Terms of Use on the site's home page.) Are there any copyright issues with playing these recordings directly from the Web? Document your findings to include in the report to your instructor.

4. Return to the Tutorial 4 Weblinks page. Use the links in the Copyrights section for Case Problem 2 to learn more about U.S. copyright law, fair use, and public domain as they relate to music. Record your findings to include in the report to your instructor.

5. Return to the Tutorial 4 Weblinks page and use the links in the Digital Audio Books Sites section for Case Problem 2 to find at least one audio book that would be suitable for teaching your students about Beethoven, Mozart, or your favorite classical composer. Note the titles and authors of the books you find along with the URLs of the pages where you found those books to include in your report.

6. Write a short report to your instructor that summarizes your findings. In your report, describe any copyright restrictions that you find and evaluate whether your use of the files in the classroom would infringe on the files' copyright. Be sure to include citations to the Web pages you visited.

7. Close your Web browser.

Find current information about mine safety issues and related government legislation.

CREATE

Case Problem 3

There are no Data Files needed for this Case Problem.

Hamilton Mining   Headquartered in Wheeling, West Virginia, Hamilton Mining operates six deep shaft coal mines in the state. The company has an excellent safety record and spends a considerable amount of money every year promoting safety in its mines. The company is aware that mining accidents can focus the public's attention on mining safety issues, and can lead to criticism of companies that operate mines. Because a mining accident can happen at any time, Hamilton Mining maintains a public relations plan that it can implement immediately when an accident occurs in the industry. You are an intern in the office of Joan Caruso, a public relations consultant who does work for Hamilton Mining. Joan has asked you to help her with some background research as she creates a proposal for integrating a mine safety Web site into Hamilton Mining's public relations program. You need to research Hamilton Mining's competitors, and then evaluate each competitor's safety information. Joan also asks you to find out whether any bills are pending in the U.S. Congress that will affect mine safety regulations because any public relations campaign must consider the impact of pending legislation. Complete the following steps:

1. Start your Web browser, go to **www.cengagebrain.com**, open the Tutorial 4 Weblinks page, and then click the Case Problem 3 link.

2. Use the links in the News Search Engines section to find at least three current (within the past three or four months) news reports about mine safety, mining accidents, or the coal mining industry in general. In a report to your instructor, summarize the major issues identified in these reports. Be sure to include citations for each article you used in your research.

3. Use your favorite search engine to find a mining company in the United States, visit its Web site, and then review the safety information provided on its Web site. Summarize this information for your instructor. Again, include a citation for the Web site you visited.

4. Return to the Tutorial 4 Weblinks page, and then click the Library of Congress THOMAS link in the Government Site section for Case Problem 3. Search the site using the phrase **mine safety**. Read one of the bills listed and prepare a one-paragraph summary for your instructor of the bill's likely effects on the mining industry. Include citations for the Web pages you visited.

5. Close your Web browser.

Case Problem 4

Create a report that summarizes current arguments for or against prison privatization.

CHALLENGE

There are no Data Files needed for this Case Problem.

Johnson for Senate Campaign You work for the campaign team of Vivianne Johnson, who is running for a seat in the state senate. One issue that promises to play a prominent role in the upcoming election campaign is privatization of the state prison system. It is important for Vivianne to establish a clear position on the issue early in the campaign, and she has asked you to prepare a briefing for her. Vivianne has no particular preference on the issue and she wants you to obtain a balanced set of arguments for each side so she can assess the political risks associated with taking each position. Complete the following steps:

1. Start your Web browser, go to **www.cengagebrain.com**, open the Tutorial 4 Weblinks page, and then click the Case Problem 4 link.

2. Choose one or more of the search engines listed to conduct a search for **privatization prisons**.

3. Examine your search results for authoritative sites that include positions on the issue. (*Hint*: You might need to follow a number of results page hyperlinks to find suitable Web pages.)

4. Find at least one Web page that states a clear position in favor of privatization, and at least one Web page that states a clear position against privatization.

5. Write a report that summarizes the arguments for each position using the content of the Web pages you visited. Include full citations for the Web pages.

6. Close your Web browser.

*Find images
for a menu
and determine
the copyright
limitations on
their use.*

CHALLENGE

Case Problem 5

There are no Data Files needed for this Case Problem.

Europa River Cruises   You have just started a summer internship in Bonn, Germany, working for Europa River Cruises. Europa operates luxury cruises on the Danube, the Rhine, and other major rivers in Europe. You have been assigned to work for Dieter Welker, the manager of restaurant operations on all of the company's cruise ships. The Europa line is famous for its fine dining and features the cuisine of different countries each night. The menus and table settings are illustrated with graphics and photos that represent the country whose food is being featured that night. Dieter is supervising a redesign of the menus and table settings for each night. He wants you to help the design team by gathering art and photos from the Web that the team might use in the illustration of the menus or design of the table settings. Complete the following steps:

1. Start your Web browser, go to **www.cengagebrain.com**, open the Tutorial 4 Weblinks page, and then click the Case Problem 5 link.
2. Click one of the links in the Image Search Engines section and use it to conduct a search for images or photos that represent France, Italy, Spain, Germany, Portugal, and Ireland.
3. Return to the Tutorial 4 Weblinks page, and repeat the search using another search engine.
4. Examine the search results for images or photos that would be suitable to use in the menu redesign assignment. Find two images or photos for each country (a total of 12).
5. When you find a suitable image, examine the Web site on which you found it to determine what copyright or other restrictions exist for using that image. (*Hint*: You need to look for restrictions that could prevent the team from using the images or photos in print; these restrictions might be different from restrictions on online use.)
6. Prepare a report that includes a brief description of each image or photo, its source, the URL of the site where you found it, and a summary of the restrictions on Europa's use of the image in printed materials. If the Web site does not include any description of restrictions, state your opinion (based on what you have learned in this tutorial) regarding what restrictions might exist on Europa's use of the image.
7. Close your Web browser.

User-Generated Content on the Internet

INTERNET

Evaluating Different Methods of Internet Communication

Case | *Shilling Social Media*

A few years ago, Kay Shilling lost her corporate job as a marketing executive when her company implemented a workforce reduction strategy. Kay contacted dozens of potential employers for months, only to discover that jobs in her field were scarce. After many disappointments, Kay began helping small businesses in her community get started with their Internet marketing, including building and maintaining Facebook pages and Twitter accounts. Kay realized that her extensive experience in marketing and social networking gave her a perfect skill set for starting a new business, which she has incorporated using the business name Shilling Social Media. Her business will offer her professional services to help new and existing small to medium-sized businesses create, maintain, and manage the online "social" side of their marketing efforts.

Kay already has the basis for the business in her home: a dedicated home office, a new laptop computer, and a smartphone, along with many references from local businesses that she has already helped. She will begin by reviewing the Internet and its many forms of communication, keeping a watchful eye on any new technologies and communication methods that she can use in running own business, or that might be appropriate for her clients' needs.

STARTING DATA FILES

There are no starting Data Files needed for this tutorial.

SESSION 5.1 VISUAL OVERVIEW

"After I finish my student teaching, I want to teach English to students in Dubai."

Pull Technology

PULL TECHNOLOGIES

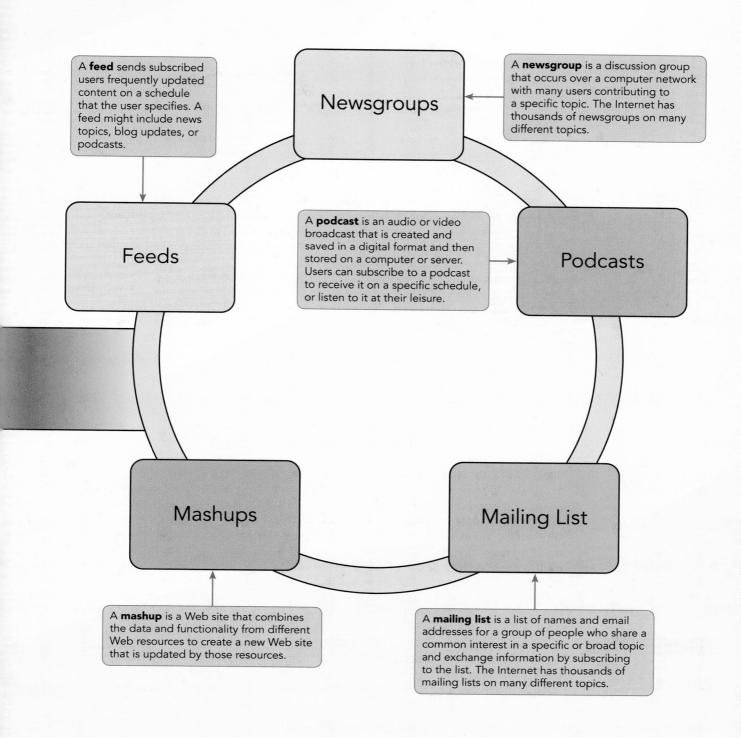

A **feed** sends subscribed users frequently updated content on a schedule that the user specifies. A feed might include news topics, blog updates, or podcasts.

A **newsgroup** is a discussion group that occurs over a computer network with many users contributing to a specific topic. The Internet has thousands of newsgroups on many different topics.

Newsgroups

A **podcast** is an audio or video broadcast that is created and saved in a digital format and then stored on a computer or server. Users can subscribe to a podcast to receive it on a specific schedule, or listen to it at their leisure.

Feeds

Podcasts

Mashups

Mailing List

A **mashup** is a Web site that combines the data and functionality from different Web resources to create a new Web site that is updated by those resources.

A **mailing list** is a list of names and email addresses for a group of people who share a common interest in a specific or broad topic and exchange information by subscribing to the list. The Internet has thousands of mailing lists on many different topics.

Push and Pull Communication

Until a few years ago, users would search the Internet for information and use links to visit a Web page or multiple Web sites to gather information. In this scenario, the Web was a resource—much like a library on a school campus—that required action on your part to get information from it. You found the sites, reviewed them, and perhaps even used your Web browser to create bookmarks so you could revisit those sites. These Web sites were mostly static, with updates being posted by the Web site's developer on a regular basis. During this time, you found the site and viewed it, and later returned to the site and checked it for updates. You used these Web sites to pull the information you wanted to your computer so you could view it.

Several years ago, with new software and imaginative ways of using existing software, the way people used the Web changed. In addition to searching for content, you could identify content you wanted and have it *sent* to you, either at your request or on a certain schedule. As more users put more information on the Web, this idea of "pushing" content to other users created a new way of using the Web for people who were "pulling" content to their computers.

You can group the Internet's many communication methods into two basic categories: push and pull. Some communication methods use **push technology** to send content to users who request it. Some examples of push technology are chat, instant messaging, online social networks, photo- and video-sharing sites, and blogs. The other communication method, which is called **pull technology** because subscribers "pull" content to their computers when they want it, includes mailing lists, newsgroups, feeds, podcasts, and mashups. Some communication methods are both push and pull, depending on who is using them. For example, the person who writes a blog is pushing content to other users, who then pull it to their computers so they can read it.

Some communication methods don't fit into neat categories based on the method they use, but you can still categorize them based on the technology they use to disseminate information or on the way the information is combined. The Visual Overview for Session 5.1 describes the pull technologies that you will learn about in this session.

Web 2.0

Some people think of pulling content as the "old" Internet—you had to find the resources and establish how you would pull the information to your computer. Over the past several years, the Web has evolved so that connected people *push* information to users who request it or just wander into it. This change is sometimes called the "new Internet" or **Web 2.0**, a term coined during a brainstorming session between representatives of O'Reilly Media and MediaLive International. During the session, Tim O'Reilly and Dale Dougherty were characterizing the changes in Web technology and how these changes affected the way people used and accessed the Web. Web 2.0 creates users who actively participate in writing the content that they are viewing—hence the term "user-generated content." Web 2.0 users not only interact with content; they also are given new and easy ways to create it. In fact, Web 2.0 isn't a "new" Internet at all. The term itself is intended to indicate a change in the way people use the Web, just like a version change in a software program indicates that a new release of the software is better than the old version. Web 2.0 applications enable users to manage and distribute information gathered from online communities to people all over the world, who then take the information and work to improve, enhance, and forward it to new users.

Web 2.0 applications vary, but they all rely in some way on the interactions of communities of people and their data. Web 2.0 includes online social networks, mashups, photo- and video-sharing sites, blogs, microblogs, feeds, and podcasts. (You will learn about these technologies as you complete this tutorial.)

TIP

You learned about another Web 2.0 application, wikis, in Tutorial 4.

Two decades ago, virtual communities were an essential part of the online experience for people using the Internet. Although these virtual communities continue to thrive, Web 2.0 has expanded the overall number and types of virtual communities and has increased their numbers dramatically. A virtual community, now more commonly called an **online social network**, provides a way for people to discuss issues and share information using the Internet or cellular networks. People who share common interests—such as the high school or college they attended, the sports they watch or participate in, their religious preferences, their careers or jobs, or even the types of diets they follow—use social networks to connect to other people with similar characteristics and interests.

Kay wants to explore the different types of Internet communication so she can share new ideas with her clients as they build their Internet-based business communications. She knows that almost all of her clients will rely on some kind of email communication with their customers, so she decides to investigate some of the Internet's email-based communication methods first.

Email-Based Communication

In Tutorial 2, you learned how to use email to communicate with other people. You can also use email-based communication to access and share other information stored on the Web. For example, you might use email-based communication to gather ideas, conduct research, or contact other people who share your interests.

One way of sharing information is to join, or **subscribe** to, a mailing list. These mailing lists are not like the ones you created in Tutorial 2, in which you grouped related individuals in your email program's address book for convenience; nor are they like the email messages that you might request and receive from Web sites to learn more about a special promotion or a new product. A mailing list uses a **list server** to send subscribers messages from other list members. Once popular for exchanging ideas on many subjects, mailing lists today are used primarily to share information about very specific subjects, such as software testing and product development. Each person who wants to join a mailing list is responsible for subscribing to the list by sending an email message to the list's administrative address or by using a Web site to request to be added to the list. A mailing list might be moderated, in which case an individual or group called the **list moderator** monitors messages sent to the list and discards inappropriate content; this type of list is called a **moderated list**. A mailing list that does not have a list moderator is called an **unmoderated list**. When a mailing list has a list administrator who oversees the list's members, the list is called a **closed list**. When anyone can subscribe to a mailing list, it is called an **open list**.

Another email-based communication is the **Usenet News Service**, or **Usenet**, which was founded in 1979 at Duke University as a way of collecting information and storing it by topic category. Usenet was one of the first large, distributed information databases in the world. A **distributed database** is stored in multiple physical locations, with portions of the database replicated in different locations. The original Usenet News Service was devoted to transmitting computing news and facilitating discussions among employees of university computing departments on topics such as operating systems and programming languages. The topic categories on Usenet originally were called newsgroups or forums. Many people still use these terms when they refer to Usenet categories, but another popular term is **Internet discussion group**. Most of these newsgroups are available to the general public; however, some newsgroups are limited to users at a specific site or to those affiliated with a particular organization.

Newsgroups are similar to mailing lists in that they accept messages from users and make them generally available to other users. However, newsgroups do not use a list server to forward copies of submitted messages to subscribers. The server that stores a newsgroup is called a **news server**; the collection of news servers connected to the

TIP

A list server runs email list software to manage the functions of a mailing list.

TIP

In a mailing list or a news-group, a series of postings on a particular issue is called a **thread**.

Internet make up Usenet. Organizations that operate news servers include most ISPs, universities, large businesses, government units, and other entities connected to the Internet. A newsgroup stores items on a server as **articles** or postings that are sorted by topic. Users pull the content they need to their computers in the form of articles posted to the newsgroup. Users can simply read these articles, or they can optionally reply to them.

When the Usenet News Service began operating in 1979, the only way to read or post articles to newsgroups was to install and run a software program, called a **newsreader**, that could manage and display the articles. Later, email programs included features that managed the articles. Now, you can easily search and read newsgroup articles by using a Web site that archives articles, such as the Google Groups directory. Google Groups stores millions of newsgroup articles dating from 1981 in its database. Figure 5-1 shows the Google Groups home page.

Figure 5-1	Google Groups home page

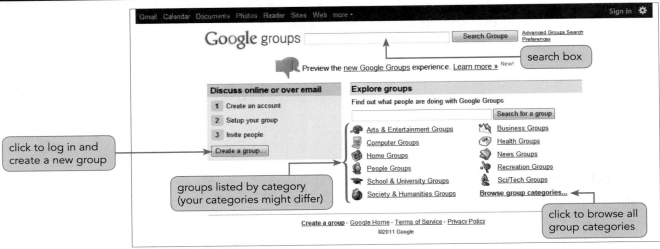

© Google

You can search the Google Groups directory by typing keywords in the search box, or you can click the general group categories to open a list of subcategories, which often lead to additional subcategories. As you drill down through the categories, you'll find a page with the individual groups. The summary for each group includes a hyperlinked group name, a brief summary paragraph with the group's focus and content, and often a note about the number of members in the group and the number of messages per month the group generates. To read the messages in a specific group, click the group's hyperlink.

Keep in mind that most groups are unmoderated; as a result, many groups contain a large number of off-topic threads, including messages that contain advertisements for unrelated products and services and messages about other topics. Unfortunately, many postings are potentially offensive to some readers. In an unmoderated list, there is no moderator to handle the disposition of objectionable material, so you must assume that job yourself.

Protecting Your Online Privacy

Joining a mailing list or newsgroup often requires you to identify yourself on a registration page before the site accepts your membership. You should consider carefully whether to provide detailed personal information when you register because most current laws do not require a Web site administrator to maintain the confidentiality of your information. In addition, your email address or your user name at the site might reveal some part or all of your entire identity. In a mailing list, messages that you send to the list are forwarded by the list server to everyone who has subscribed to the list. In some cases, your identity includes your name, location, email address, and other details about you. To protect your privacy, you should consider deleting your signature from email messages you post to a mailing list and using a Web-based email account (such as Yahoo! or Windows Live Hotmail) that does not include your name when you register for different sites. This way, you protect your "real" email address and your privacy.

Getting Information from RSS Feeds

Usenet is just one example of a feed (also commonly called a **newsfeed** or a **Web feed**) that uses pull technology to deliver changing content to users. This changing content might be from a blog, a Web site, or a news organization. The format that is used to syndicate (distribute) published content from one site to another is called **RSS**, an acronym for **Really Simple Syndication**; another format is **Atom**. Both RSS and Atom make it possible for computers to share updates. Feeds are similar to newsgroups in that they let you subscribe to content that you want to receive on your device. However, feeds differ from newsgroups because of the way that content is delivered to subscribers. Newsgroup postings are delivered via email messages, whereas feeds are delivered through a program that includes a summary and a link to the published or actual content, depending on how you choose to receive it.

Feeds are also used by organizations and individuals that create and maintain blogs, and on social networking sites as a way to publish content and alert subscribers to changes in the content.

As you learned in Tutorial 4, to receive feed content, you can install a program called an aggregator on your device. An aggregator is similar to an email program in that it requests content from feeds to which you have subscribed and displays that content in a format similar to an email message. Most Web browsers, email programs, and social networking sites have built-in aggregators that let you subscribe to, view, and remove feeds. Most Web sites that syndicate content also include built-in aggregators that you can use to search for, subscribe to, and view syndicated content using any Web browser.

To subscribe to a feed with content that you would like to view, you can use a feed directory to find a source. However, a more common method is to use the tools provided on the Web site that includes the feed. Web sites that include feeds will display a small, orange RSS or Atom icon that you can click to subscribe to the feed. Sometimes the link to subscribe to feeds is a text link with the letters "RSS" to indicate the file format of the syndicated content. Figure 5-2 shows a page from MedlinePlus, a site that includes feeds. In Internet Explorer, the Feeds button on the Command bar changes color from gray to orange when the site includes syndicated content. Clicking the arrow on the orange Feeds button opens a menu that identifies the feeds on the page by name; clicking a feed name opens a new page that displays the feed's content.

TIP

When only *part* of a Web page is coded to syndicate content, such as a sports score or a weather update, you can subscribe to it using a Web Slice (Internet Explorer) or a Webchunk (Firefox).

| Figure 5-2 | MedlinePlus page showing syndicated content in Internet Explorer |

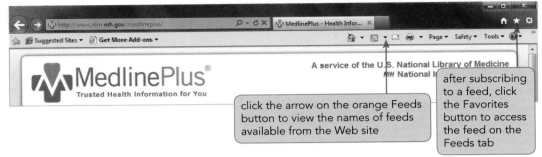

Courtesy of © Microsoft; Courtesy of U.S. National Library of Medicine, National Institutes of Health

Figure 5-3 shows the same page from MedlinePlus in Firefox. Clicking the Bookmarks button on the Bookmarks Toolbar shows that the Subscribe to This Page button is orange, which indicates that the currently displayed page contains one or more feeds. When more than one feed is available from a site, pointing to the Subscribe to This Page option opens a submenu with the names of the available feeds; clicking a feed name in the submenu opens a new page with options for subscribing to the feed.

| Figure 5-3 | MedlinePlus page showing syndicated content in Firefox |

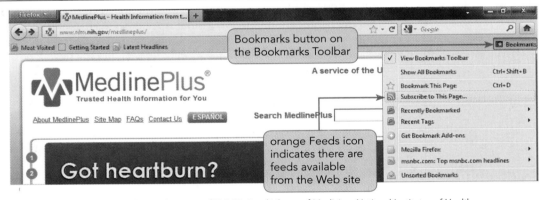

Courtesy of The Mozilla Foundation; Courtesy of U.S. National Library of Medicine, National Institutes of Health

Kay has used feeds in the past and has liked the convenience of viewing timely articles on various topics. She wants to search for feeds that might be of interest to self-employed individuals, so she decides to use a search engine to investigate this type of content.

To search for Web sites that include feeds:

1. Start your Web browser, go to **www.cengagebrain.com**, open the Tutorial 5 Weblinks page, click the **Session 5.1** link, and then click one of the links in the Search Engines section.

2. In the site's search box, type **self employment guide**, and then run the search.

3. Examine the search results and look for Web sites that include links to sites that might interest Kay, such as those dealing with general self-employment issues and home-based business guides.

4. Click one of the links to open the Web site, and then examine the page to determine if it contains any feeds. You'll know that a site contains one or more feeds when the Feeds button on the Command bar in Internet Explorer or on the Bookmarks menu in Firefox is orange in color.

Trouble? If the site you opened doesn't include any feeds, return to your search results and select another Web site until you find one that contains a feed.

5. If you are using Internet Explorer, click the **Feeds** button arrow on the Command bar, click the name of a feed of interest to view the feed's articles, and then click a link to an article that might interest Kay and scan the content. Figure 5-4 shows the feeds for the NPR News page.

Figure 5-4   **NPR News feeds page in Internet Explorer**

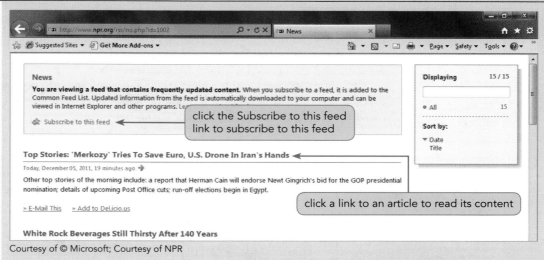

Courtesy of © Microsoft; Courtesy of NPR

6. If you are using Firefox, click the **Bookmarks** button on the Bookmarks Toolbar, click the **Subscribe to This Page** option on the Bookmarks menu, and then, if necessary, click the name of a feed of interest to view the feed's articles. Figure 5-5 shows the feeds for the NPR News page.

Figure 5-5   **NPR News feeds page in Firefox**

Courtesy of The Mozilla Foundation; Courtesy of NPR

Trouble? If the Bookmarks button is hidden, click the Firefox button on the title bar, and then point to Bookmarks on the menu.

7. Review one or more articles to see if they contain content that might interest Kay, who is self-employed. (Do not subscribe to any feeds at this time.)

8. Return to the Weblinks page for Session 5.1.

Depending on how you subscribe to a feed and the device you are using to view the feed's content, the feed's content might be displayed in different ways. With an aggregator, you might see summaries of the feed's content, similar to how you receive email messages, with links to the full articles. Clicking the link opens a page in a Web browser. Feeds are added using default settings that indicate the frequency with which to download new content from the source. You can change the feed's update schedule by changing its properties.

To cancel a feed, you just delete it. In Internet Explorer, right-click the feed's name on the Feeds tab in the Favorites Center, and then click Delete on the shortcut menu. In Firefox, right-click the button on the Favorites Bar or the feed's name on the Bookmarks Toolbar, and then click Delete on the shortcut menu.

Although Kay's personal business strategy doesn't include podcasts, she decides to investigate podcasting to see if it might be a useful technology for clients who want to provide recordings or videos on their social networking sites.

Podcasting

As you learned in Tutorial 4, MP3 is a compressed digital audio file format that greatly reduces the file size of an audio file without sacrificing the clarity of its content. When the MP3 file format became popular in the early 1990s, many people began purchasing MP3 players, which are portable devices that play MP3 files. Now, most cell phones and many other types of devices can play audio and video files.

At the same time that these types of devices became affordable and readily accessible, people who knew how to make different types of technology work on these devices found new uses for them. In the early 2000s, a group of programmers created the technical specifications necessary to encode audio recordings in feeds. Soon after, they worked toward the goal of being able to synchronize and encode audio files in feeds, which led to the development of podcasting in 2004. **Podcasting** lets a user subscribe to an audio or video feed, and then listen to it or watch it at the user's convenience on a compatible device, which might include the user's computer, or a mobile device such as an iPod or a cell phone.

Podcasting's original use was to make it easy for people to create and broadcast their own radio shows, but many other uses soon followed. Podcasts are used by the media to store and disseminate interviews with politicians and professors on specific subjects; by colleges and universities to record lectures for distance learning classes; and by movie studios to promote new movie releases. Some podcasts have different names that further identify the type of content they contain, such as a Godcast to denote a religious broadcast, a vidcast to identify a video feed, or a learncast to identify content that is educational in nature, such as a podcast produced by a university or other educational institution.

Although you can play a podcast using a media player, such as Windows Media Player or Apple's QuickTime, you will need to use software to subscribe to a podcast. This software, called a **podcatcher**, manages the schedule for downloading files to your device. When you connect your device to the Internet, the podcatcher will automatically download subscribed podcasts to your device so you can play them later.

TIP

The word "podcast" is a combination of the words "iPod" and "broadcasting," but you can play a podcast on any device with a media player.

Figure 5-6 shows the Podcasts page for iTunes, which contains podcasts in many different categories. The user can click a category to examine its available podcasts on this page. For example, clicking the Action Sports category opens a list of podcasts related to sports; clicking a link to one of the sports podcasts begins playing it. To subscribe to the podcast using iTunes, click the Subscribe button to add the podcast's feed to your iTunes Library, which in turn downloads the podcast's file and transfers it to your device.

| **Figure 5-6** | **Podcasts page for iTunes** |

podcasts grouped by categories

Kay wants to review some sites that organize podcasts by category so she can get a sense of the type of information a podcast might include and its format. One of her clients, a small hospital, is considering including interviews with doctors, who will discuss basic medical conditions, on its social networking site. Kay might advise the hospital to produce podcasts to push content to patients, so she will examine podcasting next.

To explore podcast directories:

1. On the Weblinks page for Session 5.1, click one of the links in the Podcast Directories section. Figure 5-7 shows the Podcast Directory page for LearnOutLoud.com, a site that stores audio and video podcasts on hundreds of subjects that are geared toward personal and professional education and development. You can search for podcasts by using the search box or by navigating the different podcast categories.

Figure 5-7 **LearnOutLoud.com Podcast Directory page**

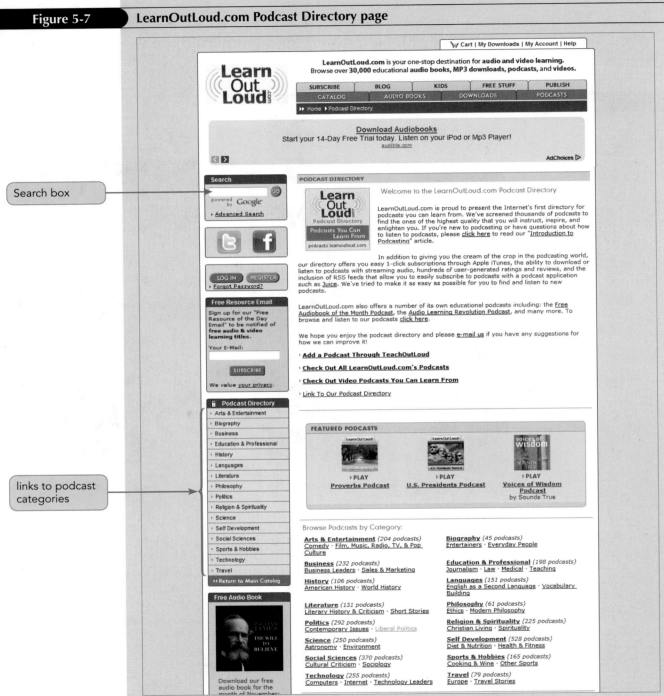

2. Use the links to categories (such as Science & Medical or Education and Professional) on the site you selected, or type keywords (such as **medical** or **physician**) in the site's search box, to explore the different categories of medical podcasts. As you are reviewing the podcasts, also note the dates of the broadcasts. You will probably notice that the broadcast dates are very recent, with some occurring on the day of or within a few days of completing this step. Because the podcasts are recent, the information they contain is current. Some sites provide archives of past podcasts that become a source for online research.

▶ **3.** If the site allows you to do so, click a podcast link to play the file. If your computer can play the podcast, it will start in a new window. Listen to the podcast for a few minutes to get a sense of the content it provides, and then close the window playing the podcast.

Trouble? If the file does not start playing, close the window that opened and skip Step 3. You need a plug-in, such as QuickTime or Windows Media Player, to play a podcast, and you need speakers to hear it.

▶ **4.** Return to the Weblinks page for Session 5.1, and then click another link in the Podcast Directories section. Explore the site to search for podcasts that might interest Kay's client.

▶ **5.** When you are finished exploring the site, return to the Weblinks page for Session 5.1.

Podcasts might be an interesting way for the physicians at the hospital to push general health information to their patients. Kay also represents a group of local real estate agents, who might be interested in another technology in which the content of two or more Web sites is combined into a single site. She decides to review this type of site next.

Mashups

When your computer runs a certain operating system, such as Windows 7, and you install software programs on that computer, the operating system and the software programs communicate with each other to handle specific tasks such as displaying content on the screen or printing. A software program uses an **application programming interface (API)** to communicate with an operating system or some other program.

An API is written by a programmer or developer with a specific goal in mind, such as displaying content on a screen or accessing a file system. When programs are developed for a specific operating system, developers might reference an API used by the operating system to print a document or display it on the screen, instead of writing the content themselves. APIs reduce the amount of coding for third-party software programs and ensure that the programs work together well.

The developers of most operating systems write new APIs and make them available to third-party developers by request. This relationship between developers wasn't always easy because the operating system developers often didn't give third-party developers what they needed to run their own programs. In addition, sometimes the APIs from one developer were not made available to other developers, and vice versa, so data was not shared between companies.

Instead of keeping data to itself, a company such as eBay or Amazon.com writes an API and makes it available to *any* developer who wants to use it—usually for free. When APIs are shared in this way, the term **Web services** describes the process of organizations communicating through a network to share data without needing extensive knowledge of each other's systems. As more companies make their APIs available, developers can use them to enhance their own sites by combining content from two or more sites. Amazon.com was the first to make APIs available to other developers, who in turn used them to link to and integrate their content with the Amazon.com Web site.

When Web content is combined in this way, the new Web site is called a mashup. In a mashup, a developer combines the services from two (or more) different sites using APIs to create a completely new site that uses features from each site. Some examples of mashups are sites that combine the "25 best companies to work for" feature from *Fortune Magazine* with an API from Google Maps that produces a map with locations of the companies; or a list of apartments available on craigslist for rent in a specific city that uses an API from Yahoo! to plot the apartments on a map with details about the apartments, such as the square footage, the number of bedrooms, and the monthly rent.

Figure 5-8 shows a site that combines an interactive map of the Las Vegas Strip from the Google Maps API with several APIs from social networking sites that provide user comments and user-posted photos and videos, along with pricing information from the individual hotels in the area, such as Caesars Palace. The resulting Web site combines all of this data for the user to make it very easy to find a hotel to stay at while visiting Las Vegas.

Figure 5-8   **Vegas Hotel Hunt page for Caesars Palace**

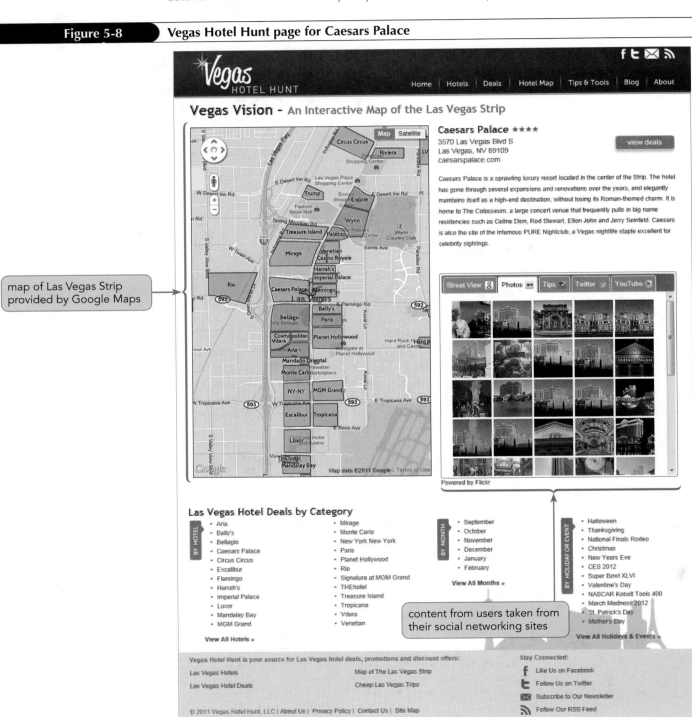

map of Las Vegas Strip provided by Google Maps

content from users taken from their social networking sites

© 2011 Vegas Hotel Hunt, LLC

Kay realizes that a mashup might be very useful for her real estate client, so she decides to review a mashup site next to see how it works. She is going to Boston next week for a conference, so she decides to use a mashup site to calculate the cost of taking a taxi from the conference center to the airport.

To view a mashup site:

▶ **1.** In the Mashups section of the Weblinks page for Session 5.1, click the **TaxiWiz** link to open the TaxiWiz home page. This site lets you calculate the cost and distance of taking a cab from one location to another in different cities. The first thing you need to do is identify the city you are visiting. You'll use Boston, MA, as the city, and calculate the estimated fare to take a taxi from the Prudential Center to Logan Airport.

▶ **2.** Click the **Select City** arrow, and then click **Boston** in the list. This sets Boston as the city and adds common starting points and destinations to the menus on the site to make it easy for users to use the site.

  Trouble? The TaxiWiz site might change over time, in which case you might use different tools to select your starting point and destination. If the site changes, use the Taxi Tips tab or link to review the current instructions, and then run the requested search as identified in the steps.

  Trouble? If the TaxiWiz site is no longer available, return to the Weblinks page for Session 5.1 and click a link in the Mashups section to visit another site. Use the tools on the site you select to explore the features of a mashup site and skip to Step 7.

▶ **3.** Click the **Starting point** arrow, and then click **Prudential Center** in the list.

▶ **4.** Click the **Destination** arrow, and then click **Logan Airport** in the list.

▶ **5.** Click the **Go!** button to submit your request. Figure 5-9 shows the page from TaxiWiz with the results of your search. This page uses Google APIs to combine a page displaying a map of Boston, MA, and the estimated route and fare for taking a taxi from the Prudential Center to Logan Airport after entering these locations into the site's form. The site generates a page that shows a map of Boston with an overlay of the route the taxi might take to arrive at the entered destination from the entered starting point, and an estimate of the fare the user might incur for the service. In addition, Google's AdSense API displays links to services that might interest the user, such as links to limo services in different cities.

Figure 5-9 | **TaxiWiz estimated fare page for Boston, MA**

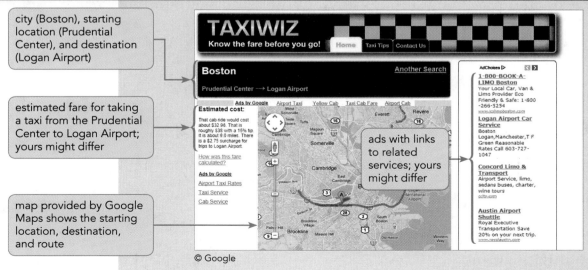

city (Boston), starting location (Prudential Center), and destination (Logan Airport)

estimated fare for taking a taxi from the Prudential Center to Logan Airport; yours might differ

ads with links to related services; yours might differ

map provided by Google Maps shows the starting location, destination, and route

© Google

6. Return to the Weblinks page for Session 5.1, and then click another link in the Mashups section and explore the Web site. Try to determine the resources the site combines, use the site to explore its features, and try to determine the intended consumer use of the site.

7. Return to the Weblinks page for Session 5.1.

You might wonder how a mashup is profitable to its developer. The developer usually includes additional APIs on the mashup site that link to Google AdSense or other content that generates revenue through customized advertising on the site, similar to the ads displayed on the right side of the TaxiWiz page in Figure 5-9. The mashup's developer most likely has an agreement with Google AdSense or another API provider to display this advertising and to share the income generated by users who click the links to these ads.

Because mashups rely on Web site data that already exists and APIs that are created by other companies, developers with the necessary programming background find mashups to be relatively easy to create and maintain, and profitable for the efforts needed to create them. For this reason, mashups constitute one of the fastest growing segments of Web sites on the Internet.

Kay wonders where she can get more information about APIs that she can use to generate new content that might be useful to her clients. Some Web sites list APIs by category, and include descriptions of the APIs and links to sites that use them. Because all of her clients rely on social networks, Kay wants to examine the APIs available for integrating social networking.

To view APIs available on the Web:

1. In the Session 5.1 section of the Weblinks page for Tutorial 5, click the **ProgrammableWeb.com** link. Figure 5-10 shows the home page, which contains a variety of information about API resources. The site also provides a directory of available APIs that you can search by API category or by using keywords.

Figure 5-10　ProgrammableWeb.com home page

Mashups link

API Directory link

search box lets you search for APIs using keywords

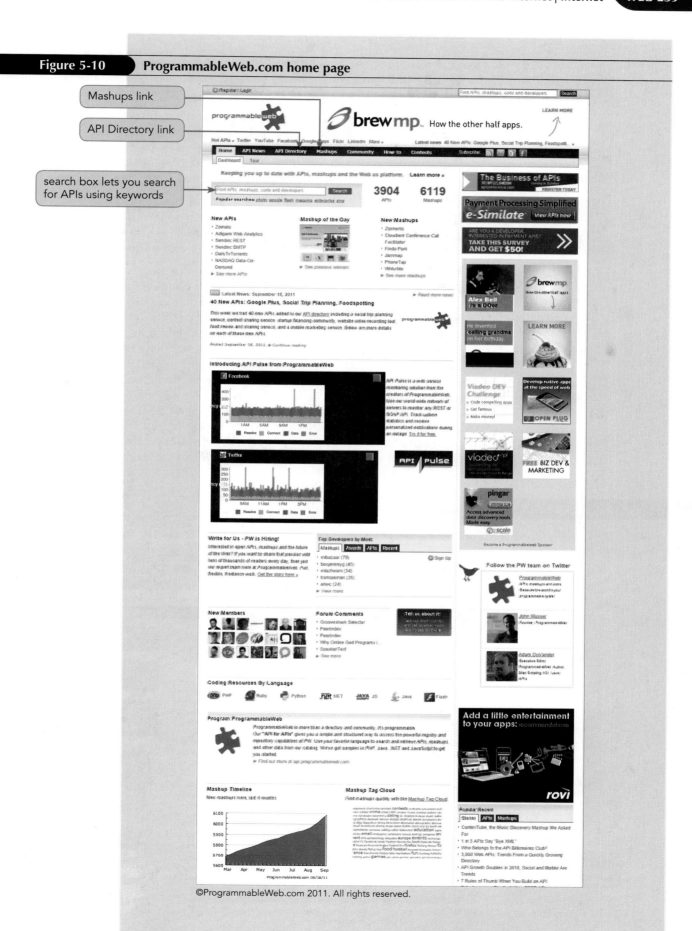

2. Near the top of the page, point to or click the **API Directory** link, and then click the **APIs By Category** link or the **By Category** link. The Web Services Directory page displays options for filtering the directory to find specific APIs.

3. In the Hide Filters section, click the **Category** arrow, scroll down the menu and click **Social**, and then click the **Filter This List** button. The filter displays APIs for the Social category. These APIs are used by developers to integrate the services from social networks with other Web sites. For example, you might use an API that displays the contacts from a social network with an API that displays a map so a user can locate a contact geographically.

4. Scroll down the page and review some of the APIs and their descriptions in the Social category. Because this list is updated daily as new APIs are added by the contributing sites, the list changes frequently. Next you will search for mashup sites.

5. Point to or click the **Mashups** link near the top of the page, and then click the **Mashup Tag Cloud** link or the **Tag Cloud** link. As developers add APIs to the site, they code them with keywords, called tags, that identify their use in a way that categorizes them. When used in the context of APIs or Web sites, a **tag** is something that a person uses to categorize a Web site, photo, post, video, or almost any other form of Web content based on the information it contains. Figure 5-11 shows a **tag cloud**, with all the tags that describe the different APIs or mashups uploaded to this site shown in an alphabetical list and a cloud arrangement. Larger words in the cloud indicate more APIs and mashups in that category. Pointing at a word in the tag cloud displays a ScreenTip that indicates the number of APIs and mashups associated with the tag. This feature gives you an idea of the relative popularity of each API or mashup category, and lets you search for all the related APIs and mashups quickly by clicking the tag that identifies the content you are searching for.

| Figure 5-11 | ProgrammableWeb.com tag cloud |

boston tag in the tag cloud

6. Point to the word **boston** in the cloud. A ScreenTip appears showing how many APIs and mashups are coded with this tag.

7. Click the **boston** tag to open a page listing other APIs and mashups that use the boston tag to describe their functionality. Scroll down the page, noticing the various sites. For example, you might see sites that find the best parking or restaurants in the city of Boston.

8. Find a site that interests you, and then click the site's name. A page opens and describes the site's content, identifies the APIs it uses and the tags that describe it, and lists the date the site was created, its author, and a link to the actual site.

9. Return to the Weblinks page for Session 5.1.

PROSKILLS

Problem Solving: How to Ensure Effective Collaboration with a Virtual Team

Many push and pull technologies make it possible for members of a virtual team to be physically separated but able to work as if everyone is in the same room. Some of the technologies you learned about in Session 5.1, and the technologies you will learn about in Session 5.2, are used by virtual teams to collaborate on projects such as market research, product development, advertising and marketing campaigns, and sales presentations.

Virtual teams often must work rapidly to accomplish tasks, so identifying which technologies team members should use to collaborate on projects is critical. For example, when collaborating on a PowerPoint presentation, the team leader must determine the best method for team members to share the file. For example, will they use email to exchange copies of the file, or will they use another method? Will routine communication and updates be conducted by email or using another method? How will team members handle urgent communication? The decision to use one technology over another has many considerations, such as ensuring that the technology is cost effective, private, and available to everyone on the team, and that all team members are proficient at using it. The leader may change as well, depending on the stage of work the team is completing, so the method of communication must be one in which the person leading the group can take it over quickly and easily.

To ensure that your virtual team is successful, decide which communication technologies the team will use to keep the flow of information moving smoothly, and then reevaluate your choices periodically to verify that the technology is complementing and enhancing the work of the team.

In the next session, you will learn about push technologies.

REVIEW

Session 5.1 Quick Check

1. Describe push technology and pull technology, and provide examples of each.
2. What are three examples of Web 2.0 applications?
3. What term is given to a series of postings on a particular newsgroup or mailing list topic?
4. When viewing a Web page in Internet Explorer and Firefox, how can you determine that the page contains one or more feeds?
5. What is a podcatcher and what does it do?
6. What is a mashup?
7. What information is provided in a tag cloud?

SESSION 5.2 VISUAL OVERVIEW

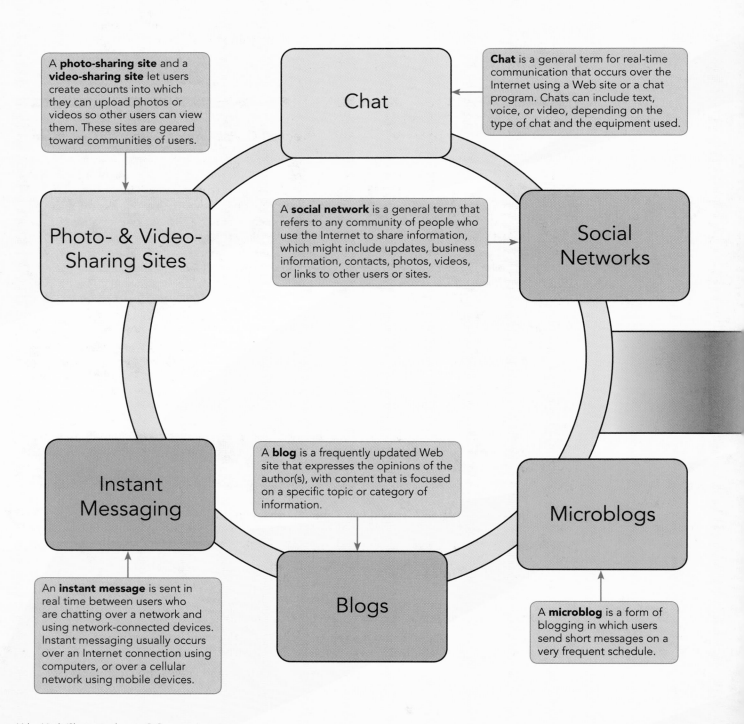

A **photo-sharing site** and a **video-sharing site** let users create accounts into which they can upload photos or videos so other users can view them. These sites are geared toward communities of users.

Chat

Chat is a general term for real-time communication that occurs over the Internet using a Web site or a chat program. Chats can include text, voice, or video, depending on the type of chat and the equipment used.

Photo- & Video-Sharing Sites

A **social network** is a general term that refers to any community of people who use the Internet to share information, which might include updates, business information, contacts, photos, videos, or links to other users or sites.

Social Networks

Instant Messaging

A **blog** is a frequently updated Web site that expresses the opinions of the author(s), with content that is focused on a specific topic or category of information.

Microblogs

An **instant message** is sent in real time between users who are chatting over a network and using network-connected devices. Instant messaging usually occurs over an Internet connection using computers, or over a cellular network using mobile devices.

Blogs

A **microblog** is a form of blogging in which users send short messages on a very frequent schedule.

PUSH TECHNOLOGIES

Internet Chat Communication

Until now, you have learned about Internet communication methods that let users pull information to their devices when they want it. You can also use the Internet to push information to users. Some of these communication methods are older and being used less frequently as new technologies take their places, but their history is important to understanding the evolution of more current methods.

Originally, the term "chat" described the act of users exchanging typed messages, or a **text chat**. The early networks that became the Internet included many computers that ran a program called **Talk** that allowed users to exchange short text messages. In 1988, Jarkko Oikarinen wrote a communications program that extended the capabilities of the Talk program for his employer, the University of Oulu in Finland. He called his multiuser program **Internet Relay Chat (IRC)**. By 1991, IRC was running on more than 100 servers throughout the world. IRC became popular among scientists and academicians for conducting informal discussions about experiments and theories with colleagues at other universities and research institutes. IRC is still widely used today around the world.

In addition to text-only chats, people in the 1990s used their Web browsers to visit a virtual **chat room**, where they could send text-only messages to other users in the room or just read the messages without contributing to the discussion. (The practice of reading messages and not contributing to the discussion is called **lurking**.) These types of sites still exist; today, however, chats can involve exchanging pictures, videos, sounds, data, and programs using a variety of technologies and methods. Some chat software lets you give control of your computer to another user so that person can use your programs or troubleshoot a problem that you are having. You can also use chat to collaborate with another user on a file as you talk to each other. Users with a sound card, speakers, and a microphone connected to their computers can participate in a **voice chat**, in which participants speak to each other in real time, much like they would using a telephone. The addition of a Web camera (also called a webcam) enables users to participate in a **video chat**, in which participants can see and speak to each other.

Different types of chat programs can be used to participate in an Internet chat. The chat program you choose and the type of chat you have (text, voice, or video) depend primarily on the software and hardware that you and other users have installed on your computers, your Internet connection types, and the conversation you plan to have (public or private). Some chat types require specific chat software and a connection to a specific server.

Instant messaging software lets users chat in real time using an Internet-connected device. The first instant messaging program, **ICQ** (pronounced "I seek you"), started in 1996 and still has millions of worldwide users. Within six months of ICQ's introduction, America Online (AOL) created its own instant messaging software called AOL Instant Messenger (AIM). AOL originally created AIM to allow its members to chat with each other, but subsequently made the software available to anyone (even those people without AOL accounts) for use on the Web. Soon Microsoft introduced MSN Messenger (called Windows Live Messenger in Windows Vista and Windows 7), Yahoo! introduced Yahoo! Messenger, and other portals and software vendors released their own products to capitalize on the continuing popularity of instant messaging. Instant messaging is now widely available, with built-in support on many social networking sites and other types of Web sites, and for many types of devices including computers and cell phones.

Most instant messaging programs are available in different versions for specific operating systems and devices, so you should select the correct version for the device on which you will use it. After starting the software, you sign in using your user name and password. Then you use the software to create or install a list of contacts.

Kay mostly communicates with her clients using email messages and phone calls, but some of her clients prefer to use instant messages to contact her. She decides to explore some popular instant messaging software programs next so she can communicate better with her clients. In addition, she is interested in learning how to integrate existing instant messaging software with social networks.

TIP

Some people use the term "IM'ing" when using instant messaging. "IM" is also used as a verb, as in "to IM a friend."

TIP

Some instant messaging software programs refer to online contacts as "buddies" or "friends."

To learn more about instant messaging software:

1. Start your Web browser, go to **www.cengagebrain.com**, open the Tutorial 5 Weblinks page, click the **Session 5.2** link, and then click a link in the Instant Messaging section.

2. Follow some of the links on the site's home page to learn more about its services. Try to determine if the service includes video and voice chat features, or if it is just text-based chat. Make sure to look for information that Kay needs, such as how to get started and on which types of devices the software works, and if it is accessible through social networking sites. Figure 5-12 shows the Windows Live Messenger home page, which includes links to other pages that describe some of the features that Kay wants to learn more about.

Figure 5-12 | Messenger home page

you can use Messenger to consolidate your social networking accounts

Messenger works on mobile devices and with other services

users can choose text or video chats with contacts from Messenger or social networks

Courtesy of © Microsoft

3. When you are finished exploring the first Web site, return to the Weblinks page for Session 5.2, and then click another link in the Instant Messaging section.

4. Follow some of the links on the site's home page to learn more about the program you selected. If you see links to videos and other interactive demos that describe the features and you have the required software to view them, click the links and watch the demos. Make sure to look for information that Kay needs, such as how to get started, on what types of devices the software runs, and options for accessing feeds from other social networking accounts.

5. When you are finished exploring the Web site, return to the Weblinks page for Session 5.2.

Another type of instant message, called a **text message**, occurs over a cellular network between users who are connected to the network using cell phones or other mobile devices. Text messaging uses different technology than instant messaging, but its communication is very similar. Text messaging lets users send and receive very short messages (usually 140 characters or less) in real time.

PROSKILLS

Written Communication: The Language of Chatting

Most people using one of the many forms of chat communication take certain shortcuts in their written messages that they should avoid using in business communication. For a conversation between friends or family members, responding to a message with only the letter "K" might indicate the sender's acknowledgement of a message that is requesting a certain action, and agreeing to complete the assigned task. This typing shortcut is fast, which is how most written chat conversations occur. Because of the speed at which chat participants react to each other's messages, it's not unusual to take other written shortcuts—such as not using capital letters, complete sentences, or proper grammar—to send your messages faster.

How you express your messages during a chat might also convey your emotional involvement in the message, as well. Messages written in all capital letters have a common interpretation of indicating that the sender is shouting or screaming the message for emphasis. Chat participants often use the same emoticons that email users find helpful to display humor and emotions in their messages. In addition, chat participants might use common acronyms as a typing shortcut for common expressions, such as "bbl" for "be back later," "c u" for "see you (later)," "lol" for "laughing out loud," "jam" for "just a minute," and "ttfn" for "ta-ta for now" (or "goodbye").

Because chat, instant messaging, email, and texting are convenient, cost effective, and widely available methods of communication, most business professionals use these methods on their cell phones and other mobile devices to communicate with clients and customers. Although the previously mentioned typing shortcuts are acceptable between friends and family, they are *never* acceptable for business communication.

The language you use when communicating in a business environment should be understandable without the use of any emoticons or other characters that express your true feelings, and should be clearly written. In addition, even though you are using a technology that is intended to convey short messages, your business communications should be written in complete sentences and use proper grammar. After you create a message, be sure to review it before sending it to make sure that a spell checker or other text correction feature didn't change any of the words in your message in a way that alters their meanings.

Voice over Internet Protocol

Some instant messaging programs include support for voice communications, using software that lets users engage in voice conversations using their software and the required equipment for engaging in a voice chat. Another option for voice calls is **VoIP**, which is an acronym for **Voice over Internet Protocol**. VoIP is frequently used as a cost-effective alternative to the traditional "landline" telephone service provided by residential and commercial phone companies. Because VoIP providers rely on the Internet as their network instead of the physical communications structure required by landlines, VoIP eliminates monthly service fees and taxes and usually includes long-distance and international calling for free or for a nominal charge. Most VoIP providers, such as the Skype service shown in Figure 5-13, include calling features that you expect from landlines, such as caller ID, call forwarding, call waiting, and voice mail services. If your landline is already provided by your cable provider, you might already be using VoIP for your telephone service.

Figure 5-13	Skype home page

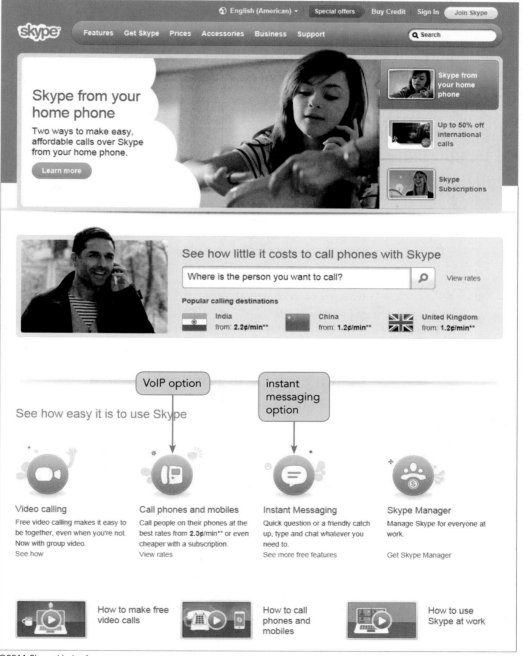

©2011 Skype Limited

For business customers, VoIP is a way to reduce costs by routing voice conversations over existing Internet networks while at the same time providing other business services such as faxing, conference calls, and Web conferencing.

The primary disadvantage of VoIP is its limitations in identifying a caller's physical location for emergency services (911) operators because VoIP uses an IP address instead of a physical location such as a person's home address to identify a call's origin. VoIP providers use Enhanced 911 service to transmit all 911 calls from their subscribers to the appropriate emergency services provider, along with the caller's telephone number and the physical address provided by the subscriber upon initiation of the VoIP service. This process is slower than what you might expect from making an emergency call from a traditional landline.

Kay knows that in addition to using a Web browser and other types of devices for chatting, she can also chat with friends from other social networks, such as Facebook.

Online Social Networks

In the past, social networks connected people with specific common interests. For example, one of the first social networks on the Internet, Classmates.com, started in 1995 as a way to connect people from specific graduating classes at high schools and colleges, and in the military.

Another early online social network, craigslist, which was created in 1995 by Craig Newmark, started as an information resource for San Francisco area residents. This online community has expanded to include information for most major cities in the United States and in countries around the world. The company started as a not-for-profit organization but was incorporated as a for-profit company in 1999. According to the site's fact sheet, craigslist retains its .org domain as a way to symbolize the relatively noncommercial nature of the service and its noncorporate culture. This mission is evident in the site's very basic design and function.

The craigslist Web site was an early pioneer, and it is still operated as a community service. Most of the revenue earned by craigslist comes from the 1 million job postings it features each month at a cost of $25 to $75 each, depending on the city in which the ad is placed, and brokered apartment listings in New York City. According to craigslist, more than 50 million people visit more than 700 craigslist sites in countries around the world each month.

Connecting with Friends

> **TIP**
>
> In 2011, Google launched its own social network, Google+, which is integrated with users' Gmail accounts and other Google services, as a competitor to Facebook.

Another early pioneer of Web 2.0, Friendster, was launched by Jonathan Abrams in 2003 and was an immediate sensation on the Web. In the same year, Google saw the advertising potential for the online social network and offered Abrams a $30 million buyout, which Abrams turned down in favor of obtaining venture capital from another source.

Members used Friendster to post profiles with information about themselves and, at their option, to upload their photos and videos. They could use the Friendster site to ask friends who were already members to link to their profiles so they could interact with each other by chatting and sharing pictures and other information. Members could invite their nonmember friends to become Friendster members, which is one reason the site grew so rapidly at first. At one point, Friendster had more than 120 million users; but as other social networking sites came online and provided new and more interactive features, Friendster's popularity rapidly declined. By 2011, Friendster's membership was fewer than 1 million members and it had moved its headquarters to Asia, where most of those members were located. In addition, Friendster discontinued its social networking features and changed its focus to a social gaming site.

Other social networking sites that use the same technology as Friendster have been enormously successful. Facebook, which began in 2004 as a closed network for college students and later was expanded to include high school students, was founded by Mark

Zuckerberg, then a student at Harvard University. After gaining new members at a rate three times faster than its competitors, the Facebook network was opened to anyone age 13 and older with an email address.

Many social networks operate in niche markets, such as networks for people speaking specific languages or living in specific geographic areas; people with certain hobbies and other interests; people of the same religious preference; and people who share other common characteristics, much like you would find in traditional peer groups. Most of these sites provide a directory that lists members' locations and interests. On some sites, a member can offer to communicate with any other member, but the communication does not occur until the intended recipient approves the contact (usually after reviewing the sender's directory information). By gradually building up a set of connections, members can develop contacts within a community. Some of these social networking sites have proven track records for re-creating (on a much larger scale) the essence of the original Internet communities.

Advertising Revenues from Social Networks

Most, if not all, social networking sites rely heavily on advertising to generate the revenue they need to operate. Successful social networks have not only catered to members' needs, but also have had an open mind with regard to advertising and creativity. In 2003, Myspace, capitalizing on its large membership of people ages 16 to 34 years old, allowed Procter & Gamble to create a profile for singer/actress Hilary Duff that included logos and links to free downloads of three of her pop songs. The profile and links were surrounded by a marketing pitch for Procter & Gamble's Secret Sparkle deodorant to a large number of people in the product's target market. In addition to personal connections and profiles, many corporations now use social networks as a way of connecting with consumers by harvesting data in user profiles and displaying relevant advertising, garnering product feedback, and offering coupons and other incentives for purchasing their products and services.

Expanding on promoting products for the first time using social networks, in 2005, the band Arctic Monkeys made history when its first single was released without an album and climbed to number one on the charts in the United Kingdom. Instead of gathering momentum from an album release or a tour, the band used its Myspace profile to "release" and publicize the single. The band used Myspace to successfully connect with its audience by capitalizing on the social network's popularity, something that had never been done before.

Facebook is a particularly attractive site for advertisers because of its large number of active users—800 million and counting—and more than 50% of its users check their Facebook pages daily. Now the largest social network in the world, Facebook has become an essential communication tool for individuals and a valuable marketing tool for corporations: Even something as commonplace as a brand of toilet paper has a Facebook page. Political candidates, grassroots campaigns, television programs, and millions of businesses have Facebook pages that are an integral part of their marketing efforts. Figure 5-14 shows the Help page for Facebook; notice how many help topics relate to business use of this social network.

TIP

Some industry analysts have estimated Facebook's annual revenues to be in excess of $1 billion, mostly from advertising.

Figure 5-14	Facebook Help Center page

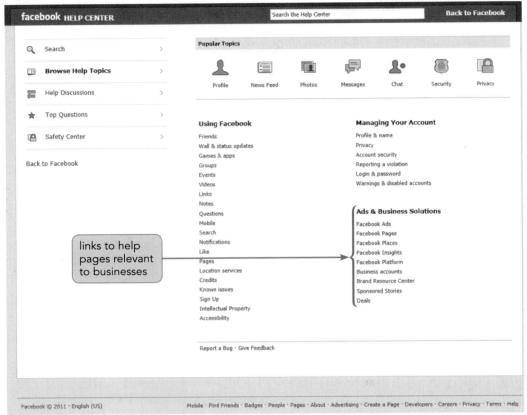

Facebook ©2011

In 2011, Facebook was still a privately held company despite purchase offers from Yahoo! and Google. Founder and CEO Mark Zuckerberg, who owns the largest share of Facebook, has stated that the company will remain private to fulfill its mission statement of providing new technologies and innovative ways to connect people in natural ways. However, in early 2012, there was speculation in the business community that Facebook would become a publicly traded company at some point in the future. The Facebook sign up page includes the slogan, "It's free and always will be." Because of the enormous success of Facebook's social network and advertising models, becoming a publicly traded company most likely will not change the way the Facebook site operates.

Online Business Networks

LinkedIn, a social network started in 2003 for business professionals, has more than 135 million individual members who use the site to make connections to other professionals and companies around the world, and to build an online résumé. More than 2 million companies around the world use the site to connect with professionals, professional networks, and other companies as a recruiting and marketing tool. LinkedIn is just one of many sites that focus primarily on professional networking, but it is the largest. Other business network sites, such as Ryze (for "rise up," with 500,000 members) and Sermo (a site restricted to credentialed U.S. physicians that has more than 120,000 members), are smaller but still connect business professionals. Users of these sites are usually seeking jobs, searching for potential business partners, recruiting workers, joining professional networks, exchanging ideas, and engaging in other business development and career activities.

Users of online business networks are not looking to build social connections to users like those on Facebook. Online business networks are used by people and organizations that are looking for specific business solutions, such as a company recruiting employees with specific skills, a vendor hoping to place its product in a particular retail outlet, or an organization searching for a consultant who can provide assistance on a specific topic. Online business networks tend to use categories that reflect these specific interests and try to make it easy for businesspeople to find the connections they need as quickly and efficiently as possible. Figure 5-15 shows the "What is LinkedIn?" page, which illustrates the ways that the LinkedIn site connects its users.

Figure 5-15   **What is LinkedIn? page**

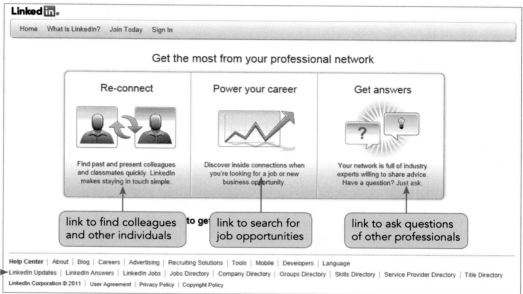

As part of promoting her business, Kay uses a LinkedIn account to connect to colleagues and clients. She hasn't explored the part of the LinkedIn site that lets users ask and answer questions, so she decides to view those pages next.

To learn more about LinkedIn:

1. On the Weblinks page for Session 5.2, click the **What is LinkedIn? page** link under the Business Networks heading. The page shown in Figure 5-15 opens.

2. In the Get answers box, click the **Just ask** link. The LinkedIn Answers page opens. Professionals can use this page to ask questions, which are mostly related to specific business needs and industries. The Browse section on the right side of the page lists questions by topic, such as "Hiring and Human Resources."

   Trouble? If LinkedIn redesigns its site and you cannot find the page described in Steps 1 and 2, click the LinkedIn Answers link at the bottom of the home page to open the LinkedIn Answers page. If this page is no longer available or requires a login, explore the parts of the LinkedIn site that are available without logging in.

> **3.** Scroll down the page and examine some of the questions posed by users. Notice that many of the questions are written in languages other than English, a fact that reflects the worldwide use of the LinkedIn site.

> **4.** On the right side of the page, click a link to a category that might interest Kay and explore some of the questions posed by users.

> **5.** Return to the Weblinks page for Tutorial 5.

Kay has several clients that will need to share pictures of items such as homes for sale, custom-designed jewelry, and company-sponsored events on their Web sites. She decides to explore sites that allow users to post and share pictures on the Web.

Sharing Pictures on the Web

As digital cameras became less expensive and more capable of producing extremely high-quality photos, many companies that provided photo-processing services, such as drugstores, began to change their offerings. They started allowing consumers to upload their digital images to a Web site and print photographs, and to purchase items sold by the site (such as coffee cups, mouse pads, and t-shirts) imprinted with those images. Eventually, new sites on the Web started offering these same services plus enhanced tools that made it easy for users to upload pictures and create more complex items, such as calendars and Web galleries. These sites, such as Shutterfly and Snapfish, let users upload pictures and print them in different ways, and also let users share their pictures with other users. Some sites, such as Flickr, have evolved even further and now let users tag images by category or person and share these photos as part of the Flickr social network or with other social networks, such as Facebook.

These sites, generally called photo-sharing sites, enable users to become part of a community by uploading their images from a digital camera or from a mobile device, and then posting them for other users to see. In many of these sites, users can add photos uploaded to a photo-sharing site and transfer them to their Facebook page or to their blog to share them with their existing networks of friends. Many of these sites let users post photos for free, up to a certain online storage limit. In this case, the site might be supported by advertisements that target users based on the content of the photographs they upload; other sites impose fees for all users.

Sharing photos on the Web can be done privately or publicly, depending on your goal. Almost every site includes features that let you post photos and restrict who can view them by sending invitations to view your gallery through email messages to authorized users. Other sites let you post your photos and make them available to any user.

Kay decides to explore the Flickr site next so that she will be prepared to discuss the functionality of a photo-sharing site with clients that will share different types of photos with their customers.

To learn more about sharing photos on the Web:

> **1.** In the Photo-Sharing Sites section of the Tutorial 5 Weblinks page, lick the **Flickr** link to open the site's home page, which is shown in Figure 5-16 (your page might differ).

Figure 5-16   **Flickr home page**

flickr from YAHOO!   The Tour   Explore   Sign In   Sign Up   [   ] Search

link to start the Flickr tour

Share your life in photos

Sign up now
or login with your ID:

● ○ ○ ○   © by The Girl In The Black Beret

Upload
More ways to get your photos online.

Multiple ways to upload your photos to Flickr—through the web, your mobile device, email or your favorite photo applications.

Discover
See what's going on in your world.

Keep up with your friends and share your stories with comments & notes. Add rich information like tags, locations & people.

Share
Your photos are everywhere you are.

Upload your photos once to Flickr, then easily and safely share them through Facebook, Twitter, email, blogs and more.

Sign up now *Free!*
or learn more

It takes less than a minute to create your free account & start sharing!

Have a Google or Facebook account? You can use them to sign in!

Community
Flickr is made of people.

Join one of over 10 million active groups to take part in the conversation, learn from our other 60 million photographers and share your own story through photos.

Privacy
Your photos are safe with us.

Who can see this photo?

Share photos only with the people you want to with our easy privacy settings. Flickr's multiple-backed storage system makes sure you never lose another photo again.

Flickr on the go
Mobile options to keep you going.

flickr
rec cor you explore

Flickr is always in your back pocket with apps for iPhone, Windows 7, and more. Or use m.flickr.com from any mobile device to share photos on the go.

Explore
The world's most interesting photos, right here.

Flickr is home to over five billion of the world's photos.

random photo gallery of posted images

information about integrating Flickr with other social networks

Sign up now   You can use your Google or Facebook account:
and remember, Flickr loves you! ♥ ♥

Still not convinced?
Take the Flickr Tour!

link to start the Flickr tour

You   Sign in   Create Your Free Account
Explore   Places   Last 7 Days   This Month   Popular Tags   The Commons   Creative Commons   Search
Help   Community Guidelines   The Help Forum   FAQ   Sitemap   Get Help

Flickr Blog   About Flickr   Jobs   Terms of Use   Your Privacy   About Our Ads   Copyright/IP Policy   Yahoo! Safely   Report Abuse

繁體中文 | Deutsch | English | Español | Français | 한글 | Italiano | Português | Tiếng Việt | Bahasa Indonesia
Copyright © 2011 Yahoo! Inc. All rights reserved.

2. Scroll down the page and examine its contents. Notice the photo gallery that appears on the page; click any image in the gallery that interests you. The page that opens will display the full-sized image along with details about the image, such as the photographer's name, where and when the photo was taken, and a caption describing the image. If the image has been posted long enough, you might see feedback about the image from other Flickr users; it is this interaction with other users that creates a social network. In addition, you might see tags that assign categories to the photo. Clicking one of these tags will open another page of photos related to that category. As users find images that interest them, they can create connections to the photographers of those images and make them part of their social network.

3. Click your browser's **Back** button to return to the Flickr home page, and then click another picture in the gallery and explore the page that opens to learn more about the photograph. When you have finished, return to the Flickr home page.

Flickr offers a tour to help new users learn to use the site. You'll explore this tour next.

4. On the Flickr home page, click the **The Tour** link at the top of the page or scroll down and click the **Take the Flickr Tour!** button at the bottom of the page.

Trouble? If you cannot find a tour on the Flickr home page, return to the Weblinks page for Session 5.2 and click a link to another site in the Photo-Sharing Sites section until you find a site with a tour or another feature that explains how the site works.

5. Follow the on-screen steps to take the tour, being sure to read the content on each page. Pay particular attention to the site's privacy settings for photographs; how to integrate the images with other social networks, such as Twitter and Facebook; and how to create blogs and groups from your photos.

6. When you reach the page that asks you to create a free account and log in, return to the Weblinks page for Session 5.2. (Do not log in or create an account at this time.)

Kay likes the features that the photo-sharing site provides and predicts that she might find creative ways for her clients to use this site. Another social network that might interest her clients is YouTube, which is an online social network for sharing videos.

Sharing Videos on the Web

Similar to photo-sharing sites, where users post photos to share with other users, a video-sharing site lets users post video content. These videos might be short clips shot from someone's cell phone, or professionally produced movie trailers, news segments, or interviews. The most popular video-sharing site, YouTube, started in 2005 as a private venture; only a year later, Google purchased it for $1.65 billion. By 2011, YouTube had more than 2 billion visitors posting and watching hundreds of millions of videos each day. As the site became more popular and more integrated with other online social networks, corporations began sponsoring pages and uploading their own material, including commercials, corporate news, product tours, and even political ads and rallies.

YouTube is now the primary place where people post and watch video content on the Web. You don't need to visit the YouTube Web site to view its content; many companies embed links to content that they have posted on YouTube, and program those links to open a new window and a media player on your device to play the video content directly from their Web page. For example, Figure 5-17 shows a video playing on the MindTap About Us page. This video, produced by Cengage Learning, includes an explanation of the company's philosophy and innovations in textbook publishing. Cengage Learning also posted this video to its accounts on other social networking sites, including Twitter, Facebook, and YouTube, and included links to these sites on the page so visitors can easily view MindTap content on these other sites.

| Figure 5-17 | Video playing on the MindTap About Us page |

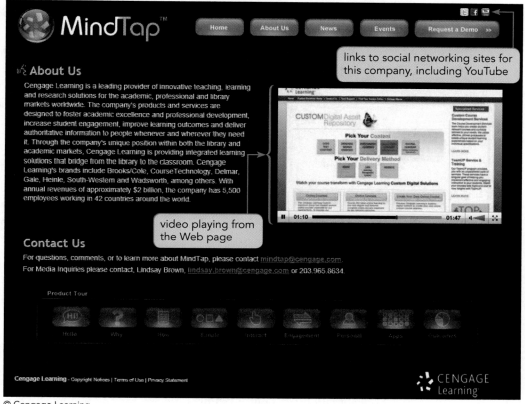

© Cengage Learning

Although YouTube is the most popular and active video-sharing site on the Internet, most other portals, such as Yahoo! and Bing, also include dedicated sites where users can post and share videos. In some cases, you'll find the same video posted on multiple sites, and also on the owner's site. For example, the video that appears in Figure 5-17 also appears on YouTube.

When YouTube first started, it was immediately popular with people who were already participating in well-established social networks. Word of mouth traveled quickly, and users began uploading and sharing video content on YouTube. The site didn't really need to advertise itself: Its innovative approach became a social network of its own, and the people using YouTube were quick and eager to pass it on. YouTube now has strategic partnerships with many major television and cable networks and music labels to broadcast their content. In addition to these partnerships, YouTube relies heavily on display ad placement, brand channels (advertising focused on a specific brand), and contests to generate revenue.

Effectively Searching Video-Sharing Sites

Aside from users posting videos of their pets doing tricks or something funny, amateur athletic events, world events, or other human interest stories, YouTube and other sites that let users post video content are also a repository for millions of commercially uploaded segments, such as professional sporting events, movie trailers, unaired alternate endings for television shows, news broadcast segments, commercials, and seminars by corporations and individuals. The videos you'll find on these sites range from low-quality videos shot with a cell phone camera to commercial-quality, high definition, professionally produced segments.

Depending on your reason for visiting a video-sharing site, you might find something that makes you laugh, or find videos to supplement or begin a research project or to increase your knowledge about a specific topic. Most video-sharing sites let users tag content, which makes it easy to find video content related to research projects or specific subjects. In addition, these sites include search tools that let you search for video content with keywords or by browsing categories, much like you would search for a podcast or blog.

When viewing content on a video-sharing site, you need to use the same skills you learned in Tutorial 3 to properly investigate the site's source and creator so you can evaluate its credibility. Most video-sharing sites include categories that let users add their videos to channels, some of which include titles such as "Science & Technology" or "Politics and Current Events." Depending on the source of these videos, they might contain information that you can deem reliable.

You can visit the Web sites for YouTube and other video-sharing sites by using the links in the Video-Sharing Sites section of the Weblinks page for Tutorial 5.

Blogs

As you learned in Tutorial 4, a blog is a Web site that is published to express the blogger's opinions about a particular topic. The blog's author, usually a person or a specific organization, often invites the blog's readers to add comments to the blog entries. A blog might chronicle a person's life or adventures and become an online personal journal, or it might function as a forum to communicate political, religious, or other opinions of groups of people. Some blogs function much like news organizations by disseminating information about a specific story or from a specific organization. A blog might contain only text and comments, but it usually includes photographs, links, videos, and other content, and lets readers integrate the blog content they are viewing into their own social networks by clicking buttons for Facebook, email, and other social networks.

Figure 5-18 shows a page from the official blog of the Federal Communications Commission, an agency that regulates interstate and international radio, television, wire, satellite, and cable communication in the United States. Notice that the blog includes tools that the blog's reader can use to repost the blog's content on other social networks. Clicking the Facebook share link, for example, lets a reader log in to a Facebook account and post the blog's content on the reader's Facebook page, thus sharing the content with other communities.

Figure 5-18 | **Official FCC Blog page**

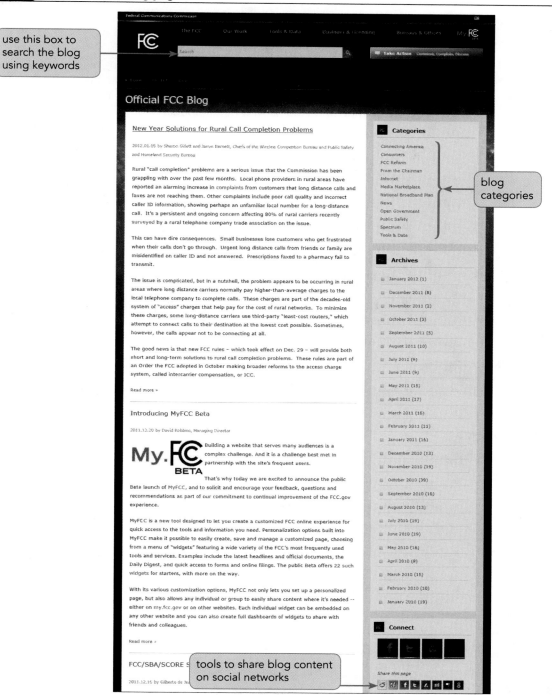

Courtesy of Federal Communications Commission

Many blogs are published using free blogging tools available from sites such as Blogger, WordPress, and Windows Live Writer to publish content to the author's own Web site or to a subdomain on the host's Web site. These blogging tools often include templates that format the blog's content and provide the blog's overall design, create a form to post comments, create a **widget** of tools to post the content on other sites, and provide code snippets to create hyperlinks and embed photos in the postings. As postings are added to the blog, they appear at the top of the comments section, with older postings appearing below the newer ones. This chronological method of posting is common to most blogs. Most blogging tools today include features that let the blog's author update the blog's content from a mobile device, making it possible for the blog's content to be updated constantly. You can use the links in the Blogs section on the Weblinks page for Tutorial 5 to visit different blogging sites.

Because anyone can write a blog, there are millions of them on the Internet. Some are from reporters working for well-known news organizations such as *The New York Times*, CNN, ZDNet, Reuters, and local newspapers in many U.S. markets. Other blogs are written by individuals who might not claim any affiliation to an organization. When searching for blogs, you should use the skills you learned in Tutorial 3 to evaluate the resources a blog contains and the credentials of its authors. Just like any other Web site, a blog might contain inaccurate or inappropriate information. Fortunately, it is easy to find blogs based on their content and authors. Google Blog Search is one resource that categorizes blogs for searching. You'll explore Google Blog Search next.

To use Google Blog Search to search for blogs:

1. In the Blog Search section of the Weblinks page for Session 5.2, click the **Google Blog Search** link.

2. If necessary, click in the search box, type **social media marketing**, and then click the search button. Google Blog Search opens a search page, similar to the one shown in Figure 5-19 (your results will differ).

| Figure 5-19 | Google Blog Search results for "social media marketing" |

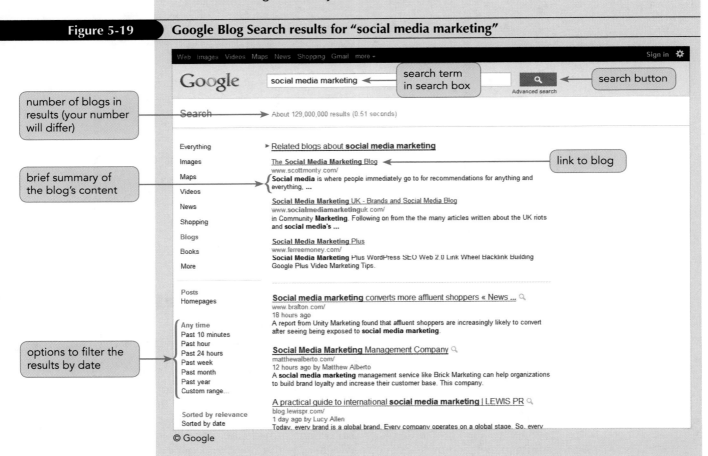

© Google

The Google Blog Search shown in Figure 5-19 returned links to millions of postings related to the search text, "social media marketing." Each blog posting includes a link to the blog's source and to the complete posting, a brief summary of the posting, and a link to the site. You can use the feature on the left side of the page to fine-tune your search to a specific time period, such as "Past 10 minutes," or a custom date that you specify after clicking the "Custom range" link.

▶ **3.** Explore some of the links to the listed blogs that contain relevant information to the search topic. Then use the evaluation skills you learned in Tutorial 3 to examine the information listed about the site and its author(s) to get a sense of the site's credentials with regard to whether this site produces expert, documented content on social media marketing research and trends, or is more geared toward expressing individual opinions.

▶ **4.** Close your browser.

Microblogs

The popularity of using blogs to create an online personal journal, combined with the proliferation of Internet-connected devices, resulted in a new type of blog called a microblog. A microblog is a form of blogging that sends short messages—usually 140 characters or less—on a very frequent schedule. Whereas a blogger might spend hours updating his or her blog daily, weekly, or monthly with long posts that include text, photos, and links, a microblogger might update his or her content hourly or even more frequently using just a few words or a single sentence. The content of a microblog differs from that of a traditional blog in that it answers the question, "What are you doing?" A microblogger might send one sentence or a few words to describe what's going on in his or her life at that exact moment, whereas a blogger might take several hours to describe a vacation or express an opinion.

Microblog postings are sometimes called **tweets**, and the act of microblogging is sometimes called **tweeting**; both terms are references to the popular microblog Web site, Twitter. The Twitter page for CengageBrain, a companion site for this textbook's publisher, is shown in Figure 5-20.

Figure 5-20   **Twitter page for CengageBrain**

user's profile

click the Follow button to subscribe to tweets from CengageBrain

retweet

statistics about this account

embedded link to another source

hashtag

© Cengage Learning

To post content using a microblog such as Twitter, you need to create an account. To read the content of someone else's microblog, you choose the option to follow that person's or organization's account. In microblogging, the term **follower** identifies a person or an organization who is receiving your updates. You don't need to create an account to view someone else's postings; you can simply go to the microblog's Web site and find his or her page of postings and read it. However, if you already have an account, you can become a follower, in which case the updates appear in your microblog account as soon as they are posted by other users. You might receive content through your account on the microblog Web page, or via instant or text messages on a wireless device.

Because many people use cell phones to post and receive content on their microblogs, and messages are usually limited to fewer than 140 characters, many microbloggers use the same text message acronyms that you find in instant messages. Just like in a blog, as you post content, it might be read by your friends or by people you don't know. It is this act of following people on a microblog that makes it social.

Postings on a microblog site, such as the Twitter site shown in Figure 5-20, show up as individual messages. The person or organization that posted the message appears in bold; in Figure 5-20, the postings are all by the user named "CengageBrain." The postings are all very short, concise messages. Some of the postings include an embedded link to a photo or video; these links are shown in red and, when clicked, load the photo or other embedded content on the user's device. Notice that the link name is just a generated link and not a URL to a site or photo.

In addition, users include user-defined keywords called **hashtags** to create topical categories that link to other messages with the same hashtags. For example, in Figure 5-20, the hashtags #professor, #technology, and #currentevents in the first, second, and third messages indicate that the author is linking messages to other messages on the Twitter network related to these categories. Clicking a hashtag provides a listing of all other messages that include the same hashtag to link together the messages and their authors. You will also find hashtags related to people's moods (such as #bummedout to indicate a letdown or #soexcited for something exciting happening) or their location (such as #Boston). Because users can create new hashtags based on any single keyword or combination of keywords (which contain more than one word, without spaces), millions of them appear in messages on the network. As users include messages with hashtags, their messages become linked together. This linking of messages and their followers, in addition to the messages themselves, creates the social network of the microblog.

Similar to the evolution of blogs, microblogs have gained popularity beyond the online personal journal and are now widely used for a variety of purposes. Many organizations, including well-known retailers and educational institutions, now use microblogs to communicate with customers, students, and other types of followers. Many actors and politicians have Twitter accounts and use them to communicate with their followers; Twitter provides a way to interact with fans and voter bases. Some microblogs, such as Yammer, are used by companies and other organizations to provide a private social network for employees to use to communicate about work-related business by restricting followers to people with valid email addresses from the organization. Other microblogs let you create private groups that also might be suitable for business communication.

TIP

A **retweet** happens when a user forwards a message to another user.

INSIGHT

Social Media: You Can't Always "Take It Back"

Although social media sites can have a very positive impact on the way their users interact with the world, they can also have a very real and very negative impact on individual users. According to Merriam-Webster Online, one definition of a scandal is the "loss of or damage to reputation caused by actual or apparent violation of morality or propriety." For centuries, individuals, groups, and organizations have been victims of scandals of all types. In the 21st century, however, the visibility of scandals has increased dramatically due to the speed at which information travels over social networks and the Internet. In the past several years, social media have quickly communicated scandals, sometimes within minutes of their occurrences. For example, consider the following news stories from 2011:

- After a major earthquake and a tsunami caused billions of dollars of damage and resulted in the deaths of thousands of people in Japan, comedian Gilbert Gottfried used his Twitter account to make jokes about the disaster. A sponsor who used Gottfried's voice in its advertising campaign terminated his contract after the incident.
- Both Congressman Christopher Lee and Congressman Anthony Weiner resigned from the House of Representatives after admitting to sending inappropriate photographs over the Internet.

Other lapses in judgment occur every day by users of social networks, but they aren't as well publicized and immediately forwarded to thousands or millions of users in an instant. News organizations regularly report about instances in which employees disparage their employers or coworkers on their personal Facebook pages, or students breach university rules and attest to their indiscretions with photographs posted on their Twitter accounts. For some people, the end result of these incidents is being fired or expelled.

The immediacy of social networks can provide important details about unfolding events, such as crises. But this immediate communication should be treated with the same respect that is found in other forums that are not electronic. Before you post something on a social network, you should consider the following:

- Evaluate who can access your comments. Even if you change your account settings to share your posts only with friends that you designate, your friends might forward your posts to other users. If you intend for your posts to be private, the only way to ensure privacy is to not post them at all.
- Consider your state of mind when posting comments. A good rule is to avoid posting comments when you are upset or angry, and to make sure that you confirm your facts. Attempts at jokes might be misinterpreted or misunderstood, especially when the reader has no way to gauge the seriousness of your comments. A comment that you posted in jest might seem real to another person.
- Don't say something online that you wouldn't say in person. The isolation of typing comments makes some people bolder and causes them to say something that they might later regret. Before submitting or sending content, consider whether you would say the same thing in exactly the same way in front of a large group of people in an auditorium. If you wouldn't, then you shouldn't say it online, either.

The most important consideration when using social media is to remember that it is very difficult to take comments back because comments you post appear in all of your friend's feeds. If you do find yourself in a situation in which you made a mistake, be quick to delete the offensive comment and to apologize to the parties involved.

You can use the links in the Microblogs section on the Weblinks page for Tutorial 5 to visit the Web sites for different microblogging sites.

Protecting Your Privacy and Identity on Social Networks

Social and business networks can be powerful tools for keeping in touch with friends and family, communicating with business associates, or locating people around the world who share your hobbies and interests. However, the very nature of these open networks can result in problems for users who are not careful about how they use them. When creating a profile on an online social network, consider the following:

- There is a strong likelihood that many people in the world share your same name and maybe even some common life details. When you contact someone as a "friend" through the network, you might not be contacting the correct person—you might just be contacting someone with the same name. Likewise, you could be contacting someone who is pretending to be someone else.

- Some sites have restricted areas or prohibit use for underage users; but with millions of users, it's likely that some of them will be able to access restricted content simply by falsifying their age. Parents need to be especially diligent to monitor the use of online social networking by minors to protect their privacy and the material they view while online. In response to this and other problems associated with minors using social networking sites, some school districts in the United States have blocked access to Facebook, Twitter, and other online social networks on their school computers in an attempt to protect children from inappropriate content and Internet predators. Many corporations and large organizations, such as the Department of Defense, also block their computers from accessing online social networks. Many do so for the sake of "security," but some admit that the blocks occur because employees waste too much time at work visiting these sites.

- **Cyberbullying**—using Internet communication such as email, text and instant messages, blogs, microblogs, or social networks to harass, threaten, or intimidate someone—is a problem usually associated with children but can involve adults as well. Most online social networks have codes of conduct that establish penalties for this type of behavior, which should be reported immediately. In addition, the site's Help section usually outlines the steps you can take to prevent cyberbullies from contacting you again and to report them to the network's administration.

- Because the nature of an online social network requires you to provide real information about yourself—your name, hometown, education, birth date, picture, and other personal information—and because this information you provide, by design, is made public, you might be putting yourself at risk for identity theft and other privacy problems. Most sites include tools that let you hide parts of your profile from other users until you give them permission to access your complete profile. Be sure to read the site's privacy policy and change the default security settings as necessary to protect your privacy in a way that makes you feel comfortable and secure when using the site. However, keep in mind that the contacts you have on these social networks have access to your information, and so do all of their contacts. A member with 20 contacts might feel comfortable sharing personal information with those 20 contacts, but must be mindful of the fact that each of those 20 contacts can share your information with their contacts—some of whom are strangers to you.

Protecting Your Reputation

In addition to protecting your privacy and identity, it's important to protect your reputation and control the information that you make available to the public. The information you post on a social network is public—and it is often archived even after you delete it. Many employers check Twitter, Facebook, and other online social networks for information that you have posted about yourself. Applicants with exemplary résumés are often passed over for interviews when their Twitter accounts or Facebook pages show them acting in ways that are inappropriate for a corporate culture.

Schools are especially careful to monitor online sites; most parents would demand action from school districts if they find that their child's teacher is participating in inappropriate online behavior, even if that behavior is on his or her "own time." Some universities have policies that prevent student athletes from creating profiles on Facebook and other sites. Although the reasons for these bans vary, one stated reason is to protect the privacy of athletes, some of whom travel significantly as part of their involvement in a student athletic program. Another stated reason is to protect the reputation of the school; some universities view student athletes as "ambassadors" of the university, and having athletes involved in inappropriate behavior documented on their online profiles could result in an embarrassment to the school and other athletes.

Another issue related to privacy is the use of your online profile by people in positions of authority. On several college campuses across the United States, students' online profiles provided proof that they violated the code of conduct agreements that they signed when they became tenants of student housing. In one case, students at North Carolina State University took pictures of themselves in a dorm room while consuming alcohol. One of the students posted pictures of the party on his Facebook page. When a university official found the pictures, they became proof of the violation to the student housing contract and proof of the students' underage drinking. In similar cases on other college campuses, the students were suspended. At some schools, students regarded this lurking by university officials on online sites as an invasion of privacy. Other schools have updated their codes of conduct to specifically authorize the monitoring of students' online profiles as a legal way of taking action against a student when inappropriate or illegal behavior is proven with information students post on their profiles.

Unfortunately, sometimes the online content that is posted about a specific person or a business might not be true, resulting in damage to his or her online reputation, or the information might be true and cause problems with job applications or required background screenings for different reasons. When the information posted is not true, you might need to employ the services of a reputation management firm to help remove it. These types of businesses are becoming more prevalent on the Internet as a way to help people and organizations monitor their online reputation and, when necessary, work to clear any offensive or negative content from online social networks, blogs, and other sites. ReputationDefender, a product of one such company that specializes in online reputation management, is shown in Figure 5-21. You can explore this site and other online reputation management firms by clicking the links in the Monitoring Your Online Reputation section of the Weblinks page for Tutorial 5.

Figure 5-21   **ReputationDefender product page**

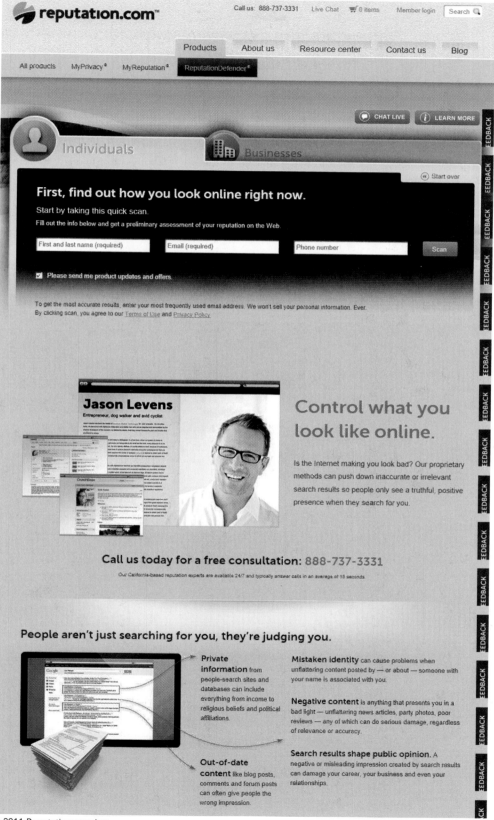

Kay is confident that she can use the information she found while exploring the different push technologies to enhance the communication strategies of her own new business and of her new clients.

REVIEW

Session 5.2 Quick Check

1. What is lurking?
2. What is VoIP? What is the primary advantage and primary disadvantage of using VoIP for residential telephone service?
3. How do most social networks earn the necessary income to run their sites?
4. What feature of a photo-sharing site makes it social?
5. What is a hashtag? How and where is it used?
6. What is cyberbullying?

Review Assignments

There are no Data Files needed for the Review Assignments.

Shilling Social Media has just been hired by the local school district's board of trustees to help identify how the district can use social media to improve communication with students and parents. The district has a Web site and in the past has relied on it to communicate information about important school events, school board elections, and other important district information. Last year, several natural disasters occurred during the school day and required immediate communication with parents, which exposed the district's lack of planning to facilitate an emergency communication method with parents. To address this problem and enhance overall communication with students and parents, the district wants to explore using social networks. Kay Shilling knows that electronic communication with minors adds a layer of complexity to any marketing campaign, so she needs to research the acceptable use guidelines and other rules of the sites the district plans to use to make sure that the district operates within established legal and site guidelines. Complete the following steps:

1. Start your Web browser, go to **www.cengagebrain.com**, open the Tutorial 5 Weblinks page, and then click the Review Assignments link.

2. Click a link in the Chat & Instant Messaging section, and then explore the site to learn about its features, paying particular attention to the district's communication needs. Determine if this site might be a good way to communicate with parents in general and during emergencies. Explore the site's terms of use (or terms of service) and privacy policies to determine if there are any limits on minors under the age of 18 or another specific age using the site. In a report, note your findings about this site in the first paragraph.

3. Return to the Weblinks page for the Review Assignments, and then choose another link in the Chat & Instant Messaging section. Repeat Step 2 to evaluate this site, and then add your findings to the second paragraph of your report.

4. Return to the Weblinks page for the Review Assignments, and then explore at least two of the sites in the Photo- & Video-Sharing Sites section. Repeat Step 2 to evaluate the site, and then add your findings to the next two paragraphs of your report.

5. Return to the Weblinks page for the Review Assignments, and then explore at least two of the sites in the Social Networks section. Repeat Step 2 to evaluate the site, and then add your findings to the next two paragraphs of your report.

6. Close your browser.

7. In the final paragraphs of your report, evaluate the information you found by answering the following questions and supporting your answers with details from the sites that you visited:

   a. Which of the communication tools that you evaluated would best fulfill the district's goal of enhancing general communication with parents? Which of the communication tools that you evaluated would best fulfill the district's goal of providing a method of communicating with parents in an emergency? Why did you make these choices?

   b. If any of the sites have policies restricting the use of the site by minors, would you still recommend that the district use the site to communicate? Why or why not?

   c. Do any of the sites that you are recommending have features that will make it easy for the district to integrate its different communication strategies with other online sites? What are these features and which sites do they integrate with?

d. For the communication tools that you recommended in Step 7a, what kind of opportunities does the district have if it chooses these tools? For example, how could the district use a photo-sharing site or a microblog?

e. Based on your research and with regard to communication with minors, are there any networks or sites that the district should not use? Why or why not?

Case Problem 1

Learn more about using tags to categorize images at photo-sharing sites.

APPLY

There are no Data Files needed for this Case Problem.

Biology II   Before Bruce Hill became a high school biology teacher, he studied and worked as a botanist who collected, analyzed, and studied the life cycle of plants. Consequently, botany is his favorite unit to teach to his high school class. A project he assigns asks his students to collect 30 samples of indigenous wildflowers and prepare a notebook that includes the plant sample, photographs of the plant in its wild state, the plant's common and scientific names, and details about the plant's habitat, growing cycle, and other pertinent information. Over the years, Bruce has amassed a large, personal collection of wildflowers and frequently uses his pictures to help students identify their own samples. During class last week, one of his students suggested that he create an account for the class on a Web site so the students could upload their photos and contribute to his collection. Bruce thinks that this is a great idea and decides to explore using a photo-sharing site on the Internet to collect the photos. Because of his interest in botany, he is also interested in connecting to other teachers who might be assigning similar projects, so he can expand his plant collection beyond the geographic area of his school. Complete the following steps:

1. Start your Web browser, go to **www.cengagebrain.com**, open the Tutorial 5 Weblinks page, and then click the Case Problem 1 link.

2. Click one of the links to a photo-sharing site and use the site to learn more about tagging photos. A good starting point is to search the site's Help feature for the word "tag" or to examine the frequently asked questions page. As you are reviewing the information you find, note the site's suggestions for tagging content. After you are finished, use the site to examine photos with tags related to botany, such as specific wildflower or plant names. If you need help determining your search text, use a search engine to find the names of flowers and plants, and then return to the photo-sharing site to enter those names and search for them.

3. After searching the site, review the site's community guidelines, its terms of use, or a similarly named page to make sure that the site is appropriate for high school sophomores who are at least 15 years old.

4. Return to the Weblinks page for Case Problem 1, and then click another site in the Case Problem 1 section. Repeat Steps 2 and 3 for the second site.

5. Close your browser.

⊕ **EXPLORE**

6. In a report containing two to four paragraphs, answer the following questions:

a. Can the photo-sharing sites you visited support the use that Mr. Hill proposes, as explained in the introductory paragraph at the beginning of this case problem? Why or why not?

b. Do either of the sites you visited have restrictions that might limit the use of the site by high school sophomores? If so, what are these restrictions?

c. Which site do you think would be better for Mr. Hill to use? Why?

d. Do you think that Mr. Hill's intention of connecting with other high school biology teachers through his photos is possible? Why or why not?

Case Problem 2

Investigate online business networks to learn more about their career-building features.

RESEARCH

There are no Data Files needed for this Case Problem.

Garrett Cordero, RN, BSN, CNP   After working for several years as a Registered Nurse, Garrett Cordero studied at Northern Arizona University to complete his master's degree in nursing. He recently finished his training and completed the licensing requirements to become a Certified Nurse Practitioner (CNP), with a specialty in pediatrics. As a pediatric CNP, Garrett will work under a physician's supervision to provide routine medical care for children under the age of 18. He worked with the university's career services department before he graduated and secured a job working for a physician in Scottsdale, Arizona. Garrett will be relocating to Scottsdale in a few weeks, and he is interested in connecting with other CNPs in the area to start building a network of friends and colleagues who can help him with his transition to his new job and his new community. He asks you to help him establish these connections. Complete the following steps:

1. Start your Web browser, go to **www.cengagebrain.com**, open the Tutorial 5 Weblinks page, and then click the Case Problem 2 link.

⊕ EXPLORE

2. Click one of the links to a professional network and explore the site to determine if the site provides specific social groups for recent college graduates in the nursing field. As you explore the site, evaluate the other resources the site offers and its ease of use. In addition, be on the lookout for links that might interest Garrett, such as relocation services, career advice, general advice for nursing professionals, or forums that let users ask questions or seek advice about nursing.

⊕ EXPLORE

3. Return to the Weblinks page for Case Problem 2, and then evaluate the resources at another site.

4. In a report containing two to four paragraphs, describe your experiences at the sites and the quality of information they provide. In your report, recommend two features at the sites for Garrett to use to prepare for his new career, and explain your choices. In addition, evaluate the overall effectiveness of the sites in terms of their career-building features.

5. Close your browser.

Case Problem 3

Find and evaluate the privacy policies at several social networking sites.

RESEARCH

There are no Data Files needed for this Case Problem.

Lakeside Police Department   Detectives at the Lakeside Police Department, which patrols an area outside of Chicago, Illinois, have received several calls in the past month from victims of identity theft. In each case, the detectives traced the initiation of the theft back to the user's social networking page. As part of the department's community education division, detectives want to offer a course in protecting users' privacy and identity on social networking sites. Because the detectives have busy caseloads, they have asked for your help in researching some precautions users can take. As part of your research, they also would like you to visit a few sites and examine their privacy controls. Complete the following steps:

1. Start your Web browser, go to **www.cengagebrain.com**, open the Tutorial 5 Weblinks page, and then click the Case Problem 3 link.

2. Several of the Case Problem 3 links are to video content posted on YouTube. If your computer can play these videos, watch at least two of them and take notes about the steps the reporter or the person being interviewed suggests for protecting a user's identity on a social networking site, such as Facebook. (*Note:* If you cannot play these videos, skip this step.)

⊕ EXPLORE

3. Return to the Weblinks page for Case Problem 3, and then choose one of the non-video links. Search the site's home page for a link that will lead to information about the site's rules of conduct. (You should not need to log in or create an account to carry out this research.) Look for links titled "Terms of Service," "Code of Conduct," "Rules and Etiquette," "Terms of Use," or a similarly named link. You might also consult the provider's Help menu or a link to a Help system. If you cannot find any rules at the site you choose, return to the Weblinks page for Case Problem 3 and choose another site to use in your search. As you review the site's rules of conduct, search for information about the acceptable rules of use, age limits of participants, language guidelines, banned topics of conversation, and other items that would be of interest in protecting a person's privacy and identity. If you could watch the videos in Step 2, use the background information you found in the videos to help guide your exploration of the site. Be sure to evaluate the resources the site provides for reporting unacceptable behavior and the site's commitment to enforcing its rules.

4. After finding the rules at the first site you selected, return to the Weblinks page for Case Problem 3 and choose another site. Search this site for its rules of conduct.

5. After finding the rules at the second site you selected, return to the Weblinks page for Case Problem 3 and choose another site. Search this site for its rules of conduct.

⊕ EXPLORE

6. In a report containing four to six paragraphs, summarize your findings about what kinds of problems can result from having information posted on an online social network, and the methods the sites recommend to prevent these problems. In your opinion, does the burden of protecting an individual's online privacy and preventing identity theft fall on the individual using the network, the network itself, or both? What kinds of problems can be prevented by following the site's recommendations? Support your recommendations with facts you found at the sites you visited.

7. Close your browser.

Examine mashups to determine how they combine sources and generate revenue.

CHALLENGE

Case Problem 4

There are no Data Files needed for this Case Problem.

Evaluating Mashup Content and Ad Placement   In this tutorial, you learned about the technology that combines content from two or more Web sites to create a mashup. Because the technology that combines mashups is relatively simple and inexpensive or free, new mashups are added to the Web every day. Some mashups are created as public services, others are created for profit. In this Case Problem, you will review two mashup sites and evaluate the content that they contain, the origin of that content, and the advertising included on the site. Complete the following steps:

1. Start your Web browser, go to **www.cengagebrain.com**, open the Tutorial 5 Weblinks page, and then click the Case Problem 4 link. Click one of the sites in the list.

2. Evaluate the content on the site to determine where the data comes from. Your evaluation of the source data can come from information posted on the site or from your analysis of the content.

3. Note whether the site includes advertising and try to determine its source. How do the ads relate to the content you are viewing on the site? Do you see any ads that are relevant to the city or town in which your computer is connected? If so, how do you think that these ads were generated? If the site doesn't include ads, does it include another feature that might generate revenue?

4. Return to the Weblinks page for Case Problem 4, and then choose another site. Use the information provided in Steps 2 and 3 to evaluate the data and ads featured on the second site.

⊕ **EXPLORE**

5. In a report containing two to four paragraphs, describe the content you evaluated in Step 2 and answer the questions in Step 3 for each Web site. How do the two sites you selected compare in terms of the information provided, their ease of use, and the advertising they feature? Use information on the sites to support your responses.

6. Close your browser.

Evaluate the resources at news organizations and compare them to directory content.

CHALLENGE

Case Problem 5

There are no Data Files needed for this Case Problem.

Evaluating Syndicated Information Resources   In this tutorial, you used directories to find information about blogs and podcasts. Almost all major newspapers and news organizations use blogs, podcasts, and feeds to provide information, in addition to their published editions and Web sites. When you are researching a specific topic, these news organizations can provide you with a broad range of information written by objective journalists, and opinions written by outside contributors and content experts. To see what information is available on the Web, you'll choose a search topic that interests you and then evaluate the information you find. Complete the following steps:

1. Start your Web browser, go to **www.cengagebrain.com**, open the Tutorial 5 Weblinks page, and then click the Case Problem 5 link.

⊕ **EXPLORE**

2. Click a link to a feed, podcast, or blog resource. Review the site's content and find a category of information that interests you. For example, you might choose to explore health, sports, science, or Internet topics. Do not subscribe to anything, but use the links to the content to see the articles and postings available for a category. For example, clicking a health category might open a page with articles or postings about health topics. Review the material that you find and evaluate it to see if it fulfills your information needs. Click the individual links to open the postings so you can read them directly. If the content is not what you need, return to the categorical listing and choose another topic until you find one that you like.

⊕ **EXPLORE**

3. Use the Web pages where the content is posted to evaluate the source of the postings. For several articles, note the author and the date the content was published, and then read a few paragraphs of each article to get a sense of whether the content expresses the author's opinion or contains objective reporting.

⊕ **EXPLORE**

4. Return to the Weblinks page for Case Problem 5, and then click a link in the Blogs, Feeds, or Podcast Search section. Use the search feature of the site you selected to search for the same topic using the category you selected in Step 2. Use the links on the search results page to review a few of the sources.

⊕ **EXPLORE**

5. In a report containing two to four paragraphs, discuss the content you viewed and evaluate the quality of the information at the news organization using the search directory. What is your impression of the content you viewed at the news organization? What is your impression of the same content you viewed using the blog, feeds, or podcast search directory? In your opinion, which option provides better information? Why?

6. Close your browser.

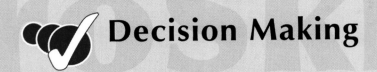 Decision Making

Evaluating Search Results

Decision making is the process of identifying, evaluating, and selecting a course of action in a specific situation or when solving a problem. The steps involved for making good decisions include the following:

1. Obtaining relevant information
2. Identifying possible courses of actions or solutions
3. Selecting the best course of action
4. Developing and implementing an action plan
5. Monitoring the result, verifying the accuracy of the decision, and taking corrective action, if needed

The Internet can be a valuable resource during the decision-making process.

Step 1: Obtaining Relevant Information

Before evaluating a potential course of action for a given situation or problem, you must gather the data and other information you need to make a decision. This data might be information that you obtain from people, reports, or other sources, such as blogs, podcasts, newsgroups, and news feeds. All of these resources can help you to understand the problem you are seeking to understand and solve.

Step 2: Identifying Possible Courses of Action or Solutions

After collecting information to help you solve a problem, you can identify courses of actions or solutions. Some decisions need to be made quickly, in which case, you must evaluate the information you find in a limited amount of time.

Step 3: Selecting the Best Course of Action

Once you have identified multiple courses of actions or solutions, you need decide on the best one. Sometimes, you might ask questions, such as:

- Which course of action make sense for the long term?
- Which course of action easily implemented, given the resources you have available?
- Are you comfortable with the course of action?

ProSkills

Step 4: Developing and Implementing an Action Plan

Once you have made a decision, you need to decide how to implement the necessary steps to put the decision into effect. You should have a pretty good idea of what the final outcome needs to look like in order to consider all relevant steps.

After making a decision, you can begin implementing a plan. As you complete your work, you can check off the required tasks as you complete them and assess your progress against the overall schedule. If you veer off schedule, you must be able to determine the cause of any problems and decide how to correct them.

Step 5: Monitoring Results and Verifying the Accuracy of the Decision

After implementing your plan, you should verify that your decision was correct and solved the problem you were working on. To assess the effect of the implemented plan, you can collect feedback from any affected parties to help you determine how well your solution worked.

PROSKILLS

Evaluating and Using Search Results in Decision Making

You make decisions every day: Some are as simple as what to eat for breakfast, and others are more complex, such as deciding which route to take from one location to another. Deciding how to get from one place to another can be a surprisingly complex decision in a city like New York. When making a decision, you should gather relevant information and then evaluate it in the context of criteria you have developed for evaluating that information to achieve the best decision outcome.

To decide which route is best, you will need to consider many factors, some of which will depend on the time of day (a taxi might be safer than the subway or walking if you are traveling late at night), how much time you have (are you on vacation and wanting to see the sights or are you late for a business meeting), and how much money you have to spend on this trip. You might also want to consider other factors, such as how many calories you will burn or what the environmental impact of your choice could be.

In Tutorials 1 through 5, you learned how to locate and evaluate information on the Internet. When faced with a problem to solve, the Internet can be a useful tool for gathering information to help you make the best decision. For example, you could use a Web site such as HopStop to find ways to navigate around a large city such as New York. The search results will provide you with many different options. For example, a search for directions in New York City will usually give you options to take the subway, a bus, a taxi, or an hourly car rental. The site will also give you specific directions for riding a bicycle or walking, which are often different in New York because the city has many one-way streets and streets that are closed to vehicular traffic.

ProSkills

When HopStop presents its directions, it will give specific information for each routing option, including:

- Estimated time duration (of the trip overall and for each leg of the trip)
- Walking time (even trips that use a bus or subway require walking to and from the station or bus stop)
- Cost (bus/subway/taxi fare or car rental fee)
- Calories burned (if you are walking)

You can use these factors to make an informed decision about which route and travel method to take, giving consideration to how much money you will spend, how long it will take you to travel, and how good you will feel after getting some exercise.

Note: Please be sure not to include any personal information of a sensitive nature in the documents you create to be submitted to your instructor for this exercise. Later on, you can update the documents with such information for your own personal use.

1. Start your browser, and then use a search engine to find and open the HopStop Web site or another Web site that helps commuters determine the best transportation method to use when navigating New York City.
2. Use the tools on the site to change the location to New York City.
3. Set your starting location as the Crowne Plaza Times Square, which is located at 1605 Broadway Avenue, Midtown, NY 10019.
4. Set your destination as the Metropolitan Museum of Art, which is located at 1000 Fifth Avenue, New York, NY 10028.
5. Compute the transportation route using the Subway/Rail only option, the Walking option, and the Taxi cost/time option. Note the distance travelled and the estimated travel time for each option. For the Taxi cost/time option, note the estimated cab fare.
6. Based on the following information, make a decision about how you would get from the Crowne Plaza Times Square hotel to the Metropolitan Museum of Art. Use the information in this ProSkills exercise and from the HopStop site to support the steps you took to make your decisions for each situation described below:
   a. You need to arrive at the museum in a hurry because you are meeting a friend there and you are running late.
   b. You are on a strict budget while visiting New York City, but it is snowing and very cold outside.
   c. It is a beautiful day and you are not in a hurry to arrive at the museum.
   d. It is late at night, and you are visiting New York City for the first time.

ProSkills

7. In an email message addressed to your instructor, describe each decision you made.

8. Evaluate the site's other options, such as its city guide and maps. Can you determine how this information is created on the site? For example, do you find any evidence of using APIs to create this information? How do you suppose that a site like HopStop earns revenue? Use specific information from the site to support your conclusions and add this content to your email message.

9. Send the email message to your instructor and close your browser.

INTERNET

The Internet and the World Wide Web

History, Structure, and Technologies

- Understand computer networks and connectivity
- Learn about domain names and Uniform Resource Locators (URLs)
- Explore the history of the Internet and the World Wide Web

In this Appendix, you will learn how computers are connected to each other in networks, how computers are identified on a network using IP addresses and domain names, and the origin of the network known as the Internet.

STARTING DATA FILES

There are no starting Data Files needed for this appendix.

Computer Networks

Computers that are connected to each other form a network. Each computer on a network uses a network interface card to create the network connection. A **network interface card** (often called a **NIC** or simply a network card) is a circuit board card or other device used to connect a computer to a network of other computers. Most computers and mobile devices have a network card built into them; for older devices, you might need to install a network card to connect the device to a network. These cards are connected to servers using cables or wireless signals. A **server** is a general term for any computer that accepts requests from other computers that are connected to it and shares some or all of its resources, such as printers, files, or programs, with those computers.

A server runs software that coordinates the information flow among the other computers in the network, which are called **clients**. The software that runs on the server is called a **network operating system**. Connecting computers this way, in which one server computer shares its resources with multiple client computers, is called a **client/server network**. Client/server networks commonly are used to connect devices in a **local area network (LAN)**, which is a network configuration in which devices that are located in close proximity to each other, such as in a home or small business, are connected to each other. Figure A-1 shows a typical client/server LAN.

Figure A-1	**Client/server LAN**

© Cengage Learning. © AAGAMIA/Getty Images.

Each computer, printer, or other device attached to a network is called a **node** or **network node**. The server can be a personal computer (PC) or a larger, more powerful computer. Most of these larger computers are called "servers" to distinguish them from desktop or laptop computers. Companies that need substantial computing power to run their applications and manage their businesses often connect hundreds or even thousands of large PCs together to act as servers.

Like any computer, servers have operating systems; however, they also can run network operating system software. Although network operating system software can be more expensive than the operating system software for a stand-alone computer, having computers connected in a client/server network can provide cost savings. For example, by connecting each client computer to a server, all of the computers can share the server-installed network printer and the media used for creating computer backups.

Most personal computer operating systems, including current versions of Microsoft Windows and Macintosh operating systems, have built-in networking capabilities. Also, some personal computer operating systems that can serve as network operating systems, such as Linux, are available on the Internet and can be downloaded and used at no cost.

Connecting Computers to a Network

Not all LANs use the same kind of cables to connect their computers. The oldest cable type is called **twisted pair cable**, which telephone companies have used for years to wire residences and businesses. Twisted pair cable has two or more insulated copper wires that are twisted around each other and are enclosed in another layer of plastic insulation. A wire that carries an electric current generates an electromagnetic field around itself. This electromagnetic field can induce a small flow of electricity in nearby objects, including other wires. This induced flow of unwanted electricity is called **electrical interference**. In twisted pair wiring, the wires are twisted because wrapping the two wires around each other reduces the amount of electrical interference that each wire in the pair might pick up from other nearby current-carrying wires. The type of twisted pair cable that telephone companies have used for years to transmit voice signals is called **Category 1 cable**. Category 1 cable transmits information more slowly than the other cable types, but it is also much less expensive.

Coaxial cable is an insulated copper wire encased in a metal shield that is enclosed in plastic insulation. The signal-carrying wire is completely surrounded by the metal shield, so it resists electrical interference much better than twisted pair cable. Coaxial cable also carries signals about 20 times faster than Category 1 twisted pair; however, it is considerably more expensive. Because coaxial cable is thicker and less flexible than twisted pair, it is harder for installation workers to handle and thus is more expensive to install. You probably have seen coaxial cable because it is used for most cable television connections. You might hear this type of cable called "coax" (pronounced "koh-axe") by network technicians.

Over time, cable manufacturers have developed better versions of twisted pair cable. The current standards for twisted pair cable used in computer networks are Category 5, Category 5e, Category 6, and Category 7 cable. **Category 5 cable** carries signals between 10 and 100 times faster than coaxial cable and is just as easy to install as Category 1 cable. **Category 5e cable** (the "e" stands for "enhanced"), **Category 6 cable**, and **Category 7 cable** are three newer versions of twisted pair cable that look exactly like Category 5 cable, but are constructed of higher quality materials so they can carry more signals up to 10 to 100 times faster than Category 1 cable. Many businesses and schools have Category 5 cable installed, but they are replacing it with Category 5e, Category 6, or Category 7 cable as they upgrade their network hardware to handle the highest LAN speeds available today. You might hear these cable types called "Cat-5," "Cat-6," or "Cat-7" cable by network technicians.

The most expensive cable type is fiber-optic cable, which does not use an electrical signal at all. **Fiber-optic cable** (sometimes called "fiber" by network technicians) transmits information by using lasers to pulse beams of light through very thin strands of glass. Fiber-optic cable transmits signals much faster than either coaxial cable or any category of twisted pair cable. Because it does not use electricity, fiber-optic cable is completely immune to electrical interference. Fiber-optic cable is lighter and more durable than coaxial cable, but it is harder to work with and more expensive than either coaxial cable or Category 5 or higher twisted pair cable. The price of fiber-optic cable and the laser sending and receiving equipment needed at each end of the cable has dropped dramatically over time. Thus, companies are using fiber-optic cable in more networks as the cost becomes more affordable; however, its main use today remains connecting networks to each other rather than as part of the networks themselves. Figure A-2 shows these three types of cable.

| Figure A-2 | **Twisted pair, coaxial, and fiber-optic cables** |

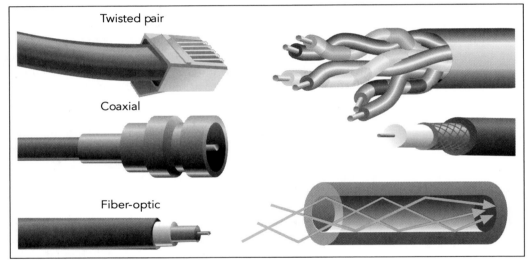

© Cengage Learning

Perhaps the most liberating way to connect computers in a LAN is to avoid using cables completely. **Wireless networks** use wireless transmitters and receivers that plug into or replace network cards to connect devices to a network without using cables. Wireless LANs are used to provide network services in many types of buildings, on school campuses, in retail outlets, and in homes and businesses. Figure A-3 shows the physical layout of a small wireless network that might be useful in a small office or a home. Connected to the wireless network are two desktop computers, two laptop computers, a shared printer, and two mobile devices. The only cable used in this configuration is the one that connects the wireless router to the Internet connection.

| Figure A-3 | A small wireless network |

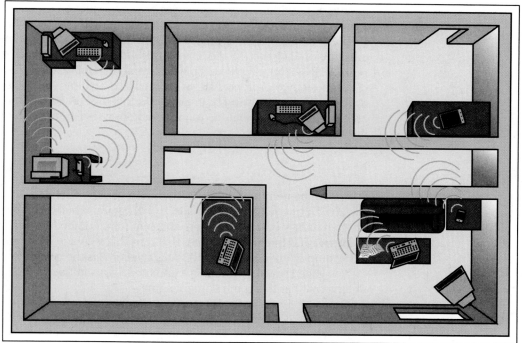

© Cengage Learning

All of these connection types—twisted pair, Category 1, coaxial, Category 5, Category 5e, Category 6, Category 7, fiber-optic, and wireless—are options for creating LANs. These LANs can, in turn, be connected to the Internet or to other, larger networks.

Understanding IP Addresses and Domain Names

Each computer on the Internet has a unique identification number, called an **IP (Internet Protocol) address**. IP addressing uses a unique number, such as 192.168.0.1, to identify each computer on the Web. Most people, however, do not use an IP address to locate a Web site. Instead, they use a domain name.

IP Addressing

Until 2011, the IP addressing system used on the Internet was called **IP version 4 (IPv4)**. IPv4 uses a 32-bit number to label each address on the Internet. The 32-bit IP address is usually written in four 8-bit parts. In most computer applications, an 8-bit number is called a **byte**; however, in networking applications, an 8-bit number is often called an **octet**.

In the binary (base 2) numbering system, an octet can have values from 00000000 to 11111111; the decimal equivalents of these binary numbers are 0 and 255, respectively. Each part of a 32-bit IP address is separated from the previous part by a period, such as 106.29.242.17. You might hear a person pronounce this address as "one hundred six dot twenty-nine dot two four two dot seventeen." This notation is often called **dotted decimal notation**. The combination of these four parts provides 4.2 billion possible addresses (256 × 256 × 256 × 256). Because each of the four parts of a dotted decimal number can range from 0 to 255, IP addresses range from 0.0.0.0 (which would be written in binary as 32 zeros) to 255.255.255.255 (which would be written in binary as 32 ones).

In the mid-1990s, the accelerating growth of the Internet created concern that the world could run out of IP addresses within a few years. Originally, the 4.2 billion addresses provided by the IPv4 rules seemed sufficient for an experimental research network. However, by 2011, the supply of IP addresses was gone.

The IETF worked on several new protocols that could solve the limited addressing capacity of IPv4 and, in 1997, approved **IP version 6 (IPv6)** as the protocol that would replace IPv4. The new IP version was implemented gradually over a 20-year period because the two protocols are not directly compatible. However, network engineers have devised ways to run both protocols together on interconnected networks. The major advantage of IPv6 is that the number of addresses is more than a billion times larger than the 4.2 billion addresses available in IPv4.

Domain Names

A **domain name** is a unique name associated with a specific IP address by a program that runs on an Internet host computer. This program, which coordinates the IP addresses and domain names for all computers attached to it, is called **DNS (Domain Name System) software**, and the host computer that runs this software is called a **domain name server**. For example, the domain name "cengage.com" is the computer connected to the Internet for Cengage Learning, which is a commercial institution (.com). No other computer on the Internet has this same domain name.

Domain names have a hierarchical structure that you can follow from top to bottom as you read the domain names from right to left. The last part of a domain name is called its **top-level domain (TLD)**. For example, DNS software on the Internet host computer that is responsible for the .com domain keeps track of the IP addresses for all of the institutions in its domain, including "cengage." Similar DNS software on the "cengage" Internet host computer would keep track of the company's other computers in its domain.

Since 1998, the **Internet Corporation for Assigned Names and Numbers (ICANN)** has been responsible for managing domain names. In the 1980s, six TLDs were created (.com, .edu, .gov, .mil, .net, and .org). Domains registered using the .com, .net, and .org TLDs have no restrictions; however, domain names that use the .edu, .gov, and .mil TLDs are restricted to certain types of organizations and for limited purposes.

In addition to these original TLDs, ICANN created and manages additional TLDs, called **general TLDs (gTLDs)**, to expand the number of TLDs. Some of the gTLDs include ones for specific countries, such as .us, which is approved for general use by any person or organization within the United States. However, the .us domain is most frequently used by state and local government organizations in the United States and by U.S. primary and secondary schools (because the .edu domain is reserved for post-secondary educational institutions). Internet host computers outside the United States often use two-letter country domain names instead of, or in addition to, the six general TLDs. For example, the domain name uq.edu.au is for The University of Queensland (uq), which is an educational institution (.edu) in Australia (.au).

The four gTLDs introduced in 2000 included .biz (for business organizations), .info (for an informational Web site created by an individual or organization), .name (for individuals), and .pro (for licensed professionals, such as accountants, lawyers, and physicians).

ICANN also created other TLDs, called **sponsored TLDs (sTLDs)**, which are maintained by a sponsoring organization other than ICANN. The three sTLDs introduced in 2000 that are sponsored by various industry organizations are .aero (for airlines, airports, and the air transport industry), .coop (for cooperative organizations), and .museum (for museums). Each of these domains is maintained by its sponsoring organization, not by ICANN. For example, the .aero domain is maintained by SITA, an air transport industry association.

Figure A-4 shows a list of the original TLDs, and some of the country and general TLDs you'll find today.

Figure A-4	Commonly used domains

Original TLDs		Country TLDs		General TLDs Added Since 2000	
TLD	**Use**	**TLD**	**Country**	**TLD**	**Use**
.com	U.S. Commercial	.au	Australia	.asia	Companies, individuals, and organizations based in Asian-Pacific regions
.edu	U.S. Post-secondary educational institution	.ca	Canada	.biz	Businesses
.gov	U.S. Federal government	.de	Germany	.info	General use
.mil	U.S. Military	.fi	Finland	.int	International organizations and programs endorsed by a treaty between or among nations
.net	U.S. General use	.fr	France	.name	Individual persons
.org	U.S. Not-for-profit organization	.us	United States	.pro	Professionals (such as accountants, lawyers, and physicians)

Internet Assigned Numbers Authority Root Zone Database, http://www.iana.org/domains/root/db/

Origins of the Internet

In the early 1960s, the U.S. Department of Defense undertook a major research project. Because this was a military project and was authorized as a part of national security, the true motivations are not known with certainty; but most people close to the project believe it arose from the government's concerns about the possible effects of nuclear attack on military computing facilities. The Department of Defense realized that the weapons of the future would require powerful computers for coordination and control. The powerful computers of that time were all large mainframe computers, so the Department of Defense began examining ways to connect these computers to each other and to weapons installations that were distributed all over the world.

The agency charged with this task was the **Advanced Research Projects Agency (ARPA)**. During its lifetime, this agency has used two acronyms: ARPA and DARPA. This book uses its current acronym: **DARPA**, for **Defense Advanced Research Projects Agency**. DARPA hired many of the best communications technology researchers, and for many years funded research at leading universities and institutes to explore the task of creating a worldwide network of computers. A photo of these dedicated computer networking pioneers appears in Figure A-5.

Courtesy of Raytheon BBN Technologies

DARPA researchers soon became concerned about computer networks' vulnerability to attack because networks at that time relied on a single, central control function. If the network's central control point was damaged or attacked, the network would be unusable. Consequently, they worked hard to devise ways to eliminate the need for network communications to rely on a central control function.

Connectivity: Circuit Switching vs. Packet Switching

One of the first networking-related topics to be researched by the DARPA scientists was connectivity, or methods of sending messages over networks. The first computer networks were created in the 1950s. The models for those early networks were the telephone companies because most early wide area networks (WANs) used leased telephone company lines to connect computers to each other. In telephone company systems of that time, a telephone call established a single connection between sender and receiver. Once the connection was established, all data then traveled along that single path. The telephone company's central switching system selected specific telephone lines, or circuits, that would be connected to create the single path. This centrally controlled, single-connection method is called **circuit switching**.

Although circuit switching is efficient and economical, it relies on a central point of control and a series of connections that form a single path. This makes circuit-switched communications vulnerable to the destruction of the central control point or any link in the series of connections that make up the single path that carries the signal.

Packet switching is an alternative means for sending messages. In a packet-switching network, files and messages are broken down into packets that are labeled electronically with codes for their origin and destination. The packets travel from computer to computer along the network until they reach their destination. The destination computer collects the packets and reassembles the original data from the pieces in each packet. Each computer that an individual packet encounters on its trip through the network determines the best way to move the packet forward to its destination.

Computers and other devices that perform this function on networks are often called routing computers, or **routers**, and the programs they use to determine the best path for packets are called **routing algorithms**. Thus, packet-switched networks are inherently more reliable than circuit-switched networks because they rely on multiple routers instead of a central point of control, and because each router can send individual packets along different paths if parts of the network are not operating.

By 1967, DARPA researchers had published their plan for a packet-switching network; and in 1969, they connected the first computer switches at four locations: the University of California at Los Angeles, SRI International, the University of California at Santa Barbara, and the University of Utah. This experimental WAN was called the **ARPANET**.

The ARPANET grew over the next three years to include more than 20 computers. The ARPANET used the **Network Control Protocol (NCP)** to enable each of those computers to communicate with other computers on the network. A **protocol** is a collection of rules for formatting, ordering, and error-checking data sent across a network.

Open Architecture Philosophy

As more researchers connected their computers and computer networks to the ARPANET, interest in the network grew in the academic community. One reason for increased interest in the project was its adherence to an **open architecture** philosophy; that is, each network could continue using its own protocols and data-transmission methods internally. The open architecture philosophy includes four key points:

- Independent networks should not require any internal changes to be connected to the Internet.
- Packets that do not arrive at their destinations must be retransmitted from their source network.
- Router computers do not retain information about the packets they handle.
- No global control will exist over the network.

This open architecture philosophy was revolutionary at the time. Most companies that built computer networking products at that time, including IBM and Digital Equipment Corporation, put considerable effort into making their networks incompatible with other networks. These manufacturers believed that they could lock out competitors by not making their products easy to connect with products made by other companies. The shift to an open architecture approach is what made the Internet of today possible.

In the early 1970s, Vinton Cerf and Robert Kahn developed a set of protocols that implemented the open architecture philosophy better than the NCP. These new protocols were the **Transmission Control Protocol** and the **Internet Protocol**, which usually are referred to by their combined acronym, **TCP/IP**. TCP includes rules that computers on a network use to establish and break connections; IP includes rules for routing of individual data packets. TCP/IP continues to be used today in LANs and on the Internet. The term "Internet" was first used in an article about TCP written by Cerf and Kahn in 1974. The importance of TCP/IP in the history of the Internet is so great that many people consider Vinton Cerf to be the father of the Internet.

A number of TCP/IP-based networks—independent of the ARPANET—were created in the late 1970s and early 1980s. The National Science Foundation (NSF) funded the **Computer Science Network (CSNET)** for educational and research institutions that did not have access to the ARPANET. The City University of New York started a network of IBM mainframes at universities called the **Because It's Time** (originally, "Because It's There") **Network (BITNET)**.

New Uses for Networks

Although the goals of the ARPANET were still to control weapons systems and transfer research files, other uses for this vast network began to appear in the early 1970s. In 1972, an ARPANET researcher named Ray Tomlinson wrote a program that could send and receive messages over the network. Email had been born and rapidly became widely used in the computer research community. In 1976, the Queen of England sent an email message over the ARPANET. The ARPANET continued to develop faster and more effective network technologies; for example, the ARPANET began sending packets by satellite in 1976.

By 1981, the ARPANET had expanded to include more than 200 networks. The number of individuals in the military and education research communities who used the network continued to grow. Many of these new participants used the networking technology to transfer files and access computers remotely. The TCP/IP suite included two tools for performing these tasks. **File Transfer Protocol (FTP)** enabled users to transfer files between computers, and **Telnet** let users log in to their computer accounts from remote sites. The first mailing lists also appeared on these networks. A mailing list is an email address that takes any message it receives and forwards it to any user who has subscribed to the list.

Although file transfer and remote login were attractive features of these new TCP/IP networks, their improved email and other communications facilities attracted many users in the education and research communities. Mailing lists (such as BITNET's LISTSERV), information posting areas (such as the User's News Network, or Usenet newsgroups), and adventure games were among the new applications appearing on the ARPANET.

Although the people using these networks were developing many creative applications, relatively few people had access to the networks. Most of these people were members of the research and academic communities. From 1979 to 1989, these new and interesting network applications were improved and tested with an increasing number of users. TCP/IP became more widely used as academic and research institutions realized the benefits of having a common communications network. The explosion of PC use during that time also helped more people become comfortable with computing.

Interconnecting the Networks

The early 1980s saw continued growth in the ARPANET and other networks. The **Joint Academic Network (JANET)** was established in the United Kingdom to link universities there. Traffic increased on all of these networks; and in 1984, the Department of Defense split the ARPANET into two specialized networks: The ARPANET would continue its advanced research activities, and the **MILNET** (for **Military Network**) would be reserved for military uses that required greater security.

By 1987, congestion on the ARPANET caused by a rapidly increasing number of users on the limited-capacity leased telephone lines was becoming severe. To reduce the traffic load on the ARPANET, a network run by the NSF, called NSFNET, merged with another NSF network, called CSNET, and with BITNET to form one network that could carry much of the network traffic that had been carried by the ARPANET. The resulting NSFNET awarded a contract to Merit Network, Inc., IBM, Sprint, and the state of Michigan to upgrade and operate the main NSFNET backbone.

A **network backbone** includes the long-distance lines and supporting technology that transport large amounts of data between major network nodes. By the late 1980s, many other TCP/IP networks had merged or established interconnections. Figure A-6 summarizes how the individual networks described in this section combined to become the Internet as it is known today.

| Figure A-6 | Networks that became the Internet |

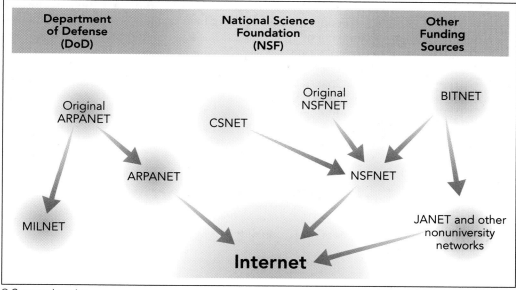

© Cengage Learning

Network Use in Business

As PCs became more powerful, affordable, and readily available during the 1980s, companies increasingly used them to construct LANs. Although these LANs included email software that employees could use to send messages to each other, businesses wanted their employees to be able to communicate with people outside their corporate LANs. The NSF prohibited commercial network traffic on the networks it funded, so businesses turned to commercial email services. Larger firms built their own TCP/IP-based WANs (wide area networks) that used leased telephone lines to connect field offices to corporate headquarters.

Today, people use the term **intranet** to describe LANs or WANs that use TCP/IP but do not connect to sites outside a single organization. Although most companies allow only their employees to use the company intranet, some companies give specific outsiders—such as customers, vendors, or business partners—access to their intranets. These outside parties agree to respect the confidentiality of the information on the network. An intranet that allows selected outside parties to connect is often called an **extranet**.

In 1989, the NSF permitted two commercial email services—MCI Mail and CompuServe—to establish limited connections to the Internet that allowed their commercial subscribers to exchange email messages with the members of the academic and research communities who were connected to the Internet. These connections allowed commercial enterprises to send email directly to Internet addresses, and allowed members of the research and education communities on the Internet to send email directly to MCI Mail and CompuServe addresses. The NSF justified this limited commercial use of the Internet as a service that would primarily benefit the Internet's noncommercial users.

People from all walks of life—not just scientists and academic researchers—started thinking of these networks as a global resource that we now know as the Internet. Information systems professionals began to form volunteer groups such as the **Internet Engineering Task Force (IETF)**, which first met in 1986. The IETF is a self-organized group that makes technical contributions to the engineering of the Internet and its technologies. The IETF is the main body that develops new Internet standards.

Although the network of networks that is now known as the Internet had grown from four computers on the ARPANET in 1969 to more than 300,000 computers on many interconnected networks by 1990, the greatest growth in the Internet was yet to come.

Growth of the Internet

A formal definition of the term "Internet," which was adopted in 1995 by the Federal Networking Council (FNC), appears in Figure A-7.

Figure A-7   **The FNC's October 1995 resolution to define the term "Internet"**

RESOLUTION: The Federal Networking Council (FNC) agrees that the following language reflects our definition of the term "Internet"

"Internet" refers to the global information system that—

(i) is logically linked together by a globally unique address space based on the Internet Protocol (IP) or its subsequent extensions/follow-ons;

(ii) is able to support communications using the Transmission Control Protocol/Internet Protocol (TCP/IP) suite or its subsequent extensions/follow-ons; and/or other IP-compatible protocols; and

(iii) provides, uses or makes accessible, either publicly or privately, high level services layered on the communications and related infrastructure described herein.

Courtesy of http://www.nitrd.gov/fnc/Internet_res.html

The researchers who had been so involved in the creation and growth of the Internet accepted it as part of their working environment, but people outside the research community were largely unaware of the potential offered by a large interconnected set of computer networks until the 1990s. Realizing that the Internet was becoming much more than a scientific research project, the U.S. Department of Defense finally closed the research portion of its network, the ARPANET, in 1995. The NSF also wanted to turn over the Internet to others so it could return its attention and funds to other research projects.

The process of shutting down the ARPANET and privatizing the Internet began in 1991, when the NSF eased its restrictions on Internet commercial activity. Businesses and individuals continued to connect to the Internet in ever-increasing numbers. Although nobody really knows how big the Internet is, one commonly used measure is the number of Internet hosts. An **Internet host** is a computer that connects a LAN or a WAN to the Internet. Each Internet host might have any number of computers connected to it. Figure A-8 shows the rapid growth in the number of Internet host computers. As you can see, the growth has been dramatic.

| Figure A-8 | Growth in the number of Internet hosts |

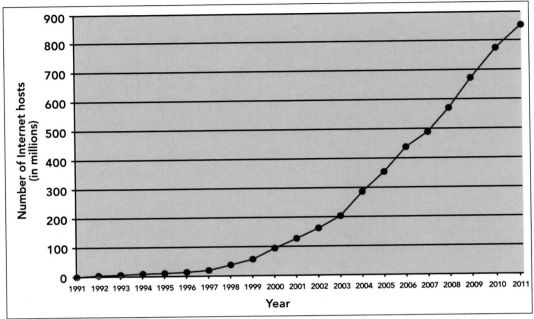

Adapted from Internet Systems Consortium (https://www.isc.org/) and other sources

The numbers in Figure A-8 probably underestimate the true growth of the Internet in recent years for two reasons. First, the number of hosts connected to the Internet includes only those computers that are directly connected to the Internet. In other words, if a LAN with 100 PCs is connected to the Internet through only one host computer, those 100 computers appear as one host in the count. Because the number and size of LANs have increased in recent years, the host count probably underestimates the growth in the number of all computers that have access to the Internet. Millions of mobile devices have features that allow them to connect to the Internet. These devices are connected through a relatively small number of Internet hosts at their wireless service providers, which is another reason why the number of devices connected to the Internet is probably underestimated.

Second, the number of computers is only one measure of growth. Internet traffic now carries more files that contain graphics, sound, and video, so Internet files have become larger. A given number of users sending video clips will use much more of the Internet's capacity than the same number of users will use by sending email messages or text files.

No one knows how many individual email messages or files travel on the Internet, and no one really knows how many people use the Internet today because the Internet has no central management or coordination, and the routing computers do not retain copies of the packets they handle. However, some companies and research organizations estimate the number of regular Internet users today to be nearly 2 billion.

The opening of the Internet to business enterprise helped increase its growth dramatically; however, another development worked hand in hand with the commercialization of the Internet to spur its growth. That development was the technological advance known as the World Wide Web.

The Evolution of the Web

Two important innovations played key roles in making the Internet easier to use and more accessible to people who were not research scientists. The first innovation, hypertext, connected the content stored on the networks and made that content more accessible. The second innovation was the Web browser itself, which provided users with a tool that made it possible to find and access that content.

Origins of Hypertext

In 1945, Vannevar Bush, who was the director of the U.S. Office of Scientific Research and Development, wrote an *Atlantic Monthly* article about ways that scientists could apply to peacetime activities the skills they learned during World War II. The article included a number of visionary ideas about future uses of technology to organize and facilitate efficient access to information. Bush speculated that engineers eventually would build a machine that he called the **Memex**, a memory extension device that would store all of a person's books, records, letters, and research results on microfilm. Bush's Memex would include mechanical aids to help users consult their collected knowledge fast and in a wide variety of ways.

In the 1960s, Ted Nelson described a similar system in which text on one page links to text on other pages. Nelson called his page-linking system **hypertext**. Douglas Engelbart, who also invented the computer mouse, created the first experimental hypertext system on one of the large computers of the 1960s. In 1976, Nelson published a book, *Dream Machines*, in which he outlined project Xanadu, a global system for online hypertext publishing and commerce. Figure A-9 includes photos of Bush, Nelson, and Engelbart—three forward-looking thinkers whose ideas laid the foundation for the Web.

| Figure A-9 | Left to right: Vannevar Bush, Ted Nelson, and Douglas Engelbart |

© Getty Images; © 2011 Samuel Dietz; Courtesy of Doug Engelbart Institute

In 1989, Tim Berners-Lee and Robert Cailliau were working at CERN—the European Laboratory for Particle Physics. Berners-Lee and Cailliau were trying to improve the laboratory's research document-handling procedures. CERN had been using the Internet for two years to circulate its scientific papers and data among the high-energy physics research community throughout the world; however, the Internet did not help the agency display the complex graphics that were important parts of its theoretical models. Independently, Berners-Lee and Cailliau each proposed a hypertext development project to improve CERN's document-handling capabilities.

Over the next two years, Berners-Lee developed the code for a hypertext server program and made it available on the Internet. A **hypertext server** is a computer that stores files written in the hypertext markup language, and lets other computers connect to it and read the files. Berners-Lee, who was familiar with **Standard Generalized Markup Language (SGML)**—a set of rules that organizations have used for many years to manage large document-filing systems—began developing a subset of SGML that he called Hypertext Markup Language (HTML).

HTML, like all markup languages, includes a set of codes (or tags) attached to text. These codes describe the relationships among text elements. For example, HTML includes tags that indicate which text is part of a header element, which text is part of a paragraph element, and which text is part of a numbered list element. One important type of tag is the hypertext link tag. A hypertext link, or hyperlink, points to another location in the same or another HTML document. HTML documents can also include links to other types of files, such as word-processing documents, spreadsheets, graphics, audio clips, and video clips.

An HTML document differs from a word-processing document because it does not specify *how* a particular text element will appear. For example, you might use word-processing software to create a document heading by setting the heading text font to Arial, its font size to 14 points, and its position to centered. The document displays and prints these exact settings whenever you open the document in the word processor. In contrast, an HTML document surrounds the text with a pair of **heading tags** to indicate that the text should be considered a heading. Many programs can read HTML documents. The programs recognize the heading tags and display the text in whatever manner that program normally displays headings. Different programs might display the heading text differently.

Like the Internet itself, standards for HTML are not controlled by any central managing organization. Standards for technologies that are used on the Web (including HTML) are developed and promulgated by the World Wide Web Consortium (W3C), an international organization formed in 1994 and sponsored by universities and businesses from around the world. Berners-Lee was appointed director of the W3C when it was formed and continues in that position today.

Evolution of Web Browsers

A Web browser displays an HTML document in an easy-to-read format in its graphical user interface. A **graphical user interface** (**GUI**, pronounced "gooey") is a way of presenting program output using pictures, icons, and other graphical elements instead of just displaying text. All personal computers now use a GUI. The GUI presented in Web browsers played an important part in the rapid growth of the Web. The first Web browsers were text-based and lacked the graphical elements, such as buttons, that make today's browsers so easy to use. Figure A-10 shows a Web page displayed in Lynx, a text-based browser that was commonly used in the early days of the Web. As you can see, it does not look very much like the Web pages displayed by Web browsers today.

Figure A-10   Web page rendered in a text-based browser

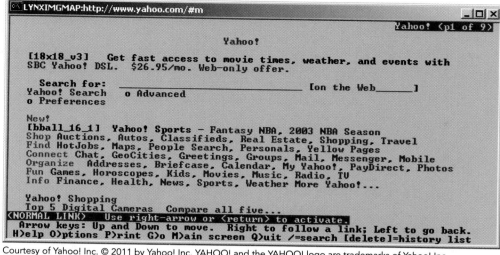

Courtesy of Yahoo! Inc. © 2011 by Yahoo! Inc. YAHOO! and the YAHOO! logo are trademarks of Yahoo! Inc.

In 1993, a group of students led by Marc Andreessen at the University of Illinois wrote Mosaic, the first GUI program that could read HTML and use hyperlinks to navigate from page to page on computers anywhere on the Internet. Mosaic was the first Web browser that became widely available for PCs. Figure A-11 shows a Web page from 1993 displayed in an early version of the Mosaic Web browser.

Figure A-11   Mosaic, the first widely available Web browser

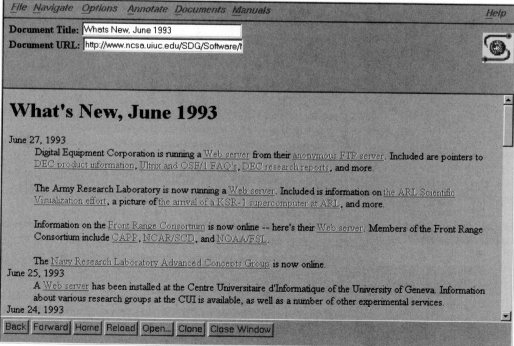

Courtesy of Pär Lannerö; Source: http://www.dejavu.org/emulator.htm

In 1994, Andreessen and other members of the University of Illinois Mosaic team joined with James Clark of Silicon Graphics to found Netscape Communications. The university was not happy when the team decided to leave the school and develop a commercial browser. The university refused to allow the team to use the name "Mosaic." Netscape's first browser was called the "Mosaic Killer" or "Mozilla." Soon after its release, the product was renamed Netscape Navigator. The program was an instant success. Netscape became one of the fastest growing software companies at the time.

Microsoft created its Internet Explorer Web browser and entered the market soon after Netscape's success. Microsoft offered its browser at no cost to computer owners using its Windows operating system. Within a few years, most users had switched to Internet Explorer and Netscape was unable to earn enough money to stay in business.

Microsoft was accused of wielding its monopoly power to drive Netscape out of business; these accusations led to the trial of Microsoft on charges that it violated U.S. antitrust laws. The charges were settled in a consent decree, but other violations by Microsoft led to a second trial in which the company was found guilty. Parts of Netscape were sold to America Online, but the browser became open-source software.

Open-source software is created and maintained by volunteer programmers, often many of them, who work together using the Internet to build and refine a program. The program is made available to users at no charge. The open-source release of Netscape is called Mozilla, which recalls the name of the original Netscape product. In an interesting turn of Web history, the Netscape Navigator browser available today is based on the Mozilla open-source software.

The proliferation of tools to make the Internet more usable led to an explosion in the amount of information stored online. The number of Web sites has grown more rapidly than the Internet itself. Figure A-12 shows the growth in the Web during its lifetime.

Figure A-12   **Growth of the Web**

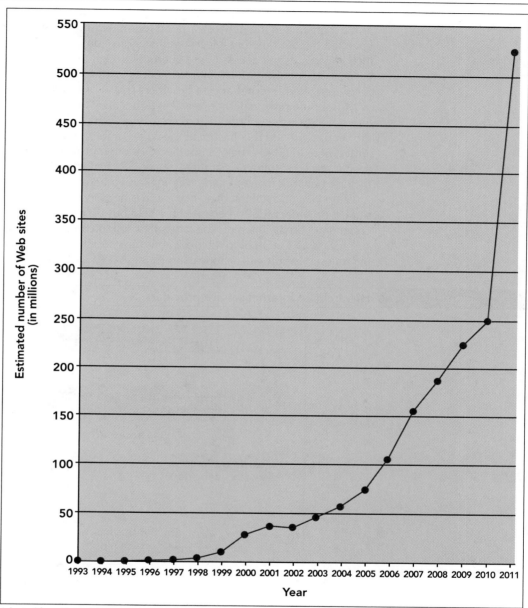

Adapted from Netcraft Web Survey (http://www.netcraft.com/survey/Reports)

After a dip between 2001 and 2002, growth in the number of Web sites resumed at its rapid rate. As individual Web sites become larger, they include many more pages. Experts agree that the number of pages available on the Web today exceeds 1 trillion, and that number is increasing faster than ever. As more people have access to the Web, commercial uses of the Web as well as its nonbusiness uses will continue to increase.

Businesses That Provide Internet Access

As NSFNET converted the main traffic-carrying backbone portion of its network to private firms, it organized the network around four **network access points (NAPs)**, which were operated by four different telecommunications companies. These four companies and their successors sell access to the Internet through their NAPs to organizations and businesses that, in turn, provide Internet access to other businesses and individuals. These firms are called **Internet access providers (IAPs)** or **Internet service providers (ISPs)**.

Most of the firms call themselves ISPs because they offer more than access to the Internet. ISPs usually provide their customers with software to connect to the ISP, browse the Web, send and receive email messages, and perform functions such as file transfer and remote login to other computers. ISPs often provide network consulting and Web design services to their customers. Some ISPs have developed a range of services that include network management, training, and marketing advice.

Large ISPs that sell Internet access and other services to businesses are called **commerce service providers (CSPs)** because they help businesses conduct business activities (or commerce) on the Internet. The larger ISPs sell Internet access to smaller ISPs, which then sell access and services to their own business and individual customers. The hierarchy of Internet service providers appears in Figure A-13.

| Figure A-13 | **Hierarchy of Internet service providers** |

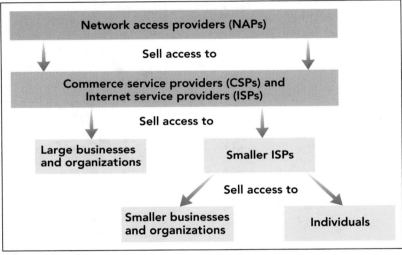

© Cengage Learning

One of the most important differences among different levels of ISPs is the connection bandwidth an ISP can offer.

Bandwidth and Types of Connectivity

Bandwidth is the amount of data that can travel through a communications circuit in one second. The bandwidth an ISP can deliver depends on the connection it has to the Internet and the connection you have to the ISP.

The available bandwidth for any type of network connection between two points is limited to the narrowest bandwidth that exists in any part of the network. For example, if you connect to an ISP through a regular telephone line, your bandwidth is limited to the bandwidth of that telephone line, regardless of the bandwidth connection that the ISP has to the Internet. Bandwidth for Internet connections is measured the same way as bandwidth for connections within networks, in multiples of **bits per second (bps)**. Common terms are **kilobits per second (Kbps)**, which is 1,024 bps; **megabits per second (Mbps)**, which is 1,048,576 bps; and **gigabits per second (Gbps)**, which is 1,073,741,824 bps.

Sometimes computer users are confused by the use of bits to measure bandwidth because file sizes are measured in bytes. As explained earlier, a byte is eight bits; it is abbreviated with an uppercase "B." A **kilobyte (KB)** is 1,024 bytes, or 8,192 bits. A **megabyte (MB)** is 1,048,576 bytes (or 8,388,608 bits), and a **gigabyte (GB)** is 1,073,741,824 bytes (or 8,589,934,592 bits).

Most LANs today run either Fast Ethernet, which operates at 100 Mbps, or Gigabit Ethernet, which operates at 1 Gbps. Some older LANs use an earlier version of Ethernet that operates at 10 Mbps. The effective bandwidth of wireless LANs depends on the distance between computers and what types of barriers the wireless signals must pass through (for example, wireless signals travel more easily through glass than steel). Most wireless LANs achieve an operating bandwidth of between 2 Mbps and 10 Mbps, although newer wireless devices with more than 100 Mbps are available. Figure A-14 shows examples of typical times required to send different types of files over different types of LANs.

Figure A-14	Typical file transmission times for various types of LANs

Type of File	Typical File Size	Wireless (7 Mbps)	Ethernet (10 Mbps)	Fast Ethernet (100 Mbps)	Gigabit Ethernet (1 Gbps)
One-paragraph text message	5 KB	Less than .1 second	Less than .1 second	Less than .1 second	Less than .1 second
Word-processing document, 20 pages	100 KB	.1 second	Less than .1 second	Less than .1 second	Less than .1 second
Web page containing several small graphics	200 KB	.2 second	.2 second	Less than .1 second	Less than .1 second
Presentation file with 20 slides and several large graphics	800 KB	1 second	.7 second	Less than .1 second	Less than .1 second
Color brochure, five pages with several color photos	2 MB	3 seconds	2 seconds	.2 second	Less than .1 second
Compressed music file (MP3 format) containing a four-minute song	5 MB	6 seconds	4 seconds	.4 second	Less than .1 second
Uncompressed music file containing a four-minute song	60 MB	1 minute	50 seconds	5 seconds	.5 second
Compressed video file containing a 10-minute interview	200 MB	4 minutes	4 minutes	17 seconds	2 seconds
Compressed video file containing a feature-length film	4 GB	1.5 hours	1 hour	6 minutes	35 seconds

© Cengage Learning

When you extend your network beyond a local area, either through a WAN or by connecting to the Internet, the speed of the connection depends on the type of connection. One way to connect computers or networks over longer distances is to use regular telephone service (sometimes referred to as **dial-up**, **POTS**, or **plain old telephone service**). Regular telephone service to most U.S. residential and business customers provides a maximum bandwidth of between 28.8 Kbps and 56 Kbps. The rates vary because the United States has different telephone companies that do not all use the same technology.

When you connect your computer, which communicates using digital signals, to another computer through a telephone line, which uses analog signals, you must convert the signals from one form to the other. The device that performs this signal conversion is a **modem**, which is short for "modulator-demodulator." Converting a digital signal to an analog signal is called **modulation**; converting that analog signal back into digital form is called **demodulation**. A modem performs both functions; it acts as a modulator and a demodulator.

Some telephone companies offer a higher grade of service that uses one of a series of protocols called **Digital Subscriber Line (DSL)** or **Digital Subscriber Loop (DSL)**. The first technology that was developed using a DSL protocol is called **Integrated Services Digital Network (ISDN)**. ISDN service has been available in various parts of the United States since 1984. Although considerably more expensive than regular telephone service, ISDN offers bandwidths of up to 256 Kbps. ISDN is much more widely available in Australia, France, Germany, Japan, and Singapore than in the United States because the regulatory structure of the telecommunications industries in those countries encouraged rapid deployment of this new technology.

All technologies based on the DSL protocol require the implementing telephone company to install new equipment at its switching stations, which can be very expensive. New technologies that use the DSL protocol are currently being implemented around the world. One of those, **Asymmetric Digital Subscriber Line** (ADSL, also abbreviated **DSL**), offers transmission speeds ranging from 16 to 640 Kbps from the user to the telephone company, and from 1.5 to 9 Mbps from the telephone company to the user.

Businesses and large organizations often obtain their Internet connection by connecting to an ISP using higher-bandwidth telephone company connections called **T-1** (1.544 Mbps) and **T-3** (44.736 Mbps) connections. (T-1 and T-3 were originally acronyms for Telephone 1 and Telephone 3, respectively, but few people use these terms any longer.) Companies with operations in multiple locations sometimes lease T-1 and T-3 lines from telephone companies to create their own WANs to connect their locations to each other.

T-1 and T-3 connections are much more expensive than POTS or ISDN connections; however, organizations that must link hundreds or thousands of individual users to WANs or to the Internet require the greater bandwidth of T-1 and T-3 connections. Smaller firms can save money by renting access to a partial T-1 connection from a telephone company. In a partial T-1 rental, the connection is shared with other companies.

The NAPs operate the Internet backbone using a variety of connections. In addition to T-1 and T-3 lines, the NAPs use newer connections with bandwidths of more than 1 Gbps—in some cases exceeding 10 Gbps. These connection options use fiber-optic cables, and are referred to as OC3, OC12, and so forth. **OC** is short for **optical carrier**. NAPs also use high-bandwidth satellite and radio communications links to transfer data over long distances.

A group of research universities and the NSF now operate a network called **Internet2** that has backbone bandwidths greater than 10 Gbps. The Internet2 project continues the tradition of the DARPA scientists by sponsoring research at the frontiers of network technologies.

A connection option available in the United States and some other countries is to connect to the Internet through a cable television company. The cable company transmits data in the same cables used to provide television service. Cable can deliver up to 10 Mbps to a user and can accept up to 768 Kbps from a user. Cable connections usually deliver speeds between 500 Kbps and 3 Mbps, although some cable companies offer guarantees of higher speeds (for higher monthly fees). These speeds far exceed those of existing POTS and ISDN connections, and are comparable to speeds provided by the ADSL technologies currently implemented by telephone companies and other companies that rent facilities from the telephone companies.

Another option that is commonly used in remote geographic areas where cabled connections are more difficult to install is connecting by satellite, which uses satellites orbiting the earth to send and receive signals from dishes mounted on rooftops. Using a satellite-dish receiver, users can download at a bandwidth of approximately 400 Kbps. In the early days of satellite Internet access, users could not send information to the Internet using a satellite-dish antenna, so they needed to also have an ISP account to send files or email. Today, most satellite ISPs install transmitters on the dish antenna. This allows two-way satellite connections to the Internet. Because satellite connections are affordable and easy to install, they are used now throughout the world, and not just in remote geographic areas.

The actual bandwidth provided by all these Internet connection methods varies from provider to provider and with the amount of traffic on the Internet. During peak operating hours, traffic on the Internet can become congested, resulting in slower data transmission. The bandwidth achieved is limited to the lowest amount of bandwidth available at any point in the network. To picture this, think of water flowing through a set of pipes with varying diameters, or traffic moving through a section of highway with a lane closure. The water (or traffic) slows to the speed it can maintain through the narrowest part of its pathway.

Figure A-15 shows typical file transmission times for various types of Internet connection options. The speeds shown are examples of what a user can expect on average during download operations. Faster Internet connections cost significantly more money than slower connections.

| Figure A-15 | Typical file transmission times for various types of Internet connections |

Type of File	Typical File Size	POTS (25 Kbps)	ISDN or Satellite (100 Kbps)	Residential Cable or DSL (300 Kbps)	Business Leased T-1 (1.4 Mbps)
One-paragraph text message	5 KB	2 seconds	.4 second	.2 second	Less than .1 second
Word-processing document, 20 pages	100 KB	33 seconds	8 seconds	3 seconds	Less than .1 second
Web page containing several small graphics	200 KB	1 minute	16 seconds	6 seconds	Less than .1 second
Presentation file with 20 slides and several large graphics	800 KB	4 minutes	1 minute	22 seconds	Less than .1 second
Color brochure, five pages with several color photos	2 MB	11 minutes	3 minutes	1 minute	Less than .1 second
Compressed music file (MP3 format) containing a four-minute song	5 MB	28 minutes	7 minutes	2 minutes	Less than .1 second
Uncompressed music file containing a four-minute song	60 MB	6 hours	1.5 hours	28 minutes	.4 second
Compressed video file containing a 10-minute interview	200 MB	19 hours	5 hours	2 hours	1 second
Compressed video file containing a feature-length film	4 GB	16 days	4 days	30 hours	25 seconds

© Cengage Learning

Figure A-16 summarizes the bandwidths, costs, and typical uses for the most common types of connections currently in use on the Internet. Some companies offer **fixed-point wireless** connections, which use technology similar to wireless LANs. Although fixed-point wireless service is not yet widely available, some companies are offering it to both business and residential customers.

Figure A-16	Types of Internet connections

Service	Upstream Speed (Kbps)	Downstream Speed (Kbps)	Capacity (Number of Simultaneous Users)	One-Time Start-up Costs	Continuing Monthly Costs
Residential-Small Business Services					
POTS	28–56	28–56	1	$0–$20	$9–$20
ISDN	128–256	128–256	1–3	$60–$300	$50–$90
ADSL	100–640	500–9,000	1–20	$50–$100	$40–$500
Cable	300–1,500	500–10,000	1–10	$0–$100	$40–$300
Satellite	125–150	400–500	1–3	$0–$800	$40–$100
Fixed-point wireless	250–1,500	500–3,000	1–4	$0–$350	$50–$150
Business Services					
Leased digital line	64	64	1–10	$50–$200	$40–$150
Fixed-point wireless	500–10,000	500–10,000	5–1,000	$0–$500	$300–$5,000
Fractional T-1 leased line	128–1,544	128–1,544	5–180	$50–$800	$100–$1,000
T-1 leased line	1,544	1,544	100–200	$100–$2,000	$600–$1,600
T-3 leased line	44,700	44,700	1,000–10,000	$1,000–$9,000	$5,000–$12,000
Large Business, ISP, NAP, and Internet2 Services					
OC3 leased line	156,000	156,000	1,000–50,000	$3,000–$12,000	$9,000–$22,000
OC12 leased line	622,000	622,000	Backbone	Negotiated	$25,000–$100,000
OC48 leased line	2,500,000	2,500,000	Backbone	Negotiated	Negotiated
OC192 leased line	10,000,000	10,000,000	Backbone	Negotiated	Negotiated

© Cengage Learning

Locating and Evaluating Health Care Information on the Internet

OBJECTIVES

- Use and expand the skills you learned in Tutorials 3 and 4
- Visit Web sites to find information about a disease or medical condition
- Evaluate the resources you find
- Examine the resources provided by a credentialing site to evaluate health care information on the Web

Some Web sites provide information about medical care, prescription drugs, and related health topics. Many doctors and other health care professionals have concerns about the quality of medical and health resources available on the Internet because anyone can post anything on the Web—there are no requirements for or restrictions on giving medical advice in this manner. Many health information Web sites include incorrect or incomplete information about health issues.

When you need information about a specific disease or medical condition, you can use one of the many sites on the Internet to conduct your research. In some cases, you might visit sites that are associated with credible research institutions, medical facilities, and universities. Sites in these categories include the Medical College of Wisconsin HealthLink, WebMD, and the Mayo Clinic. When you visit the sites of these organizations, you can read about the specific disease or medical condition that interests you, and often you will find links to other sites that provide more information. For example, if you are trying to learn about emphysema, a condition commonly associated with smoking cigarettes, one of these sites might provide information about the condition and links to other Web sites, such as the American Lung Association, where you can get more detailed information.

Just like any other Web site, you must carefully evaluate the quality of the resources and the information it provides. Sometimes you can make these determinations easily. For example, the American Lung Association is a well-known health organization that was founded

STARTING DATA FILES

There are no starting Data Files needed for this assignment.

in 1904 to fight tuberculosis and other lung diseases using donations and resources from public and private sources, foundations, and government agencies. Other resources, however, might be more difficult to evaluate because you might not be familiar with them. Fortunately, accrediting agencies that evaluate health information sites have their own Web sites that provide information about medical sites. Two of these sites are the Health on the Net (HON) Foundation and the URAC Health Web Site Accreditation. You can use the resources at these sites and other credentialing sites to evaluate health resources you find on the Internet. In some cases, the credentialing site might let you search its database to locate sites that it has already deemed credible using its own sets of rules, guidelines, and quality standards.

In this assignment, you will select a specific disease or medical condition that interests you (or your instructor might provide one for you to use), find information about it, and then use a credentialing site to evaluate its resources.

1. Visit at least two health information sites to obtain information about the disease or medical condition you selected. You can use your favorite search engine or directory to find the sites. Gather the information and evaluate the quality of the information and the quality of the Web site from which you obtained it.

2. Visit at least one credentialing or accreditation site and review its contents. Write a summary that describes how the site operates and evaluate whether the site accomplishes its goals.

3. Visit a site maintained by the U.S. government that offers health care information, such as the U.S. Centers for Disease Control and Prevention (CDC) or the U.S. National Institutes of Health MedlinePlus. Explore the site you selected and then write a review of the site in which you describe how the government-sponsored site is different from the privately operated sites you already visited. Provide your responses in a report for your instructor.

Evaluating Encyclopedia Resources on the Internet

OBJECTIVES

- Use and expand the skills you learned in Tutorials 3, 4, and 5
- Explore the content requirements and processes for published encyclopedia resources
- Examine the content of and quality controls for a collaborative encyclopedia Web site
- Evaluate encyclopedia resources available on the Web and their role in research

In Tutorials 3, 4, and 5, you learned techniques for locating and evaluating information on the Internet. When evaluating the information, you learned methods to ensure that it is complete, thorough, unbiased, and free from security threats such as viruses. As you search for information, you must assume responsibility for interpreting and analyzing the information you collect to make sure that it meets these criteria.

When you use Google or another search engine to search for information about a topic, chances are very good that your search results will include links to information that is posted on Wikipedia. Wikipedia, which began in 2001, is a much younger "encyclopedia" than its published counterparts, such as *World Book Encyclopedia* (which is more than 95 years old) or *Encyclopedia Britannica* (which is more than 220 years old). *World Book Encyclopedia* and *Encyclopedia Britannica* have established standards for research and information that rely on accredited and credentialed authors for content, subject matter experts for thorough reviews of that content, and editorial boards of experts in various fields to set standards for content. This established process of writing and reviewing greatly reduces problems related to bias or inaccuracies.

Wikipedia, on the other hand, does not apply these same types of standards to its content. The content that you find in Wikipedia might be written and reviewed by a casual user or an expert. According to the Wikipedia Web site, since its creation in 2001, over 82,000 people have actively contributed to more than 19 million articles in more than 270 languages. As a result of this collaboration, Wikipedia is one of the largest resource sites on the Internet. This collaboration of individuals has resulted in an enormous accumulation of knowledge. However, because material is freely contributed by people who might *not* be subject matter experts, and edited and reviewed by people with their own unique perspectives and biases, Wikipedia's content is subject to different quality standards than you might find in other publications.

STARTING DATA FILES

There are no starting Data Files needed for this assignment.

In this assignment, you will explore some of the pros and cons of using a collaborative site such as Wikipedia as a resource when conducting research.

1. Use your favorite search engine or directory to find the Web site for *World Book Encyclopedia*, and then use the "About Us," "Board," "Reviews," or other similarly named links on the publisher's Web site to learn about its contribution requirements and other quality assurance policies. (You might need to review several pages at the site to get a full picture of the encyclopedia's quality assurance standards.) Pay particular attention to author and reviewer credential requirements, review processes that ensure quality content, and any processes listed for making corrections to the published works.

2. Return to your search engine, and then find the Web site for *Encyclopedia Britannica*. Use the guidelines in Step 1 to evaluate the contribution requirements and quality assurance policies for this Web site.

3. Return to your search engine, and then search using the term **Wikipedia quality issues** and explore the links to learn about some controversies that have arisen as a result of Wikipedia's collaborative nature. Be sure to review material that details specific problems that have occurred and try to understand, what, if any, measures Wikipedia has taken to resolve these problems.

4. Referring back to the information you gathered in Steps 1 and 2 and the research you did in Step 3, what is your opinion of the use of traditional encyclopedias such as *World Book Encyclopedia* or *Encyclopedia Britannica* when compared to an online collaborative project such as Wikipedia? What role does each encyclopedia play in the field of research? How would you use each of these sources when conducting research? What level of confidence do you place in each source, and why? Provide your responses in a report for your instructor.

OBJECTIVES

- Use and expand the skills you learned in Tutorials 3, 4, and 5
- Learn about the Mars Student Imaging Project
- Find distance learning programs at your school or in your area
- Consider ways that distance learning can enhance education

Advances in Distance Learning

The Internet has enhanced the way that students in grades kindergarten through 12 learn about and participate in scientific research. The National Aeronautics and Space Administration (NASA) began its historic Mars Exploration Rover Mission, which is a long-term robotic exploration of the planet Mars, in June, 2003 and successfully landed a rover on the planet surface in January, 2004. NASA teamed with the Mars Education Program at Arizona State University to offer students in the United States the opportunity to participate in the Mars Student Imaging Project (MSIP). MSIP lets students in grades 5 through college sophomore level work in teams with scientists on the Mars project and choose a site on the Mars planet that they would like to map (photograph) from an orbiting rover. Archived data is also available for students to use in research projects. Students participate in the project through distance learning, which is made possible through video conferencing, chats, and teleconferencing. Students complete their projects by writing and submitting a final scientific report for publication in the online MSIP Science Journal.

STARTING DATA FILES

There are no starting Data Files needed for this assignment.

In this assignment, you will explore the Mars Student Imaging Project site and other distance learning sites that you find on the Internet. Then you will consider the future of using distance learning to enhance the education of grade school and college students.

1. Use your favorite search engine to locate the Mars Student Imaging Project Web site, and then explore the site to learn more about the project. Which Internet technologies make this project possible for students located in the United States?

2. Use your search engine to explore distance learning opportunities at your own school or at other colleges and universities in your area. How do these programs compare to the Mars Student Imaging Project? Which Internet technologies make these programs possible? Are all students able to participate in distance learning programs? Why or why not?

3. Based on your findings, determine other ways schools can use the Internet to enhance the education of grade school and college students. Are there technological impediments that prevent this method of learning? If so, what are they? What advantages do these types of programs offer students and educators? Provide your responses in a report for your instructor.

The Future of the Semantic Web

OBJECTIVES

- Use and expand the skills you learned in Tutorials 1, 3, and 4
- Review Web sites with information about the Semantic Web
- Use the skills you learned in this book to evaluate the resources you find
- Draw conclusions about the future of the Semantic Web based on your research

Tim Berners-Lee, widely regarded as the founding father of the Web, has been active in promoting and developing a project that blends technologies and information to create a next-generation Web, which he calls the **Semantic Web**. Today, people are the primary users of the Web as a communication medium. An increasing portion of the traffic on the Internet, however, is computers communicating with other computers. The Semantic Web is intended to facilitate automated computer-to-computer communication that can support all types of human activity.

The Semantic Web project, as currently conceived, would result in words on Web pages being tagged with their meanings (the meanings of words are called **semantics**, thus the name "Semantic Web"). These tags would turn the Web into a huge computer-readable database. People could use intelligent programs called **software agents** to read the Web page tags to determine the meaning of the words in their contexts. For example, a software agent could be given an instruction to find an airline ticket with certain terms (such as a specific date, destination city, and a cost limit). The software agent would launch a Web search and return an electronic ticket that meets the criteria. Instead of a user having to visit several Web sites to gather information, compare prices and itineraries, and make a decision, the software agent would automatically do the searching, comparing, and purchasing.

The key elements that must be added to Web standards so that software agents can perform these functions (and thus create the Semantic Web) include a well-defined tagging system and a set of standards. Many researchers working on the Semantic Web project believe that Extensible Markup Language (XML) could work as a tagging system. Unlike HTML, which has a common set of defined tags (for example, <h1> is the tag for a level-one heading), XML tags are defined by users. Different users can create different definitions for the same XML tag. If a group of users agrees on a common set of definitions, they can all use the same XML tags. For the Semantic Web to work, everyone must agree on a common set of XML tags that will be used on the Web. Semantic Web researchers call this common set of tag definitions a **resource description**

STARTING DATA FILES

There are no starting Data Files needed for this assignment.

framework (RDF). An **ontology** is a set of standards that defines, in detail, the relationships among RDF standards and specific XML tags within a particular knowledge domain. For example, the ontology for cooking would include concepts such as ingredients, utensils, and ovens; however, it would also include rules and behavioral expectations, such as identifying ingredients that can be mixed using utensils, the resulting product that can be eaten by people, and ovens that generate heat within a confined area. Ontologies and the RDF would provide the intelligence about the knowledge domain so that software agents could make decisions as humans would.

In this assignment, you will search for information about the Semantic Web and evaluate its potential for future use.

1. Use your favorite search engine to find sites with information about the Semantic Web, XML, RDF, and the term "ontology" as it is used in this area of research (the term "ontology" is used in philosophy and other disciplines, so you will need to use some of the techniques you learned in Tutorial 3 to narrow your results). Prepare a report that summarizes your findings on each of the four topics. Include citations for at least two Web pages for each of the four topics in your report.

2. For each of the eight (or more) Web pages you cited in the report required by the previous step, evaluate the quality of the information you obtained and evaluate the overall quality of the Web site from which you obtained it. Summarize your evaluations in your report. Be sure to include the reasons for your evaluations and explain how you performed the evaluations.

3. Using the information you have gathered about the Semantic Web, evaluate the likelihood that it will become a useful part of the Web within the next 10 years. Include a summary of your evaluation in your report and cite the Web sources that support your arguments.

GLOSSARY/INDEX